SAVING THE FREEDOM OF INFORMATION ACT

Enacted in 1966, the Freedom of Information Act (or FOIA) was designed to promote oversight of governmental activities, under the notion that most users would be journalists. Today, however, FOIA is largely used for purposes other than fostering democratic accountability. Instead, most requesters are either individuals seeking their own files, businesses using FOIA as part of commercial enterprises, or others with idiosyncratic purposes like political opposition research. In this sweeping, empirical study, Margaret Kwoka documents how agencies have responded to the large volume of non-oversight requesters by creating new processes, systems, and specialists, which in turn has had a deleterious impact on journalists and the media. To address this problem, Kwoka proposes a series of structural solutions aimed at shrinking FOIA to re-center its oversight purposes.

Margaret B. Kwoka is the Lawrence Herman Professor in Law at The Ohio State University Moritz College of Law. Her research on FOIA has been published in the *Yale Law Journal* and *Duke Law Journal*, featured in The New York Times, and has received the Harry J. Kalven Jr. Prize for Empirical Scholarship from the Law and Society Association. She has served on the federal FOIA Advisory Committee, testified before Congress in FOIA oversight hearings, and litigated FOIA cases, including a recent victory before the US Court of Appeals for the Ninth Circuit.

Saving the Freedom of Information Act

MARGARET B. KWOKA
The Ohio State University Moritz College of Law

CAMBRIDGE
UNIVERSITY PRESS

CAMBRIDGE
UNIVERSITY PRESS

University Printing House, Cambridge CB2 8BS, United Kingdom

One Liberty Plaza, 20th Floor, New York, NY 10006, USA

477 Williamstown Road, Port Melbourne, VIC 3207, Australia

314–321, 3rd Floor, Plot 3, Splendor Forum, Jasola District Centre, New Delhi – 110025, India

103 Penang Road, #05–06/07, Visioncrest Commercial, Singapore 238467

Cambridge University Press is part of the University of Cambridge.

It furthers the University's mission by disseminating knowledge in the pursuit of education, learning, and research at the highest international levels of excellence.

www.cambridge.org
Information on this title: www.cambridge.org/9781108482745
DOI: 10.1017/9781108697637

First published 2021

A catalogue record for this publication is available from the British Library.

ISBN 978-1-108-48274-5 Hardback
ISBN 978-1-108-71089-3 Paperback

"To my parents, Anita Marie Benvignati and John Edward Kwoka, Jr. Thank you."

Contents

Acknowledgements

I owe an enormous debt of gratitude to so many for helping me bring this project to fruition.

To begin, at the University of Denver, which I called my academic home for a wonderful eight years, thank you to Dean Bruce Smith and the College of Law, to the Hughes-Ruud Research and Development Committee, and to my wonderful colleagues. Their collective support of my work – intellectual and financial – was critical at every stage.

Additional thanks to The Ohio State University Moritz College of Law community for welcoming me and championing my efforts to turn the ideas in this book into meaningful government reform.

Thank you also to my many generous colleagues in the greater academic community who clarified my thinking, pushed me to fill my gaps, and provided me with their insights, including on earlier articles that formed the building blocks for this book. These colleagues include Bita Amani, Rebecca Aviel, Kent Barnett, Emily Bremer, Fred Cheever, Bernard Chao, Alan Chen, Ming Chen, Roberto Corrada, Patience Crowder, K.K. DuVivier, Nancy Ehrenreich, Brian Feinstein, Rashmi Goel, Nicole Godfrey, Sheila Hyatt, Danielle Jefferies, RonNell Anderson Jones, Beto Juárez, Margot Kaminski, Heidi Kitrosser, Seth Kreimer, Christina Koningisor, Tammy Kuennen, Stephen Lee, Nancy Leong, Kevin Lynch, Justin Marceau, David McCraw, Jon Michaels, Rachel Moran, Helen Norton, Nicholas Parrillo, Mary-Rose Papandrea, Justin Pidot, Dave Pozen, Nantiya Ruan, Tuan Samahon, Michael Sant'Ambrogio, Miriam Seifter, Bijal Shah, Peter Shane, Dave Shultz, Derigan Silver, Michael Siebecker, Scott Skinner-Thompson, Joyce Sterling, Chip Stewart, Chris Walker, and Sonja West.

To the many journalists, lawyers, and government officials who offered me their time and wisdom in sharing their on-the-ground perspectives and experience, thank you for helping me understand the many angles of FOIA practice.

I am also indebted to dozens of students who have made this work possible. Editors at the Yale Law Journal and the Duke Law Journal, in particular, helped me to hone my early ideas and lay the groundwork for the research that appears in this volume. In addition, generations of research assistants at the University of Denver have passed this project down from one team to another for the past seven years, tirelessly making FOIA requests, tracking responses, following up with agencies, cleaning data sets, analyzing results, and meticulously keeping track of a truly massive undertaking. For this, I deeply thank, in roughly chronological order: Caroline Marfitano, Elizabeth Weil, Patrick Sweet, Leah Perczak, Nathan Fall, Sydney Boyle, Elena Engel, Jacob Goldstein, Adriana Levandowski, and, with special thanks for hanging in there with me to the bitter end, Kate Googins.

Thank you also to the team at Cambridge University Press, starting with my editor Matt Gallaway who solicited the work in the first instance, as well as Cameron Daddis, Claire Sissen, Neena Maheen, and Michael Goldstein for production and editing assistance.

And finally, I have been graced with the support of my amazing family, including my chosen family, and X and Z. In particular, I owe this book to the support of César Cuauhtémoc García Hernández, who is and has given me everything.

Introduction

Emma Quezada and her three US citizen children were living in the home she owns in the United States when she consulted an attorney and found she was eligible for lawful permanent resident (LPR) status – that is, to become a green-card holder. LPRs have many coveted rights in the United States, including work authorization, the ability to travel internationally, and a path to citizenship. Quezada's attorney filed her application to become an LPR; but to complete the process, Quezada needed to provide evidence that she was lawfully admitted into the country the first time she entered the United States. To get that documentation, Quezada filed a request with the US Citizenship and Immigration Services (USCIS) agency under the Freedom of Information Act (FOIA), asking for a record of her admission. Then, she waited twenty-two months, all while lacking the security of a green card.[1] She finally became a named plaintiff in a class action lawsuit brought to enforce FOIA's mandate that the government respond to requests for information within twenty business days.[2]

WM was a noncitizen from El Salvador when the government began deportation proceedings against him. The problem is that WM had previously registered for Temporary Protected Status (TPS), a type of immigration benefit, which entitled him to a hearing on his asylum claim in the United States. His attorney filed a FOIA request with USCIS seeking documentation of his TPS registration and, while waiting for those records, also sought relief in federal court from his imminent deportation. But while proceedings unfolded, the Department of Homeland Security (DHS) deported WM back to El Salvador. After his removal from the United States, the records arrived, and WM's attorney discovered documentation

[1] Complaint at para. 59, Brown v. U.S. Customs & Border Prot., 132 F. Supp. 3d 1170 (N.D. Cal. 2015) (No. 3:15-cv-01181).

[2] *Id.* at para. 59–60.

that his TPS status had been erroneously terminated. His attorney believes that had they received these records sooner, WM would not have been deported.[3]

You may be thinking these stories are strange. After all, these individuals are amid agency proceedings where the same agency already has possession of these relevant records. Does the agency not have an obligation to turn these records over? Or can these individuals not obtain them through discovery? Are these records not just personal records they should be able to easily access? And, most relevant here, why FOIA? Why is FOIA the tool that these individuals used to obtain their immigration histories?

Odd stories about FOIA are not unusual. Here's another one. John Patrick Gavin is a lifelong financial analyst who, around the year 2000, founded his first of a series of companies that sells information about publicly traded companies to investors. Where does he get this information? FOIA. Not just some information, but loads of it. In the most recent iteration of his business model, *Probes Reporter*, Gavin explains his research process: "Each year we file about 2,500 FOIA requests and hundreds of administrative appeals with the SEC [Securities and Exchange Commission]."[4] Previously, *The New York Times* reported that under an earlier version of his business, he was charging "upward of $50,000 a year" for these services.[5]

But wait, FOIA? Why is Gavin using FOIA to get public records about public companies? How is it possible that public records are a commodity that can be obtained for free or very little cost, and resold for tens of thousands of dollars in what is essentially arbitrage masquerading as government oversight? How many other businesses exist with products that consist not of private goods, but of public records? (Hint: A lot.)

This book and the years of research before it were prompted by three basic observations I made during my years as a FOIA litigator and then FOIA scholar. First, the federal government receives more and more FOIA requests every year. Indeed, it is safe to say we are closing in on an annual count of a million requests within the next few years. If that's the case, FOIA must be doing some important work; it must be serving someone's interests well enough for them to keep coming back for more. Second, it is harder than one might imagine to answer the questions, "Who uses FOIA?" or, "What records do people seek under FOIA?" So armed with basically no actual knowledge, we imagine that FOIA is mostly used for the purpose it was created: public oversight by the press and maybe a small group of watchdog groups or other civil society organizations facilitating democratic participation. And

3 Brief for Am. Immigration Lawyers Ass'n as Amicus Curiae Supporting Appellees at 12–13, Hajro v. U.S. Citizenship & Immigration Servs., 811 F.3d 1086 (9th Cir. 2015) (Nos. 11-17948, 12-17765).

4 *Our Research Process*, PROBES REPORTER, https://probesreporter.com/our-research-process (last visited Nov. 16, 2020).

5 Gretchen Morgenson, *Deafened by the S.E.C.'s Silence, He Sued*, THE NEW YORK TIMES (May 28, 2006), www.nytimes.com/2006/05/28/business/yourmoney/28gavin.html.

third, and this is where the rubber meets the road, while some celebrate the number of requests made as evidence of FOIA's success, the costs associated with FOIA and loud complaints by news media about how badly FOIA is failing have caused significant criticisms of the law, verging on advocacy of its demise.

Over the past several years, I set out to answer the unanswered questions. Who uses FOIA and what records are they trying to obtain? I have done this, ironically, by making hundreds of FOIA requests for agencies' FOIA logs and related records. I now have data that covers about three-quarters of the federal government's total requests. I can give you the quick upshot: FOIA largely is not used to promote democratic accountability. My best estimate – and I have now spent a lot of time trying to get to this estimate – is that news media are less than 3 percent of requesters government-wide. Instead of requesters seeking to inform the public about government activities, the bulk of requesters look more like Emma Quezada, WM, and John Patrick Gavin.

Let me be clear: These uses of FOIA are completely legitimate, legal, and may often be in the public interest in the more broadly defined sense. For example, individuals requesting their own records are often doing so as part of seeking a government benefit or defending against a government enforcement action. These uses often promote fairness and accuracy in decision-making processes, dignity for individuals in agency proceedings, and a sort of procedural legitimacy of agency actions. Businesses using FOIA may be using it to ensure greater compliance with legal requirements, and even those just trying to learn about their competition may use the information in ways that benefit consumers by improving the marketplace. Yet, these requesters are not trying to obtain information to make the general public more aware of government actions.

The foundational problem for government transparency is that the volume of these non-oversight-minded requesters undermines FOIA's efficacy. On the practical side, given that agencies are overwhelmed by requests, they necessarily engage in triage. Rational responses to volumes of nonoversight requesters includes creating processes, systems, and specialists who speak to the volume of routine requests, not one-off media requests about a pressing timely topic. In fact, agencies often do not have the resources or technology to best serve the specialized interests of news media. Conversations I had with agency officials confirm this reality. They are trying to build a system that deals with the bulk of requests, not necessarily those most important to FOIA's mission.

Relatedly, the impact on the media is palpable. Delay and administrative burden are by far the biggest complaints journalists raise about the law, and those concerns are directly related to agencies' resource constraints. At DHS, a senior FOIA official explained that because systems are set up to optimize routine nonoversight requests that come in in droves, he thinks that "true" FOIA requests mostly end up in the backlog, and "the backlog is masked with routine requests."[6] There is, I believe, a direct connection between vast numbers of routine, nonoversight FOIA requests and the difficulties the news media face in effectively using the law.

And then there are theoretical problems. The fact that FOIA is mostly used in ways not imagined to be at the heart of its purpose is a big part of what gives the strongest critiques of FOIA legs to stand on. Nonoversight requesters detract from advocates' assertions that FOIA is worth its considerable costs. And they are what leads to questioning about whether FOIA is accomplishing its goal. Helen Foster, a former FOIA official at three different department-level agencies, when asked what would surprise the public about FOIA if they knew, stated it bluntly: "People don't understand that it's impossible. The goal of the statute as it is currently implemented can't be done. … FOIA is the Titanic, it sank years ago."[7]

When we think about where FOIA stands today, we have to place these extremely high-volume nonoversight requesters at the center of the discussion. Doing so, it turns out, provides numerous insights both about how FOIA works and how it could work better, but also about how we might reimagine the relationship between the administrative state and the public. People who need agency information – members of the public I refer to as "information constituents" – are not limited to people engaging in public oversight of government activities. Yet, oftentimes their only option is to use a statute designed for that purpose, and not with them in mind. As the examples above suggest, it often ends badly – it is not a process that works well for the agencies (think of Foster's Titanic analogy), it is not a process that works well for the information constituents (think of Quezada and WM), and it certainly is not good for FOIA. This book reimagines the future of the government's relationship with its information constituents. It proceeds in three parts.

Part I consists of my full-throttled defense of FOIA. This is a case worth making. A fundamental flaw with any sort of cost-benefit discussion with respect to FOIA is that the costs may be hard to quantify, but at least it is possible to take a stab at tabulating the value of government officials' time, FOIA personnel, office operations, and similar resources. FOIA's benefits, though, are nearly impossible to quantify. It is hard to know how much knowledge the public gains from FOIA requests. Many news stories involving records requested under FOIA fail to mention that a FOIA request was involved in reporting, because journalists do not show all their work when they write. Moreover, how do we quantify the value of particular pieces of knowledge to the public? And there are a myriad of nonoversight benefits FOIA is currently providing, as this book details, which are equally if not more

6 Interview with Dr. James V. M. L. Holzer, Deputy Chief FOIA Officer, Jimmy Wolfrey, Senior Dir., FOIA Operations and Mgmt. & Amy Bennett, Public Liaison, U.S. Dep't of Homeland Sec., in Washington D.C. (June 5, 2019).

7 Telephone Interview with Helen Foster, Former Chief Privacy and FOIA Officer & Chief Administrative Officer, U.S. Dep't of Housing and Urban Development (May 14, 2019).

difficult to quantify. As a result, any discussion of whether FOIA is "worth it" is a discussion that stacks the deck from the beginning.

That said, there is a lot of evidence that FOIA is, even in its highly imperfect state, serving very significant interests. Chapter One details the theoretical and political origins of FOIA, explaining its vital role in a modern democratic society and the motivations behind the law. FOIA is not just a creation of the contemporary administrative state; it is rooted in the great Enlightenment-era political philosophers and comes of age in times of crises in US democracy. Chapter Two dives into the oversight uses of FOIA, drawn primarily from a series of interviews with news media requesters who use FOIA particularly effectively and who have found pockets of great success. This chapter reveals telling narratives where FOIA had great impact, particularly in uncovering government waste and abuse, learning about private influence over government decision-making, and revealing national security and law enforcement activity. There is a substantial body of evidence amassed here that FOIA is, indeed, very much worth saving.

Part Two of this book reports the most complete data ever collected concerning FOIA requesters and FOIA requests in the United States. In Chapter Three, I provide a government-wide overview of FOIA requesters. Interesting patterns emerge. First, this chapter documents the volume of news media requesters across the government, in what is the most comprehensive effort to tabulate an estimate of journalists use of FOIA. Then, the chapter documents the dominant uses of FOIA across the federal government, since it is not the news media.

At the highest level of generality, agencies can be grouped into three categories: benefits agencies, law enforcement agencies, or regulatory agencies. And, at this bird's-eye level, my data show that benefits and law enforcement agencies are disproportionately inundated with first-person FOIA requests; that is, requests for records about the requesters themselves, whether they concern the requester's own law enforcement records, medical files, immigration files, or family history. This group of agencies includes all major components of DHS, Veterans Affairs, Department of State, Social Security, and the Equal Employment Opportunity Commission (EEOC). These are requesters like Quezada and WM. Regulatory agencies, on the other hand, tend to receive high volumes of commercial requests, or requests for records to be used as part of a profit-making enterprise. These include agencies like the SEC, the Environmental Protection Agency (EPA), and the Food and Drug Administration (FDA). These requesters tend to use FOIA to fuel consulting, due diligence, or industry advising services, or they are businesses whose sole business model is to request records under FOIA and resell them at a profit, like Gavin's various enterprises.

Chapters Four through Eight take an in-depth look at each of these subsets of voluminous requests. Chapter Four is dedicated solely to the question of immigration, which now drives around half of all requests submitted to the federal government each year. Understanding FOIA's role in the immigration context is essential to understanding the state of FOIA today. Chapter Five focuses on the substantial areas of non-immigration first-person use of FOIA, primarily in the areas of benefits, employment discrimination, and genealogy research. Chapter Six turns to commercial requesters, which are businesses that use FOIA to obtain information that they privately benefit from in the commercial marketplace. And Chapter Seven looks at the subset of those commercial requesters who, like Gavin, request records under FOIA and resell them at a profit as their primary business model. Finally, Chapter Eight rounds out the discussion by acknowledging an important reality; some agencies have truly idiosyncratic information constituencies. This chapter explores issues such as public research databases, political opposition research, requests between different arms of government, curiosity requesters, and the legitimate (if often overstated) problem of requesters aiming to harass officials or abuse FOIA processes. These sorts of information constituencies may beg for bespoke solutions to information delivery.

Part III explains the import of knowing what work FOIA does, and what work it does not do. The central argument is that rather than trying to squeeze all of the public's needs for government information into FOIA, reform efforts should focus on requiring or incentivizing agencies to meet nonoversight information needs head-on through tailored mechanisms crafted outside of FOIA. Under this view, no one should be denied the opportunity to avail themselves of FOIA, but if there were better alternatives to access particular information that members of the public routinely want, these would-be requesters would no longer need to resort to FOIA. This approach would reduce (perhaps vastly) the number of FOIA requests that are made and free up FOIA offices' resources to better serve FOIA's core mission. As sort of an additional benefit, in many cases they would better serve the private interests at stake and could be more efficient for agencies, too.

Chapter Nine details the growing criticism of FOIA and the need for fundamental reform. It describes how the glut of nonoversight requesters is at the center of this debate, not on its margins. And it makes the case that structural solutions aimed at shrinking FOIA to recenter on oversight purposes is the way forward. Chapters Ten through Twelve address a series of strategies agencies can use – or Congress can require – to accomplish this type of reform. Chapter Ten takes on affirmative (or proactive) disclosure. In many contexts, particularly with respect to routine requests by commercial requesters, one can easily imagine a targeted affirmative disclosure initiative that would address the needs of information constituencies by publishing, on an ongoing basis, whole categories of frequently requested records. Chapter Eleven tackles reform to agency adjudication practices, including the possibility of administrative discovery and other processing modifications that would eliminate the need for individuals seeking government benefits or defending against enforcement to resort to FOIA to obtain their own records. Finally, Chapter Twelve discusses an array of other specialized procedures agencies can create to address information needs outside the FOIA process.

Forcing all information needs into the FOIA queue muddies the waters of any debate over whether FOIA resources are being well spent and obfuscates sensible agency strategies to reduce the need to rely on FOIA. This book describes not only what needs to be done, but how to do it. As it stands, there is little reason for agencies to look for alternatives to FOIA. Routine requests – the kinds that noncitizens are making by the hundreds of thousands for their immigration files, that businesses are flooding the SEC, EPA, and FDA with each year, that the Social Security Administration (SSA) see most often from amateur genealogists – are often the easiest to fulfill. As a result, agencies fare better in reporting their overall success rates under FOIA when they have lots of routine requests, including faster processing times, higher release rates, and fewer administrative appeals and legal challenges.

Certainly, there is no evidence that agencies consciously avoid non-FOIA alternatives to make their FOIA performance look better, but there is no question that the system is set up with performance metrics that favor jamming nearly everything into FOIA. Agency officials confirm the lack of incentives for finding alternatives to FOIA. Congress has a role in considering new reporting requirements, proactive disclosure requirements, and even private enforcement regimes. Agencies have a role in reimagining information delivery as a core function. Meanwhile, the public has a role in demanding an administrative state that serves its information constituents – us.

PART I

FOIA And Democracy

1

Why Free Information?

A. DEMOCRACY AND TRANSPARENCY

In the late eighteenth century, on the eve of the French Revolution, a Swiss-born banker by the name of Jacques Necker was serving a short-lived appointment as the French Director-General of Finance. In that role, Necker advocated balancing the government's ordinary budget as a means of increasing public confidence, and using debt – secured at a lower interest rate as a result of the balanced budget – to finance extraordinary circumstances, namely, at the time, the French involvement in the American Revolutionary War.[1]

His commitment to increasing public confidence in the solidity of government finance led him to an act of radical government transparency. In 1781, Necker published the *Compte Rendu*, or "Report," which was in effect an accounting of the budget of the French government. The publication was of such an unprecedented nature that publishers reproduced an unheard of twenty thousand copies, which quickly sold out. Influential Protestant pastor Jean-Paul Rabaut Saint-Étienne declared that the publication showed "the effect of sudden light in the midst of darkness," invoking a metaphor of light still used today in government transparency discussions.[2]

While Necker's *Compte Rendu* came under fire for alleged misrepresentations about French governmental debt, Necker remained immensely popular, and committed to the idea that "the preservation of secrecy was, in effect, the rescue of despotism."[3] Indeed, his later ouster from a government post is thought to have contributed to the uprising of the French Revolution itself.[4]

1 Simon M. Schama, Citizens: A Chronicle of the French Revolution 92 (1989).
2 *Id.*
3 *Id.* at 95.
4 *See* Darius Von Guettner, The French Revolution 19 (Carolyn Glascodine ed., 1st ed. 2015).

Necker found himself in a moment where government transparency – then referred to as publicity – was essentially invented.[5] Eighteenth-century Europe was characterized by the age of Enlightenment, in which prevailing wisdom departed from the historical model using faith as the central method of understanding the world. Instead, Enlightenment thinkers promoted science and reason, believing rationality in decision-making was the way of the future. This intense period of intellectual engagement gave rise to the work of great philosophers, including political philosophers.[6]

Relatedly, during this period, Europe experienced the advent of representative forms of government, the origins of modern-day democracies. The Enlightenment thinking certainly fueled these movements. On the earlier end, the English Revolution of 1688 led to the adoption of the Bill of Rights, divesting some of the monarchy's absolute power and preserving more power for Parliament.[7] And on the later end, the French Revolution overturned the monarchy and led to the establishment of the French Constitution and a representative democracy.[8] Similar transformations were occurring in countries throughout the world, including, of course, the United States establishing a republican form of government after the revolutionary war.

By the late eighteenth and early nineteenth centuries, leaders across Europe began to articulate the need for more publicity of governmental activities. For example, in 1772, Charles J. Fox, a leading British Parliamentarian who was greatly influenced by and supportive of the American Revolutionary War and the French Revolution, spoke tellingly of the role of the public in representative democracies. After reaffirming a commitment to following the will of the people as an elected representative, he declared, "[O]ne thing is most clear, that I ought to give the public the means of forming an opinion." Likewise in 1804, Prussian king Frederick William III told his own ministers "that a decent publicity is for both government and subjects the surest guaranty against the negligence and spit of subaltern officials and deserves to be promoted and protected by all means."[9]

The thinking of these leaders in reimagining the relationship between government and its citizenry was not in isolation. As representative democracies came into

[5] Sandrine Baume, *Transparency in the Handling of Public Affairs: Origins and Meaning of a Requirement*, RUTGERS U.:1ST GLOBAL CONF. ON TRANSPARENCY RES., May 19–20, 2011, at 9.

[6] John J. Patrick, *Connecting Science and Free Government in Citizenship Education: Teaching about Our Legacy from the Age of Enlightenment*, SOC. STUD. DEV. CTR., Nov. 6, 1987, at 4–6.

[7] *Id.* at 6.

[8] Jean-Louis Halpérin, *Legal Interpretation in France under the Reign of Louis XVI: A Review of the Gazette des Tribunaux*, in INTERPRETATION OF LAW IN THE AGE OF ENLIGHTENMENT: FROM THE RULE OF THE KING TO THE RULE OF LAW 21, 21–24 (Yasutomo Morigiwa et al. eds. 2011).

[9] JÜRGEN HABERMAS, THE STRUCTURAL TRANSFORMATION OF THE PUBLIC SPHERE: AN INQUIRY INTO A CATEGORY OF BOURGEOIS SOCIETY 84 (Thomas Burger & Frederick Lawrence trans., 1991) (1962).

being, philosophers began articulating transparency as a foundational element of legitimate government. Immanuel Kant, in his 1795 essay entitled "Perpetual Peace," theorized a set of governing principles that in his view would lead to, as the title suggests, a lasting peace between and within states. Transparency takes on an outsized presence in this relatively short work, as Kant explains that the legitimacy of the laws that govern the state, private individuals, and the relations between them depend on publicity.[10] This is, in essence, the democratic aim of transparency.

But not only does Kant's vision require publicity – or public disclosure – of government laws and policies, but it also holds publicity out as the means of harmonizing two potentially conflicting claims: moral rights and political rights. Moral rights are based in a theoretical frame of promoting welfare and avoiding harm, whereas political rights are determined by the practical inquiry of what can be workable in governing a population. Kant acknowledges the possible divergence between moral and political rights but finds publicity to be the answer:

> All Maxims which require Publicity in order that they may not fail of their end, are in accordance with both right and politics united with each other. For if these maxims can only attain their end by publicity, they must be comfortable to the common end of the public, which is happiness; and it is the special problem of politics to put itself into agreement with the public, and to make the people contented with their condition. But if this end is to be attained only by publicity, as the means of removing all distrust of political maxims, these maxims must also be in harmony with the right of the public; for the union of the ends of all is only possible in the harmony established by right.[11]

That is, through publicity, or transparency, the public knows of the governmental policy, and the government cannot create policies that would be contrary to the public interest if they are to be known, or they will not be accepted. Publicity itself turns mere political rights into political rights that are also consistent with moral rights. For Kant, publicity is a key component of a just governance.

Jean-Jacques Rousseau had a similar view of transparency as the promoter of more moral and just governance.[12] Indeed, in 1772, Rousseau attributed the success of smaller states to the inherent nature of their transparency, because in small states "all the citizens know and watch over one another . . . the leaders can see for themselves the evil that is being done, the good they have to do; and . . . their orders are carried

[10] Immanuel Kant, Perpetual Peace: A Philosophical Sketch 138–39 (William Hastie trans., 1891) (1795).

> All actions relating to the right of other men are wrong, if their maxim is not compatible with publicity. This principle is not to be regarded merely as ethical, and as belonging only to the doctrine of virtue, but it is also to be regarded as juridical and as pertaining to the rights of men. For a maxim cannot be a right maxim which is such that I cannot allow it to be published.

[11] *Id.* at 147.

[12] Baume, *supra* note 5, at 10

out before their eyes."[13] By contrast to small states, "[a]ll great peoples, crushed by their own mass, suffer either from anarchy … or from subordinate oppressors."[14]

Thus, for Kant and Rousseau, transparency or publicity is not only necessary to ensure the ability to exercise democratic oversight but indeed itself functions to regulate state actors. Where officials know their actions will come to public light, they will not abuse their power or act in interests other than the public interest. We can think of this transparency as a form of regulating the behavior of government officials.[15]

Some fifty years later, the transformation of the dominant political system to republican forms of government having taken place, English philosopher and political reformer Jeremey Bentham took up the theory of publicity as a primary component of his work. While Bentham agrees with Kant and Rousseau that publicity is the means to ensure that the will and interest of the people are carried forward, he also emphasizes the role of publicity in fostering public trust in government. "Suspicion," he writes in his 1843 essay entitled "Of Publicity," "always attaches to mystery. … For why should we hide ourselves if we do not dread being seen?"[16] Transparency, then, can also serve the independent aim of enhancing public trust.

There are strong connections between these early philosophers' conceptions of publicity and modern-day justifications offered for transparency regimes. For example, echoing concerns of democratic accountability, Alexander Meiklejohn, a twentieth-century political philosopher, uses the frame of First Amendment protections for freedom of speech to explore some aspects of access to public information. Meiklejohn asserted that the First Amendment is "concerned, not with a private right, but with a public power, a governmental responsibility."[17] And in order to exercise that responsibility, among other actions, "[w]e, the people who govern, must try to understand the issues which, incident by incident, face the nation."[18]

Yet there has also been some significant divergence in modern transparency theory. To begin, the very terminological shift between publicity and transparency is itself meaningful. Publicity, as a term, necessarily has a focus on the effect on the listener. As Jürgen Habermas explained, "[t]he subject of this publicity is the public as carrier of public opinion; its function as a critical judge is precisely what makes

[13] Jean-Jacques Rousseau, The Government of Poland 11 (Willmoore Kendall trans., 1972) (1782).

[14] *Id.*

[15] I, with Bridget DuPey, separately explore the concept of government transparency as a regulatory mechanism in *Targeted Transparency as Regulation*, 48 Fl. St. L. Rev. 389 (2021).

[16] Jeremy Bentham, 2 The Works of Jeremy Bentham, 310 (John Bowring ed., 1843).

[17] Alexander Meiklejohn, *The First Amendment is an Absolute*, 1961 The Sup. Ct. Rev. 245, 255 (1961).

[18] *Id.*

the public character of proceedings—in court, for instance—meaningful."[19] That is, publicity examines the public's ability to influence government, to understand issues of public importance, to judge the correctness of the actions they observe, and to trust in government.

That publicity is really about the experience of the listener is particularly evident in Bentham's work. When Bentham talked of publicity, he meant quite literally the act of publicizing the activities of government. To that end, he advocated the publication of certain official documents allowing the public to physically view certain proceedings and provide their own account.[20]

Transparency, as a term, instead turns the lens in the other direction, examining the state and its degree of openness. It appears to articulate not a means to an end as publicity does but rather a way of being that itself is the goal of good governance. The theory of a "transparent state" that it "removes the obstructions that keep the government hidden and the public imperfectly informed."[21] But because, as Max Weber wrote, "[b]ureaucratic administration always tends to exclude the public, to hide its knowledge and action from criticism as well as it can," legal rights must be established to ensure the public's access to government information.[22]

B. THE FREE PRESS

As the theoretical justification for publicity or transparency demonstrates, democracy does not just happen by giving people the right to vote. A population needs the means by which they can be informed of important public issues and the activities of their elected leaders. Without that information, the right to vote does very little good. A representative democracy, however, presupposes that democracy will be exercised through intermediaries. Indeed, the very premise of electing a representative is to have an intermediary filter the interests of the population up to the governmental level, that is, to represent the people in the government.

But intermediaries, albeit less formal, were also contemplated in filtering information down from government to the people (i.e., operationalizing "publicity" or "transparency"). In this instance, rather than elected representatives, the press was always imagined performing this function: to decide what government information is important, to make it digestible, and to inform the people so they can exercise their basic oversight responsibilities.

[19] Habermas, *supra* note 9, at 2.

[20] Bentham, *supra* note 16, at 315.

[21] Mark Fenster, The Transparency Fix: Secrets, Leaks, and Uncontrollable Government Information 4 (2017).

[22] Max Weber, Economy and Society: An Outline of Interpretive Sociology 992 (Guenther Roth & Claus Wittich eds., 1978).

Indeed, the conceptual role of a free press as essential to a democratic society grew up in tandem with the republican form of representative government.[23] From 1720 to 1723, in the midst of the political shifts in Europe, two English journalists, John Trenchard and Thomas Gordon, published a series of essays under the pseudonym Cato.[24] Among the wide-ranging topics the letters covered, Cato addressed freedom of speech, famously declaring that "freedom of speech is the great bulwark of liberty; they prosper and die together."[25]

While freedom of speech is the nominal topic of that essay, it is no coincidence that journalists made this early declaration about the importance of free speech; free speech rights and press freedoms have long gone hand in hand. In fact, as a leading scholar on press freedoms Professor David Anderson has documented, in the early formulations of fundamental rights in the United States, press freedoms – not freedom of speech – were the central preoccupation.[26]

As early as 1768, Cato's own words were transformed into a statement about the centrality of press freedoms in the colonies. That year, a leading radical newspaper in Boston published an accusation against the Royal Governor of the Colony of Massachusetts, to which the Royal Council responded by asking the House to refer the matter for grand jury prosecution for seditious libel. The House not only refused but, led by radical Sam Adams, adopted the following resolution: "The Liberty of the Press is a great Bulwark of the Liberty of the People: It is, therefore, the incumbent Duty of those who are constituted the Guardians of the People's Rights to defend and maintain it."[27]

The central role of the press was reaffirmed as the colonies agitated for independence. On the eve of the American Revolutionary War, First Continental Congress delegates, then presided by Henry Middleton, addressed the people of the province of Quebec in an attempt to recruit allies in the war. The address described the democratic values that they sought in the brewing conflict, and in so doing, announced five "invaluable rights." Among them was the freedom of press:

> The last right we shall mention, regards the freedom of the press. The importance of this consists, besides the advancement of truth, science, morality, and arts in general, in its diffusion of liberal sentiments on the administration of Government, in its ready communication of thoughts between subjects, and its consequential

[23] David A. Anderson, *The Origins of the Press Clause*, 30 UCLA L. Rev. 455, 463 (1983).

[24] Christopher S. Grenda, *Thinking Historically about Diversity: Religion, the Enlightenment, and the Construction of Civic Culture in Early America*, 48 J. Church & St. 567, 579 (2006).

[25] Thomas Gordon & John Trenchard, *No. 15. Saturday, February 4, 1721. Of Freedom of Speech: That the Same is Inseparable from Publick Liberty*, *in* Cato's Letters or Essays on Liberty, Civil, or Religious, and Other Important Subjects 79, 81 (Ronald Hamowy ed., Liberty Fund 1995).

[26] Anderson, *supra* note 23, at 464 (1983).

[27] *See* Leonard W. Levy, Legacy of Suppression: Freedom of Speech and Press in Early American History 69 (1960).

promotion of union among them, whereby oppressive officers are shamed or intimidated, into more honourable and just modes of conducting affairs.[28]

This early declaration is consistent with Cato's contention that freedom of the press was foundational to a democratic governance structure. Professor Anderson points to the significance of the fact that freedom of press is given center stage, while freedom of speech – the First Amendment's better-known right – is nowhere mentioned.[29]

Cato's famous "bulwark of liberty" phraseology returned in the form of codified rights, but again, referring to protections for freedom of the press. Two of the state constitutions – Virginia and North Carolina – adopted during the Revolutionary War used the phrase; for example, Virginia's constitution provided "that the freedom of the Press is one of the greatest bulwarks of liberty, and can never be restrained but by despotick Governments."[30] Indeed, of the eleven state constitutions adopted during the Revolutionary War, nine included provisions on freedom of the press, but only one had a dual clause protecting not just the press but speech more generally.[31] That one state, Pennsylvania, ended up providing the model on which the federal First Amendment was drafted, but the press was the animating concern during the debate about the bill of rights.[32] As Professor Anderson explained, "freedom of the press was viewed not merely as a desirable civil liberty, but as a matter integral to the structure of the new government."[33]

At the time that press freedoms began to acquire these legal protections, however, "the press" was less like journalism and more like the trade of printers; indeed, the word "press" referred most directly to the technological innovation that made wide dissemination of publications possible – the printing press.[34] That is not to say, however, that the role of the printing press was wholly distinct from the role of modern-day journalism; the two share many of the most important features. Indeed, the historical role of the press demonstrates that it had a particularly revered role in society.

To begin, the printing press – "the press" of colonial America – was much more than a new pastime. "As glimmerings of the Enlightenment began to appear in the seventeenth century, the technology of printing was portrayed by some as a virtual

[28] Bernard Schwartz, 1 The Bill of Rights: A Documentary History 223 (1971).

[29] Anderson, *The Origins of the Press Clause*, *supra* note 23, at 464.

[30] Schwartz, *supra* note 28, at 235, 287.

[31] Anderson, *The Origins of the Press Clause*, *supra* note 23, at 464.

[32] U.S. Const. amend. I ("Congress shall make no law respecting an establishment of religion, or prohibiting the free exercise thereof; or abridging the freedom of speech, or of the press; or the right of the people peaceably to assemble, and to petition the government for a redress of grievances."); Anderson, *The Origins of the Press Clause*, *supra* note 23, at 473.

[33] Anderson, *The Origins of the Press Clause*, *supra* note 23, at 488.

[34] Jeffrey A. Smith, Printers and Press Freedom: The Ideology of Early American Journalism 41 (1988).

panacea."[35] Printers, the owners of the presses, assumed a sort of public role, in the word of one such press, permitting the population a means of "asserting all their just Rights, redressing Grievances, detecting Error, advancing useful Knowledge, and making an Appeal to the Reason and Justice of the whole Race of Mankind."[36] That is, printers filled the role we think of as journalistic and popular oversight.

And, of course, printers had a wildly influential role in the American Revolutionary War. One of Benjamin Franklin's central preoccupations was setting up presses.[37] Printed pamphlets have long been credited with solidifying the secession movement. These pamphlets, reproduced by printers and distributed widely, included Thomas Paine's infamous *Common Sense*, and John Dickinson's *Letters from a Farmer in Pennsylvania*.[38] It was the outsized role of printers – publishers both of newspapers and of these influential pamphlets – that led historian David Ramsay to declare in 1789 that "in establishing American independence, the pen and press had merit equal to that of the sword."[39]

To be sure, there has been a changing vision of what constitutes "the press." While printers, largely engaged in reproducing texts and selling them for small profits, were "the press" at the time the press clause was adopted in the First Amendment, those printers nonetheless filled the same role that modern-day journalists – now thought of as "the press" – do.[40] They served as a means to vocalize dissent, hold government accountable, and produce the collective wisdom necessary for the population to engage in democratic governance.

The centrality of the press to American democracy thus stems from a long-standing tradition of protecting a free press. Independence from government and political parties, journalistic integrity, and a commitment to the public interest have always characterized the press in the United States.[41] The press has thus earned a revered place in American society.

It should come as no surprise, then, that the press continues to enjoy special treatment in the law. The press is sometimes the subject of extra constitutional protections that stem directly from their roles as journalists. For example, a state may favor one viewpoint over another when it is engaged in journalism,[42] and, although the Supreme Court has not definitively weighed in, courts of appeals recognize a journalistic privilege against revealing confidential sources.[43]

[35] *Id.* at 42.

[36] *Id.* at 18 (quoting the Connecticut Gazette).

[37] *Id.* at 17, 44.

[38] Robert G. Parkinson, *Print, the Press, and the American Revolution*, *in* Oxford Research Encyclopedia of American History, at 4 (2015).

[39] *Id.* at 1.

[40] David A. Anderson, *Freedom of the Press*, 80 Tex. L. Rev. 429, 447–48 (2002).

[41] *Id.* at 483.

[42] Ark. Educ. Television Comm'n v. Forbes, 523 U.S. 666, 669 (1998).

[43] United States v. Caporale, 806 F.2d 1487, 1504 (11th Cir. 1986); Zerilli v. Smith, 656 F.2d 705, 710-12 (D.C. Cir. 1981); Miller v. Transamerican Press, Inc., 621 F.2d 721, 725 (5th Cir. 1980); Silkwood v. Kerr-McGee Corp., 563 F.2d 433, 438 (10th Cir. 1977).

But much more often, First Amendment protections of speech apply nominally to everyone but have special salience for the press. While there is a public right of access to courtrooms, for example, the press can be given preferential access to the exclusion of others.[44] Press members are also particularly well suited to take advantage of the right to publish information of public concern regardless of whether it was initially obtained illegally, so long as the publisher was not involved in the illegal activity.[45] For example, as with *The New York Times* publication of the Pentagon Papers, a classified account of the US involvement in Vietnam that was famously leaked by Daniel Ellsberg, journalists are those most likely to receive and publish illegally leaked or stolen information.[46]

The press's special role in American society is also recognized in countless statutory and even administrative rules that privilege journalists' rights as protectors of the public's interest in governance and oversight. State laws and judicial decisions grant press privileges to resist subpoenas; government institutions – including the White House, Congress, state governments, and law enforcement agencies – all give press preferential access including to press rooms, to briefings, and to observe important governmental functions; and federal and state laws prevent search warrants from targeting newsrooms in all but extraordinary circumstances.[47] The press are also exempt from various government imposed burdens including certain taxes, campaign finance laws, and antitrust limitations.[48] It is thus fair to say that historically, culturally, and legally, the press have occupied a particularly salient role in facilitating American democratic governance.

C. LEGISLATING FREEDOM OF INFORMATION

Open government laws fit comfortably within a tradition of privileging the press as stand-ins for the public and facilitators of democratic governance, especially because they specially contemplated the interests of the news media and in some instances give them preferential access to government records. In fact, the news media are heavily invested in FOIA, from its creation to its continued vitality. Because the press has a central and revered place in American democracy, the intertwinement of the press with FOIA further elevates the law's importance to American governance, even though, as is evident from the history, legal rights to public records is a relatively new innovation.

The US Constitution was ratified amid the very European movement toward representative democracy that gave rise to theories of government transparency. Yet, a right of public access to government information was hardly baked into American

[44] Richmond Newspapers, Inc. v. Virginia, 448 U.S. 555, 581 n.18 (1980).
[45] *See generally* N.Y. Times Co. v. United States, 403 U.S. 713 (1971).
[46] *Id.* at 749–51 (Burger, J., dissenting).
[47] Anderson, *Freedom of the Press, supra* note 40, at 487.
[48] *Id.*

democracy. It is true that James Madison famously said that "[a] popular Government, without popular information, or the means of acquiring it, is but a Prologue to a Farce or a Tragedy; or, perhaps, both."[49] Yet the quote is often misapprehended by mapping those words onto a contemporary understanding of freedom of information laws and right to know regimes. Madison was in fact not talking about handing over government records to whomever asks, but rather was applauding the state of Kentucky for endeavoring to provide a public education to its citizens.[50] Neither Madison nor his contemporaries contemplated opening up the federal government for public inspection.[51]

Rather, the framers believed in an informed citizenry, but the means of acquiring information were wholly separate from notions of access and transparency. As Michael Shudson carefully documented, the founders considered, for example, the postal system to be a means of circulating information, particularly with favorable rates for the distribution of newspapers.[52] Other innovations, like patent protections, and, as illustrated by Madison's quote, public education, were thought important to an informed citizenry.[53] Principally, however, direct democracy was not the ideal; rather, elections were designed to allow voters to know the character of the candidates, to vote for a trusted official who would make decisions in the voter's place.[54] That is why the framers referred not to democracy, but to a republican form of government.

Around the turn of the twentieth century, the concept of transparency began to enter into American administrative law, but rather than focusing on the state, the light was shone on private corporations.[55] In 1903, the Bureau of Corporations was established with its regulatory activities limited largely to collecting and disseminating information about corporate trade practices. The thinking was that public scrutiny would keep companies from engaging in illicit practices, thereby serving as a sort of soft form of regulation.[56] Using transparency as a form of regulation only grew in popularity, particularly in the consumer context. Investigative journalism like Upton Sinclair's exposé on the meatpacking industry in his infamous book *The Jungle* spurred a movement for greater corporate accountability.[57] Yet, rather than substantive regulations, the legislative reactions were largely around disclosure and

[49] Letter from JAMES MADISON TO W.T. BARRY (Aug. 4, 1822) (on file with the Library of Congress), hwww.loc.gov/resource/mjm.20_0155_0159/?sp=1&st=text.

[50] Michael Doyle, *Misquoting Madison*, LEGAL AFFAIRS (July/August 2002), www.legalaffairs.org/issues/July-August-2002/scene_doyle_julaug2002.msp.

[51] *Id.*

[52] *See*, MICHAEL SHUDSON, THE RISE OF THE RIGHT TO KNOW: POLITICS AND THE CULTURE OF TRANSPARENCY, 1945–1975, at 54 (2017).

[53] Doyle, *supra* note 50.

[54] SHUDSON, *supra* note 52.

[55] David Pozen, *Transparency's Ideological Drift*, 128 YALE L.J. 100, 109 (2018).

[56] Robert L. Rabin, *Federal Regulation in Historical Perspective*, 38 STAN. L. REV. 1189, 1283–84 (1986).

[57] *Id.* at 1226–27.

transparency. Thus, food and drug labeling laws and inspection regimes were implemented as a result.[58]

Even what is perhaps the most famous quote attached to modern understandings of freedom of information and the public's right to know was not about government, but about business. Justice Louis Brandeis, invoking a metaphor still very popular in freedom of information conversations, stated that "[s]unlight is said to be the best of disinfectants; electric light the most efficient policeman."[59] Brandeis's concern, though, was the concentration of power among investment bankers, especially with the consolidation of certain industries including banks and railroads, not government oversight.

Thus, throwing open the doors of government agencies for the public to peer in was neither part of the republican form of government contemplated by the founding fathers, nor the type of transparency that most concerned legislators and jurists around the turn of the twentieth century when the administrative state began to take its modern form.

The swell of the administrative state, however, was certainly bound up with the advent of FOI and right-to-know legislation, but it was President Franklin Delano Roosevelt's New Deal programs that provoked the reaction.[60] For a time prior to 1937, the Supreme Court was acting as a check on the accumulation of government power, routinely striking down New Deal programs as unconstitutional. In 1937, however, Justice Owen Roberts changed his views of the programs, widely known as the "switch in time that saved nine" because of Roosevelt's threat to increase the number of justices under his so-called court packing plan. Thus, with the Supreme Court no longer consistently reigning in Roosevelt's administrative growth, checks on that power had to come from other sources.[61]

Thus was born the Administrative Procedure Act (APA), enacted after great debate in 1946 precisely to address concerns about unchecked government power, a fear augmented by the conflicts with communist and totalitarian governments abroad. Indeed, an authoritative historical account of the enactment of the APA described the law as the result of "a pitched political battle for the life of the New Deal."[62] In keeping with the trend of transparency as form of regulation – this time aimed at the government – the APA contains various public disclosure requirements. For example, the hallmark notice-and-comment rulemaking procedures represent an attempt to alert the public to an agency's proposed regulations and allow direct democratic input.

58 *Id.* at 1243–44.
59 Louis D. Brandeis, *What Publicity Can Do*, Harper's Weekly 10, 10 (Dec. 20, 1913).
60 George B. Shepherd, *Fierce Compromise: The Administrative Procedure Act Emerges from New Deal Politics*, 90 Nw. U. L. Rev. 1557, 1582 (1996).
61 *Id.* at 1560–76.
62 *Id.* at 1560.

In fact, FOIA was itself not truly a standalone law, but rather technically an amendment to the APA, which itself contained the original provision purporting to grant a right of public access to government records. That provision required "matters of official record . . . [to] be made available to persons properly and directly concerned" but excepted records "required by statute" to be withheld as well as "information held confidential for good cause found."[63] But the results of the information access provision of the APA were certainly disappointing. In practice, it functioned more as a "withholding [statute] than as a disclosure statute," being cited as authority to withhold just about anything the agency did not want to reveal.[64]

Yet, this original APA access provision planted the seed of access to government records as part of the law that some supporters referred to as a "bill of rights" for individuals facing the increasingly powerful administrative state.[65] It demonstrates the inextricable link between the growth of the administrative state – itself a democratic challenge never envisioned by the framers – and the advent of transparency laws – a remedy equally foreign at the framing of the Constitution.

Other important factors were at play in the impetus for passing FOIA, however, and many of them centrally concerned the changing landscape of the news media and the resulting advocacy of journalists. Although journalism in the United States had always been characterized by independence from government and political parties, as Professor Mark Fenster has carefully documented, it was not until the wake of World War II when the US news media formed a strong professional identity as such.[66]

In the late 1800s, the *Associated Press* (AP), the major wire service from which most news outlets obtained national news, had joined forces with a European news cartel under which each service agreed on territorial limits to their newsgathering and distribution. But the other members of the cartel had ties to national governments that had the potential to affect the independence of their reporting. As time went on, AP was both concerned about the integrity of the news it obtained under the cartel agreement and also facing stiffer competition from another US wire service not subject to cartel restrictions.[67]

The AP's general manager Kent Cooper managed to withdraw from and then essentially defeat the European wire service cartel, and with that shift in the industry "the American press turned evangelical."[68] The evangelism centered on press

63 S. Rep. No. 88–1219, at 10 (1964).
64 *Id.*
65 Joanna L. Grisinger, The Unwieldy American State: Administrative Politics since the New Deal 10–11 (2012).
66 Mark Fenster, *The Transparency Fix: Advocating Legal Rights and Their Alternatives in the Pursuit of a Visible State*, 73 U. Pitt. L. Rev. 443, 451–66 (2012).
67 *Id.* at 451–52.
68 *Id.* at 454.

independence and the right to free information. Kent Cooper himself authored an article published in *Life* magazine in 1945 entitled "Freedom of Information," in which he advocated for a broad range of rights, including the freedom to "seek out news."[69] That same year, the United Nation's Human Rights Commission created a Subcommission on Freedom of Information, and in 1948 a Conference on Freedom of Information was held in the Geneva Convention. Now situated in the postwar political climate, advocates for press freedoms also used the rhetoric of freedom of information to provide a direct contrast to press as propaganda, a threat made real by the Cold War. Mostly, however, these early efforts were an attempt to export American-style reporting around the world, and to promote the American values the free press was thought to have enshrined.[70]

A bit later, the freedom of information movement turned inward, again at the behest of the press. In the early 1950s, the American Society of Newspaper Editors (ASNE), the leading press organization, formed a Freedom of Information Committee, which quickly began to investigate the question of government secrecy in the United States.[71] The committee employed Harold Cross as its legal advisor who, in that capacity, authored a groundbreaking 1953 book, *The People's Right to Know*.[72] In the book, he described the current state of information access rights under a patchwork of federal and state statutes, administrative regulations, and court decisions.[73] Importantly, he documented the woeful inadequacy of these rights with respect to the needs of the press. At the conclusion of the book, Cross called on Congress to "legislate freedom of information for itself, the public, and the press."[74]

If it is not the actual founding fathers, it is Representative John Moss, then, who might be considered the founding father of FOIA. He was the champion of public information access and led a nearly decade-long campaign that ended in FOIA's passage, beginning with his 1955 appointment as the Chair of the new Subcommittee on Government Information of the Government Operations Committee, a position for which he heavily lobbied.[75] His interest in the issue is traced to his own experience as a member of Congress requesting and being denied access to information held by government agencies.[76] Some accounts also trace his

69 Kent Cooper, *Freedom of Information: Head of Associated Press Calls for Unhampered Flow of World News*, LIFE MAG. 55 (Nov. 13, 1944).

70 Fenster, *supra* note 66, at 443, 451–66.

71 *Id.*

72 James S. Pope, *Foreword* to HAROLD L. CROSS, THE PEOPLE'S RIGHT TO KNOW: LEGAL ACCESS TO PUBLIC RECORDS AND PROCEEDINGS, at viii (1953).

73 CROSS, *supra* note 72, at 19–37 (describing statutes, judicial decisions, regulations, and opinions of attorneys general as the various sources from which a right to know had in some circumstances arisen).

74 *Id.* at 246.

75 Michael Lemov & Nate Jones, *John Moss and the Roots of the Freedom of Information Act: Worldwide Implications*, 24 SW. J. INT'L L. 1, 11–12 (2018).

76 SHUDSON, *supra* note 52, at 39–40.

motivations to two very public instances of government attempting to control public access to information related to the Cold War.[77]

Regardless of subjective motivation, his public statements were unequivocal. He proclaimed a right of access to information foundational to democracy: "If the people and their elected representatives have the right to find out what their government is planning and doing, we live under a democracy."[78] This message resonated widely. Indeed, Moss capitalized on the Cold War rhetoric of the time, invoking the term "paper curtain" to describe government secrecy around post–World War II military efforts, and particularly the development of the atomic bomb. In an obvious attempt to reference the "iron curtain" used to describe the Soviet grip on much of Eastern Europe, "paper curtain" likened government secrecy to the totalitarianism that was at war with American values. In fact, Moss went further and invoked instances where the Soviet government was more transparent than the government in the US, and even directly compared certain Pentagon publicity campaigns to Soviet government style propaganda.[79] Moss thus viewed transparency in government as an essential component of a free and democratic society.

Moreover, Moss understood the inextricable ties between access to government information, democratic oversight, and the role of the press. Journalists made up the bulk of the subcommittee's staff, including reporters from the *Washington Post* and both national wire services,[80] and Harold Cross himself became its legal advisor.[81] The subcommittee deployed journalists to investigate and document problems of government secrecy to support the legislative efforts.[82] Journalist complaints made up more than a third of all complaints the subcommittee documented,[83] and Moss

77 Michael R. Lemov, People's Warrior: John Moss and the Fight for Freedom of Information and Consumer Rights 49 (2011). The first such instance was President Eisenhower's establishment of an office designed to secure cooperation from businesses and the press in refraining from publishing "strategic information" that might help Cold War enemies. *Id.* The second was a Department of Defense memorandum requiring government officials and contractors to only release information that makes a "constructive contribution" to Cold War defense. *Id.* These instances prompted public and press outrage. *Id.*

78 Shudson, *supra* note 52, at 59.

79 *Id.* at 47–49.

80 *Id.* at 41, 44–45.

81 Fenster, *supra* note 66, at 464; *see also* Sam Archibald, *The Early Years of the Freedom of Information Act: 1955 to 1974*, 26 Pol. Sci. & Pol. 726, 727 (1993) ("The newspaper-reporter staff members [of the Moss committee] had collected information [about government secrecy] by investigation, interview and research, then reported the results in clear language, just as they had done while writing for newspapers.").

82 *See* Lemov, *supra* note 77, at 56–57 (describing Moss's strategy of "demonstrating a pervasive problem and then calling on the government … to explain why the problem should not be fixed").

83 Michael Doyle, The Freedom of Information Act In Theory and Practice 33–34 (May 2001) (unpublished M.A. thesis, Johns Hopkins University) (on file with author) (articulating these two as the "most common theories … undergirding information access," but adding a third suggested theory centering on public ownership claims on government information).

routinely called journalists to testify in public hearings.[84] Moreover, journalists jumped to the defense of the subcommittee when efforts were made to abolish it.[85] Moss treated journalists as his partners in this endeavor.

After a decade-long fight, Congress passed the 1966 Freedom of Information Act, and the formal legislative history of FOIA echoes the very same themes of democratic oversight and press facilitation of public participation in governance. The House of Representatives Report that accompanied the passage of the bill declared that "[a] democratic society requires an informed, intelligent electorate, and the intelligence of the electorate varies as the quantity and quality of its information varies."[86] Likewise, the Senate Report explained that "[a]lthough the theory of an informed electorate is so vital to the proper operation of a democracy, there is nowhere in our present law a statute which affirmatively provides for a policy of disclosure."[87] Upon signing the bill into law, President Johnson reaffirmed the oversight and democracy enhancing goals of the act: "[A] democracy works best when the people have all the information that the security of the Nation permits … I signed this measure with a deep sense of pride that the United States is an open society in which the people's right to know is cherished and guarded."[88]

Moss announced from the House floor when FOIA was passed: "The list of editors, broadcasters and newsmen and distinguished members of the corps who have helped develop the legislation over these 10 years is endless," and then personally thanked individual journalists at a variety of major news outlets and journalist associations.[89] Another Congressman explained the importance of the press making use of the new law: "it will take vigorous action by the … Nation's press to make our objectives [in passing FOIA] a reality."[90]

The Supreme Court has repeatedly reaffirmed this view of FOIA's role: "The basic purpose of FOIA is to ensure an informed citizenry, vital to the functioning of a democratic society, needed to check against corruption and to hold the governors accountable to the governed."[91] It has further opined "FOIA is often explained as a means for citizens to know 'what the Government is up to.' This phrase should not be dismissed as a convenient formalism. It defines a structural necessity in a real democracy."[92]

[84] *See* Lemov, *supra* note 77, at 56–57 (describing Moss's strategy of "demonstrating a pervasive problem and then calling on the government … to explain why the problem should not be fixed").

[85] *Id.* at 60.

[86] H.R. Rep. No. 89–1497, at 12 (1966).

[87] S. Rep. No. 88–1219, at 8 (1964).

[88] Subcomm. on Admin. Practice & Procedure, 93d Cong., Freedom of Information Act Source Book: Legislative Materials, Cases, Articles 1 (Comm. Print 1974).

[89] 112 Cong. Rec. 13,642–43 (1966) (statement of Rep. Moss).

[90] *Id.* at 13,655 (statement of Rep. Hall).

[91] NLRB v. Robbins Tire & Rubber Co., 437 U.S. 214, 242 (1978) (citations omitted).

[92] Nat'l Archives & Records Admin. v. Favish, 541 U.S. 157, 171–72 (2004).

Congress's primary goal of promoting oversight of government, particularly the ability to ferret out malfeasance in office, was yet again evidenced in the first significant amendments to FOIA, which were passed in 1974 over President Ford's veto.[93] At the time, the Watergate scandal loomed large, enhancing Congress's distrust of claimed needs for secrecy: "As in the Watergate debacle, the umbrella of 'national security' is now being raised in the veto message to cover the real reasons for the bureaucrat's opposition to the public's right to know."[94]

Modern FOI regimes around the world largely followed the US example. While the US FOIA was third (after Sweden and Finland), it was by far the most influential.[95] In fact, it has catalyzed the global movement toward domestic and transnational transparency regimes. Over 100 countries have passed their own FOI laws, and international institutions such as the European Union, the African Union, and the United Nations among others, have likewise codified public access into their governance.[96]

What is more, in many countries, FOI is no longer confined to statutory governance, but instead is integrated into constitutional design,[97] and scholars have argued that a right of access to government information can or should be elevated to a constitutional right in the United States as well.[98] Beyond domestic constitutions, international courts have declared access to information to be a human right.[99] Even in an essay entitled "Against Transparency," influential constitutional law scholar Larry Lessig acknowledges that "transparency has become an unquestionable bipartisan value."[100]

93 Preliminary House action on Presidential Veto, November 18, 1974, 120 Cong. Rec. H10705–H10706 (1974).

94 *Id.*

95 Sweden boasts the very first FOI law, its Freedom of the Press Act that was included in its constitution in 1766. *The Swedish Press Act: 250 Years of Freedom of the Press*, GOV'T OFFICES OF SWED. (June 1, 2016), www.government.se/articles/2016/06/the-swedish-press-act-250-years-of-freedom-of-the-press.

96 *Alphabetical and Chronological Lists of Countries with FOI Regimes*, FREEDOMINFO.ORG (Sept. 28, 2017), www.freedominfo.org/2017/09/chronological-and-alphabetical-lists-of-countries-with-foi-regimes.

97 *See, e.g., Legislation*, INFO. COMM'R, REPUBLIC OF SLOVN., www.ip-rs.si/en/legislation (last visited Nov. 16, 2020) (stating that Slovenia's FOI regime is defined in the Constitution of the Republic of Slovenia).

98 *See, e.g.*, Thomas I. Emerson, *The First Amendment and the Right to Know: Legal Foundations of the Right to Know*, 1976 WASH. U. L.Q. 1, 14 (1976) (arguing for a constitutional basis rooted in the First Amendment for the public's right to access government information).

99 In 2006, the Inter-American Court of Human Rights declared access to government information to be included within the basic human right of free thought and expression. Reyes v. Chile, Merits, Reparations, and Costs, Judgment, Inter-Am. Ct. H.R. (ser. C) No. 151, para. 77 (Sept. 19, 2006). The European Court of Human Rights did the same in 2009. *See Társaság a Szabadságjogokért v. Hungary*, 37374/05, Eur. Ct. H.R. ¶ 39 (2009).

100 Lawrence Lessig, *Against Transparency*, THE NEW REPUBLIC (Oct. 8, 2009), http://newrepublic.com/article/70097/against-transparency.

Outside of government, a civil society invested in protecting transparency rights has sprung up, working shoulder to shoulder with journalists and news media to continue to advocate for openness in government. Transparency International, an aptly named NGO focused on anti-corruption, has more than 100 national chapters across the globe.[101] In the United States, the Sunlight Foundation works to "make our government and politics more accountable and transparent to all."[102] The Electronic Frontier Foundation's "transparency work" is dedicated to using FOI laws "to shine light on government activities."[103] In short, transparency has won the day.

D. THE RESULTING STATUTORY RIGHT

What Congress eventually passed as FOIA can be seen either as radically ambitious or as disappointingly modest, or perhaps most truthfully, some combination of the two. It both applies broadly, giving every member of the public rights to request information, and narrowly, applying only to executive branch agencies. It appears to cover all topics with limited numbers of exemptions, but those exemptions can be shockingly broad. And it requires of the government a prompt and painless process, but fails to deliver effective enforcement of that obligation.

Significantly, the act begins not with its most well-known provision allowing the submission of requests for government records, but with two sets of affirmative obligations placed on all agencies to make certain records available to the public without the need for a request to be made.[104] First, FOIA mandates that certain records be published in the Federal Register.[105] These include binding agency regulations and general statements of policy or interpretive guidance documents.[106] Second, FOIA requires that other categories of records be made "available for public inspection," and this provision was revised in 1996 to require that the records be available in "an electronic format."[107]

This latter provision is known as the reading room provision, because agencies historically met their obligations by maintaining a physical room open to the public in which these records could be inspected. Now, agencies maintain so-called electronic reading rooms, or a designated portion of their website on which they

[101] *Overview*, TRANSPARENCY INTERNAT'L, www.transparency.org/whoweare/organisation (last visited Nov. 16, 2020).

[102] *Our Mission*, SUNLIGHT FOUND., https://sunlightfoundation.com/about (last visited Nov. 16, 2020).

[103] *Transparency*, ELEC. FRONTIER FOUND., www.eff.org/issues/transparency (last visited Nov. 16, 2020).

[104] 5 U.S.C. § 552 (2018).

[105] *Id.* at §552(a)(1).

[106] *Id.*

[107] *Id.* at § 552(a)(2).

post records for public inspection.[108] The categories of records originally enumerated to be made available in this way included agency orders in the adjudication of cases, other guidance documents, and administrative staff manuals that affect the public. Later, in the 1996 amendments, Congress added the requirement of disclosure of frequently requested records.[109]

Collectively, the affirmative provisions of FOIA are actually quite telling. The Court has explained that the affirmative obligations "represent[] a strong congressional aversion to 'secret [agency] law.'"[110] Indeed, Judge Easterbrook, a prominent jurist, once opined that the "indexing and reading-room rules indicate that the *primary objective* [of the statute] is the elimination of 'secret law.'"[111]

Yet, Congress hardly confined FOIA's reach to these governing documents that directly affect the rights of the public. In its third set of obligations imposed on agencies, the statute sweepingly mandates that agencies produce any other agency records to any person who submits a valid request for them, subject to a limited set of enumerated exemptions.[112] Importantly, "any person" means any person, natural or legal.[113] The innovation this embodies is that no particular legal standing or interest in the records is necessary to make a request. In fact, the purpose of the request is irrelevant to the requester's right to access government records.[114]

In addition, Congress was committed to providing a strong remedy for improper denials of requests made under the law, and accordingly provided the right of any person denied access to requested documents to file a lawsuit in federal court.[115] Indeed, Congress cited the lack of strong judicial remedy as one of the primary failings of the old APA access provision.[116] One member of Congress touted FOIA's review provision, explaining that "for the first time" in history "a citizen will no longer be at the end of the road when his request for a Government document arbitrarily has been turned down by some bureaucrat."[117]

Perhaps most strikingly, FOIA departed from the well-accepted standards of review for other administrative actions, nearly all of which involve some level of deference to the agency's decision, and instead mandated de novo review of all

[108] U.S. Dep't of Justice, Guide to the Freedom of Information Act: Proactive Disclosures 6 (Apr. 11, 2019).

[109] *See* 5 U.S.C. §552 (a)(2) advisory committee's note to 1996 amendment (requiring a yearly report on efforts taken by the DOJ to encourage compliance).

[110] NLRB v. Sears, Roebuck & Co., 421 U.S.132, 153 (1975).

[111] Frank H. Easterbrook, *Privacy and the Optimal Extent of Disclosure under the Freedom of Information Act*, 9 J. Legal Stud. 775, 777 (1980) (emphasis added).

[112] 5 U.S.C. § 552(a)(3).

[113] *Id.* at § 551(2).

[114] *See* EPA v. Mink, 410 U.S. 73, 80 (1973), *superseded by statute*, 5 U.S.C. § 552 (b)(1)(B); U.S. Dep't of Justice v. Reporters Comm'n for Freedom of Press, 489 U.S. 749, 772 (1989).

[115] 5 U.S.C. § 552(a)(4)(B).

[116] *See, e.g.*, H.R. Rep. No. 89–1497, at 5 (1966) ("Above all, there is no remedy available to a citizen who has been wrongfully denied access to the Government's public records.").

[117] 112 Cong. Rec. 13,659 (1966) (statement of Rep. Gallagher).

agency actions withholding requested records under FOIA.[118] Again, Congress made this choice for a reason. Review that ensured that "the propriety of the agency's action" was decided by a court prevented, in the view of Congress, that review from becoming "meaningless judicial sanctioning of agency discretion."[119] Indeed, in the 1974 amendments to the law, Congress reasserted de novo review in the face of a Supreme Court decision undermining courts oversight of national security claims.[120]

And finally, the act demonstrates Congress's commitment to removing barriers to access to the extent possible. After reports that agencies were charging exorbitant fees for some requests, Congress adopted a set of fee provisions in a set of 1986 amendments to FOIA that remain in effect in largely the same form today.[121] The provision establishes three categories of requesters: (1) a preferred, news media and educational requesters category, which can be assessed only fees for actual costs of duplication of records; (2) a disfavored commercial requester category, which is subject to fees covering the cost of duplication as well as personnel time to search for the records as well as review them for necessary redactions; and (3) a final category of all other requesters who can be charged fees for duplication and search but not review.[122] On top of this striated fee structure, Congress also required agencies to waive any otherwise applicable fees for any request that is in the public interest, "because it is likely to contribute significantly to public understanding of the operations or activities of the government."[123]

The fee categories are telling insofar as they are directly linked to the theory of FOIA as a democracy enhancing tool of oversight and accountability. As the House of Representatives official analysis of the law explained, "the effect of the changes in fee and fee waiver policies will be to increase use of the FOIA by the press and by public interest and other nonprofit organizations as well. An increase in government oversight by these groups . . . is fully intended."[124] Congress intended to lower – and in many cases eliminate entirely – the financial barriers to effective oversight.

Despite these bold and ambitious provisions, FOIA has also proved quite modest in other ways. Most notably, its exemptions to mandatory disclosure, while only numbering nine listed categories in the act, have been interpreted to cover a very broad swath of government information. The listed exemptions to disclosure cover

[118] 5 U.S.C. § 552(a)(4)(B).

[119] 111 Cong. Rec. 26,823 (1965).

[120] *See* Margaret B. Kwoka, *Deferring to Secrecy*, 54 B.C. L. Rev. 185, 198–200 (2013) (detailing the history of de novo review, and the 1974 amendments regarding the standard of review).

[121] 5 U.S.C. § 552(a)(4)(A).

[122] *Id.* at § 552(a)(4)(A)(ii).

[123] *Id.* at § 552(a)(4)(A)(iii) (stating that to qualify, the request must also not be "primarily in the commercial interest of the requester.").

[124] Analysis of the Fees and Fee Waivers Amendments to the Freedom of Information Act Included in the Anti-Drug Abuse Act of 1986 (HR 5484), 132 Cong. Rec. H9455–05 (1986) (statement of Rep. English).

the following records: (1) those that are properly classified pursuant to an executive order; (2) certain internal personnel rules or practices; (3) those records exempted from disclosure by another statute; (4) trade secrets or confidential commercial or financial information; (5) records that would be subject to a claim of privilege in litigation; (6) files that if released would constitute a "clearly unwarranted invasion of personal privacy"; (7) certain law enforcement records; (8) records related to bank examinations; and (9) geological data concerning wells.[125] Moss himself lamented even the length of the list of exemptions, believing that only military and diplomatic secrets should have been incorporated into the law.[126]

Yet, the list of protected material itself has in the end proved less overreaching than the application of each exemption. Tellingly, of those requests that are processed, agencies claim exempt material, either in whole or in part, in 63.5 percent of substantive responses.[127] Moreover, individual exemptions have been applied broadly, by agencies and by courts, perhaps explaining the high rate of exemption use by agencies.

For example, exemption 5, which covers privileged material, is one of the most cited exemptions because of the so-called deliberative process privilege.[128] This privilege, designed to protect the agency decision-making process, covers records that are both pre-decisional and deliberative, but should not cover factual material or records created after an agency decision was made. Yet, its overuse is so well acknowledged that Congress recently took up the cause, amending FOIA to provide that the privilege cannot be applied to records more than 25 years old, an attempt to curb the growing secrecy this privilege has fostered.[129]

Likewise, over-classification is a problem of such a magnitude that it is acknowledged by those inside and outside the government security and military agencies.[130] Yet, courts have proven unwilling to second-guess agency classification decisions, despite their clear power to review them.[131] Similar accounts can be found throughout the list of bases for withholding records from the public. Thus, how to address the problem of over withholding is one matter that has been the subject of near constant debate among legislators and advocates concerned with government transparency.

[125] 5 U.S.C.§ 552(b) (2018).

[126] Shudson, *supra* note 52, at 61.

[127] U.S. Dep't of Justice, Office of Info. Policy, Summary of Annual FOIA Reports for Fiscal Year 2019, at 7 (2019) [hereinafter 2019 FOIA Reports Summary].

[128] *Id.* at 7 (citing exemption 5 as the fourth most cited exemption, after the two privacy exemptions, and one subset of the law enforcement exemption).

[129] FOIA Improvement Act of 2016, Pub. L. No. 114–185, § 6, 130 Stat. 538 (2016).

[130] *See* Susan Nevelow Mart & Tom Ginsburg, *[Dis-]Informing the People's Discretion: Judicial Deference under the National Security Exemption of the Freedom of Information Act*, 66 Admin. L. Rev. 725, 752–64 (2014) (detailing evidence of pervasive overclassification).

[131] *Id.* at 764; Kwoka, *supra* note 120.

Another matter of continued efforts at reform is the performance of agencies in responding to requests in a timely fashion. Though the law requires an agency to respond within twenty business days, the average processing time across the federal government exceeds that timeframe.[132] Even for simple requests, the average processing time in the last fiscal year was thirty-nine days, and for complex requests almost half of all requests take more than 100 days to process.[133] At some particular agencies, average response times are much longer. Despite Congress's repeated attempts to address issues of timeliness, sometimes through penalties or incentives and sometimes through reporting requirements, backlogs and delay remain serious concerns for the requester community.[134]

Yet, FOIA's ambition, its breadth, and its ease of use still remain powerful. Despite its limitations, as the next chapter will detail, it has managed to be a tool for exactly the type of oversight and democratic participation that were imagined not just by Congress, but by the original philosophers on representative democracies. Understanding the way in which requesters were thought to facilitate these lofty goals and how an influential group of requesters, whom I dub oversight requesters, are using FOIA effectively are key to understanding what about FOIA is worth saving and how to accomplish that goal.

[132] 5 U.S.C. § 552(a)(6)(A)(i).

[133] 2019 FOIA Reports Summary, *supra* note 127, at 11–12.

[134] *See* 5 U.S.C. §552 advisory committee note to 1996 amendments (requiring the Attorney General to submit an annual report detailing the efforts undertaken by the Department of Justice to encourage agency compliance with this section).

2

FOIA as Oversight

A. THE NEWS MEDIA MAY COMPLAIN, BUT THEY USE FOIA

Much of the remainder of this book will detail how, despite the law's clear underlying intent, FOIA is largely used for purposes other than democratic oversight. Indeed, the actors thought so central to the project of government transparency – the news media – make up a tiny fraction of FOIA requesters government-wide. But before that stark reality is laid bare, it is worth exploring what the news media and other oversight requesters are still accomplishing using FOIA, regardless of its limitations. As it turns out, FOIA remains a powerful tool for many journalists.

To begin, while journalists as a fraction of FOIA requesters may seem small, news stories that use FOIA are not at all insignificant. In one of the best snapshots capturing the power of FOIA requests, the Society of Professional Journalists examined daily news coverage for a month-long period in a diversity of media outlets including print and television, different geographic locations, and various market sizes. The research gathered data from a total of 4,445 articles and stories and found that nearly one out of every five print stories relied on public records, as did one in ten television stories. It was even more likely that stories reported by large and mid-sized news organizations relied on public records, and these reported figures may well undercount the reliance on public records because, as the researchers found, "[o]nly in rare cases" did the story "clearly state[] that the information was taken from public records. . . ."[1]

Others have similarly documented significant news media engagement with FOIA. Non-profit News Media for Open Government (previously known as the Sunshine in Government Initiative), has catalogued hundreds of news stories that were made possible by information obtained under FOIA, ranging from health and

[1] Ian Marquand, *FOI and Daily News Coverage*, Soc'y of Prof'l Journalists, www.spj.org/opendoors5.asp# (last visited Apr. 20, 2020).

safety concerns to national security matters.[2] It also started a Tumblr of "FOIA-Powered Stories," which identify stories that were made possible by FOIA, ending each blurb by explaining what the public would not have learned but for FOIA. For example, "Without FOIA, the public might not have known federal agencies are teaming up with local law enforcement to scan license plates of people attending gun shows," and "Without FOIA, the journalists would not have obtained the report showing a drop in [opioid] enforcement had been noted within the Justice Department."[3]

Similarly, researcher James Hamilton compiled a dataset of more than 12,500 entries to the Investigative Reporters and Editors annual prize competitions and searched for use of FOIA or open records requests as part of the underlying reporting. He found that public records requests played a role in fourteen percent of submissions, and that reporting that involved records requests were more likely to produce tangible results such as laws passed, policy changes, audits, investigations, or personnel decisions.[4]

That said, observers have certainly also recognized that news media use of FOIA has not been as robust as we might like or imagine. Syracuse University's Transactional Records Access Clearinghouse (TRAC) founded the FOIA Project, which has tracked news media activity in filing lawsuits under the law. At one point in time, the FOIA Project reported a notable decrease in FOIA litigation by news media under the Obama administration as compared with the Bush administration, even while FOIA litigation overall was increasing. Between 2005 and 2012, traditional news media only brought between three and nine FOIA suits a year.[5]

However, a strict count of news media organizations and reporters likely underrepresents the media use of FOIA because news outlets also rely on significant FOIA activity by third-party nonprofits who use FOIA to do oversight work that is then reported on in mainstream media. Tomas Susman, Director of the American Bar Association's Governmental Affairs Office, succinctly described this phenomenon: "The news services in some ways have outsourced their investigative work."[6] To take one small example, non-profit and frequent FOIA requester Judicial Watch pried loose official calendars of one of the top prosecutors in the office of Special Counsel Mueller, who was appointed to investigate the Trump campaign ties to Russia, and

2 *SGI FOIA Storybase*, News Media for Open Gov't, foropengov.org/stories (last visited Apr. 20, 2020).

3 Without FOIA, withoutfoia.tumblr.com (last visited Apr. 20, 2020).

4 James T. Hamilton, *FOIA and Investigative Reporting*, *in* Troubling Transparency: The History and Future of Freedom of Information 117 (David E. Pozen & Michael Schudson eds., 2018).

5 *Media Making Fewer Challenges to Government Secrecy in Federal Court*, FOIA Project (Mar. 14, 2013), foiaproject.org/2013/03/14/media-making-fewer-challenges-to-government-secrecy-in-federal-court.

6 *Id.*

The New York Times then reported on their contents, making digestible an otherwise difficult to understand set of records.[7]

Despite the dip under Obama, TRAC's data shows a robust media presence even as traditionally defined in recent years. Particularly under the Trump administration, news media were more active than ever in filing FOIA lawsuits. In 2018, TRAC reported that over the previous four years, news media lawsuits jumped nearly threefold, having previously accounted for a relatively steady 3.5 percent of all FOIA lawsuits, and hitting a record 10.8 percent in 2015.[8]

Interestingly, the traditional news media that do use FOIA most are precisely the kinds of major journalism organizations one might expect. Max Galka, who runs a project called the FOIA Mapper, collected the largest single database of FOIA requester identities ever compiled and coded the requesters carefully into a set of categories. In the news media category, the top ten general interest media outlets by volume of requests were (in descending order): the *Associated Press*, *The Wall Street Journal*, *Bloomberg*, *The Nation*, *The New York Times*, *USA Today*, *The Hill*, *The Washington Post*, *Buzzfeed*, and *ProPublica*.[9]

There are, however, a small number of even more frequent requesters categorized as news media who are relatively recent entrants into the FOIA landscape. These are news organizations whose primary mission is to publicize information obtained under FOIA; there are two prominent ones that are prolific requesters: *MuckRock* and *The Black Vault*. In fact, *MuckRock*, if properly counted as news media, is the largest news media requester in Galka's study.[10]

There are even new oversight-oriented organizations that cropped up expressly to use FOIA to hold the Trump administration to account. American Oversight described itself as "the top Freedom of Information Act litigator investigating the Trump administration," and it regularly appears as a frequent requester on recent FOIA logs, the records agencies keep of FOIA requests that they receive.[11] For instance, American Oversight submitted 102 requests to the Office of Information Policy (OIP) at the Department of Justice (DOJ) in a one-year period.[12] Similarly, The Protect Democracy Project, while less singularly focused on FOIA, is a post-Trump administration organization that uses FOIA heavily as part of its mission to hold the administration "accountable to the laws and longstanding practices that

7 Adam Goldman et al., *6 Things That Calendars from the Special Counsel's Office Tell Us*, N.Y. Times (May 15, 2019), www.nytimes.com/2019/05/15/us/politics/special-counsel-calendars.html.

8 *News Reporters Drive Growth in Media FOIA Litigation*, FOIA Project (Jan. 9, 2017), foiaproject.org/2017/01/09/news-reporters-drive-growth-in-media-foia-litigation.

9 Max Galka, *Who Uses FOIA? – An Analysis of 229,000 Requests to 85 Government Agencies*, FOIA Mapper (Mar. 13, 2017), foiamapper.com/who-uses-foia.

10 The only other outlier is Greenwire, an environment and energy news publication, which ranks third overall, but is a special interest news media outlet. *Id.*

11 *About*, American Oversight, www.americanoversight.org/about (last visited Apr. 20, 2020).

12 U.S. Dep't of Justice, Office of Info. Policy, Freedom of Information Act Responses to Feb. 26, 2018 Request by Margaret B. Kwoka (on file with author) [hereinafter OIP Data].

have protected our democracy . . . ."[13] It submitted 113 requests to OIP that same year.[14] These organizations may be properly classified as new media or perhaps as the nonprofit feeder organizations that so often provide the oversight work that fuels news stories. Regardless of categorization, as oversight requesters, they are definitely making frequent use of FOIA.

Data regarding lawsuits filed under FOIA, rather than requests at the administrative level, similarly track these trends. Indeed, traditional news media still have a strong presence. TRAC identifies *The New York Times*, the Center for Public Integrity, and the *Associated Press* as the consistently top news media FOIA plaintiffs.[15] Among reporters filing lawsuits in their own name, however, new media outlets make a substantial appearance. For example, Jason Leopold, then of *VICE News* (now at *Buzzfeed*), had filed thirty-two lawsuits as of 2018.[16] In smaller numbers, other new media outlets like *ProPublica* and *MuckRock* make appearances.[17] Notably, advocacy groups that often feed news stories were found to file FOIA suits more often than media. These groups include Judicial Watch, the American Civil Liberties Union (ACLU), and the Electronic Privacy Information Center, among others.[18]

There are also journalists who make such voluminous use of FOIA that they compete with some of the corporate uses described in later sections of the book. In fact, the government has occasionally referred to these reporters as "try[ing] to monopolize the system" or, even more colorfully, labeling one such requester as a "FOIA terrorist."[19] But any examination of their use of FOIA reveals apparent public-interest and government-oversight oriented purposes behind these requests.

As to the "monopolizer" – so labeled in an official Department of Defense Annual FOIA Report[20] – Nick Turse described how beginning in 2012 he sought information about American military bases located in Africa. After his inquiries and follow-ups went unanswered six months later, he was directed by an agency official to submit a FOIA request. When he began submitting requests it took years to receive any response at all, and so he kept filing them. But all was not in vain. After "dozens" of requests, Nick Turse published a story demonstrating that US Africa

13 *About Us*, The Protect Democracy Project, protectdemocracyproject.org/about/ (last visited Apr. 20, 2020).

14 OIP Data, *supra* note 12.

15 *News Reporters Drive Growth in Media FOIA Litigation*, FOIA Project (Jan. 9, 2017), foiaproject.org/2017/01/09/news-reporters-drive-growth-in-media-foia-litigation.

16 *Id.*

17 Greg Munno, *FOIA Suits Jump In 2014*, FOIA Project (Dec. 22, 2014), foiaproject.org/2014/12/22/foia-suits-jump-in-2014.

18 *Id.*

19 Nick Turse, *How a Simple Request Got Me Blacklisted by the Pentagon*, The Intercept (Apr. 20, 2016), theintercept.com/2016/04/20/how-a-simple-request-got-me-blacklisted-by-the-pentagon.

20 Dep't of Def., Chief Freedom of Information Act Officer Report to the Department of Justice 13 (2016).

Command's personnel were, with some regularity, engaging in illegal, dangerous, and untoward behavior. Incidents included excessive drinking with dangerous and even fatal incidents that followed, solicitation of prostitutes, and even sexual assault.[21] His reporting detailed previously unknown incidents of great public concern regarding military conduct abroad.[22]

As to the "FOIA terrorist," Jason Leopold heard from a source inside an agency that the source's superior sent out an email referring to Mr. Leopold as such.[23] In one instance, the Department of State offered to partially fulfill one particularly contentious request he had submitted, if he agreed never to file another request.[24] But he is undoubtedly engaged in journalism. He is currently a reporter with *Buzzfeed*, previously at *Vice* and other outlets, where his rogue reporting style has evidently caused him all manner of difficulties, but there is no question his career has been dedicated to ferreting out government misconduct.[25]

The government's complaints about individual requesters are not new, however. In 1993, the Defense Intelligence Agency pinned its failure to reduce its backlog on the "117 requests from Mark Sauter on the Vietnam and Korean War era POW/MIA issue" which were, "complicated and voluminous."[26] Sauter, however, has written numerous articles about previously undisclosed details surrounding prisoners of war in the Korean War, and has even authored a book on the subject.[27] Family members of missing servicemen are waging ongoing legal battles in part as a result of the information Sauter has pried loose.[28] Even these new media, nontraditional media, and high-volume media requesters are, in fact, often using FOIA precisely as intended.

Part Two of this book contains a detailed account of media requesting using the data gathered for this study. To preview, there is no question that those numbers reveal media use of FOIA government-wide to be low – less than 3 percent of all requests. That said, the data also show that media requesting is much more

21 Turse, *supra* note 19.

22 Nick Turse, *Tomgram: Nick Turse, AFRICOM Behaving Badly*, TomDispatch.com (Apr. 21, 2015), www.tomdispatch.com/blog/175984/tomgram%3A_nick_turse%2C_africom_behaving_badly.

23 Michael Morisy, *Requester's Voice: Jason Leopold: The "FOIA Terrorist" Shares his Transparency Secrets*, MuckRock (July 12, 2013), www.muckrock.com/news/archives/2013/jul/12/jason-leopold-foia-terrorist-shares-his-transparen/.

24 Staff of H.R. Comm. on Oversight and Gov't Reform, 114th Cong., FOIA Is Broken: A Report 8 (2016).

25 He has detailed his colorful, deceitful, and unconventional path into journalism in a published memoir. Jason Leopold, News Junkie (2014).

26 Memorandum from Def. Intelligence Agency on Freedom of Info. Backlogs to Assistant Sec'y of Def. (Public Affairs) (Oct. 12, 1993) (on file with author).

27 *See generally* Mark Sauter & John Zimmerlee, American Trophies (2013).

28 Tom O'Connor, *America's Missing Korean War Veterans Could be in Russia, Family Says*, Newsweek (Aug. 11, 2017), www.newsweek.com/america-missing-war-veterans-could-be-russia-family-648966.

significant at some agencies, even upwards of a quarter or a third of all requests submitted to the agency.[29] Moreover, pockets of significant media requests can be found even in some unexpected agencies, such as the Defense Department's Office of the Secretary/Joint Chiefs or the Secret Service, where security-related concerns might lead to an assumption that FOIA requests would not bear much fruit.[30] And finally, at some agencies core oversight requesters are numerous, but are not made up of journalists; rather, they are watchdog groups and nonprofit advocacy groups working on a particular topic. This trend holds particularly true among environmental and animal protection organizations, who make voluminous requests to divisions of the Department of Agriculture and the Department of the Interior.[31]

But while the data are set out in great detail in Part II of this volume, the data simply do not tell the whole picture. A single media request may yield dividends in the public's understanding of government activities. A single media request may lead to policy changes that protect health and safety, curb law enforcement excess, or improve the functioning of government. To better understand how some of the most effective media requesters are using FOIA, I interviewed about a dozen journalists who, by and large, are using FOIA more and more effectively than average reporters. I also interviewed two lawyers who work in house at major media outlets who litigate FOIA denials on behalf of their reporters. What follows is an account of the promise of FOIA.

1. *Uncovering Government Waste and Abuse*

Perhaps the most straightforward use of FOIA is when journalists obtain documents that demonstrate waste and abuse of government resources. It is the quintessential oversight of government power – the public's interest in the expenditure of their tax dollars. It also can lead to the downfall of elected officials, political appointees, and career government employees, changing the landscape of the federal workforce.

Abuse can start at the top. Among the many scandals that erupted around Trump-appointed Environmental Protection Agency (EPA) Administrator Scott Pruitt, one focused on his use of a particularly elite government resource: his security detail. *E&E News* initially broke a story describing how Pruitt requested extra security detail upon assuming his new role, moving from "portal-to-portal" coverage, which is basically nine-to-five while on the job, to a twenty-four-hour detail. In an early follow-up – long before the EPA Inspector General's Office began

[29] The details of these results can be found *infra* Ch. 3, pt. B.

[30] DOD Office of the Secretary/Joint Chiefs received 29.4 percent of its requests from news media and the Secret Service received 20.7 percent of its requests from journalists. *See* U.S. Dep't of Def., Office of the Sec'y/Joint Chiefs of Staff, Freedom of Information Act Response to Mar. 20, 2018 Request by Margaret B. Kwoka (on file with author); FOIA Logs 2018, U.S. Secret Serv., U.S. Dep't of Homelannd Sec., www.secretservice.gov/press/foia/library.

[31] *See infra* Ch. 3, pt. B.

investigating – Kevin Bogardus at E&E News used documents obtained under FOIA to show just how much the extra security measures were costing the taxpayer. The records revealed that Pruitt spent nearly twice as much on security in his first three months in office as did his two immediate predecessors in the job. His total for just those three months was $832,735.40, as compared to Gina McCarthy's $465,165.04 and Lisa Jackson's $423,490.62.[32]

As Bogardus explained, "I got, essentially, the first documented proof that Scott Pruitt's security detail was costing a lot of money."[33] Knowing the expenditure was so much more than previous security details, Borgardus set out using FOIA to determine if the additional expenditures were justified. He described filing more FOIA requests looking for documentation about what threats were being investigated and how serious those threats were, leading to additional reporting that the threats being investigated were, in fact, not more serious than previous officials received. He described what he thought the public should take away from the reporting he did based on records obtained under FOIA: "I'd hope they understood that a 24/7 security detail for an EPA Administrator, you know, may not have been justified. And also was costing a lot of money."[34]

These initial stories, widely reported by other outlets once broken, led to an investigation by the EPA's Inspector General which found "[f]ailure to properly justify the level of protective services provided to the Administrator has allowed costs to increase from $1.6 million to $3.5 million in just 11 months."[35] That is, Bogardus's initial assessment from documents obtained under FOIA proved to be precisely correct. While it was far from the only scandal Pruitt found himself mired in, this scandal was one of the "barrage of investigations and audits" that caused him to resign as EPA Administrator.[36]

Abuse can also cover the much more mundane, and FOIA has proven to be a tool for uncovering lower level, career employees' conduct as well. Scott MacFarlane, *NBC News* investigative reporter, filed FOIA requests to the Inspectors General at twelve federal agencies requesting records concerning wider-spread misconduct and computer misuse involving federal workers watching pornography on their computers at work. As MacFarlane wrote, "[t]he records obtained and reviewed by the I-Team showed about 100 workers admitted surfing pornography while on the job.

32 Kevin Bogardus, *Big Spike in Security Spending for Pruitt*, E&E News (July 5, 2017), www.eenews.net/stories/1060056958.

33 Telephone Interview with Kevin Bogardus, Reporter, E&E News (Mar. 22, 2019).

34 *Id.*

35 U.S. Envtl. Prot. Agency, Office of the Inspector Gen., Report No. 18-P-0239, EPA Asserts Statutory Law Enforcement Authority to Protect Its Administrator but Lacks procedures to Assess Threats and Identify the Proper Level of Protection (2018).

36 Laura Strickler, *Scott Pruitt's $3.5 Million, 24/7 Security Detail Not Justified, Says EPA Watchdog*, NBC News (Sept. 4, 2018), www.nbcnews.com/politics/donald-trump/scott-pruitt-s-3-million-24-7-security-detail-not-n906211.

In many cases, the surfing consumed hours of an employee's time each day."[37] A few cases even involved criminal behavior because the images involved minors.

Importantly, agencies treated these infractions with large disparities, sometimes invoking penalties as minor as a written reprimand.[38] Just weeks later, the US House Oversight Committee unanimously approved a bill requiring the US Office of Management and Budget to issue new guidelines prohibiting the viewing of pornography on government computers.[39] Importantly, the legislators cited MacFarlane's reporting as prompting their legislative action.[40]

While straightforward, this use of FOIA is invaluable. Both Bogardus and MacFarlane indicated that their stories were made possible almost entirely by FOIA. Both stories illustrate how this kind of reporting can prompt public, administrative, or even legislative actions. And both demonstrate the power of documentation. An anecdote may be powerful, but the records complete the picture.

2. *Revealing Influence Over Government Decision-Making*

Another very prominent use of FOIA by journalists is to uncover outside pressure over government officials' decisions. In fact, *New York Times* First Amendment Fellow Al-Amyn Sumar identified as one of the prime categories of journalists who "really benefit from FOIA" those who "report on ... influence and lobbying."[41] One reason FOIA is so powerful in this context is because requests typically concern "email correspondence that certain agency officials have had with people outside of the agency," which "are not easily subject to exemption."[42] These types of FOIA requests can yield dividends for the public, which has a keen interest in whether official policy decisions are being made based on the relevant legal considerations or whether there is some sort of improper or even illegal influence by private or special interests.

Charles Seife has spent his career on investigative journalism in science, now still freelancing from his academic post, and has particular expertise in the Food and

[37] Scott MacFarlane et al., *Dozens of Federal Employees Watched Abundance of Porn on the Job in Recent Years*, NBC Wash. (Feb. 24, 2017), www.nbcwashington.com/investigations/Dozens-of-Federal-Employees-Watched-Abundance-of-Porn-on-the-Job-in-Recent-Years-414743293.html.

[38] *Id.*

[39] H.R. Rep. No. 115-81, at 2 (2017). The bill subsequently died in committee. Eliminating Pornography from Agencies Act, H.R. 680, 115th Cong. (2017) (last action on Apr. 6, 2017); Scott MacFarlane, *U.S. House Committee Backs Ban on Porn Viewing at Work by Federal Employees*, NBC Wash. (Mar. 9, 2017), www.nbcwashington.com/investigations/House-Oversight-Committee-Approves-Bill-to-Stop-Federal-Employees-From-Viewing-Porn-on-the-Job-415803513.html.

[40] H.R. Rep. No. 115-81, at 2 n.11 (2017).

[41] Telephone Interview with David McCraw, Deputy Gen. Counsel, N.Y. Times, and Al-Amyn Sumar, First Amendment Fellow, N.Y. Times (May 3, 2019).

[42] *Id.*

Drug Administration (FDA). So, when the FDA approved marketing of Eteplirsen, a new drug to treat the rare childhood disease Duchenne muscular dystrophy, over a contrary recommendation of its own experts, he wanted to know more.[43]

To fill in some of the history, in April 2016, the FDA's advisory panel, which makes recommendations on whether to approve new drugs as safe and effective – the relevant legal standard – voted seven to three not to approve the drug because the drug company's clinical trial involved only twelve boys.[44] But just a few months later, in September 2016, the FDA went against that recommendation and approved the drug. First, Janet Woodcock, director of the Center for Drug Evaluation and Research, overruled the advisory opinion, and then FDA Commissioner Robert Califf upheld Woodcock's determination. As *The New York Times* reported, "[t]he approval was so controversial that FDA employees fought over it, a dispute that was taken to the agency's commissioner, Dr. Robert M. Califf, who ultimately decided that it would stand."[45]

Commissioner Califf's final decision was published, and notes, among other things, that "Dr. Woodcock heard and read all the scientific evidence, including the detailed views of Dr. Unger and the review team; yet she came to a different conclusion."[46] It also noted, but dismissed as unfounded, the review board's procedural concerns, including that Woodcock was involved or even interfered with its early stages of review, and that she may have caved to pressure from the patient community or concerns about the financial solvency of the drug company sponsor.[47]

Without underlying records, however, it was impossible to evaluate the claims of improper influence. Seife filed a FOIA request for FDA documents about the approval of the drug. After having to go to court over the agency's refusal to comply, FDA began "releasing thousands of never-before-seen documents regarding the most controversial drug approval in many years."[48] What did those records show? Most astonishingly, an email from John Jenkins, then head of the Office of New Drugs, to Commissioner Califf alleges that Woodcock bypassed agency procedures, ignored the findings of the review team, and succumbed to improper influence from

43 Declaration of Charles Seife at 1, *Seife v. Food & Drug Admin*, No.. 87, 1:17-cv-3960-JMF (S.D.N.Y. May 28, 2018).

44 Andrew Pollack, *Advisors to F.D.A. Vote against Duchenne Muscular Dystrophy Drug*, N.Y. Times (Apr. 25, 2016), www.nytimes.com/2016/04/26/business/muscular-dystrophy-drug-fda-sarepta-eteplirsen.html.

45 Sabrina Tavernise, *F.D.A. Approves Muscular Dystrophy Drug That Patients Lobbied For*, N.Y. Times (Sept. 19, 2016), www.nytimes.com/2016/09/20/business/fda-approves-muscular-dystrophy-drug-that-patients-lobbied-for.html.

46 Memorandum from Robert M. Califf, Comm'r of Food and Drugs, Food & Drug Admin., to Janet Woodcock, Dir., Ctr. for Drug Evaluation & Research, Food & Drug Admin., et al. 4 (Sept. 16, 2016), www.accessdata.fda.gov/drugsatfda_docs/nda/2016/206488_summary%20review_redacted.pdf.

47 *Id.* at 6-8.

48 Charles Seife, *FDA Documents Reveal Depths of Internal Rancor Over Drug's Approval Process*, Undark (Aug. 2, 2017), https://undark.org/2017/08/02/fda-eteplirsen-janet-woodcock.

the patient community and drug company sponsor. Speaking to Califf's ultimate decision to uphold Woodcock's approval of the drug, Jenkins writes:

> On page 4 you state "there is also abundant evidence that Dr. Woodcock heard and read all the scientific evidence..." This implies she took these actions BEFORE reaching a decision on the application, which is clearly not correct given her statement to the review team of her intention to overrule them and approve the drug BEFORE they had completed their reviews.[49]

That is, Jenkins asserts that Woodcock had made her decision before the review team's findings were even available, thus undercutting any possibility that it was based on a scientific assessment. Jenkins went further, concerning the findings of no improper influence:

> As to your footnote 23 [regarding allegations that the sponsor's solvency influenced her decision], there are direct statements that Janet made to the team that contradict the statements you reference from your interview with her. I am happy to discuss these statements with you further. In addition, Janet has had frequent private conversations with the sponsor and the stakeholder community. To my knowledge, she has not documented the substance of those conversations to the record, as is required by FDA regulations. That leaves a gap of knowledge to evaluate the concerns raised by the review team and Dr. Borio.[50]

What, then, should the public make of this? According to Seife, "[e]ven with the understanding that Jenkins' perceptions are clearly colored by his antipathy for Woodcock, the newly released documents would seem to illuminate a bureaucracy whose procedural and scientific rules were broken, one after the other, by an administrator determined to get a drug approved."[51] Without FOIA, there may have been no way of knowing the level of influence alleged to have impacted FDA's decision. In an area where health and safety are on the line, that is no small question.

Sometimes FOIA sheds light on questions of influence and decision-making that make the front pages and possibly their way to the Supreme Court. One prime example concerns the administration of the 2020 census. Back in 2017, while speculation circulated that the Trump administration might heed long-time Republican calls to add a question to the census concerning US citizenship status, senior officials were denying such proposals were being discussed and Commerce Secretary Wilber Ross had previously opined that it would hurt response rates.[52]

49 Email from John Jenkins, Dir., Office of New Drugs, Food & Drug Admin., to Robert Califf, Comm'r, Food and Drugs, Food & Drug Admin. (Sept. 14, 2016), www.documentcloud.org/documents/3911805-2017-07-24-FDA-Production.html#document/p1/a365947.

50 *Id.*

51 Seife, *supra* note 48.

52 Danny Vink & Andrew Restuccia, *Leading Trump Census Pick Causes Alarm*, Politico (Nov. 21, 2017), www.politico.com/story/2017/11/21/trump-census-pick-causes-alarm-252571.

Then, in December 2017, Justin Elliott at *ProPublica* broke the story that the Justice Department, through a letter authored by DOJ official Arthur Gary to the Census Bureau, was urging the inclusion of a citizenship question based on a need for the data to better enforce the Voting Rights Act.[53] The revelation sparked outrage, pushback, claims that the proposal would sabotage the census, and more.

But Justin Elliott explained to me that "the letter was signed by some ... career administrative official ... And so, you couldn't tell [] who was driving the policy."[54] So he filed a FOIA request. Lo and behold, it was a "political appointee named John Gore who was actually behind this."[55] Elliott broke that story, too, writing that "[t]he letter was drafted by a Trump political appointee who is best known for his work defending Republican redistricting efforts around the country."[56] In fact, at his previous law firm job, he was "best known for defending a range of Republican state redistricting plans that were attacked as racial gerrymandering by opponents."[57]

In short, the emails obtained by Elliott under FOIA which formed the basis for this story were the first indication that the citizenship question was likely politically motivated, rather than coming from career DOJ staff concerned with the enforcement of civil rights laws. As Elliott said to me, "that was very newsworthy."[58] As if to underscore the importance, those records, along with many more obtained after the fact in discovery, became relevant in the litigation over the citizenship question which then made its way up to the United States Supreme Court.[59] It also provided a lead for further investigations that revealed that Ross himself prompted the DOJ request authored by Gore, solidifying the political nature of the decision.[60]

Perhaps even more striking, sometimes FOIA shows how agencies are pressured to make so-called "secret law." In July 2014, financial reporter Zach Mider, at *Bloomberg News*, began to break a series of stories concerning the enforcement of a ban on federal contracting with companies that reincorporate in lower tax jurisdictions abroad, known as "inversions."[61] Ingersoll-Rand, an American

[53] Justin Elliott, *Trump Justice Department Pushes for Citizenship Question on Census, Alarming Experts*, ProPublica (Dec. 29, 2017), www.propublica.org/article/trump-justice-department-pushes-for-citizenship-question-on-census-alarming-experts.

[54] Telephone Interview with Justin Elliott, Reporter, ProPublica (Apr. 19, 2019).

[55] *Id.*

[56] Justin Elliott, *The Trump Appointee behind the Move to Add a Citizenship Question to the Census*, ProPublica (Mar. 7, 2018), www.propublica.org/article/john-gore-trump-appointee-citizenship-question-census.

[57] *Id.*

[58] Telephone Interview with Justin Elliott, *supra* note 54.

[59] *See* Dep't of Commerce v. New York, 139 S. Ct. 2551, 2562 (2019).

[60] Michael Wines, *New Emails Show Push by Trump Officials to Add Citizenship Question to Census*, N.Y. Times (July 24, 2018), www.nytimes.com/2018/07/24/us/census-citizenship-question.html.

[61] *See, e.g.*, Zachary R. Mider, *Tax Runaways Win Billions in U.S. Contracts Despite Bans*, Bloomberg News (July 7, 2014), www.bloomberg.com/news/articles/2014-07-08/tax-runaways-win-billions-in-u-s-contracts-despite-bans.

manufacturing company that reincorporated in Bermuda, had been one of the examples lawmakers had pointed to when crafting the ban, and yet Mider found that Ingersoll-Rand was still being awarded contracts. His initial reporting made clear that companies were often taking advantage of legal loopholes to continue bidding for federal contracts, and Ingersoll-Rand claimed it had conducted an "exhaustive legal analysis" that resulted in their conclusion that they were not subject to the prohibition on contracting at all.[62] The Ingersoll-Rand representative, however, "declined to share the firm's reasoning or say whether the government endorsed this view."[63]

Mider wanted more answers. Eventually the Department of Homeland Security (DHS) voluntarily provided a letter to Mider that was written by an agency lawyer, opining that "after reviewing a legal brief submitted by Ingersoll-Rand, he does 'not have a reason to disagree' with the company's assertion that it's eligible for contracts."[64] The agency would not comment further and Mider decided to turn to FOIA. He filed a request for the legal brief submitted by Ingersoll-Rand, the reasoning of which DHS had apparently adopted. Interestingly, when the company was notified of Mider's request, it offered to provide the document to him directly if he would drop his ongoing effort to obtain it under FOIA.[65] In that way, it was a bit of a proxy win under FOIA, but the results were nonetheless hugely illuminating.

The Ingersoll-Rand brief, the reasoning of which DHS had endorsed, urged an argument that the entire law banning federal contracting with inverted companies was invalid.[66] It also advanced two other arguments that would make it essentially pro forma for any company to fit within one of the existing exemptions to the ban. But as Mider said to me, "there was no kind of public declaration that this law is without effect," even though, in DHS's legal opinion, that's precisely the result.[67]

Whether it is a secret legal standard advocated for by an interested party, a seemingly legalistic policy proposal that turns out to be politically motivated, or a questionable health and safety decision motivated by desperate parents and drug company profits, there is no question the public views governmental action differently when it knows what motivated or influenced it. These uses of FOIA are invaluable to the public's understanding of government action, and evaluations of the job their officials are performing.

[62] *Id.*

[63] *Id.*

[64] Zachary R. Mider, *Ingersoll-Rand Cleared for U.S. Contracts Despite Inversion*, Bloomberg News (Dec. 22, 2014), www.bloomberg.com/news/articles/2014-12-22/ingersoll-rand-cleared-for-federal-contracts-despite-inversion.

[65] Zachary R. Mider, *U.S. Sided with Tax-Avoiding Companies Over Contracting Ban*, Bloomberg News (July 6, 2015), www.bloomberg.com/news/articles/2015-07-06/u-s-sided-with-tax-avoiding-companies-over-contracting-ban.

[66] *Id.*

[67] Telephone Interview with Zachary Mider, Reporter, Bloomberg News (Apr. 16, 2019).

3. *Shedding Light on Security and Policing*

Perhaps some of the most surprising FOIA success stories concern national security and law enforcement. Without doubt, FOIA's reputation in this area is less than stellar. David Pozen has, for example, argued that FOIA "contributes to a culture of adversarialism and derision surrounding the domestic policy bureaucracy while insulating the far more secretive national security agencies, as well as corporations, from similar scrutiny."[68] Indeed, he documents the broad interpretations courts have given national security and law enforcement exemptions to FOIA, and critiques the secrecy of the national security state, both of which strongly support the notion that FOIA does too little to curb secrecy in this area.[69]

My own prior work supports the notion that courts are much too reticent to look behind agency claims of national security harm in FOIA cases,[70] and one need not look far to find plenty of support for the notion that over classification is a rampant and largely unchecked problem. To be sure, some reporters I have spoken with support the view that FOIA is of little use in these areas. *Newsweek*'s Jeff Stein bluntly told me, "those of us who report on intelligence agencies and activities, we just don't use [FOIA] much."[71] That said, he also credited the ability to write a historical and investigative book about the prosecution of five Green Berets for murder of an alleged double agent in the Vietnam war to FOIA:[72] "I don't think I could have done the book without it, actually."[73] Still, he uses it very little today in his reporting.[74]

So, when I noticed that one of the top news media FOIA plaintiffs in recent years is *New York Times* national security reporter Charlie Savage, I was surprised. I asked David McCraw, Vice President and Deputy General Counsel of *The New York Times*, who serves as the paper's top newsroom lawyer, why the seeming contradiction. "Our people who cover the intelligence community," he said, "I think are more likely to file FOIAs."[75] He observes that intelligence agencies are often more reticent to turn over documents without a FOIA request because they want the legal cover of being able to say "FOIA requires it, or a judge has required [it], or the AUSA is telling us we need to do this."[76] Since these agency officials are more

68 David E. Pozen, *Freedom of Information beyond the Freedom of Information Act*, 165 U. Penn. L. Rev. 1097, 1097 (2017).
69 *Id.* at 1118.
70 *See, e.g.*, Margaret B. Kwoka, *The Procedural Exceptionalism of National Security Secrecy*, 97 B.U. L. Rev. 103, 139 (2017).
71 Telephone Interview with Jeff Stein, Nat'l Sec. Correspondent, Newsweek (Mar. 14, 2019).
72 *See generally* Jeff Stein, A Murder In Wartime: The Untold Story that Changed the Course of the Vietnam War (1993).
73 Telephone Interview with Jeff Stein, *supra* note 71.
74 *Id.*
75 Telephone Interview with David McCraw & Al-Amyn Sumar, *supra* note 41.
76 *Id.*

fearful of turning over records without a legal mechanism, when the reporter is "not getting anywhere through the front or side doors, as it were, if you're reporting" then they file a FOIA request.[77] That is, intelligence agencies are more reluctant to hand over records through *any* mechanism, and FOIA is the only legally obligatory one.

Investigative reporter Seth Freed Wessler gave a concrete example of precisely that phenomenon. After having asked the Coast Guard for data about the number of people stopped and detained at sea, he was told "we can't just send it to you . . . but if you FOIA us, we'll send it to you. And then, they did."[78] Sarah Scoles, a freelance science writer and contributor to *Wired*, told me she files between five and ten FOIA requests a year, mostly to defense and intelligence agencies, as well as the National Aeronautics and Space Administration (NASA).[79] She noted that the Air Force was particularly helpful in her experience, contradicting what one might assume about military agencies' openness to public records requests.[80]

Some top media and oversight organizations are working almost exclusively in the national security arena. The National Security Archive, a non-profit research institute at George Washington University, uses FOIA almost exclusively to uncover and publicize security related information.[81] *The Black Vault*, the seventh highest media requester government-wide according to Max Galka's study at the FOIA Mapper,[82] is a website dedicated entirely to using FOIA to uncover previously classified records and records concerning UFOs.[83] The Electronic Privacy Information Center maintains a steady focus on surveillance and uses FOIA to great effect.[84] The ACLU does the same, as part of its National Security Project.[85]

Consistent with these observations, Seth Kreimer focused on national security as part of his compelling research detailing how FOIA comprises one aspect of the "ecology of transparency," having provided the "building blocks for accountability regarding abuses during the first five years of political stasis regarding the [Global War on Terror]" after September 11, 2001.[86] In that work, he documented how "FOIA [has been] a force to be reckoned with" and cites important court victories that led to the release of records about Guantanamo detainees, prisoner abuse, and surveillance.[87] Notably, Kreimer identified some of these very organizations – the ACLU, the *Associated Press*, National Security Archive, EPIC, the Electronic

77 *Id.*

78 Telephone Interview with Seth Freed Wessler, Freelance Investigative Reporter (Apr. 10, 2019).

79 Telephone Interview with Sarah Scoles, Freelance Science Writer (Mar. 18, 2019).

80 *Id.*

81 Nat'l Sec. Archive, nsarchive.gwu.edu (last visited Nov. 19, 2020).

82 Galka, *supra* note 9.

83 The Black Vault, www.theblackvault.com (last visited Nov. 19, 2020).

84 Elec. Privacy Info. Ctr., epic.org (last visited Nov. 19, 2020).

85 *National Security Project*, Am. Civil Liberties Union, www.aclu.org/issues/national-security (last visited Apr. 20, 2020).

86 Seth F. Kreimer, *The Freedom of Information Act and the Ecology of Transparency*, 10 U. Pa. J. Const. L. 1011, 1017 (2008).

87 *Id.* at 1024.

Frontier Foundation, Center for Constitutional rights, and Judicial Watch, among others – as the “most effective requesters” in this arena.[88]

Powerful examples of FOIA revelations in the security context abound. “From the moment indigenous protesters gathered to resist the Dakota Access pipeline in North Dakota, they faced heavy-handed tactics from law enforcement and private security hired by the pipeline company. As the protests grew, so did the campaign to surveil and repress them.”[89] This is the opening of *The Intercept*’s nine-part investigative reporting series on the policing of the Standing Rock Sioux water protector protests of a major oil pipeline project that would run near reservation lands and degrade environmental quality in the region. The reporting series focuses on the use of government power to intervene in a controversial dispute at the intersection of big business (oil), environmental protection (water), and Native American land rights.[90]

Interestingly, public records requests, including FOIA requests at the federal level, played an important part in the reporting. When the Federal Aviation Administration (FAA) enacted a no-fly zone over the protest area, Will Parrish, one of the lead journalists of the series, described his comparatively greater success using state-open records laws, but nonetheless cited an important federal FOIA request that formed the basis of part seven of the series.[91]

Under FOIA, records were released that demonstrated that the request for a no-fly zone at Standing Rock “generated controversy within the agency.”[92] One of the emails from a specialist at the FAA said he planned to deny the request for a no-fly zone, “there being no hazard from the ground to [aircraft]” but wanted everyone on board because it was a “high profile event.”[93] When a request to renew the no-fly zone was submitted, another official expressed concerns that “some of the involved tribes are arguing that the FAA’s action to implement a [no-fly zone] was driven not by a genuine safety/security threat, but rather by the desire of local [law enforcement] handling the situation to prevent the protesters from using drones to surveil unlawful actions on the part of [law enforcement] that infringe on the protesters’ First Amendment rights.”[94]

Parrish explained to me the importance of understanding that the FAA was not even sure it had authority to grant the no-fly zone, and the types of rationales that local law enforcement were trying to use.[95] “Then it turns out that … some FBI

[88] *Id.*

[89] Stephanie Harris et al., *Oil and Water*, The Intercept, theintercept.com/series/oil-and-water/timeline/ (last visited Apr. 20, 2020).

[90] *Id.*

[91] Alleen Brown et al., *Police Used Private Security Aircraft for Surveillance in Standing Rock No-Fly Zone*, The Intercept (Sept. 29, 2017), theintercept.com/2017/09/29/standing-rock-dakota-access-pipeline-dapl-no-fly-zone-drones-tigerswan/.

[92] *Id.*

[93] *Id.*

[94] *Id.*

[95] Interview with Will Parrish, Freelance Investigative Journalist (Feb. 25, 2019).

folks had met with FAA administrators and played at least some role in convincing them to authorize the no-fly zone. So, those records were very interesting and useful."[96] He further elaborated that a lot of people use FOIA very successfully, "even in the case of someone like me who [covers the] gray area around national security."[97] He further cited the work of Nick Turse, discussed above, who uses FOIA "really extensively to report on the military."[98]

Traditional international security efforts are also the subject of successful FOIA requests. In 2011, the Obama administration authorized the targeted drone killing of al-Qaeda linked Anwar al-Awlaki, the first American citizen deliberately killed on the order of a president without a criminal trial since the Civil War.[99] This action sparked vast public debate about whether such killing was justified on the evidence. One central government claim was that al-Alwaki was behind a plot to blow up a US airliner on Christmas 2009, ultimately unsuccessful, which was carried out by Umar Farouk Abdulmutallab, now known as the "underwear bomber."[100]

In 2017, *New York Times* journalist Scott Shane reported on records obtained under FOIA which contained summaries of interviews of Umar Farouk Abdulmutallab.[101] As Shane described, the documents obtained under FOIA "suggest that the Obama administration had ample firsthand testimony" about al-Awlaki's involvement.[102] Moreover, Shane explained that because the interviews were conducted simply through persuasion to talk – with great success – they "play into the debate President Trump has renewed about whether torture is ever necessary to get useful information from terrorism suspects."[103] Granted, it took *The New York Times* two years of litigation to obtain these documents, but the public learned a great deal about US counterterrorism abroad.

Some of the most pressing national security issues now arise in the realm of immigration. In this arena, too, news media have been using FOIA to particularly good effect. Seth Freed Wessler's work provides an exemplar. In 2016, Wessler published a series of investigative stories in *The Nation* revealing a pattern of negligent medical care leading to the preventable deaths of noncitizens serving criminal sentences in immigrant-only private prisons contracted to be run for the Bureau of Prisons (BOP).[104] The series of stories itself describes the role of FOIA.

96 *Id.*
97 *Id.*
98 *Id.*
99 Scott Shane, *Inside Al Qaeda's Plot to Blow Up an American Airliner*, N.Y. Times (Feb. 22, 2017), www.nytimes.com/2017/02/22/us/politics/anwar-awlaki-underwear-bomber-abdulmutallab.html.
100 *Id.*
101 *Id.*
102 *Id.*
103 *Id.*
104 Seth Freed Wessler, *Special Investigation: Dying in Private Prisons*, The Nation, www.thenation.com/special/private-prison-deaths/ (last visited Apr. 20, 2020).

Wessler had heard about substandard medical care in these facilities anecdotally, but had difficulty getting access to the facilities or confirming the accounts.[105] So he filed a FOIA request in 2012 with the BOP asking for records pertaining to deaths of inmates in privately run, immigrant-only facilities.[106] BOP delayed answering his request – as he told me, "I was told constantly ... yes, it's coming, we're working, we're working. But months and then years passed, and still, no documents."[107] So he finally found a lawyer to represent him pro bono and he filed a lawsuit in 2014,[108] and in 2015 BOP began producing what ended up being over 9,000 pages of healthcare records, constituting medical files for 103 men who died in these facilities.[109]

Wessler had the medical files reviewed by physicians, and of the seventy-seven files that were complete enough to evaluate, thirty-eight were found to involve inadequate medical care and for twenty-five of them – one third of the total – physicians reviewing the file concluded that the medical deficiencies likely contributed to the inmate's death[110] Wessler's series not only reports these shocking figures, but tells the stories of some of these men: of a massive stroke left untreated for a critical six hours until a man was brain-dead upon arrival at the hospital; of persistent serious complaints and visits to the medical unit with critical symptoms over nearly five months before a man was diagnosed with severe metastatic stomach cancer that killed him; of a man with documented and severe mental illness who went untreated until he hung himself from a bedsheet while in solitary confinement.[111]

The revelations in this series of stories led to at least one civil suit for wrongful death against the private prison operator[112] and also likely influenced the DOJ decision to end its reliance on private prison operators for BOP facilities,[113] though that policy was rolled back when the Trump administration took office and then reinstated under Biden. Regardless, Wessler's work provoked a national conversation about the private prison industry, and, as Wessler explained to me, "FOIA was

[105] Seth Freed Wessler, *A Guide to Our Investigation of Deaths Inside Immigrant-Only Prisons*, Type Investigations (Jan. 28, 2016), www.typeinvestigations.org/blog/2016/01/28/guide-investigation-deaths-inside-immigrant-prisons/.

[106] *Id.*

[107] Telephone Interview with Seth Freed Wessler, *supra* note 78.

[108] *Id.*

[109] Freed Wessler, *A Guide to Our Investigation*, *supra* note 105.

[110] *Id.*

[111] Seth Freed Wessler, *This Man Will Almost Certainly Die*, The Nation (Jan. 28, 2016), www.thenation.com/article/privatized-immigrant-prison-deaths/.

[112] Seth Freed Wessler, *Family Sues Private-Prison Operator Over Deaths at Immigrant-Only Facilities*, The Nation (Mar. 15, 2016), www.thenation.com/article/family-sues-private-prison-operator-over-deaths-at-immigrant-only-facilities.

[113] Seth Freed Wessler, *The Justice Department Will End All Federal Private Prisons, Following a 'Nation' Investigation*, The Nation (Aug. 18, 2016), www.thenation.com/article/justice-department-to-end-all-federal-private-prisons-following-nation-investigation.

central" to reporting this series of stories. "I did a lot of field reporting, but much of that field reporting stemmed from leads gleaned from documents produced in the FOIA."[114]

Without doubt, FOIA fights over exempt materials, classified records, intelligence sources and methods, and even agencies' refusal to admit or deny the existence of records (referred to as the "Glomar" response), are difficult hurdles in the national security realm. But reporting on national security is generally difficult. Sometimes FOIA is the only way, and these reporters are taking full advantage.

B. WHY FOIA

So-called FOIA Terrorist Jason Leopold has explained that, "[t]here is a sort of myth that exists in newsrooms that the Freedom of Information Act doesn't work well in reporting because if you're reporting a topic or issue, it needs to be reported now."[115] And certainly, the media have lodged vociferous complaints about delay, over-withholding, and resource-intensive fights as barriers to accessing records under FOIA. So why, then, do they still turn to FOIA? Not all of them do, of course. But for those I spoke with who use FOIA so effectively, their answers are illuminating. Mostly, it boils down to this: there aren't better alternatives.

Of course, FOIA is not the only transparency law, nor are laws the only way that information reaches the public. Government information reaches the public through agencies' affirmative or proactive disclosure, through whistleblowers and leakers, through congressional oversight, and through other transparency laws covering open meetings, advisory committees, and other such matters. Sometimes, these mechanisms prove extremely powerful. The Mueller report on Trump's ties to Russia is now available in bookstores across the country.[116] Edward Snowden's massive leak concerning NSA surveillance has led to legal changes and corporate policy shifts.[117]

Certainly, these mechanisms could be enhanced and serve, in some ways, to preempt the need for some amount of FOIA requesting. Affirmative disclosure requirements could be substantially strengthened, whistleblowers and leakers could be better protected, and congressional monitoring could take on a larger role. Professor Pozen also suggests conditioning the legal effect of documents on their

[114] Telephone Interview with Seth Freed Wessler, *supra* note 78.

[115] Jennifer Peters, *"FOIA Terrorist" Jason Leopold Shines a Light in the Dark*, NEWS MEDIA ALLIANCE (Sept. 18, 2017), www.newsmediaalliance.org/jason-leopold-shines-light/.

[116] *See generally* ROBERT S. MUELLER, III, U.S. DEP'T OF JUSTICE, REPORT ON THE INVESTIGATION INTO RUSSIAN INTERFERENCE IN THE 2016 PRESIDENTIAL ELECTION (2019).

[117] *See, e.g.*, Julian Hattem, *Spying after Snowden: What's Changed and What Hasn't*, THE HILL (Dec. 25, 2016), thehill.com/policy/technology/310457-spying-after-snowden-whats-changed-and-what-hasnt.

prior publication creates another powerful incentive;[118] we do have some such requirements and more could be done in this regard.

Even if, however, attention was given to strengthening alternative transparency and oversight mechanisms, FOIA would remain unique. None of the aforementioned mechanisms allows the agenda to be set by a government outsider. Affirmative disclosure mandates essentially require a prediction of what categories or kinds of records will be most important for public oversight. Leakers and whistleblowers are government insiders whose own views on what the public should know may be outside the norm, and in any event their willingness to disclose depends not on the public's interest but often on their own tolerance for substantial personal risk. By contrast, FOIA provides a method for a member of the public, or ideally the press representing that public interest, to specify the subject of inquiry.[119] These actors do not harbor the same insider concerns about embarrassment or institutional legitimacy of government agencies. Perhaps even more importantly, as my conversations with reporters demonstrated, is that FOIA is judicially enforceable. While judicial review is often less robust than many would hope, it has still proven a powerful tool for reporters across a wide range of topics.

That FOIA remains vital for reporters is evidenced by their explanations of when they make a FOIA request. "When do we use it?" Scott MacFarlane of *NBC* said, "When we realize there's no other way to get that item."[120] Charles Seife, investigative science journalist and journalism professor, explained that science journalism is typically non-adversarial, because scientists want reporters to write about their work.[121] Because of that, there was no culture of "whistleblowers to kind of cultivate in the same way," – that is, alternatives did not exist – "so I used FOIA quite a bit to open up those stories."[122] Seth Freed Wessler, freelance investigative journalist, described to me that getting government agency officials to open up can be difficult: "[D]ocuments are a way to force that opening, to access a level of detail that makes it possible to build a narrative, to tell a close to the ground story that straight interviews can't do alone."[123]

Justin Elliot of *ProPublica* described how one benefit of FOIA is that reporters do not need to cultivate relationships with sources that those same reporters may then be reluctant to jeopardize by writing something the source would not like.[124] In his words: "I guess one of the things that I like about FOIA, at least sort of in theory, is that it doesn't require … access."[125] He elaborated that, "I don't need to be, like,

[118] Peters, *supra* note 115.

[119] 5 U.S.C. § 552(a)(3)(A) (2018).

[120] Telephone Interview with Scott MacFarlane, Investigative Reporter, NBC Wash. (Mar. 22, 2019).

[121] Telephone Interview with Charles Seife, Professor, N.Y.U. (Feb. 15, 2019).

[122] *Id.*

[123] Telephone Interview with Seth Freed Wessler, *supra* note 78.

[124] Telephone Interview with Justin Elliott, *supra* note 54.

[125] *Id.*

friends with Steven Bannon to get him to tell me something; I can just ask for some record and theoretically get it and write a story about it."[126]

Zach Mider of *Bloomberg* had a less rosy view of the results of his FOIA requests, but nonetheless feels the law is invaluable. "I think the big thing is [that] the actual requests themselves are not usually very helpful, but the fact that you can make them, and the fact that the government's aware that you can make them, has probably [] a kind of beneficial effect of [agencies'] assuming … that the public actually has a right to know things, you know?"[127]

For these reporters, there simply weren't alternatives to FOIA. They didn't have a whistleblower or an insider source, there was no willing participation of agency officials. The documents were crucial to telling the story. FOIA remained imperfectly unique.

C. WHAT MAKES AN EFFECTIVE OVERSIGHT REQUESTER

Reporters I spoke to use FOIA very regularly. Will Parrish described his requesting routine: "I've gotten to a point where I have an Excel sheet, you know, that's constantly tracking dozens of different records requests of FOIAs and has become, you know, at least a significant part of what I do as a journalist."[128] Seth Freed Wessler explained that, "for big, long term investigative projects, FOIA has been an essential part of my process."[129] Scott MacFarlane says he files FOIA requests, "[o]n an average, probably … once or twice a day, but you know, sometimes it's 10 one day, and then I won't do another one for two weeks."[130]

Kevin Bogardus credits his FOIA practice for how he got hired for his current position at *E&E News*. "I said, I'm going to use FOIA so much. I'm going to FOIA this, I'm going to FOIA that … To their credit, the editors were excited about that, and they supported me in that process going forward, I mean, greatly."[131] He likes to use hashtag #foiaforever and the saying "every day is #foiafriday."[132] FOIA Friday, for him, is the first Friday of every month when he files five to eight requests to a dozen or more agencies for records he routinely seeks.[133] It is no doubt also partly ideological. As David McCraw of *The New York Times* has said publicly, "[s]imply, we feel that using this law is an essential part of our mission."[134]

[126] *Id.*
[127] Telephone Interview with Zachary Mider, *supra* note 67.
[128] Telephone Interview with Will Parrish, *supra* note 95.
[129] Telephone Interview with Seth Freed Wessler, *supra* note 78.
[130] Telephone Interview with Scott MacFarlane, *supra* note 120.
[131] Telephone Interview with Kevin Bogardus, *supra* note 33.
[132] *Id.*
[133] *Id.*
[134] *News Reporters Drive Growth in Media FOIA Litigation*, FOIA PROJECT (Jan 9, 2017), foiaproject.org/2017/01/09/news-reporters-drive-growth-in-media-foia-litigation.

Every reporter I spoke with who uses FOIA effectively described it as simply one of their many reporting tools. Seife elaborated that "FOIA really gives you specifics to create a narrative around something that you know happened. Like fraud or kind of a revolving door, or things like that. If you can pinpoint one nice, really concrete example that allows you to have that microcosm to explain the macrocosm of the broader problem."[135] Sarah Scoles similarly described her uses of FOIA as fitting into a broader investigative picture: often she is looking for contracts with businesses in an industry she is investigating; records that are related to a breaking news story but when she senses there may be a larger aspect to it that is less timely that might produce a follow-up; or she turns to FOIA when a source says something off the record or says just enough to know that there is something more she wants to look into.[136]

These accounts strongly support Professor Kreimer's theory of FOIA as "functioning within a broader ecology of transparency," where leaked or publicized information may set the stage for enough knowledge about what to request, and responses to requests or to FOIA litigation may lay the groundwork for further investigation and information gleaned from other institutions.[137] For example, Seth Freed Wessler described how the medical records he received under FOIA for inmates who died in privately run BOP facilities then allowed him to identify individuals to interview about specific incidents.[138]

So, what other strategies do these effective news media requesters use? One key component is the development of expertise. When I asked Scott MacFarlane how often he uses documents obtained through FOIA as part of his reporting, he responded: "A higher percentage every day. I'm getting better at this. . . . I bet it's between ten and twenty percent."[139] Similarly, Will Parrish described his improved results under FOIA over time: "My understanding has just matured a lot, you know, of how these – you know, the different entities function, and who's involved in what, what they're likely to put in public records, what they're not likely to put in public records."[140]

Deep expertise in the underlying subject matter is also crucial. Parrish separately identified his knowledge of the field as a key factor: "[M]y theories about what governments are doing have become more accurate also, and I think that's really the main thing that's led me to be more successful, is that I think it's essential to have some sort of mental map of what is happening."[141] Charles Seife echoed the

[135] Telephone Interview with Charles Seife, *supra* note 121.
[136] Telephone Interview with Sarah Scoles, *supra* note 79.
[137] Seth F. Kreimer, *The Freedom of Information Act and the Ecology of Transparency*, 10 U. Pa. J. Const. L.1011, 1015–16 (2008).
[138] Telephone Interview with Seth Freed Wessler, *supra* note 78.
[139] Telephone Interview with Scott MacFarlane, *supra* note 120.
[140] Telephone Interview with Will Parrish, *supra* note 95.
[141] *Id.*

sentiment: "When you get really familiar with an agency or a process, sometimes you kind of know the pipelines through which, kind of, the bad stuff happens."[142]

Consistent with that view, I asked David McCraw of *The New York Times* what made some of his reporters more successful than others, and expertise was a big part of his response: "Most of our heavy FOIA users are sophisticated ... [O]ur reporters who have been on [a]beat for a long time and have a really sophisticated understanding of the agencies and areas they cover. A FOIA request that gets them a five-page document may actually have a nugget that no one else would appreciate or see."[143]

Time is also a huge factor. No one is able to use FOIA to report the news today, or even next week. The reporters I spoke with uniformly talked about how FOIA was useful for longer-term investigative work, but not for reporting breaking or daily news. Wessler spent more than two years waiting for the records that formed the basis for his series about medical treatment in private prisons.[144] It took Zach Mider almost a year to find out what rationale Ingersoll-Rand advanced for its exemption from the ban on contracting for inverted companies.[145]

Resources also matter. Scott MacFarlane said it succinctly: "[F]ollow up is more often than not required."[146] Most cited "pestering"[147] or calling "to check on things"[148] as producing results. The reporters I talked to had a wide variety of experience in terms of whether or how often they administratively appeal or file FOIA litigation to challenge agency withholding. MacFarlane indicated he most often appeals when he gets a "no records" response but he knows records exist; sometimes he even has an example and will send it to the agency to say this is a record you should have found in your search.[149] Bogardus says, "I'm in the thousands of FOIA requests just at *E&E News*. I don't even know if I'm in the double digits in appeals yet." It just usually is not worth his time. Both Justin Elliot and Scott MacFarlane noted that, although they had not been involved with FOIA litigation, they both work at organizations that have FOIA litigation capacity, something they felt was important as an option.[150]

Reporters who do invoke the courts strongly emphasized the power of the judicial system in FOIA battles. Charles Seife was blunt: "Honestly, I think that there's a small number of really hardcore users who have the power of litigation behind them."[151] He litigated his first FOIA case pro se, but after that found pro bono

[142] Telephone Interview with Charles Seife, *supra* note 121.
[143] Telephone Interview with David McCraw & Al-Amyn Sumar, *supra* note 41.
[144] Telephone Interview with Seth Freed Wessler, *supra* note 78.
[145] Telephone Interview with Zachary Mider, *supra* note 67.
[146] Telephone Interview with Scott MacFarlane, *supra* note 120.
[147] Telephone Interview with Justin Elliott, *supra* note 54.
[148] Telephone Interview with Sarah Scoles, *supra* note 79.
[149] Telephone Interview with Scott MacFarlane, *supra* note 120.
[150] *Id.*; Telephone Interview with Justin Elliott, *supra* note 54.
[151] Telephone Interview with Charles Seife, *supra* note 121.

counsel.[152] He noted that since he has had an academic position with time and resources behind him, he has been able to fight FOIA cases in court.[153] Wessler similarly believes his willingness to go to court makes the difference in his FOIA practice: "I have been able to use FOIA aggressively because I've built relationships with attorneys at firms and law school clinics who represent me pro bono."[154] He noted that in one case, when trying to get the medical records from private prison deaths, "It didn't require a judicial order. It was the suit itself that compelled the action, that led to the release of full medical files of people who had died."[155]

David McCraw had the most birds-eye view of FOIA litigation, handling all FOIA matters for *New York Times* reporters. *The New York Times* has been among the top – if not the top – media litigator under the law in recent years.[156] I asked him why they litigated so much more than their media competitors with similar numbers of requests. He explained that they do their own newsroom litigation in house, rather than invoking outside counsel which has been the industry trend. "We … work as our own little law firm," he explained, "we want to be hands-on, and we think that a good role for us."[157] He also noted that *The Times* is now in its eleventh year having a First Amendment Fellow program, which was initially started "to address what we saw was the increasing problem of government secrecy."[158] "FOIA," he added, "overwhelmingly is the main part of our litigation."[159]

He also highlighted a perverse role of litigation under the law: provoking the agency into any kind of response at all. "In most of our cases, we simply haven't got a timely response, and the only tool we have to get the government agencies to move in a timely fashion is to sue."[160] He calls the fee to file a federal lawsuit "the concierge fee," because it essentially forces the agency to skip that request ahead in line.[161] Moreover, he thinks the results are better: "[T]he threat of having a federal judge actually look at the response that we get or the failure to respond is often enough to get a much better FOIA response than what we get otherwise."[162] Finally, even when they do not get a judicial order, he asserts that they "get more creative solutions from the [government attorneys] than we get from the FOIA officers."[163] In one case they agreed a Central Intelligence Agency (CIA) historian would review

152 *Id.*
153 *Id.*
154 Telephone Interview with Seth Freed Wessler, *supra* note 78.
155 *Id.*
156 *See, e.g.*, David McCraw, *How the Times Uses FOIA to Obtain Information the Public Has a Right to Know*, N.Y. Times (Sept. 2, 2019), https://www.nytimes.com/2019/09/02/reader-center/foia-freedom-of-information-public-records.html.
157 Telephone Interview with David McCraw & Al-Amyn Sumar, *supra* note 41.
158 *Id.*
159 *Id.*
160 *Id.*
161 *Id.*
162 *Id.*
163 *Id.*

the records for responsiveness, instead of a FOIA officer, a solution McCraw found satisfying.[164]

These reporters are no doubt exceptional in the world of FOIA. They are using the law in its most intended fashion. They are developing expertise not only in their fields, but in the process of requesting and fighting for the records. And they are deploying strategies that are shaking loose documents of great public import, and from which we all benefit as we watch over our government. As Professor Kreimer said, however, "[t]o press a recalcitrant administration for disclosure under FOIA requires time, money, and expertise."[165] Not all reporters have those luxuries, but these reporters, at least, show some of the remaining promise of FOIA.

164 *Id.*

165 Kreimer, *supra* note 137, at 1020.

PART II

Who Makes a Million FOIA Requests

3

It Is Not the News Media

This chapter is the most complete accounting of who uses FOIA ever compiled. It provides the most comprehensive available statistics and paints a picture across federal government agencies. This account reveals a striking reality: Mostly, FOIA is used for purposes that have nothing to do with government oversight. Below is a necessarily imperfect yet revealing attempt to quantify what percentage, government-wide, of FOIA requesters are journalists. By contrast, it details similar estimations for other, much more dominant groups of FOIA requesters including individuals requesting their own records, whom I call "first-person" requesters, and commercial requesters. It further explains the wide variation of requester populations between agencies. While subsequent chapters in this part delve into who these other requesters are and what they are seeking, this Chapter provides the bird's-eye view of our million FOIA requesters.

A. STUDYING FOIA USERS

It is harder than one might imagine answering the questions "Who uses FOIA?" and "What records do people seek under FOIA?" At any given agency, the folks working in the FOIA office generally have a very good idea who their requesters are. But agencies perform a myriad of important functions, which results in the creation and retention of widely varying types of records. In turn, any given agency's particular record sets and principle activities determine who the bulk of its requesters are and what they seek. Even FOIA officers typically do not know who is making the bulk of requests at any agency other than their own. As such, a trans-substantive, government-wide picture of FOIA requesters sheds important light on FOIA's operation for government insiders and outsiders alike.

1. *Data Availability*

The Department of Justice's (DOJ) Office of Information Policy (OIP), tasked with overseeing FOIA compliance government-wide, does not collect information about or require reporting on who is using FOIA or what kinds of records are being sought. That choice is logical. Congress's statutory reporting requirements cover a wide variety of metrics, including number of requests made, processed, and pending; average response times for simple and complex requests and breakdowns of response times in various increments; outcomes of those requests whether granted, denied, or granted in part; bases for withholding invoked by the agency including frequency of each basis; requests for special processing be it expedited processing or fee waivers; fees collected by the agency; staff hours spent processing requests; and other matters as well.[1] Nowhere, however, does Congress or the DOJ require agencies to report who is using FOIA at their agency or what records are being requested.

Agencies, for their part, necessarily have to keep a list or log of FOIA requests, both for practical reasons and to meet statutory requirements to "establish a system to assign an individualized tracking number for each request received" and provide the tracking number to the requester.[2] Many, if not most, agencies publish some version of their logs on their websites, typically on their FOIA page. However, most publicly available logs are missing fields that would be crucial to answering basic questions about how FOIA is actually used at the agency. Requester names, organizational affiliations, and request subject matters – or at least one or two of those important fields if not all three – are often missing. Frequently, the logs will mirror the statistics that agencies are required to report: request date, closed date, tracking number, and other details focused on timing and agency processing.

Moreover, those agencies that post their logs do not post their logs in a uniform format. Not only do they report different fields of data about each request, but some agencies post logs in Excel, some in Word, some in PDFs – either digitally-created or, worse, scanned. Thus, any attempt to combine datasets across agencies is at best difficult, and at worst impossible. The best effort thus far came from Max Galka, a data visualization expert and founder of the website *FOIA Mapper*, who combined FOIA logs from eighty-five agencies totaling 229,000 requests, using only logs that contained both the requester name and requester organization. Indeed, even requiring only those two fields limited him to using eighty-five of the 142 agencies for which he had obtained some version of a FOIA log.[3] He then used various tools to categorize each requester, reporting out aggregate statistics about requester identities.

1 5 U.S.C. §§ 552(e)(1)(A)–(Q) (2018).

2 *Id.* at § 552(a)(7)(A).

3 Max Galka, *Who Uses FOIA? – An Analysis of 229,000 Requests to 85 Government Agencies*, FOIA Mapper (March 13, 2017), foiamapper.com/who-uses-foia/.

He described the heroic effort it took to get as far as he did, and yet what he did still falls far short of a comprehensive analysis of the federal government requester population. For example, the Department of Homeland Security (DHS) now receives nearly half of all federal government requests but is barely represented in Galka's study, which includes less than 4,000 requests directed to US Immigration and Customs Enforcement (ICE) and no requests directed to US Citizenship and Immigration Services (USCIS) or US Customs and Border Protection (CBP).[4] Moreover, Galka's study does not reach the question of what kind of information these requesters are seeking at all. There is no doubt the FOIA Mapper study adds to the understanding of the FOIA requester landscape, but it also demonstrates the serious limitations to the available data.[5]

2. *Methodology*

To work around the lack of publicly available data and the problem of data uniformity, I submitted my own FOIA requests seeking FOIA logs from federal agencies, requesting a standard set of data fields be included.[6] These requests were made in rounds, organically formulated based on discrete studies I conducted. To begin, I did an early study focused on commercial requesters. As I began making these requests in 2014, I requested Calendar Year (CY) 2013 data. For the select group of agencies included in that study, because I had already obtained useable

4 *Id.*

5 *Id.*

6 Though I tweaked various formulations of my request over time, in the end my standard request asked for logs that included the following fields:

1. The FOIA request identification number;
2. The name of the requester;
3. The organizational affiliation of the requester, if there is one;
4. The date on which the request was made;
5. The subject matter of the request;
6. Whether a privacy waiver or authorization for release under the Privacy Act was submitted in conjunction with the request;
7. The result of each FOIA request, whether granted, granted in part, denied, withdrawn or otherwise disposed;
8. If not granted in full, the reason for the denial or partial denial;
9. The date on which the request was resolved;
10. The category assigned to the request for the purpose of making a determination about the applicability of FOIA fees. These categories would therefore include "commercial use" requesters, "educational or noncommercial scientific institution[s]" and "representative[s] of the news media," as well as requesters eligible for reduction or waiver of fees under 5 U.S.C. § 552(a)(4)(A)(iii);
11. Indication of whether a fee waiver was requested and, if so, whether that request was granted; and
12. Dollar amount charged to requester for responding to the request and the date of the invoice.

data and analyzed it, I relied on my previous data for their inclusion in this volume.[7] Next, I conducted a study focused on first-person use of FOIA.[8] Requests for this study were made in 2016, and because I had learned from my first study that agencies could produce Fiscal Year (FY) data more easily than CY data, I requested FY 2015 data in those requests. Like with my study of commercial users, for those agencies included in my study of first-person requesters, I relied on my previous work for their inclusion in this volume.[9]

For this volume's much larger, more comprehensive accounting of FOIA users across the federal government, I created a database of all agencies listed on the DOJ's FOIA Reports website as submitting an annual FOIA report and separately reporting components of agencies listed therein.[10] Because I compiled this list in 2017 when the FY 2017 Annual Reports were not yet released, I relied upon the FY 2016 Annual FOIA Reports list.[11] For every department or agency report that broke down its data into components, I listed each component separately. In total, there were 407 FOIA reporting agency components. Of those, seventeen did not have an annual report available, though they were listed as being subject to the reporting requirement. Of the remaining 390, for all components that received 500 or more FOIA requests and for which I did not yet have useable data, I submitted a new FOIA request for the FY 2017 FOIA logs for that agency or component.[12]

I gave the FOIA request process at least a year, and in many cases more than a year, to see what data I could obtain. Where I was not receiving responses from an agency, multiple attempts to contact each agency were made by both phone and by email. For agencies that produced an incomplete response (e.g., a spreadsheet

[7] Those agencies include the Securities and Exchange Commission (SEC), the Food and Drug Administration, the Environmental Protection Agency (EPA), the Defense Logistics Agency, the National Institutes of Health, and the Federal Trade Commission.

[8] *See infra* pt. C(1) for a detailed discussed of first-person FOIA use.

[9] These agencies include US Citizenship and Immigration Services, Customs and Border Protection, Immigration and Customs Enforcement, Social Security Administration, Equal Employment Opportunity Commission (EEOC), Wage and Hour Division, Occupational Safety and Health Administration, and the Adminitration for Children and Families.

[10] There are two exceptions for which I did not break down the data into separate components but reported the agencies as a whole. These two agencies broke down their reporting by region, but the FOIA logs I obtained covered all regions, and regions do not perform different types of functions, and so I did not break down those two agencies into their regional components. These agencies were the EPA and the EEOC.

[11] These can be found at *Annual FOIA Reports FY 2016*, U.S. DEP'T OF JUSTICE, www.justice.gov/oip/annual-foia-reports-fy-2016 (last visited July 16, 2020).

[12] In addition, I submitted a select few requests to components below the 500 request mark purely out of my own interest. These included: US Census Bureau, US Agency for International Development, National Aeronautics and Space Administration, Department of Education's Office of Federal Student Aid, and the Office of Personnel Management, which did not report a tally for total requests received in Fiscal Year 2016.

without certain fields I requested) or an inaccessible response (e.g., a paper copy or scanned PDF that could not feasibly be converted to Excel), the agency was either contacted again, or I submitted an administrative appeal, or both. In almost no case could I obtain a log that had all the fields I requested. When I obtained data sufficiently complete to allow me to, at a minimum, analyze FOIA requester identities and, in most cases, the subject matter of their requests, I typically surrendered in my attempt to obtain other fields after exhausting administrative options. Notably, in one instance where an agency claimed the requester's names were exempt from disclosure under a special withholding statute, I obtained pro bono counsel, sued in court, and won.[13]

In total, I requested a year's worth of data from eighty-five agencies or agency components (hereinafter, agencies). At forty-six agencies, I obtained sufficiently complete data in response to my FOIA requests to contribute to our understanding of who uses FOIA and what records they seek. At ten more agencies, although I was unable to obtain useable data in response to my FOIA requests, a publicly available log was sufficiently detailed to be helpful in understanding FOIA users at that agency. At four more, I combined the data I received with a publicly posted log for completeness. In this volume, I report on data I have been able to analyze from those sixty total agencies.[14]

3. *Agencies*

The breadth of the data covers the vast majority of FOIA requests across the federal government. In FY 2016, the annual reports from each agency report on a government-wide total of 788,769 requests.[15] The agencies for which I am reporting data analysis in this volume received 577,892 of those requests in FY 2016, or seventy-three percent of the government's total. Moreover, for three other high-volume agencies for which I do not have data, I have found other ways of ascertaining their requester population and will report the results of those inquiries as well.[16] Thus, very few high-volume agencies are omitted from this study.

[13] Kwoka v. Internal Revenue Serv., 1:17-cv-1157-DLF, 2018 U.S. Dist. LEXIS 167547 (D.D.C. Sept. 28, 2018); denial of attorney's fee award reversed by Kwoka v. Internal Revenue Serv., 989 F.3d 1058 (D.C. Cir. 2021).

[14] For a full accounting of all agencies to whom I directed requests and the results of those requests, see Appendix A. For the twenty-five agencies from which I was unable to obtain useable data, I received no response from thirteen of them despite multiple attempts at contact, five provided an inaccessible response insofar as the data was not machine readable, seven provided an incomplete response insofar as the data did not cover the entire agency or were so incomplete that no analysis was possible.

[15] U.S. Dep't of Justice, Office of Info. Policy, Summary of Annual FOIA Reports for Fiscal Year 2016, at 5 (2016) [hereinafter 2016 FOIA Reports Summary].

[16] As described *infra* these agencies are Executive Office for Immigration Review, National Archives and Records Administration, and Cybersecurity and Infrastructure Security Agency.

As for agencies that are included in this study, I report data on seven of the nine agencies that received more than 20,000 requests in FY 2016, which I refer to as an "extremely high-volume FOIA agency." Immigration enforcement agencies top the list by volume of requests (and are gaining in their total share of FOIA requests over time). These are principally the three components of DHS: USCIS, CBP, and ICE. In FY 2016 USCIS reported 166,732 requests, CBP 66,690, and ICE 63,385, making them the top three agencies by volume across the federal government. Benefits-oriented agencies come in next. The Social Security Administration (SSA) ranked sixth-highest by volume of requests with a reported 29,631 in FY 2016 and the Veterans Health Administration (VHA) ranked seventh with 28,091. Then, the US Department of State (27,856) and the US Army (25,755) close out the extremely high-volume FOIA agency list.

Of the nine extremely high-volume FOIA agencies, I was only unable to obtain data from two. The first is the National Archives and Records Administration (NARA), which rang in at 49,966 in FY 2016, placing it fourth. As discussed below, however, it is possible to discern what drives NARA requests from other evidence. The second is the Executive Office for Immigration Review (EOIR), the adjudicative agency for immigration matters housed in the DOJ, which received 35,500 in FY 2016, placing it as the fifth-highest volume FOIA agency that year. Like with NARA, it is possible to understand EOIR FOIA requesters without a full accounting of their FOIA logs. Thus, I will report below the findings regarding requesters at all nine of the extremely high-volume FOIA agencies.

The next group of agencies, which I label "high-volume" FOIA agencies, received between 10,000 and 20,000 FOIA requests a year in the baseline FY 2016 year. Of the eight agencies in this category, I report data on five of them. These five include two primarily law enforcement agencies: the Equal Employment Opportunity Commission (EEOC) has the thirteenth-highest volume of requests at 17,680 and the Federal Bureau of Investigations (FBI) is fourteenth at 15,202. The other three are large regulatory agencies: the Securities and Exchange Commission (SEC) ranks fifteenth with 14,458 requests; the Environmental Protection Agency (EPA) is sixteenth with 10,403 requests, and the Food and Drug Administration (FDA) rings in at seventeenth with 10,374 requests.

The three high-volume agencies for which I was unable to obtain useable data are the Center for Medicare and Medicaid Services (CMS), which received 17,917 requests in FY 2016, ranking it as the twelfth-highest volume agency; the National Protection and Programs Directorate (NPPD), a division of DHS, which received the tenth-highest volume of requests at 19,557; and the Farm Service Agency (FSA), received the eleventh-highest volume of requests, 18,463. For the NPPD, I am able to use other indicators to explain the volume of requests received, but unfortunately have no reliable way to report on the requester populations at CMS or FSA.

Next, thirty-six agencies fall into the "medium-volume FOIA agency" category, encompassing those agencies that received between 1,000 and 10,000 requests in FY 2016. Of these, I report data on twenty-eight but was unable to obtain data for eight. These agencies cover a wide range of functions. Those that I report here are, in descending order of volume of requests: the US Navy, the Federal Aviation Administration, the Occupational Safety and Health Administration (OSHA), the Internal Revenue Service, the Bureau of Prisons, the Defense Logistics Agency, the Pension Benefit Guaranty Corporation, the US Coast Guard, the National Labor Relations Board, the Federal Emergency Management Agency (FEMA), the Wage and Hour Division (WHD) of the Department of Labor, the Federal Motor Carrier Safety Administration, the Forest Service (FS), the Bureau of Indian Affairs, the Office of the Secretary/Joint Chiefs of Staff at the Department of Defense, the US Postal Service, the US Marshals Service, the US Secret Service, the Department of the Treasury's Office of the Comptroller of the Currency, the National Institutes of Health (NIH), the Federal Trade Commission (FTC), the Animal and Plant Health Inspection Service (APHIS), the Bureau of Alcohol, Tobacco, Firearms and Explosives, Fish and Wildlife Service (FWS), the Centers for Disease Control and Prevention, OIP, and the Department of Justice, the Department of Housing and Urban Development (HUD), and the Mine Safety and Health Administration.

The remaining agencies are "small-volume FOIA agencies," which received between 500 and 1,000 requests in FY 2016. Of the twenty-two agencies in this category, I report on fourteen and do not have data for the remaining eight. The ones I report are: the Small Business Administration, the National Park Service, the Department of the Treasury's Departmental Offices, the General Services Administration (GSA), the Bureau of Land Management (BLM), the Federal Communications Commission (FCC), the Criminal Division of the Department of Justice, the Nuclear Regulatory Commission (NRC), the Department of Defense's Inspector General, the Transportation Security Administration (TSA), the Federal Reserve, the US Consumer Product Safety Commission, the Employee Benefits Security Administration, and the Defense Information Systems Agency. Beyond these agencies, I submitted requests to another ten agencies with less than 500 requests in FY 2016, which I would consider a negligible FOIA volume but where I was simply interested. Of those, I report on six: the Federal Deposit Insurance Corporation (FDIC), the Administration for Children and Families, the US Census Bureau, the Agency for International Development, the National Aeronautics and Space Administration, and the headquarters office of the Department of Education's Office of Civil Rights.

This is, to date, the most comprehensive attempt to catalogue FOIA requesters and what records they seek across the federal government.[17] The holes that exist in this data are dwarfed by the vast light that is shed on how transparency works in the

[17] *See* Appendix A for a complete list of agencies from which I sought data, their size as measured by requests received in Fiscal Year 2016, and the results of those attempts.

United States, for whom it works, and for whom it works less well. Below is a brief overview of this accounting, the details of which are explored in subsequent chapters.

B. NEWS MEDIA PRESENCE

Without a doubt, news media use of FOIA remains important. Chapter 2 of this volume details the various ways the news media use FOIA particularly effectively, and with an especially important impact on the public's oversight of government activity. However, the numbers bear out another stark reality. By volume, the news media represent a small, even tiny fraction of FOIA requesters. The short answer is that journalists file only 2.6 percent of federal FOIA requests.[18] The long answer is more complicated, and detailed below, but yields the same result. That is to say, the vast, vast majority of FOIA requesters are not journalists.

Overall, I am able to report news media data on fifty-two out of the total sixty agencies included in this study. For twenty-nine agencies, the agency designated each requester on their log as part of a certain category of requesters for fee purposes. The news media fee category has a capacious definition, including "any person or entity that gathers information of potential interest to a segment of the public, uses its editorial skills to turn the raw materials into a distinct works, and distributes that work to an audience."[19] News media status is often designated separately on FOIA logs or, less frequently, is combined with educational requesters because those groups share preferential fee status. Where the agency designated news media or news media/educational requesters, I simply used the agency's own count of those requesters.[20] At twenty-three agencies, no fee categories or requester categories were designated on the logs, so I hand-designated those requesters with an organizational affiliation that was apparently a media outlet and used those designations to tally media requesters. At eight agencies, the FOIA logs neither report the category of requester nor the organizational affiliation, and thus I am unable to provide a percentage of news media requesters for those agencies. The fifty-two agencies for which I have a news media count include three extremely high-volume FOIA agencies, four high-volume FOIA agencies, twenty-five medium-volume FOIA agencies, and twenty small-volume FOIA agencies. The full accounting of news media requester data is provided at Appendix B.

[18] *See* Appendix B.

[19] 5 U.S.C. § 552(b)(4)(A)(i)(III). It goes to give a broad range of nonexhaustive examples, as well as specify any methods of delivery of the news are acceptable and freelance journalists should generally be able to avail themselves of this status as well. *See id.*

[20] There is one exception to this general practice. For data received from the Office of the Inspector General at the Department of Defense, the agency count of media requesters was so incomplete that it was discarded and my own count was used instead. This is the only instance where I substituted my own count for an agency count.

To be sure, these counts are highly imperfect. In some ways, the numbers provided by agencies often overcount media requesters. To begin, for those agencies that group news media and educational requesters together, the educational requesters represent an obvious overcount.[21] In addition, agencies are inconsistent about categorizing nonprofit or advocacy organizations; most do not count those organizations as news media, but some do. The statutory definition of news media is so broad that it likely should include these organizations, but regardless, it creates inconsistency across agency data.[22]

However, without doubt, for those agencies at which I hand counted media requesters, there is likely a measurable undercount. The biggest undercounted category consists of reporters who do not list an organizational affiliation. I identified media requesters solely using organizational affiliation, and so if a reporter did not list one, I would not have flagged their request as a media request. Regardless of imperfections in the data, however, these estimates demonstrate that across the federal government media requests are a tiny fraction of all FOIA requests.

The overall percentage of media requesters, however, is not the only remarkable finding in this data. When broken down, media data reveals interesting trends. First, the fraction of media requesters is generally substantially higher at agencies with smaller-volume FOIA practices. For example, at some of the extremely high-volume FOIA agencies, the proportion of media requesters is below 1 percent. At CBP, my hand count yielded a .02 percent rate, and at ICE a 0.1 percent rate. The VHA, another extremely high-volume FOIA agency, by its own count, received 1.2 percent news media requests. High-volume agencies report slightly higher rates of news media requests: the SEC's own count reports 2.6 percent,[23] the EPA's own count has 3.5 percent media requesters, and the FDA is the only significantly higher reporting agency, with 12 percent media requests. A closer examination of the FDA data,

[21] *See* 5 U.S.C. §552(a)(4)(A)(ii)(II).

[22] *See* 5 U.S.C. § 552(a)(4)((A)(ii) ("'[A] representative of the news media' means any person or entity that gathers information of potential interest to a segment of the public, uses its editorial skills to turn the raw materials into a distinct work, and distributes that work to an audience. In this clause, the term 'news' means information that is about current events or that would be of current interest to the public.").

[23] In arriving at this number, I made one significant alteration to the SEC's own designations. John Patrick Gavin, requesting in his own name, is the proprietor of a business called SEC Probes, which sells access to information about SEC investigations to mostly other commercial clients, and therefore, in my view, is properly classified as a commercial requester. If he were included in media requesters as the SEC designates him, news media requests at the SEC would comprise 23 percent of all requests, because Gavin alone makes a fifth of the SEC's FOIA requests. U.S. Sec. & Exch. Comm'n, Freedom of Information Act Response to Sept. 5, 2014 Request by Margaret B. Kwoka (on file with author); FOIA Logs, U.S. Sec. & Exch. Comm'n, www.sec.gov/foia/docs/foia-logs.htm (select "2013" and "2014). The dataset compiled includes the months between January 2013 and December 2013, representing CY 2013.

however, reveals significant inconsistencies in the agency's own reporting, inconsistencies that likely lead to substantial overcounting of media requests.[24]

But as the agencies' overall FOIA volume decreases, the proportion of media requests appears to increase. At medium-volume agencies, media percentages creep up toward and even crack double digits. OSHA reports 4.6 percent media requests, FEMA 4.6 percent, and WHD 6.3 percent. Even more interesting, a couple of agencies dealing with primarily security and defense are seeing particularly vigorous media use: the DoD's Office of the Secretary/Joint Chiefs has a whopping 29.4 percent media requests, and the Secret Service has 20.8 percent media requests, running contrary to the general assumptions that FOIA is least effective for the media when covering security-related topics.

Some other significant media uses are found in the category of medium-volume FOIA agencies: NIH reports 5.3 percent of requests from news media, FTC 14.2 percent, FWS 19.3 percent, DOJ's OIP 21.4 percent, and HUD's headquarters 13.9 percent. Certainly, some agencies in this category have a smaller media presence in their FOIA offices, but overall medium-volume agencies in my study see an average of 4.5 percent of requests from news media, higher than the overall average by quite a bit. Small-volume FOIA agencies are even more significant in this regard. They average 12.8 percent of requests from news media, also evidencing some agencies with particularly heavy media presence: GSA has 16.5 percent requests from news media, BLM 11.4 percent, FCC 29 percent, NRC 12.2 percent, TSA 12.9 percent, and FDIC 8.1 percent to name a few.

A second interesting facet of the media data is that new media outlets, online or otherwise nontraditional media, are often the most frequent users of FOIA. *MuckRock*, a sort of journalistic FOIA-portal platform, often tops the list.[25] *MuckRock* alone accounts for 6.5 percent of all requests at the FCC, 4.6 percent at the DoD's Office of the Inspector General, 3.9 percent at OIP, and 1.7 percent of all requests at TSA. But even *MuckRock* is absent at some of the highest-volume FOIA agencies: accounting for only four requests at CBP, for example. Other new media organizations with significant presence include *Buzzfeed*, *Politico*, *Bloomberg*, and *ProPublica*. Traditional media outlets are still present, however. Regularly appearing on media requester lists include: *Associated Press*, *The New York Times*, *The Washington Post*, *USA Today*, *The Hill*, and various TV and radio outlets.

A third finding in media data as it bears on this study is that at some agencies there are very significant numbers of requests coming from public interest, accountability, advocacy, or otherwise oversight-minded non-profit organizations, who still fall

[24] For example, Washington Information Source (WIS), a requester I believe is properly classified as commercial, received news media status for 269 of its 344 requests and commercial status for the remainder. U.S. Dep't of Health & Human Servs., Food & Drug Admin. Freedom of Information Act Response to June 24, 2014 Request by Margaret B. Kwoka (on file with author).

[25] *See about MuckRock*, MUCKROCK, www.muckrock.com/about (last visited Nov. 19, 2020).

under the umbrella of what I refer to as "oversight requesters," even though they are not news media organizations. These organizations often serve the same function as journalists, bringing matters of concern regarding government activity to public attention. Indeed, non-profits, among other activities, often provide information of public concern directly to media outlets to reach a broader audience, thereby serving as a sort of media auxiliary.

Interestingly, this dynamic reaches its apex at certain environmental regulatory agencies, notably excluding the EPA. At the Department of Agriculture, both FS and APHIS evidence this trend. At FS, the agency reports 114 news media requests in the study year, representing 6.5 percent of all requests. But my own hand tabulations of oversight nonprofit requests yielded an additional 368 such requests, a category comprising 21.0 percent of requests.[26] These organizations include, for example, the Western Watersheds Project (fifty-three requests), WildEarth Guardians (thirty-seven requests), the Center for Biological Diversity (twenty-six requests), and the Grand Canyon Trust (twenty requests). Put together, news media and other oversight requesters, therefore, total more than a quarter of all requests at the agency. At APHIS, similarly, my hand tabulation of news media requests yielded 120 requests or 7.3 percent, but oversight nonprofits made 399 or another 24.3 percent of requests, totaling 31.6 percent of all requesters. The nonprofits at this agency focused in particular on animal welfare and protection. This list is dominated by People for the Ethical Treatment of Animals (181 requests), Animal Legal Defense Fund (thirty-one requests), and the American Society for the Prevention of Cruelty to Animals (twenty-eight requests), to name a few.[27]

Similarly, at the Department of Interior (DOI), both BLM and FWS are dominated by oversight nonprofit requesters. At BLM, the top three requesters, all oversight nonprofits, make up 24.0 percent of all requests to the agency, yet none are counted as media requests. At FWS, news media are already reported at a high 19.3 percent by the agency, but my own count of oversight requesters yielded 198, or another 31.4 percent requests. Together, media and other oversight requesters at FWS made more than fifty percent of all requests to the agency, the only data I found that cracked a majority oversight use. Notably, at both BLM and FWS, the organizations most frequently requesting records under FOIA also overlap heavily with those at the Forest Service.[28]

26 A spot check of news media requesters indicated minimal overlap; that is, these oversight nonprofits were, by and large, not designated as news media.

27 U.S. Dep't of Agric., Animal & Plant Health Inspection Serv., Freedom of Information Act Response to Feb. 15, 2018 Request by Margaret B. Kwoka (on file with author); U.S. Dep't of Agric., Forest Serv., Freedom of Information Act Response to Feb. 15, 2018 Request by Margaret B. Kwoka (on file with author).

28 U.S. Dep't of Interior, Bureau of Land Mgmt., Freedom of Information Act Response to Mar. 6, 2018 Request by Margaret B. Kwoka (on file with author); U.S. Dep't of Interior, Fish & Wildlife Serv., Freedom of Information Act Response to Mar. 6, 2018 Request by Margaret B. Kwoka (on file with author).

There are various reasons why these agencies are amenable to so much oversight use of FOIA by nonprofits. Among the various issue-oriented public interest groups, some of the most organized focus on civil rights and environmental issues.[29] Civil rights matters are not governed nearly as much by agency action, regulatory structures, or administrative enforcement, but rather tend to be battles waged in the courts. Environmental issues, however, largely play out in the realm of administrative law, and thus agency records bear heavily on those issues. Accordingly, the data suggest a greater oversight use of FOIA at agencies that work on issues that are the focus of a well-organized civil society.

Researchers are a group generally difficult to count, but often act in a similar public oversight requester role. These include academics, historians, and authors of nonfiction work in longform journalism or books. At the FBI, an agency where organizational affiliations are not available and thus a news media total is impossible to count, some of the top requesters fall in this category. For example, Nina Seavey, a researcher and documentary filmmaker at George Washington University, made 730 requests in one year, accounting for 3.5 percent of all requests to the FBI during that time period. Other familiar media names also made significant numbers of requests to the FBI, including *MuckRock* (754 requests), Jason Leopold (175), and *Mother Jones Magazine* (122).

Similarly, at the Department of State, six of the seven top requesters work for the National Security Archive, a nonprofit research group housed at George Washington University. Collectively, those six researchers made 199 requests in a year, constituting 2.6 percent of all requests to State. This data set also did not include organizational affiliations and thus no news media count could be made, but researchers as an oversight mechanism were still evident in the logs.

On the whole, however, the numbers make crystal clear that most requesters are not oversight requesters, much less media requesters. Moreover, at those agencies that receive the lion's share of FOIA requests – and which drive the numbers of FOIA requests across the federal government – media are even less likely to be present in significant proportions. Rather, other requesters with much more routine, non-newsworthy, non-public-oversight-minded purposes are dominating the FOIA landscape.

C. THE OTHER REQUESTERS

Surveying sixty agencies' FOIA data reveals one stark reality: although the news media are not making the majority of requests anywhere, those who are making the majority of requests differ greatly by agency. Indeed, FOIA is a trans-substantive law, yet its use is extremely substance-specific. That is, the process FOIA creates is

[29] *See generally* Steven M. Teles, The Rise of the Conservative Legal Movement: Battle for Control of the Law 22–57 (2008).

one-size-fits-all; every agency must accept the same form of request and abide by the same requirements in responding. Yet, the records agencies hold vary widely based on the agency's principal activities, and their information constituencies – that is, the sector of the public that is interested in the agency's records – varies accordingly.

At the highest level of generality, agencies can be grouped into one of three categories: benefits agencies, law enforcement agencies, or regulatory agencies. And, as described in the next four chapters, at this bird's-eye view, the data included in this study shows that benefits and law enforcement agencies are disproportionately inundated with first-person FOIA requests; that is, FOIA requests for records about the requester themself. Regulatory agencies, on the other hand, tend to receive high-volumes of commercial requests, or requests for records to be used as part of a profit-making enterprise. But many agencies also defy this easy categorization. Some agencies' FOIA practices are particularly idiosyncratic. A niche segment of the public can have a niche interest or need for records the agency holds; these unique information constituents can come to dominate the FOIA practice at a particular agency. In this way, it is helpful to understand FOIA reforms must go beyond a one-size-fits-all solution. In this rest of this Chapter, I attempt to quantify the dominant groups of requesters, and in the chapters that follow, to qualitatively describe them.

1. *First-Person FOIA*

When people need their own government files, they flock to FOIA. They use FOIA to get their own medical files, their own law enforcement records, their own immigration dossiers, and records about their own claims or complaints. This category of FOIA requests, which I call "first-person FOIA requests," has long been recognized as common. DOJ issued guidance about how to handle first-person requests starting in 1980,[30] and agencies have developed some specialized procedures for the filing of first-person requests. For example, because the privacy exemption is designed to protect the individual's interest, it cannot be invoked to withhold information about the requester themself. As a result, agencies typically require a first-person FOIA requester to submit a certification verifying the requester's identity, ensuring no personal information is disclosed to a third party.[31]

There is no doubt that individuals seeking their own records from government files can be characterized as engaging in oversight requesting. After all, an individual seeking their own records to make their best case for government benefits eligibility

[30] *See* U.S. Dep't of Justice, Office of Info. Policy, *FOIA Counselor: Privacy Act/FOIA, Conflict or Harmony?*, 1 FOIA UPDATE 3 (Jan. 1, 1980), www.justice.gov/oip/blog/foia-update-foia-counselor-privacy-actfoia-conflict-or-harmony.

[31] *See, e.g.*, *Certification of Identity Form, DOJ-361*, U.S. DEP'T OF JUSTICE, www.fbi.gov/file-repository/u-s-department-of-justice-form-361-certification-of-identity.pdf/view (last visited Nov. 19, 2020).

is holding the government to account in making the correct benefit determination. This type of personal accountability with respect to government actions is incredibly valuable. It helps individuals feel the process is fair, ensures a full opportunity to be heard, and furthers more accurate decision-making. As described in greater detail below, it promotes due process like values vis-à-vis an individual dealing with their government.

In describing this type of oversight, however, it becomes clear that it facilitates largely a sort of personal accountability, rather than the public accountability that results from obtaining information and publicizing it widely for use in the democratic process. Personal accountability and personal oversight is not at the heart of FOIA's envisioned purpose. But even if it were, the following chapters describe the ways in which FOIA fundamentally fails to effectively deliver important personal accountability because its design is a poor match for these requesters' needs.

These are very sympathetic requesters. Their interest in the information is plain. Indeed, these are requesters for whom obtaining the requested information is often a high stakes matter. They are not on a fishing expedition or wasting the government's resources. Part III describes why this and other groups of unintended FOIA users pose a problem for FOIA. But this part will describe, in no uncertain terms, why FOIA is a problem for this group of users. It was not designed for their uses, and it is doing a (mostly) poor job at serving them.

Before delving into the reasons why individuals need their personal information from the government's records and why they turn to FOIA to get it, it would be remiss not to admit some tiny fraction of first-person requests move from the personal accountability category to the public accountability category. Sometimes a pattern of individual problems emerge from FOIA requests intended to serve only the requester that can lead to public oversight actions, such as political mobilization, aggregate litigation, or systemic legal reform. However, the evidence amassed for this study suggests the vast majority of the requests never make it past the individual requester and never touch on public oversight, but rather serve personal accountability objectives.

Overall, first-person requesters are the single largest cohesive group of requesters government wide. In sum, they constitute about two-thirds of all requests submitted to the federal government. But they are not always easy to identify. First-person requests are not designated as such on nearly any agency FOIA log, are not subject to a separate categorization for purposes of assessing fees, and often submit requests through a representative such as a lawyer. Thus, for each agency, I separately examined the data for patterns that would reveal first-person requesting.

There are various ways in which first-person requesting reveals itself in the logs. One way to find first-person requests is to identify redactions on FOIA logs themselves that are invoked under FOIA's privacy exemption, exemption 6, which allows agencies to withhold information "the disclosure of which would constitute a clearly unwarranted invasion of personal privacy."[32] The DOJ, which is responsible for issuing guidance on FOIA policy to agencies government-wide, opined that "FOIA requesters, except when they are making first-party requests, do not ordinarily expect that their names will be kept private; therefore, release of their names would not cause even the minimal invasion of privacy necessary to trigger the balancing test."[33] Thus, for some FOIA logs, a (b)(6) designation as the justification for withholding a requester's name indicates a first-person request.

In other instances, a (b)(6) designation in the subject matter field of the request is indicative of first-person requesting. This is particularly true where a representative of the individual, such as their lawyer, makes the request on their behalf, but the subject matter of the request is an individual's name. In such instances we can be reasonably confident these are first-person requests because if the subject matter of a request is an individual, only the individual or their representative would be able to access those records for privacy reasons; no one else would be making a third-party request for records about a private individual in the regular course of events.

Another indicator of first-person requesting at some agencies is designation of a request as both a FOIA request and a Privacy Act request. The Privacy Act (PA) is a statute designed to give individuals certain procedural rights with respect to their own records held within government agencies.[34] Among them is a right of access, and so any request designated as a joint FOIA/PA request is necessarily a first-person request. While any request designated as a joint FOIA/PA request will necessarily be first-person, the inverse is not true; those requests designated only as a FOIA request can still be first-person requests because the Privacy Act only applies to a subset of agency records defined in the statute, not all agency records, and only applies to citizens or permanent residents of the United States.[35] Still, at some agencies, the FOIA/PA designation is a useful proxy for first-person requesting.

Finally, there are some agencies for which the data indicates groups of nearly certain first-person requesters by subject matter, because the subject matter of the request is of such a nature that only the person the records concern would be able to access the file under the relevant legal framework, FOIA or otherwise. For example, as described in greater detail below, at the EEOC, a request for a "charge" file is almost certainly a first-party request because of statutory access restrictions to those records.

[32] 5 U.S.C. § 552(b)(6).

[33] U.S. Dep't of Justice, Office of Info. Policy, FOIA Guide, 2004 Edition: Exemption 6 (May 2014), www.justice.gov/oip/foia-guide-2004-edition-exemption-6.

[34] 5 U.S.C. § 552a; *see also* U.S. Dep't of Justice, Office of Privacy & Civil Liberties, Overview of the privacy act of 1974 (2015).

[35] *See* 5 U.S.C. § 552a(a)(2) (applying the privacy act terms to "a citizen of the United States or an alien lawfully admitted for permanent residence"); § 552a(a)(5) (applying the Privacy Act terms only to a "system of records," which means "a group of any records under the control of any agency from which information is retrieved by the name of the individual or by some [unique] identif[ier].").

Of the sixty agencies for which I have data (which account for 577,892 requests in my baseline year of FY 2016), I was able to identify a quantifiable number of first-person requesters at twenty-eight of them. At an additional nine, I was able to identify noticeable examples of first-person requests, but not able to quantify them. Using only the total number of quantifiable first-person requests and adjusted for FY 2016 baseline request totals, 387,625 of the 577,982 requests included in the study are first-person, totaling 67.1 percent.[36] This both over and undercounts in important ways. For example, it undercounts obvious first-person requests at agencies for which I cannot identify a reliable count method and thus are simply not counted in this total. On the other hand, it overrepresents some of the agencies that receive the highest total volume of first-person requests, which are included in this study, whereas smaller volume FOIA agencies not included in the study are unlikely to have significant numbers of first-person requests. A full list of how first-person FOIA requests were identified can be found at Appendix C.

Despite limitations, this somewhat back-of-the-envelope math reveals that first-person requesting is undeniably driving FOIA totals – to the tune of approximately two-thirds of all requests. As described in greater detail below, all indicators suggest that first-person requesting is only increasing over time, particularly driven by immigration-related requesting. The account in the following two chapters documents the dominant drivers of first-person requesting as well as the ways in which FOIA fails to adequately meet the needs of this group of information constituents.

2. *FOIA, Inc.*

Business and commercial interests have long found great utility in FOIA. Various studies across decades have documented significant amounts of commercial requesting. In 1972, a Congressional Research Service report identified 43 percent of approximately 1,500 requests surveyed as coming from businesses,[37] and in 1978 the General Account Office (GAO) similarly concluded 58 percent of approximately 2,500 requests examined were commercial in nature.[38] These studies notably included law firm requesters, without differentiation between lawyers representing individual interests and those representing corporate interests. Nonetheless these

[36] By "adjusted for FY 2016 totals," I mean the following: because the data for which I am reporting on each agency is not the same time period (it ranges from 2013 to 2017, depending on the agency), I took the fraction of each agency's total requests that were first-person in the time period for which I have data, and multiplied that fraction by the total for 2016 so that the weighted number of first-person requests was adjusted for the proportion of total requests the agency represented over the same time period.

[37] Michael Doyle, The Freedom of Information Act: In Theory and Practice 78–79 (May 2001) (unpublished M.A. thesis, Johns Hopkins University) (on file with author).

[38] Elmer B. Staats, U.S. Gov't Accountability Office, LCD-78-120, B-173761, Government Field Offices Should Better Implement the Freedom of Information Act, at *ii (1978).

findings led the GAO to declare FOIA "is being used mostly by businesses and law firms – sometimes for purposes not contemplated by Congress."[39]

Fast-forward thirty years, and two studies found similar results in the early twenty-first century. One journalist collected data from eleven federal agencies and concluded commercial requesters were often the most frequent.[40] Another 2005 study of FOIA logs at seventeen agencies conducted by a nonprofit found about two-thirds of requests were commercial.[41] Various media outlets have also asserted FOIA is predominately used to serve business interests,[42] or that "corporate interests now drive the release of information."[43]

Despite a long history of using FOIA, commercial requesters were not formally recognized as a distinct category until Congress passed the 1986 amendments to the law, which established the first set of fee categories, including a category of charges applicable to records "requested for commercial use."[44] This category remains in the current version of the law,[45] and the Office of Management and Budget has interpreted the commercial use provision to include "use that furthers the commercial, trade or profit interests of the requester or person on whose behalf the request is made."[46] Under the fee provision, commercial requesters may be charged "reasonable standard charges for document search, duplication, and review," unlike news media who can only be charged for duplication, and all other requesters who can be charged for search and duplication, but not review.[47] That is, commercial requesters unsurprisingly have the most onerous fee provision, designed to fully compensate the agency for the expense associated with fulfilling the request.

As the existence of the commercial use fee provision implies, nothing whatsoever about commercial use of FOIA is inappropriate, much less unauthorized. Indeed, the commercial use of FOIA, while not at all emphasized at FOIA's original enactment, was acknowledged at least briefly, by two members of Congress, one

39 *Id.*

40 Doyle found that at the EPA, 87.9 percent of requesters were commercial; at the FDA, that 26.0 percent were filed by what Doyle labels FOIA-service companies (what this book characterizes as "information resellers"); and that attorneys comprised the highest-volume population of requesters at the Department of Health and Human Services. Doyle, *supra* note 37, at 70–71, 97.

41 Coal. of Journalists for Open Gov't, Frequent Filers: Businesses Make FOIA Their Business 1 (July 3, 2006), available at www.humanrightsinitiative.org/programs/ai/rti/international/laws_papers/intl/businesses_make_foia_their_business.pdf.

42 Michael Moss, *Public Eye: Federal Service Gets Wider Use by Sleuths, Snoops – and Senators*, Wall St. Journal, Jan. 3, 1996, at A1.

43 Kevin G. Hall & Kevin Johnson, *Open-Records Law Morphs into Tool for Corporations, Advocates*, McClatchy D.C. (June 17, 2015), www.mcclatchydc.com/news/politics-government/article24781393.html.

44 *See* 132 Cong. Rec. S14296–98 (1986).

45 5 U.S.C. § 552(a)(4)(A)(ii).

46 The Freedom of Information Reform Act of 1986; Uniform Freedom of Information Act Fee Schedule and Guidelines, 52 Fed. Reg. 10,012, 10,017–18 (Mar. 27, 1987).

47 5 U.S.C. § 552(a)(4)(A).

of whom inquired whether the maritime industry could use the law to learn about certain government subsidies and another of whom noted the potential for a contractor who submitted an unsuccessful bid for government work to learn the reasons why.[48] Indeed, the commercial use of FOIA is entirely legitimate and lawful.

Moreover, there is no doubt that, like with other categories of requesters, commercial requesters may at times be serving public oversight purposes as well. A business might use FOIA to learn about agency performance or actions and then use that information to submit comments to a pending rulemaking, for example. Or a company may uncover agency misconduct and report it to Congress or the media, sparking accountability actions by public bodies. Companies may also use information gleaned under FOIA in the course of litigating over agency policy measures that affect the general public, not just actions that affect their own business interests. There is no question that business is an organized force in legislative and regulatory policy decisions, and appropriately so. Additionally, sometimes companies use FOIA in ways that look more like the private – not public – oversight uses discussed in the context of first-person requesting. The bleed between these categories is most apparent with lawyers using FOIA to uncover documents germane to their corporate client's case.

Indeed, lawyers are one of the hardest groups of requesters to conceptually classify. On the one hand, lawyers are, of course, themselves mostly operating or working for a for-profit business. As such, one could view them as all commercial requesters because they use FOIA as part of their profit-making enterprise. Indeed, this may well be the reason the earliest surveys of requesters found such high commercial use – it appears lawyers were uniformly counted as business uses of FOIA.[49] Yet, most agencies treat lawyers – in my view appropriately – as mere agents of the clients they represent, the client being the true party in interest in the request.[50] Thus, where clients are individuals facing government consequences, looking for government benefits, or trying to obtain access to other opportunities, the interests served by the request are more properly categorized as individual interests and first-person FOIA requesters. For that reason, these requesters do not tend to be charged fees, even though the requests come from law firms.[51] For example, USCIS does not charge fees for A-File requests as a categorical matter, even though most

48 Doyle, *supra* note 37, at 46.

49 Elmer B. Staats, *supra* note 38; Doyle, *supra* note 37, at 46, 66.

50 *But see* U.S. Dep't of Health & Human Servs., Admin. for Children & Families, Freedom of Information Act Response to Arpil 15, 2016 Request by Margaret B. Kwoka (on file with author) (as an outlier in this regard, categorizing immigration lawyers, almost certainly representing individuals, as commercial requesters).

51 For example, at EEOC, in the study year only 297 requesters were charged any fees at all out of 17,026 total requests even though law firms make up the majority of top requesters. U.S. Equal Emp't Opportunity Comm'n, Freedom of Information Act Response to April 14, 2016 Request and Nov. 15, 2016 Administrative Appeal by Margaret B. Kwoka (on file with author).

such requests come from lawyers on behalf of their clients.[52] By contrast, law firms filing FOIA requests on behalf of business clients are, by definition, representing commercial or corporate interests and are typically treated as such.[53] This study does the same. As such, law firms are included in the discussion of commercial requesters only where their clients are evidently for-profit enterprises themselves.

Some such corporate lawyers will be using FOIA in a private (not public) oversight manner, to hold an agency accountable in its relationship with the client, be it in fighting for benefits like permits, contracts, or grants, or defending against enforcement. This relationship, like first-person FOIA private oversight, serves important ends, ensuring agency proceedings are fair and accurate vis-à-vis the rights of the public. They do not, however, typically result in public oversight, or knowledge production that benefits the general public about government activities or conduct.

These caveats aside, the evidence amassed in this study (and detailed in much greater depth in Chapters 6 and 7) makes clear that most commercial requesting serves purely private interests and hardly ever serves public oversight interests. To be sure, commercial requesting may serve very important private interests. Those private interests may even have derivative benefits to the public in the form of a more competitive marketplace, more informed business practices, or improved products or services available to the public. But these requests almost never go to the heart of FOIA's envisioned purpose.

Because the statute imposes a separate category of fees on commercial requesters, agencies often (but not always) designate their commercial requesters as such on agency FOIA logs. This was the sole method used to identify commercial requesters for the purposes of this study. That is, the agency's own designation of a requester as commercial was taken at face value, with very few exceptions noted in the discussion of the agency data. Thus, only those agencies for which I was able to obtain a fee category designation are included in the commercial requester count.

52 Interview with Jill Eggleston, Assistant Ctr. Dir., Freedom of Info. & Privacy Act Unit, Nat'l Records Ctr., U.S. Citizenship & Immigration Servs., U.S. Dep't of Homeland Sec., in Lee's Summit, Mo. (June 12, 2019); Electronic Reading Room, U.S. Citizenship & Immigration Servs., www.uscis.gov/about-us/electronic-reading-room (filter by "FOIA Logs"). The dataset compiled includes the months between October 2014 and September 2015, representing FY 2015.

53 At MSHA, where most law firm requesters are requesting commercial information, firms are largely categorized as commercial requesters. U.S. Dep't of Labor, Mine Safety & Health Admin., Freedom of Information Act Response to April 15, 2016 Request by Margaret B. Kwoka (on file with author). Similar trends exist at OSHA. U.S. Dep't of Labor, Occupational Safety & Health Admin., Freedom of Information Act Response to Arpil 19, 2016 Request by Margaret B. Kwoka (on file with author). At the Federal Trade Commission, 192 of 253 law firm requesters were charged commercial request fees. *See* Fed. Trade Comm'n, Freedom of Information Act Responses to Sept. 29, 2014 and Feb. 12, 2015 Requests by Margaret B. Kwoka (on file with author).

Of the sixty agencies included in this study (which account for 577,892 requests in my baseline year of FY 2016), I was able to obtain logs that included a requester fee category identifying commercial requesters for thirty of them. At an additional nine agencies, notable examples of commercial requesters were evident and can be cited, but counts were unavailable. Using only those commercial requesters designated by an agency log, counted as such, and adjusted for the FY 2016 baseline, reveals 46,231 commercial requests of the total 577,982 in the study, or 8.0 percent. Certainly, there are significant numbers of requests that are commercial in nature at agencies that did not have fee category designations, and this total undercounts in that way. But at the largest volume FOIA agencies, immigration and in particular first-person immigration requesting, is dominating the landscape, and given that first-person requesting can be counted at around two-thirds of all requesting, it should not come as a surprise that commercial requesting is comparatively smaller.

That said, while commercial requesting does not rival first-person requesting, more than 46,000 requests a year from business interests is still clearly significant. In addition, at large regulatory agencies, as well as agencies that administer government grants and contracts, commercial requesting dominates, sometimes overwhelmingly. A full list of the agencies at which commercial requests were identified and tallies specific to each agency can be found at Appendix D. In addition, a discussion of exactly what drives commercial requesting, how records requested by businesses are used, and how FOIA appears poorly matched to commercial information needs appears in later chapters.

3. *Idiosyncratic Requesters*

The final category of requesters documented in this study is, indeed, not truly a category at all. It is those that defy easy categorization. While the previously discussed uses of FOIA dominate across the federal government, variations between the populations of information constituents at different agencies are enormous. Indeed, the challenge of this study has been to find the common threads between agencies, to generalize a phenomenon that is often very agency-specific, and to identify similarities between often disparate groups of requesters. But there is a category worth talking about separately: the idiosyncratic requesters.

Some agencies simply have a lot of requests coming from a particular interest, perspective, information constituency, or even a particular individual. If you talk to the FOIA officials, they know who their requesters are and what they want. They may find some of these requesters frustrating – at times even abusive of the process – or they may simply understand that the records their agency holds are unique and the interest in them will be similarly unique. Regardless, the idiosyncrasy is worth highlighting because, despite common trends identified in this study, some parts of the FOIA world are beyond simple categorization.

Chapter 8 will describe these requesters. Some of them are research-driven public interest federal records databases that look either like resellers or like libraries or like news media, depending on which angle you take. Some of them are political parties, or even other parts of government – even other parts of the same federal department. Some significant amount of FOIA requesting is driven by the story of human curiosity. These requesters believe in our basic civic interest in learning about some aspect of the world. And yes, some requesters may be abusing a public process. It is worth seeing these uses of FOIA for who they are. But they are not quantifiable in any meaningful way across government. Rather, the stories of these requesters are the accounts themselves.

* * *

The following five chapters reveal a deep need for government information for a host of reasons apart from government oversight. The federal government is a vast repository of records and knowledge, and information constituencies who want access abound. Because FOIA is always an option, it gets used when there is no better option. It is the option of last resort. It is not designed for these requesters, not tailored to the records they want, and not necessarily serving them well. And, largely, FOIA has been hijacked to serve these other – often very worthy – needs. Without understanding these information constituents, one cannot understand what work FOIA is doing. And without knowing the current state of play, reforms will continue to nibble around the edges of the sinking *Titanic*.

4

Immigration

"You can't see what's going on in FOIA in government if you have immigration records included," said the second-in-command at the Department of Homeland Security (DHS) Privacy Office.[1] Otherwise put, immigration is so dominant in FOIA that it either explains or obscures FOIA practices, depending on how you look at it. Indeed, it is difficult to overstate the degree to which immigration-related requests – namely requesters seeking their own immigration files – are driving FOIA numbers government-wide. Most apparently, immigration requests are responsible for the overwhelming volume of requests at the DHS components – including US Citizenship and Immigration Services (USCIS), Immigration and Customs Enforcement (ICE), Customs and Border Protection (CBP), and others. And since DHS now receives nearly half of the federal government's total requests, that alone suggests immigration's outsized presence. But beyond DHS, immigration requests are also contributing a significant volume of requests at the State Department, the Department of Justice (DOJ), and, to a lesser extent, some fraction of requests at the Department of Health and Human Services (HHS) and the Department of Labor (DOL).

Taking DHS alone, it now receives nearly half of all FOIA requests filed across the federal government.[2] And its numbers are only increasing. In Fiscal Year (FY) 2015, the year for which data is reported in this study, it received 281,138 requests representing thirty-nine percent of the federal government's total.[3] But in 2016, that

1 Interview with Dr. James V.M.L. Holzer, Deputy Chief FOIA Officer, Jimmy Wolfrey, Senior Dir., FOIA Operations and Mgmt. & Amy Bennett, Public Liaison, U.S. Dep't of Homeland Sec., in Wash. D.C. (June 5, 2019).

2 U.S. Dep't of Justice, Office of Info. Policy, Summary of Annual FOIA Reports for Fiscal Year 2018, at 3 (2018) [hereinafter 2018 FOIA Reports Summary].

3 U.S. Dep't of Justice, Office of Info. Policy, Summary of Annual FOIA Reports for Fiscal Year 2015, at 2 (2015) [hereinafter 2015 FOIA Reports Summary].

number jumped to 325,780, or forty-one percent of all FOIA requests;[4] in 2017 it rose again to 366,036 or forty-five percent of all requests;[5] in 2018, it received 395,751 or forty-six percent of the government's total;[6] and in 2019, it cracked 400,000 requests (400,246 to be precise),[7] which represents forty-seven percent of the total requests across the federal government.[8] That is, DHS is a dominant – and increasing – presence in the requester landscape.

In FY 2015, the reporting year, ninety-five percent of requests received by DHS were directed to the three principal immigration enforcement components: USCIS, which processes applications for visas, permanent residence, and naturalization; ICE, which enforces immigration laws in the interior; and CBP, which enforces immigration laws at the border.[9] At those three components, the FOIA logs reveal that nearly all of the requests are first-person requests. At USCIS, 163,050 of the total 165,233 requests in FY 2015 had a subject matter withheld to a privacy exemption, indicating a first-party request.[10] Similarly, at ICE, 98,928 of 100,762, or ninety-eight percent, of all FOIA requests were for "records pertaining to (b)(6)(b)(7)(C)" (the two privacy exemptions) or a variation on that formulation.[11] And at CBP, where data was obtained from the FOIAOnline platform, 97.1 percent of the subject matters of the requests were listed as "under Agency review," presumably because of privacy concerns.[12]

Indeed, DHS itself has consistently described "[t]he vast majority of requests sent to DHS" as "first-party records, meaning that requesters are seeking copies of information about themselves previously submitted to the government or records that document their interactions with agency officials."[13] DHS's FOIA report identified the immigration components as receiving "the bulk of FOIA requests from

[4] U.S. Dep't of Justice, Office of Info. Policy, Summary of Annual FOIA Reports for Fiscal Year 2016, at 2 (2016).

[5] U.S. Dep't of Justice, Office of Info. Policy, Summary of Annual FOIA Reports for Fiscal Year 2017, at 3 (2017).

[6] 2018 FOIA Reports Summary, *supra* note 2.

[7] U.S. Dep't of Homeland Sec., 2019 Freedom of Information Act Report 2 (Feb. 2020) [hereinafter DHS 2019 FOIA Annual Report].

[8] 2018 FOIA Reports Summary, *supra* note 2.

[9] U.S. Dep't of Homeland Sec., 2015 Freedom of Information Act Report, at ii (Feb. 2016) [hereinafter DHS 2015 FOIA Annual Report].

[10] FOIA Library, U.S. Immigration & Customs Enf't (Oct. 3, 2017), www.ice.gov/foia/library (follow "ICE FOIA Logs" tab) [hereinafter ICE Data]. The dataset compiled included the months between October 2014 and September 2015, representing FY 2015.

[11] *Id.*

[12] FOIAOnline, foiaonline.gov/foiaonline/action/public/search/advancedSearch (under "Look Up By" select "Agency" then search for "CBP – U.S. Customs and Border Protection") [hereinafter CBP Data]. The dataset compiled includes the months between October 1, 2014 and September 30, 2015, representing FY 2015.

[13] U.S. Dep't of Homeland Sec., Departmental Freedom of Information Act (FOIA) Backlog Reduction Plan: 2020–2023, A Business Modernization Roadmap 5 (2020) [hereinafter DHS Backlog Reduction Plan].

individuals seeking immigration related records,"[14] and most recently, the department's backlog reduction plan explained that "[r]equests for A-file [immigration] material comprise the vast majority of DHS's FOIA workload."[15] To underscore the extent of the first-person requesting at DHS, a top DHS privacy official estimated to me that a full ninety-six percent of DHS requests – department-wide – were first-person requests, nearly all of them about immigration.[16]

The identities of the requesters also confirm the dominance of first-person immigration requesting. At USCIS, ICE, and CBP, the most frequent requesters are all immigration law firms.[17] Indeed, at these agencies, significant numbers of law firms are making over 100 requests a year. For example, at ICE there are sixty-seven such firms, the highest volume of which made 871 requests logged in the year's worth of data reported in this study.[18] At USCIS, some requesters topped 1,000 in a year.[19] These firms are predominantly small law firms, typically with a handful of attorneys (but almost never more than twenty) that handle exclusively immigration matters.[20]

Interestingly, a fourth component of DHS has emerged as a significant player in first-person immigration requests in very recent years. DHS's Office of Biometric Identity Management (OBIM) is a component for which FOIA requests have never been separately designated in DHS's annual FOIA reports.[21] OBIM was created in 2013 and holds biometric identification data for use by other DHS components and other federal and state law enforcement.[22] Prior to 2019, its requests were reported as National Protection and Programs Directorate (NPPD) requests which, in this study's baseline year, FY 2016, numbered 19,557,[23] and then under the

[14] 2015 FOIA Reports Summary, *supra* note 3, at ii.

[15] DHS Backlog Reduction Plan *supra* note 13, at 5.

[16] Interview with Dr. James V.M.L. Holzer, Jimmy Wolfrey & Amy Bennett, *supra* note 1.

[17] ICE Data, *supra* note 10; CBP Data, *supra* note 12; Electronic Reading Room, U.S. Citizenship & Immigration Servs., www.uscis.gov/about-us/electronic-reading-room (filter by "FOIA Logs") [hereinafter USCIS Data]. The dataset compiled includes the months between October 2014 and September 2015, representing FY 2015.

[18] ICE Data, *supra* note 10.

[19] USCIS Data, *supra* note 17.

[20] *See, e.g.*, *Services*, Rudolph, Baker & Assocs. LLP, jamesbrudolph.com/en/servicios (last visited Nov. 20, 2020); Law Office of Robert B. Jobe, jobelaw.com (last visited Nov. 20, 2020); Law Offices of Manuel Solis, manuelsolis.com/en (last visited Nov. 20, 2020).

[21] *See* DHS 2015 FOIA Annual Report, *supra* note 9, at ii; U.S. Dep't of Homeland Sec., 2016 Freedom of Information Act Report, at vii (Feb. 2017); U.S. Dep't of Homeland Sec., 2017 Freedom of Information Act Report, at vii (Feb. 2018); U.S. Dep't of Homeland Sec., 2018 Freedom of Information Act Report, at vii (Mar. 2019) [hereinafter DHS 2018 Annual FOIA Report]; DHS 2019 FOIA Annual Report, *supra* note 7, at 5, 14, 29.

[22] *Office of Biometric Identity Management*, U.S. Dep't of Homeland Sec. (Aug. 27, 2020), www.dhs.gov/obim#.

[23] *See* email from Amy Bennett, Acting Dir., FOIA Policy, Compliance & Training, U.S. Dep't of Homeland Sec. (Apr. 8, 2020) (on file with author). Bennett also noted that "[t]here has been a massive increase in these requests over the last few years."

Cybersecurity and Infrastructure Security Agency (CISA) when CISA took over NPPD's responsibilities.[24] Starting in 2019, DHS's central Privacy Office took over processing OBIM requests directly, in part to respond to an increasing backlog at that component, and in part to create a method of training FOIA processors on high-volume routine requests.[25]

As a result, the Privacy Office, which was not included in this study because of the tiny volume of requests received in this study's baseline year, jumped from receiving 1,448 in FY 2018 to 43,024 in FY 2019.[26] CISA (previously NPPD), went from 37,516 requests in FY 2018[27] to 353 requests received in FY 2019.[28] Thus, OBIM is accounting now for more than 40,000 requests per year and growing, and, as described in further detail below, these requests are of the same first-person immigration nature as the requests to USCIS, ICE, and CBP.

DHS is clearly the largest player in first-person immigration requests, but it is not the only one. Outside DHS, the single biggest recipient of first-person immigration requests is the Department of State. There, the FOIA logs available were deeply imperfect and difficult to decipher.[29] Yet, they revealed that immigration-related records dominate the subject matters of the request; a full 63.5 percent of requests contained one of the following immigration terms: visa, I-130, passport, I-94, or A File.[30] Of these, "visa" was by far the most common term, appearing alone in more than half of all requests.[31] Moreover, nearly two-thirds of requests are first-person as evidenced by the redaction of the name of the requester in the logs.[32]

[24] DHS 2019 FOIA ANNUAL REPORT, *supra* note 7, at 5 n.2.

[25] Interview with Dr. James V.M.L. Holzer, Jimmy Wolfrey & Amy Bennett, *supra* note 1. OBIM requests used to be counted under the NPPD/CISA component of DHS in its Annual FOIA Report. *Id.*

[26] DHS 2019 FOIA ANNUAL REPORT, *supra* note 7, at 14.

[27] DHS 2018 FOIA ANNUAL REPORT, *supra* note 21,at 6.

[28] DHS 2019 FOIA ANNUAL REPORT, *supra* note 7, at 14.

[29] Virtual Reading Room, U.S. Dep't of State, foia.state.gov/Search/Search.aspx (search for "FOIA Log" select "FOIA LOG - CASES RECEIVED BETWEEN 1/1/2014 AND 12/31/2014") [hereinafter State Data].

The reason for the difficulty is twofold. First, I was unable to obtain logs in response to my FOIA request, so I used a set of publicly available logs for the only year that was posted on their website, 2014. Second, the logs were posted in a non-machine-readable PDF file which I used optical character recognition software to convert. That process, however, required many hours of hand-cleaning for the results to be coherent. Even with that effort, I ended up with one list of names of requesters for those requests where they were non-exempt and one list of subject matters for all requests, but only the first line if the subject of the request was multiple lines. I calculated the exempt requester names using the difference in the number of subject matters and the number of names, since exempt requester names simply did not show up.

[30] An I-130 is a form to petition for a noncitizen relative and an I-94 is a CBP arrival or departure record.

[31] State Data, *supra* note 29. "Visa" appeared 4185 out of 7,561 times, representing 55.3 percent of all requests. *Id.*

[32] *Id.* Of 7,561 requests in the logs I obtained, 4,865 of the requesters' names were redacted under (b)(6), FOIA's principal privacy exemption, representing 64 percent. *Id.*

While the format of the data does not permit reporting how many of the immigration-related requests are first-person and vice versa, a look at the underlying data shows nearly a one-to-one matchup. Most requests with redacted requester names are for "Immigration records regarding [redacted]" or "I-130 visa petition regarding [redacted]" or "Visa records regarding [redacted]."[33] To be sure, some immigration related requests are filed by family members, some may be genealogical or historical research, but when the requester name is redacted we can be fairly confident that the requester is seeking their own records. Scaled up to today's total requests at the State Department, if about two-thirds are first-person immigration requests, that would translate to about 18,000 such requests a year to State.[34]

The Department of Justice is the locus of another enormous tranche of first-person immigration requests. It houses the Executive Office for Immigration Review (EOIR), which is the division that runs immigration courts.[35] These courts, which are administrative tribunals, adjudicate removal cases and the Board of Immigration Appeals (BIA), also housed in EOIR, hears appeals from those adjudications.[36] EOIR receives by far the biggest share of all FOIA requests directed to DOJ; in FY 2016, 35,500 out of a total 73,103, or 48.5 percent.[37] That number has grown to 55,499 in FY 2019, or 58.3 percent of DOJ's total.[38] While I have been unable to obtain FOIA logs from EOIR, the nature of the agency's activities combined with interviews with immigration attorneys strongly suggest that, just as with DHS, these are nearly all first-person requests for immigration records pertaining to an individual.[39] Thus, DOJ's overall numbers are driven in large part by first-person immigration requesting.

First-person requests can also be found in smaller – but still significant – numbers in other departments. Two in particular stand out: DOL and HHS. At the Administration for Children and Families (ACF) at HHS, 551 of 851 requests (sixty-five percent) in the studied year were for immigration records, and most of the requesters that filed multiple requests were the same set of immigration firms

[33] *Id.*

[34] State received 27,856 requests in FY 2016; if sixty-four percent were first-person that would mean 17,827 first-person requests were among them. U.S. Dep't of State, Freedom of Information Act Annual Report Fiscal Year 2017, at 40.

[35] *About the Office*, U.S. Dep't of Justice (Aug. 14, 2018), www.justice.gov/eoir/about-office.

[36] *Id.*

[37] U.S. Dep't of Justice, Annual Freedom of Information Act Report Fiscal Year 2016, at 25.

[38] U.S. Dep't of Justice, Annual Freedom of Information Act Report Fiscal Year 2019, at 18.

[39] *See, e.g.*, Telephone Interview with Robert Blackshear, Atty's, Law Firm 2 (Apr. 19, 2017). *See also How to Submit a Request*, U.S. Dep't of Justice (Aug. 12, 2020), www.justice.gov/eoir/foia-submit%20a%20request (enumerating answers to frequently questions, including "How do I request records about myself?").

represented on the USCIS, ICE, and CBP logs.[40] The reason ACF holds immigration-related records is because its Office of Refugee Resettlement (ORR) is responsible for caring for unaccompanied noncitizen minors found in the United States,[41] a function that gained particular publicity when it was charged with housing minors who arrived with families but who were separated at the border.[42] ORR thus holds records that pertain to the child's immigration status and sometimes that of their family.

At Labor, the Employment and Training Administration (ETA) processes Foreign Labor Certifications, which is a requirement for employers seeking to hire foreign workers on employment-based visas.[43] While ETA does not process the visas, the certification does involve collection of information about the foreign national applicant the employer is seeking to hire.[44] As a result, Labor holds some immigration-related records. While I was unable to obtain FOIA logs at ETA, ETA receives the third-highest volume of FOIA requests of all DOL components,[45] and from speaking with senior FOIA officials at Labor, it appears those numbers are driven by first-person immigration requesting.[46]

To sum up, immigration-driven first-person requesting alone is over half the federal government's total FOIA requests, and is growing in absolute numbers in proportion to total FOIA requests every year. These requesters are responsible for nearly all of DHS's requests, and are driving significant numbers at State, DOJ, HHS, and Labor. Thus, there is no understanding the reality of FOIA today without understanding first-person immigration requests.

To explore the underlying reasons for these requests, I interviewed immigration attorneys engaged in relatively frequent FOIA requesting.[47] Attorneys explained to me they almost always file multiple requests about the same client to different agencies or components of agencies, including the ones just described. Some

40 U.S. Dep't of Health & Human Servs., Admin. for Children & Families, Freedom of Information Act Response to April 15, 2016 Request by Margaret B. Kwoka (on file with author).

41 *Unaccompanied Alien Children*, Office of Refugee Resettlement, www.acf.hhs.gov/orr/programs/ucs (last visited Nov. 20, 2020).

42 U.S. Dep't of Health & Human Servs., Office of Inspector Gen., OEI-BL-18-00511, Separated Children Placed in Office of Refugee Resettlement Care 1 (Jan. 2019).

43 *About Foreign Labor Certification*, U.S. Dep't of Labor, Emp't & Training Admin. (Jan. 6, 2020), www.foreignlaborcert.doleta.gov/about.cfm.

44 *Id.*

45 ETA received 1,360 requests in FY2016, coming in third after OSHA and WHD. U.S. Dep't of Labor, Freedom of Information Act Annual Report for Fiscal Year 2016.

46 Telephone Interview with Ginger McCall, Former Att'y Advisor, Office of the Solicitor, U.S. Dep't of Labor (May 10, 2019).

47 The results of these interviews were originally reported in greater detail in a previous study, alongside documentation of the relevant IRB approval. *See* Margaret B. Kwoka, *First-Person FOIA*, 127 Yale L.J. 2204, 2227 (2018). Pursuant to protocols approved by the Institutional Review Board at the University of Denver, all interviews with attorneys are cited to pseudonyms. The interviews with reporters and government officials use the interviewee's actual names.

attorneys automatically file with at least two if not all three of the major DHS components: USCIS, ICE, and CBP.[48] More than one attorney noted the increasing utility of requests to OBIM, which at least one attorney asserted produced better results because the requests are submitted with a fingerprint which is used to locate the responsive records.[49] Attorneys also mentioned sometimes requesting with agencies outside of DHS, such as State.[50] Thus, attorneys were nearly unanimous that for each client, two, three or more FOIA requests were usually needed depending on the circumstances.

These attorneys confirmed that they are using FOIA almost exclusively to request their clients' own files on behalf of the clients, with some limited number of requests submitted for the immigration records of their client's family member.[51] The records these requesters are seeking are mostly contained in a noncitizen's "Alien File" or "A-File"; this file is the official immigration record held by the government on each noncitizen.[52] It contains records of prior applications for visas or other immigration benefits, notes taken by immigration officials on any interactions the individual may have had with agency officials (including official interview notes), and documentation of prior official entry to or exit from the United States or apprehension by border officials, among other records.[53]

The accounts given by the lawyers I talked to underscore the importance of first-person requesting in the immigration context. As DHS's Privacy Office itself describes, A-file and other first-person immigration request information may be necessary for "applications for benefits and appearance in immigration court" and are often "personally critical and time-sensitive."[54] Lawyers confirm these two categories of cases for which records obtained under FOIA are the driving force behind these requests; that is, removal cases where the government is attempting to deport a noncitizen, and noncitizens seeking to access certain immigration benefits such as a new or different visa or application for naturalization.

48 Telephone Interview with Russel Flores, Att'y, Law Firm 1 (Apr. 14, 2017); Telephone Interview with Gloria Glen, Att'y, Law Firm 1 (May 1, 2017); Telephone Interview with Elizabeth Hilton, Att'y, Law Firm 1 (May 2, 2017).

49 Telephone Interview with John Rivera, Att'y, Law Firm 5 (June 1, 2017); Telephone Interview with Robert Blackshear, *supra* note 39; *See* email from Amy Bennett, *supra* note 23 (explaining that OBIM requests are "usually requesters seeking A-File numbers based on fingerprint cards").

50 Telephone Interview with William Yates, Att'y, Law Firm 4 (May 24, 2017).

51 Telephone Interview with Peggy Brewer, Att'y, Law Firm 3 (May 19, 2017); Telephone Interview with Robert Blackshear, *supra* note 39; Telephone Interview with Russell Flores, *supra* note 48; Telephone Interview with Gloria Glen, *supra* note 48; Telephone Interview with Elizabeth Hilton, *supra* note 48.

52 DHS Backlog Reduction Plan., *supra* note 13, at 5.

53 Geoffrey Heeren, *Shattering the One-Way Mirror: Discovery in Immigration Court*, 79 Brook. L. Rev. 1569, 1604–07 (2014).

54 DHS Backlog Reduction Plan, *supra* note 13, at 4.

To start with removal proceedings, lawyers' use of immigration records illuminates how FOIA serves the same purpose in these cases as discovery would in a civil or criminal case in court.[55] Lawyers need their clients' own prior statements to immigration officials, their clients' past applications for benefits, and the records of any criminal justice involvement the government has about their clients.[56] These records are crucial to preparing a defense; they allow the lawyers to research any inconsistencies, analyze whether the government has properly categorized certain criminal matters, and prove certain facts about the noncitizen's immigration history.[57] Because ICE attorneys are not required to turn these records over to the noncitizen, FOIA is the only option.

One lawyer I talked to described how the government is, in fact, often incorrect about whether certain state crimes are sufficient basis to support removal, since state statutes vary greatly between them and numerous offenses are inconsistently described under state law.[58] In those cases, seeing the conviction records on which the government is relying is crucial to mounting a defense.[59] But that is just one example; litigating without the results of a FOIA request is like litigating blindfolded. For that reason, one lawyer said that the immigration judges he appears before typically ask to ensure he filed a FOIA request as to a given case.[60]

By the numbers, FOIA requests connected to pending removal cases appear to be a small fraction of first-person immigration requests. Only USCIS tracks these requests separately, and in the year for which data is included in this study, only three perecent of total requests were designated as related to pending removal proceedings.[61] That said, three percent of USCIS requests these days amounts to more than 6,000 requests a year alone.[62] Moreover, for every one of those requests, there are likely two or three more to other immigration agencies for the same noncitizen. And, USCIS's designation likely undercounts those requests tied to pending proceedings because to qualify for this priority tracking a requester must submit certain documentation of a pending court date.[63] Thus, requests pertaining to pending removal proceedings are surely substantial, even if other types of first-person immigration requests far outnumber them.

[55] *See* Heeren, *supra* note 53, at 1622–24.

[56] *Id.*

[57] *Id.*

[58] Telephone Interview with Robert Blackshear, *supra* note 39.

[59] *Id.*

[60] Telephone Interview with Russell Flores, *supra* note 48.

[61] *See* USCIS Data, *supra* note 17. In fiscal year 2015, USCIS did not begin tracking these requests separately as "track 3" requests until April, and thus only five months of data are used in calculating this figure. The raw numbers are 2,599 "track 3" requests, that is, requests related to a pending deportation proceeding, out of 82,402 total requests over that five-month period. *Id.*

[62] *Id.*

[63] U.S. Citizenship & Immigration Servs., Freedom of Information Act Request Guide 6 (2019).

Beyond defending against removal, first-person immigration requesting is used to obtain documents needed in connection with a pending or anticipated application for some sort of affirmative immigration benefit. These applications might be a petition for an immigrant visa from abroad,[64] an affirmative claim for asylum,[65] an adjustment of status from a nonimmigrant visa to a permanent resident visa (also known as a green card),[66] or an application for naturalization.[67] Lawyers representing clients seeking these benefits were equally adamant about FOIA's crucial role.

There are two principal ways in which documents obtained under FOIA are important in these instances. The first is akin to FOIA's role in removal proceedings: to confirm eligibility and obtain necessary details to make the best case possible for the benefit sought. For example, if someone is seeking to adjust their status from a nonimmigrant visa to a permanent resident visa, they will want copies of records pertaining to their original visa to ensure the new application contains all the correct details and is consistent with past submissions.[68]

Moreover, lawyers want to ensure eligibility. For example, they use FOIA to confirm that the government does not have records suggesting criminal history or other reasons why the applicant would not be eligible for a particular visa or for naturalization.[69] Or, if someone who is undocumented and entered the United States without a visa of any sort wants to apply for permanent residence, they are required to leave the United States before submitting an application.[70] Many times, however, individuals have had previous interactions with the border patrol. They may have been apprehended and sent back over the border without knowing what legal process was used; but the legal process can make all the difference. A voluntary return would not prevent them from obtaining a green card; an expedited removal, on the other hand, would.[71] Knowing precisely what happened is crucial before someone takes the risky step to leave the country in order to submit their application, and multiple attorneys cited the absolutely necessity of FOIA in these circumstances.[72]

64 8 U.S.C. §§ 1153, 1154 (2018).

65 *Id.* at § 1158.

66 *Id.* at § 1255(a).

67 *Id.* at § 1421.

68 Telephone Interview with Robert Blackshear, *supra* note 39.

69 *See, e.g., id.* (explaining that his firm will not file an application for naturalization without the results of FOIA requests unless the client signs a waiver because it is so risky).

70 8 U.S.C. §§ 1153, 1154; *see also id.*; 8 U.S.C. § 1255 (allowing persons to apply from within the United States if admitted at entry).

71 *See* 8 U.S.C. § 1182(a)(9)(C)(i) (barring permanently from obtaining admission to the United States, including on a green card, anyone who has previously been removed after being unlawfully present for more than one year); *see also Voluntary Departure*, U.S. Citizenship & Immigration Servs., www.uscis.gov/tools/glossary/voluntary-departure (last visited Nov. 20, 2020) (describing a less formal process that is not enumerated in the INA).

72 *See, e.g.*, Telephone Interview with Russell Flores, *supra* note 48. (citing the severity of the consequence of leaving the country and not being able to return when deciding "whether to

The second reason FOIA is so important for applicants for immigration benefits is to obtain records the noncitizen needs to submit with the application, but which they no longer have in their possession. Sometimes those records are previous applications, such as to support a family-based petition for a visa,[73] or sometimes they are proof of lawful entry needed for a green card application.[74] Regardless, they are records that the noncitizen may have had in their possession in the past, but which the agency retains and which are needed in conjunction with the new submission. As one attorney put it, "a lot of people lose paperwork over the course of the twenty years that they're waiting for their petition [for a family member] to become current [on the waiting list]."[75]

These accounts document why FOIA is so critically important to noncitizens with matters before an immigration agency, be it defending against enforcement (removal) or seeking benefits the agencies administer. Records obtained under FOIA promote fairness and accuracy in these adjudications and agency determinations, as they bring to bear the full adversarial process that is a hallmark of our judicial system. FOIA has been described by Professor David Pozen as conferring "due process benefits" in these situations, but he notes that "FOIA itself is ill-suited to the task."[76] Indeed, that likely understates the ways in which FOIA fails to serve individuals' interests adequately.

One serious – sometimes catastrophic – limitation of FOIA is timeliness. In a recent class certification order, a district judge, noting that FOIA was "the only way a noncitizen can obtain an A-File," described the serious problems that result from agencies' long delays in responding to requests.[77] He cited, as examples: clients who remain detained (imprisoned) for longer periods of time because of the delay; the risk of deportation someone faces if they have to delay filing an application for asylum or other relief; prolonged family separation for clients waiting to naturalize in order to file a petition for an immediate family member; the inability to travel to visit a sick family member because of the risk related to re-entry; and the loss of public assistance associated with lack of proof of immigration status.[78]

Lawyers with whom I spoke cited the very same concerns. Indeed, every single immigration lawyer I spoke to had clients for whom a response to a FOIA request

put them in the limelight of immigration"); Telephone Interview with Peggy Brewer, *supra* note 51 (explaining that "before they leave the U.S., we prioritize FOIA").

[73] *Petition for Alien Relative, I-130*, U.S. Citizenship & Immigration Servs., www.uscis.gov/sites/default/files/document/forms/i-130.pdf (last visited Nov. 20, 2020).

[74] *Official Site for Travelers Visiting the United States: Apply for or Retrieve Form I-94, Request Travel History and Check Travel Compliance*, U.S. Customs & Border Prot., i94.cbp.dhs.gov/I94 (last visited Nov. 20, 2020).

[75] Telephone Interview with Peggy Brewer, *supra* note 51.

[76] David Pozen, *Freedom of Information beyond the Freedom of Information Act*, 165 U. Pa. L. Rev.1097, 1137–38 (2017).

[77] Nightingale v. U.S. Citizenship & Immigration Servs., 333 F.R.D. 449, 453 (N.D. Cal. 2019).

[78] *Id.* at 453–54.

came too late to help their case.[79] For those lawyers with detained clients, the responses almost never came in time,[80] and many detained clients prefer to give up and return to their home countries rather than wait in detention for needed documents to fight their case, thereby preventing a lawyer from even ascertaining what relief from removal might be available.[81]

Beyond the removal context, delays in obtaining documents under FOIA present significant risk for those clients seeking affirmative immigration benefits too. For clients who want to naturalize, each day that passes waiting for documents in response to FOIA requests represents additional risk that an intervening event might compromise their immigration status.[82] For undocumented clients who are seeking to adjust their status to permanent residence, the risk is even more obvious; while waiting to get necessary documentation for a visa for which they do in fact qualify, they could be apprehended and deported.[83]

Critically, lawyers cited examples in which the response to a FOIA request came so late they had to act on the client's behalf without the requested records. Sometimes, when the records finally came, lawyers would have done something differently. These situations are particularly troubling, suggesting the outcomes of cases might be different – less fair and accurate – because of the timing of the response to a FOIA request. As one lawyer said, "there ... [have] been times where guys have been removed and then the FOIA result comes back and my strategy would have been different."[84] Another lawyer explained that she submitted an application for a visa for one client before the response to a FOIA request was obtained, and once she got it, she realized she should have submitted an additional application for a waiver in connection with the client's immigration history that was previously unknown.[85] These are, to say the least, highly prejudicial outcomes for individuals in these situations.

For exactly these reasons there have been numerous lawsuits, including multiple class actions, over the timeliness of responses under FOIA in the immigration context.[86] In a recent such class action certified against USCIS, plaintiffs assert that

[79] Telephone Interview with Robert Blackshear, *supra* note 39; Telephone Interview with Peggy Brewer, *supra* note 51; Telephone Interview with Russell Flores, *supra* note 48; Telephone Interview with Gloria Glen, *supra* note 48; Telephone Interview with Elizabeth Hilton, *supra* note 48; Telephone Interview with John Rivera, *supra* note 49; Telephone Interview with William Yates, *supra* note 50.

[80] Telephone Interview with Robert Blackshear, *supra* note 39; Telephone Interview with Gloria Glen, *supra* note 48; Telephone Interview with John Rivera, *supra* note 49; Telephone Interview with William Yates, *supra* note 50.

[81] Telephone Interview with Russell Flores, *supra* note 48.

[82] Telephone Interview with Robert Blackshear, *supra* note 39.

[83] Telephone Interview with Russell Flores, *supra* note 48.

[84] Telephone Interview with Robert Blackshear, *supra* note 39.

[85] Telephone Interview with Peggy Brewer, *supra* note 51.

[86] *See, e.g.*, *Groups File Lawsuit Challenging Failures of CBP To Respond to FOIA Requests*, AM. IMMIGRATION COUNCIL (Mar. 13, 2015), www.americanimmigrationcouncil.org/news/groups-

some FOIA requests have been pending for more than a year, and routinely, requests are pending for many months.[87] Such allegations are not surprising; DHS's most recent annual report reveals that processing within the twenty business day deadline is the exception, not the rule.[88] To take just USCIS, even for requests designated to the simple track, only 16,840 out of 34,773 requests – less than half – were processed within that timeframe.[89] For complex requests, which is the designation given to most USCIS requests, only 41,950 out of 181,691 – or twenty-three percent – were processed within twenty business days.[90]

The timing of responses under FOIA is not the only problem for noncitizens seeking their immigration records. Records processing under FOIA often leads to incomplete production. Over-withholding records is a pervasive problem – well documented and spanning administrations – across the federal government.[91] Lawyers I spoke with cited examples where information they believe is crucial was withheld, sometimes because existing records were simply not located, and sometimes because the agency redacted information the lawyer believed the client was entitled to. These omissions can have devastating consequences. For one lawyer, a client was removed based on records that were not located or produced under FOIA, but which were later used by the agency against the client.[92] Another lawyer cited the redactions of the names of immigration officers who interacted with his client as preventing him from cross-examining them about what happened in those encounters.[93] A third lawyer said his own clients' previous statements to immigration officials were routinely redacted, prompting him to observe: "How do I properly prepare them for a direct and cross examination?"[94]

Whether or not these decisions under FOIA to redact or not produce certain records were lawful, clients and their lawyers almost never have the resources to challenge the decisions under FOIA. To do so requires a separate proceeding, beginning with an administrative appeal at the agency level, and potentially requiring a lawsuit brought under FOIA in federal court.[95] Lawyers cannot justify charging

file-lawsuit-challenging-failures-cbp-respond-foia-requests; Nightingale v. U.S. Citizenship & Immigration Servs., 333 F.R.D. 449 (N.D. Cal. 2019).

87 *Nightingale*, 333 F.R.D. at 455.

88 DHS 2019 FOIA Annual Report, *supra* note 7, at 2.

89 *Id.* at 22.

90 *Id.* at 23.

91 *See, e.g.*, Ted Bridis, *Obama Administration Sets New Record for Withholding FOIA Requests*, PBS (Mar. 18, 2015), www.pbs.org/newshour/rundown/obama-administration-sets-new-record-withholding-foia-requests.

92 *See* Telephone Interview with Robert Blackshear, *supra* note 39.

93 Telephone Interview with William Yates, *supra* note 50.

94 Telephone Interview with Robert Blackshear, *supra* note 39; Telephone Interview with Russell Flores, *supra* note 48 (explaining that "they don't give you the interview" of his clients).

95 5 U.S.C. § 552(a)(4).

their clients, most of whom are resource-strapped, for that additional time, and oftentimes the clients cannot wait for an additional process to unfold.[96]

The numbers bear this experience out. At DHS, in the most recent annual report, despite receiving just over 400,000 FOIA requests, the agency only received 6,240 appeals.[97] This tiny fraction of appeals is despite the fact that only 32,233 requests were granted in full, meaning all others were either completely or partially denied.[98] Thus, when information is withheld or records are not produced, it is highly unlikely that individuals seeking their own files are going to be able to effectively mount a challenge or ultimately obtain any improperly withheld information. As such, the information individuals get under FOIA is almost necessarily going to skew toward being incomplete.

First-person immigration requests are driving FOIA numbers across the federal government. They are driving FOIA practice at the largest-volume agencies, and the agencies with the biggest increases in requests received year over year. They are also critically important for the requesters. They can mean the difference between remaining with the families and separation, the difference between incarceration and freedom, or the difference between safety and death. For society, these requests represent a method – albeit highly imperfect – to provide basic protections of fairness and accuracy in agency determinations. But FOIA was not designed with hundreds of thousands of requesters asking for their own immigration history files, one by one. Because they were not imagined as the bulk of requesters, FOIA was also not designed to meet these crucial needs well. And it doesn't. It is better than nothing, but it also often fails these requesters, sometimes catastrophically. And this story is the story of what FOIA is actually doing, by the numbers, today.

96 *See* Telephone Interview with Robert Blackshear, *supra* note 39 (explaining that the firm "[r]arely" appeals a FOIA denial because "[t]he problem is time and money"); Telephone Interview with Russell Flores, *supra* note 48 ("[M]y clients, quite frankly, can't even pay me for an appeal to the FOIA, let alone going to [court]."); Telephone Interview with Gloria Glen, *supra* note 48 ("We haven't [appealed a FOIA denial] because A, we don't have the time, and B, I've never been paid to do that."). *But see* Telephone Interview with William Yates, *supra* note 50. ("We've done some [FOIA appeals], but . . . they're not too successful.").

97 DHS 2019 FOIA Annual Report, *supra* note 7, at 14, 17.

98 *Id.* at 15.

5

Other First-Person Requesting

Immigration is such an outlier in FOIA practice it defies easy comparison. There are, however, many other circumstances in which people use FOIA to get information about themselves. In these contexts, agencies can be roughly grouped by type of first-person FOIA use. To be sure, some of these other agencies do receive first-person requests analogous to immigration requests; that is, requests made in conjunction with defending against enforcement and attempting to secure agency administered benefits. This section begins by detailing the agencies for which those two analogous uses apply, and then fills out the rest of the first-person FOIA requesting picture by describing trends across various federal agencies evidenced in the data obtained for this study.

Importantly, like with immigration requests, these other first-person requesters typically have very legitimate, even critical, needs for the records. But as this Chapter will make clear, the uses these requesters are making of the records they receive serve largely private goals, rather than FOIA's central purpose of providing public knowledge about government activities. These private needs for government records are dominant across various types of agencies including law enforcement, benefits agencies, and others. And they dwarf the number of requests that are made for the purpose of engaging in public oversight.

A. AGENCIES AS POLICE

Beyond the immigration context, there are other agencies that act in a policing fashion, and it is at those agencies that first-person uses dominate in an analogous way. Before delving into the agencies showing this trend, it is worth clarifying that – with one notable exception – those agencies that engage in law enforcement activities in the regulatory context are not included in this description, as the FOIA requests at those agencies tend to be filed by regulated industry and their representatives, not from individuals seeking their own file. While these regulatory agencies will be discussed later in the commercial context, it is worth acknowledging that there is overlap between these two groups; that is, companies asking for records about investigations of themselves, for example, could be described as first-person. But as the later discussion will reveal, most commercial use is not first-person in the same way, and, in any event, a first-person commercial requester defending against enforcement is differently situated than an individual facing an administrative action.

The one exception to this rule is the Internal Revenue Service (IRS). The IRS, like the Department of Homeland Security, enforces federal law against individuals. And, like with the immigraiton enforcement agencies, the IRS receives substantial first-person requests in connection with those enforcement proceedings. To begin, the agency itself designated a full 2,914 out of its 7,913 – or 36.8 percent – as first-person in nature. That number, however, very likely undercounts first-person requesting by a significant margin. Indeed, the dominant repeat requesters among the remaining requests are tax attorneys, a sizeable portion of which are certain to be first-person in nature, as these attorneys are representing individuals with a tax dispute before the IRS, whether an audit appeal, a penalty assessment, or a collection on tax debts.[1]

Tax attorneys I interviewed described how they use FOIA as part of their representation. The attorneys I spoke with – identified as routine FOIA requesters from the IRS logs – all represent both individuals and companies in tax disputes as part of longstanding law practices, and use FOIA to get their own clients' files.[2] The records in the file can prove useful in uncovering, for example, evidence that the IRS did not follow the right procedures in assessing a penalty,[3] statements made by other potentially responsible taxpayers such as in innocent spouse cases,[4] and the investigative records needed to help a client appeal an audit, particularly when the client went through the initial audit without a lawyer.[5] Sometimes attorneys are able to get records less formally, for example from the IRS agent working on the client's audit case, but mostly attorneys report needing to rely on FOIA.[6] And, while the attorneys I spoke with represent both indivdiuals and businesses, most reported that the

1 U.S. Dep't of Treasury, Internal Revenue Serv., Freedom of Information Act Response to order in *Kwoka v. Internal Revenue Serv.*, 1:17-cv-1157-DLF, 2018 U.S. Dist. LEXIS 167547 (D.D.C. Sept. 28, 2018); IRS FOIA Logs, INTERNAL REVENUE SERV., https://www.irs.gov/privacy-disclosure/irs-foia-logs [hereinafter IRS Data].

2 Telephone Interview with Gideon Price, Att'y, Law Firm 14 (Jan. 12, 2021); Telephone Interview with Walker Glenn, Att'y, Law Firm 15 (Jan. 12, 2021); Telephone Interview with Tate Rowe, Att'y, Law Firm 16 (Jan. 12, 2021); Telephone Interview with Chandler Soto, Att'y, Law Firm 17 (Feb. 4, 2021).

3 Telephone Interview with Tate Rowe, *supra* note 2.

4 Telephone Interivew with Chandler Soto, *supra* note 2.

5 *Id.*; Telephone Interview with Tate Rowe, *supra* note 2; Telephone Interview with Gideon Price, *supra* note 2.

6 *See, e.g.*, Telephone Interview with Walker Glen, supra note 2; Telephone Interview with Tate Rowe, *supra* note 2.

majority of clients they serve are individuals.[7] FOIA requests to the IRS are therefore overwhelmingly first-person requests.

Beyond the regulatory policing context, there are four other agencies that receive substantial first-person FOIA requests connected to their general welfare policing activities: the US Army, the US Navy, the Veterans Health Administration (VHA), and the Transportation Security Administration (TSA). In the baseline year for this study, FY 2016, the VHA rang in with the seventh-highest volume of requests at 28,091, the US Army was ninth with 25,755 requests, and the US Navy came in eighteenth with 9,605. The TSA is a much smaller-volume agency, ranking 66th with only 769 requests.[8] At each of these agencies, reports concerning particular incidents, accidents, or policing interactions are frequently the subject of first-person requests.

The data on FOIA requesting at the US Army is deeply imperfect, and thus quantifying first-person requests was impossible. But the data does reveal that at least 22.7 percent of all Army requests appear to concern a Military Police Report.[9] Military Police are the law enforcement branch of the Military, and enforce general laws including policing traffic, investigating crimes, and responding to emergencies on military property, including bases in the United States and abroad.[10] Military Police Reports are filed when there is a potential crime investigated, just as police reports are filed by local law enforcement.

As to most of the Military Police Reports requested, the Army Logs simply designated the subject of the request as "Request for MP Rpt"[11] or "MPR" with a particular report number attached.[12] Some subject matter designations are more revealing, however, and demonstrate that the requester is asking about incidents involving themselves, such as when the requester was listed as "requesting a copy of a MP report he filed when someone did damage to his POV while parked at the Motor Pool,"[13] or "M.P. Report for 30 Nov 12 pertaining to himself."[14]

7 *See, e.g.*, Telephone Interivew with Chandler Soto, *supra* note 2.; Telephone Interview with Gideon Price, *supra* note 2.

8 *Annual FOIA Reports FY 2016*, U.S. Dep't of Justice, www.justice.gov/oip/annual-foia-reports-fy-2016 (last visited July 16, 2020).

9 Specifically, at the very least 3,822 out of 16,828 requests in the Calendar Year 2013 logs obtained for this study concerned Military Police Reports as indicated by containing one of a long list of related keywords for which the data was screened. However, since they are not uniformly labeled, there are clearly more subject matters pertaining to these reports that do not contain the various keywords for which the subjects were searched. *See* U.S. Dep't of Def., U.S. Army, Freedom of Information Act Response to Oct. 6, 2014 Request by Margaret B. Kwoka (on file with author) [hereinafter Army Data].

10 *See generally* Military Police: 31B, U.S. Army, www.goarmy.com/careers-and-jobs/browse-career-and-job-categories/legal-and-law-enforcement/military-police.html (last visited Nov. 20, 2020).

11 *See, e.g.*, Army Data, supra note 9, at Request No. FP-13-008143.

12 *See, e.g.*, *id.* at Request No. FP-13-008184.

13 *Id.* at Request No. FP-13-008402.

14 *Id.* at Request No. FP-13-009043.

These occasional glimpses suggesting these reports are mostly requested in a first-person capacity are confirmed by the directions given by the base at which the Military Police are trained for the Army, the Joint Base Lewis-McChord in Washington State. The base states that these reports, along with Accident Investigation Forms, "may be released to any person named in the report, legal and registered owners of the vehicles involved, owners or property damaged in an accident or their representatives." It then describes that any request will be forwarded to the FOIA office for review prior to release.[15] Thus, these requesters are likely to be nearly all first-person in nature, and they number in the thousands, if their numbers are proportional to today's total Army requests.[16]

The Navy logs reveal a similar pattern. In the year included in this study, 3,000 requests out of 9,719 requests – or 30.9 percent – had the requester's name redacted under FOIA's privacy exemption, indicating that the request is first-person in nature.[17] While the data obtained from the Navy is formatted in such a way that specific analysis of subject matters of those requests proved impossible, a rough look through the data suggested a majority of those requests concern either "accident" or "incident" reports that would be filed by military police.[18]

At the VHA, the agency categorizes the subject matters of their requests and designates one group as requests for Police/Uniform Offense Reports, which numbered 3,787 in the year for which data were obtained, representing 14.3 percent of the VHA's total requests.[19] Of those, 65 percent were designated as made under both FOIA and the Privacy Act, indicating at least that number is first-person in nature.[20] Like with other agencies, these reports are typically made by VA police officers in the course of investigations into incidents on VA property.[21]

TSA receives a fraction of the number of requests the major branches of the military and the VA do, but nonetheless a similar percentage – 25.3 percent – are first-person in nature as indicated by the names of the requesters redacted from the logs for privacy reasons.[22] Of those, most of the subject matters appear to seek video

[15] *Directorate of Emergency Services*, Joint Base Lewis-McChord, www.lewis-mcchord.army.mil/des/le_polices_services.htm (last visited Nov. 20, 2020).

[16] If 22.7 percent of Army requests are for Military Police Reports, translated to the most recent request totals, 22.7 percent of FY 2019's 25,680 requests would be 5,829 requests.

[17] U.S. Dep't of Def., U.S. Navy, Freedom of Information Act Response to Apr. 18, 2016 Request and Nov. 1, 2016 Administrative Appeal by Margaret B. Kwoka (on file with author) [hereinafter Navy Data].

[18] *Id.*

[19] U.S. Dep't of Veterans Affairs, Veterans Health Admin., Freedom of Information Act Response to Apr. 15, 2016 Request by Margaret B. Kwoka (on file with author) [hereinafter VHA Data].

[20] *Id.*

[21] U.S. Dep't of Veterans Affairs, VA Handbook 0730/ 3, Security and Law Enforcement 8 (2014).

[22] U.S. Dep't of Homeland Sec., Transp. Security Admin., Freedom of Information Act Response to Feb. 26, 2018 Request by Margaret B. Kwoka (on file with author); U.S. Dep't of Homeland

of security at an airport for an incident involving the requester.[23] Thus, it appears these records pertain to the TSA's policing function and the interaction of TSA police with the requester.

The specific needs for these records are not revealed in the logs, nor are they easily ascertained as the identity of the requesters are obscured (and typically not represented by law firms), but one might surmise the same types of uses as individuals have for police reports from state and local law enforcement agencies.[24] For example, many people need police reports to make insurance claims, as with auto accidents, or victims may need police reports to pursue civil lawsuits. Potential criminal defendants may also want police reports, though typically these are available from the prosecution during the court martial trial discovery process rather than going through FOIA.[25]

While these four agencies provide helpful examples of this dynamic of requesting, they are almost certainly not the only agencies across the federal government to have a policing function among their primary roles. Those agencies that act more like local police, but on federal property, are likely to receive lots of requests for police reports and records of citizen-police interactions from the individuals concerned, just as local police departments do. This set of requests can be considered an analog to some of the immigration requests, at least insofar as individuals are looking for files that document their past interactions with federal law enforcement. In that way, they may be engaged in private oversight, that is, holding the agency accountable privately in their dealings with the requester. But they are not, by and large, securing records to publicize widely the agency's activities or invoke the democratic process of holding agencies accountable.

B. AGENCIES AS BENEFITS ADMINISTRATORS

The other group of first person requesters analogous to immigration requesters are those requesters seeking their own files as part of their bid to receive a particular agency benefit, only at these other agencies the benefits are largely monetary rather than visa or immigration status changes. For these requesters, it appears that by obtaining their own files from government agencies they can verify they are

Sec., Transp. Security Admin., FOIA Reading Room, www.tsa.gov/foia/readingroom (search for FOIA Logs - FY 2017) [hereinafter TSA Data].

23 *Id.*

24 *See, e.g.*, Benjamin R. Beede, *Police, Military*, *in* ENCYCLOPEDIA OF MILITARY SCIENCE 1109, 1109 (Kurt G. Piehler ed., 2003) (flagging as the major difference between civilian and military law enforcement the fact that military police run jails and prisons, but concluding they are otherwise analogous).

25 *See generally* U.S. DEP'T OF DEFENSE, JOINT SERV. COMM. ON MILITARY JUSTICE, 2019 MANUAL FOR COURTS-MARTIAL UNITED STATES, at II-67 (providing broad discovery rights about military charges).

receiving the correct benefits, challenge the benefits they are receiving, or apply for subsequent benefits.

At least six agencies included in this study have significant groups of first-person requesters that fall in this category. Four of them administer programs disbursing federal funds to individuals with circumstances that qualify for their particular federal programs, and evidence significant numbers of requests designed to facilitate access to those benefits: the Pension Benefit Guaranty Corporation (PBCG), the Federal Emergency Management Agency (FEMA), the Small Business Administration (SBA), and the Social Security Administration (SSA). At two others, the situation is slightly different because the requesters are using FOIA to get records from one agency as part of a bid for government benefits administered by a different agency: these include the Veterans Health Administration (VHA) and the National Archives and Records Administration (NARA). At each agency, first-person requesters seeking access to government benefits drive a significant fraction of the agency's total FOIA requests.

The PBCG essentially provides insurance for private defined-benefit pension plans and, when those plans fail, take over administering direct payments to plan participants.[26] At PBCG, 16.7 percent of requesters in the study year, which numbered 1,640 total, appear to be first-person requesters as evidenced by the privacy redaction of the requester's name in the log.[27] Yet, this number is likely a significant undercount of first-person requesters for two reasons: first, it does not appear from the logs that all first-person requester's names are redacted; and, second, many first-person requests are being made through representatives.[28]

The agency itself has in the past described its requester base as dominated by pension plan participants seeking access to their own records, presumably at least in part to verify accuracy, understand the benefits to which they are entitled, or better position themselves to contest the agency's benefits determinations.[29] To a large degree, the burden of these requests has been diminished by the agency's efforts to meet these information needs in other ways, efforts that are discussed in further detail in Chapter 10, but nonetheless first-person requesting is still very present at this agency. Another group of requesters at this agency, numbering 104 in the year for which data was obtained, are requesting 1099-R forms for deceased family members

[26] *Who We Are*, U.S. PENSION BENEFIT GUAR. CORP., www.pbgc.gov/about/who-we-are (last visited Nov. 23, 2020).

[27] Pension Benefit Guar. Corp., Freedom of Information Act Response to Mar. 26, 2018 Request by Margaret B. Kwoka (on file with author) [PBGC Data].

[28] One such example is discussed in greater detail with respect to income verification requests, *infra* Ch. 5, pt. G: Access to Private Services; *see also* PBGC Data, *supra* note 27.

[29] *See, e.g.*, PENSION BENEFIT GAUR. CORP., 2010 CHIEF FOIA OFFICER REPORT 2 (2010) ("[T]he majority of PBGC's requests come from pension plan participants seeking to access records pertaining to themselves and their pension plans.").

in order to file final tax returns.[30] These requesters do not fit neatly in the first-person box, because their request concerns their family member, but they serve similarly private ends and seek the records to submit as part of a separate governmental process.

FEMA's requester logs display a similar dominance of first-person requesting for private purposes. FEMA administers benefits designed to provide disaster relief and recovery assistance.[31] Out of 2,352 requests in the data year obtained, 401 had a redacted requester name indicating a first-person request.[32] Beyond that, however, around 1,360 requests came from law firms that apparently represent individuals in various capacities who are likely to be requesting their own files.[33] Sliced differently, the data reveal that 1,600 of the total requests pertain to a "claim" made to FEMA, and are thus highly likely to be first-person in nature, either filed alone or by their representative.[34] While some of these requesters are seeking records to resolve disputes with third-party insurers, discussed in greater detail below,[35] some are clearly attempting to secure benefits (or contest benefit denials) from FEMA itself. As FEMA explains, claimants can appeal disaster assistance decisions.[36] Thus, requests for claim files, seemingly about two-thirds of FEMA's total requests, are important sources of information for benefits claimants and recipients contesting agency decisions.

Like PBGC and FEMA, SBA issues monetary benefits. At SBA that assistance primarily comes in the form of guaranteeing certain private loans issued by banks to small businesses, loans that would otherwise be difficult to obtain on the private market.[37] Unfortunately, the data reflecting 969 requests in the study year do not provide a means for quantifying first-person requests. However, the FOIA logs reveal many requests with subject matters such as "I need a copy of my original loan document"[38] or "Applicant requests a copy of the credit report in regards to disaster

30 PBGC Data, *supra* note 27.

31 *About Us*, U.S. Fed. Emergency Mgmt. Assistance (Aug. 27, 2020), www.fema.gov/about-agency.

32 U.S. Dep't of Homeland Sec., Fed. Emergency Mgmt. Agency, Freedom of Information Act Response to Apr. 13, 2018 Request by Margaret B. Kwoka (on file with author) [hereinafter FEMA Data].

33 *Id.*

34 *Id.*

35 *See infra* pt. H.

36 *Request Records through the Freedom of Information Act or Privacy Act*, U.S. Fed. Emergency Mgmt. Assistance (June 22, 2020), www.fema.gov/about/offices/administrative/foia; *Frequently Asked Questions (FAQs)*, DisasterAssistance.gov (Nov. 19, 2020), www.disasterassistance.gov/help/faqs.

37 *Loans*, U.S. Small Bus. Admin., www.sba.gov/funding-programs/loans (last visited Nov. 23, 2020).

38 U.S. Small Bus. Admin., Freedom of Information Act Response to Mar. 6, 2016 Request by Margaret B. Kwoka (on file with author) [hereinafter SBA Data], at Request No. SBA-2017-000236.

application number [XXX]"[39] or "I need a copy of my promissory note from my SBA account Loan# [XXX]."[40] At this agency it has been more difficult to ascertain the possible purposes of making first-person requests for SBA loan information pertaining to the requester, but it is clear this practice is pervasive in the FOIA logs. Like at the other agencies, one can presume it is likely a mix of requesters seeking to contest benefits or access additional benefits from the agency itself and requesters seeking to use these documents to access third-party services.

SSA provides a final example of an agency that receives first-person FOIA requests from individuals seeking benefits from that agency. While this type of request is also not possible to quantify from the logs, SSA's website details how to make a FOIA request "[i]f you need your records regarding your claim for Social Security benefits."[41] These are likely fewer in number than other first-person uses at SSA described in greater detail below, but nonetheless are a nontrivial presence. An informal conversation with an SSA FOIA official revealed FOIA is typically used in this way when a minor child needs their deceased parent's information to make a derivative claim for benefits.

Finally, two other agencies demonstrate how FOIA requests for records can facilitate claiming benefits at a federal agency other than the agency to which the request is directed. At the VHA, a subset of first-person requests for medical records (which are generally discussed in further detail below) are clearly made for the purposes of obtaining Social Security Disability benefits or contesting the denial of those benefits. Many of the most frequent requesters at the VHA are lawyers making such requests on behalf their clients. For example, Binder and Binder, which made 139 requests in the study year, specializes in Social Security Disability claims.[42] Thus, a portion of requests, admittedly small compared to the overall volume of requests at the VHA, are filed for the purposes of obtaining or contesting the denial of government benefits, albeit at a different agency – the SSA.

At NARA the numbers in this regard are striking and perhaps surprising. While data was not obtained for this study, an interview with Kevin Pratt, Assistant Director for Military Records at the National Personnel Records Center, explained that his unit receives the majority of all NARA requests, numbering between 30,000 and 50,000 per year over the past several years. Of those FOIA requests, about half of them are seeking records necessary to claim the work opportunity tax credit, which is a tax benefit available to employers who hire a veteran.[43] As such, thousands – even tens of thousands – of requests a year are facilitating this benefit claim that is directed to a different agency, the IRS.

[39] *Id.* at Request No. SBA-2017-001508.

[40] *Id.* at Request No. SBA-2017-001225.

[41] *Guide to FOIA at SSA*, Soc. Sec. Admin., www.ssa.gov/foia (last visited Nov. 23, 2020).

[42] VHA Data, *supra* note 19.

[43] Telephone Interview with Kevin Pratt, Assistant Dir. for Military Records, Nat'l Peronnel Records Ctr., Nat'l Archives & Records Admin. (June 17, 2019).

C. AGENCIES AS EMPLOYERS

All agencies are, of course, employers. Indeed, scattered throughout every agency's FOIA log is undoubtedly a set of first-person requesters who are agency employees who want their personnel, disciplinary, or hiring records, or applicants for jobs who want the records about why their applications were denied. Even in many agencies where requests are dominated by other first-person interests or other interests such as commercial interests, some of these employment-related requests also appear scattered throughout the logs. At some agencies, officials have cited examples of these requests as constituting some of their first-person requests even where they are not evident from the logs.[44]

At two relatively smaller volume FOIA agencies included in this study, however, employment-related first-person requesting clearly drove a significant portion of FOIA practice. Moreover, requests at these agencies illustrate the kinds of employment-related requests other agencies may receive in small percentages of their total requests, but nonetheless are likely to exist across the federal government. These two agencies are the Department of Defense's (DoD) Office of Inspector General (OIG) and the Forest Service (FS) at the Department of Agriculture.

OIG received only 739 requests in the study year, but requesters' names were redacted in 418 of them, representing 56.6 percent of requesters.[45] Given the OIG's function as an internal investigator for the Defense Department, perhaps unsurprisingly, these first-person requesters are often asking for investigation files about themselves, complaints they filed, or their own whistleblower reports. For example, typical request summaries in the logs describe requests for "AR 15016 investigation conducted against myself, (b)(6)"[46] or "Status of his Whistleblower Reprisal Complaint against former employer, (b)(6)."[47] These types of records clearly arm employees with records they need to resolve a dispute with their employer, be it about their own alleged misconduct or the agency's.

At the FS, out of 1,724 requests there are 74 that are designated as jointly processed under FOIA and the Privacy Act.[48] The subject matters of those requests are plainly job related, either pertaining to rejected applicants or employment problems.

[44] *See, e.g.*, Telephone Interview with Eugene Baime, Supervisory Att'y., FOIA/PA Section, Office of the Gen. Counsel, Fed. Bureau of Prisons, U.S. Dep't. of Justice (Mar. 3, 2020) (estimating that BOP staff make hundreds of requests a year oftentimes pertaining to equal employment opportunity concerns or other investigations); *see also* U.S. Dep't of Justice, Fed. Bureau of Prisons, Freedom of Information Act Response to Feb. 20, 2018 Request by Margaret B. Kwoka (on file with author).

[45] U.S. Dep't of Def., Office of the Inspector Gen., Freedom of Information Act Responses to Feb. 20, 2018 Request by Margaret B. Kwoka (on file with author).

[46] *Id.* at Request No. DODOIG-2017-000198.

[47] *Id.* at Request No. DODOIG-2017-000252.

[48] U.S. Dep't of Agric., Forest Serv., Freedom of Information Act Response to Feb. 15, 2018 Request by Margaret B. Kwoka (on file with author).

A typical request of this nature asks for "a copy of the applications and/or resume of all the applicants selected for the Vacancy Announcements [listed]"[49] or "any and all records, documentation, transcripts, etc., involving employment harassment allegations made by (b)(6)."[50] These types of first-person requests demonstrate that the requester is attempting to inform themself or arm themself with respect to an actual or potential employment dispute with the agency.

One can easily imagine, and anecdotal evidence strongly supports this inference, that most other agencies are experiencing scattered requests of this nature on a routine basis as well. Conversations with agency officials routinely cite employees or applicants for agency jobs as a source of FOIA requests. For example, one agency official at the VHA noted an uptick in requests from rejected job applicants.[51] And isolated examples of these types of requests appear on the face of logs at various agencies in smaller quantities.

D. AGENCIES AS HEALTH CARE PROVIDERS

Some agencies act as direct health care providers and thus hold vast personal medical records for the individuals they serve. At these agencies, sometimes huge numbers of first-person requesters are using FOIA to access their own medical files. Among agencies included in this study, two in particular demonstrate this trend strongly: the Veterans Health Administration (VHA) and the Bureau of Prisons (BOP).

The VHA receives the vast majority of all requests to the VA as a whole. In the data year obtained, the VHA accounted for 86 percent of all VA requests, totaling 26,395 requests. Of those, a full 20,325 (or 77 percent) were designated as joint FOIA and Privacy Act requests, making them first-person in nature, and of those, 16,624 (or 81 percent) concerned veterans' medical records. That is, there is simply a huge volume of requesters seeking their own medical files.

While certain smaller pockets of requests for medical files at the VHA are evidently sought to facilitate access to other government benefits (such as disability claims) or third-party services (such as insurance), the vast majority of these requests are highly likely made by individuals seeking them for their own purposes, such as to bring past records to new health care providers (continuity of care) or simply to retain records for personal use or understanding.

Certainly, at BOP continuity of care and personal understanding of health records appears to dominate. There, the data obtained for this study makes quantifying either first-person requesters or requests for medical records impossible. However, a

[49] *Id.* at Request No. 2017-FS-WO-00034-FP.

[50] *Id.* at Request No. 2017-FSWO 00072 FP.

[51] Interview with Michael Sarich, FOIA Dir., Veterans Health Admin., U.S. Dep't of Veterans Affairs., in Arlington, Va. (July 23, 2019).

top BOP FOIA official, Eugene Baime, interviewed for this study, helpfully reviewed the unredacted records to provide estimates in this regard. To begin, he stated in no uncertain terms that "the vast majority of our request[s] are first party requests."[52] Indeed, his close review of about 750 pages of FOIA logs estimated between 55 percent and 60 percent of all requests were first-person or representatives of the individual's concerned (as indicated by the consent provided by the individual in question).[53] Baime also estimated that at least half of all requests made to BOP come by mail rather than email, due to the fact that inmates are not permitted to contact BOP by email, thereby indicating a high rate of current inmate requests.

Notably, of all requests, in a recent three-month sample Baime examined, approximately 40 percent of requests were for medical records.[54] He explained that a good portion of these requests are "continuity of care" requests. These types of requests are requests from previously incarcerated individuals who need their records to give to a new health care provider for continuing treatment or individuals expecting to be released soon and who want to take their health records with them.[55] Some much smaller number may pertain to potential civil claims or lawsuits about medical treatment or other conditions of confinement.[56]

Certainly, these agencies typify the need individuals have for access to their own medical files, but they are not the only federal agencies that provide direct health care services. One could imagine there may be similar trends at other agencies that have similar missions, including, for example, the Indian Health Service,[57] Immigration and Customs Enforcement Health Service Corps,[58] Peace Corps,[59] and the Military Health System,[60] all of which provide direct medical care to certain populations or constituencies. While this study does not have the data to support a claim that first-person requests for medical files are pervasive at these other agencies, the trends that are evident from VHA and BOP suggests that such a demand exists, and that absent other mechanisms for retrieving one's own health information, FOIA will be routinely used to request medical records.

52 Telephone Interview with Eugene Baime, *supra* note 44.

53 Email from Eugene Baime, Supervisory Att'y, FOIA/PA Section, Office of the Gen. Counsel, Fed. Bureau of Prisons, U.S. Dep't. of Justice, to Margaret B. Kwoka (Apr. 13, 2020) (on file with author).

54 *Id.* Specifically, he found 300 requests concerned medical records out of a sample of 786 requests.

55 *Id.*

56 *Id.*

57 *About IHS*, Indian Health Serv., www.ihs.gov/aboutihs (last visited Nov. 23, 2020).

58 *ICE Health Service Corps*, U.S. Immigration & Customs Enf't (Nov. 5, 2020), www.ice.gov/ice-health-service-corps.

59 *Health and Safety*, Peace Corps, www.peacecorps.gov/volunteer/health-and-safety (last visited Nov. 23, 2020).

60 *About the Military Health System*, Health.mil, www.health.mil/About-MHS (last visited Nov. 23, 2020).

E. AGENCIES AS ARCHIVES

Agencies sometimes unwittingly serve functions not imagined as part of their mission. Archival services is one of those side functions, and where archives exist, FOIA requesters seek records as part of their genealogy research to learn about their own families and family histories. This use is evident at three agencies with data included in this study: SSA, where it drives thousands of FOIA requests a year, BOP, and the Census Bureau.

At SSA, the agency received 22,044 requests in the year for which data was obtained. Of those, 11,080 were for the SS-5 form for an original social security card application, and another 4,448 were for Numident records, which are the extracted data from those SS-5 forms.[61] Together, these requests constitute 70.4 percent of all requests received by the SSA. While the purpose behind these requests is not immediately apparent from the logs, other indicators support genealogy research as a driving force. First, the requesters are far less concentrated, meaning many individuals are seeking these records on their own rather than through a lawyer representing them in an agency proceeding or third-party dispute.[62] Second, the agency's own website answers questions about using FOIA for genealogy research.[63] And third, prominent genealogy websites like Ancestry.com and Genealogy.com refer customers to the SSA website to make a request directly for SS-5 and Numident records.[64] Given the individualized nature of the requesting, it is very likely this is the significant driver of the volumes of requests for these records.

While SSA dominates by the numbers, genealogy research is present elsewhere in the federal government as well. The Census Bureau is a very small volume agency, having received only 292 requests for the year for which data was obtained. But 49, or almost 17 percent of those requests, were first-person, as indicated by the agency redacting the requester's name on the log under the privacy exemption.[65] Of those, the subject matters nearly all expressly pertain to genealogy research or for particular family records. They read, for example, "Information about family,"[66] or, "Obtain census records for family."[67]

[61] U.S. Soc. Sec. Admin., Freedom of Information Act Response to April 15, 2016 Request and March 17, 2017 Administrative Appeal by Margaret B. Kwoka (on file with author).

[62] *See id.*

[63] *Can You Provide a Copy of a Deceased Person's Social Security Number Application for Genealogical Research?*, Soc. Sec. Admin., https://faq.ssa.gov/en-US/Topic/article/KA-02585 (last visited Nov. 23, 2020).

[64] *U.S., Social Security Applications and Claims Index, 1936–2007*, Ancestry, http://search.ancestry.com/search/db.aspx?dbid=60901 (last visited Nov. 23, 2020); Rhonda R. McClure, *SSDI SS-5 Applications*, Genealogy.com (Jan. 11, 2001), www.genealogy.com/articles/over/heard011101.html.

[65] FOIA Logs, Fiscal Year 2013, U.S. Census Bureau, www.census.gov/about/policies/foia/foia_library/foia_logs.html.

[66] *Id.* at Request No. DOC-CEN-2013-000637.

[67] *Id.* at Request No. DOC-CEN-2013-001165.

Similarly, at BOP, while no numbers are available estimating the extent of the practice, FOIA Attorney Eugene Baime said that among first-person requesters, "one of the ones we get from family members quite a bit is genealogy type research about a family member formerly incarcerated in the past."[68] As such, it is clear that SSA is not alone in getting significant numbers of first-person requests that serve the personal interests of the requester in their quest to find out more about their own family.

F. THIRD-PARTY LITIGATION

Sometimes agencies hold records about individuals that are useful for those individuals in their quest to seek private remedies from third-party actors. These include personal injury, discrimination, and insurance disputes, among others. While a smattering of these types of requests is evident across a wide range of agencies, five agencies in particular display significant numbers of requests intended to vindicate rights against third parties. Moreover, these agencies demonstrate the breadth of these kinds of requests in the interests that are served.

The Equal Employment Opportunity Commission (EEOC) is a natural place to begin. It receives a relatively large volume of FOIA requests – 17,025 in the study year – and a full 95 percent of those requests are for a "charge file," which is the EEOC's investigative file for a charge of discrimination lodged by an employee against an employer under one of various civil rights statutes.[69] For statutory reasons, only the employee who filed the charge of discrimination and, in much more limited circumstances, the employer against whom the charge was filed, can obtain this file.[70] As such, these are first-person requests by definition.

One unique aspect of the EEOC's role in these third-party disputes is that, with the sole exception of claims brought under the Equal Pay Act, an employee is required to file a charge of discrimination with the EEOC prior to bringing a lawsuit to enforce anti-discrimination statutes like Title VII of the Civil Rights Act.[71] Only once the EEOC has completed its investigation (and decided not to pursue a lawsuit

[68] Telephone Interview with Eugene Baime, *supra* note 44.

[69] U.S. Equal Emp't Opportunity Comm'n, Freedom of Information Act Response to April 15, 2016 Request and Nov. 15, 2016 Administrative Appeal by Margaret B. Kwoka (on file with author) [hereinafter EEOC Data]. These statutes include Title VII of the Civil Rights Act, the Age Discrimination in Employment Act, the Americans with Disabilities Act, the Equal Pay Act, and the Genetic Information Nondiscrimination Act. *See also Laws Enforced by EEOC*, U.S. Equal Emp't Opportunity Comm., www.eeoc.gov/laws/statutes/index.cfm (last visited Nov. 23, 2020).

[70] *Freedom of Information Act*, Equal Emp't Opportunity Comm., www.eeoc.gov/foia (last visited Nov. 23, 2020) (explaining that "[y]ou can only request a charge file if you are the person who filed the charge . . . , or the employer who was accused of discrimination . . . , and the EEOC has completed its investigation of the charge of employment discrimination.").

[71] *Filing a Charge of Discrimination with the EEOC*, Equal Emp't Opportunity Comm., www.eeoc.gov/filing-charge-discrimination (last visited Nov. 23, 2020).

itself) is the employee issued a notice of right to sue which allows them to proceed to federal court within ninety days.[72] And, for statutory reasons, it is only during that ninety-day period that a charging party can file a FOIA request for the investigative file.[73]

All top requesters at the EEOC are employment law firms, and interviews with several employment lawyers reveal the importance of FOIA to their practice. Lawyers are unanimous that filing a FOIA request is essential for any client who has gone through the EEOC process and wants to file a lawsuit against their employer.[74] The records contained in the charge file include the employer's "position statement," which is essentially the employer's legal brief stating its response to the charge of discrimination, and any documents the employer submitted such as their EEO policies, employee's personnel file, or other evidence pertaining to the charge.[75] Some employment law firms are, indeed, very frequent filers, filing hundreds, sometimes pushing a thousand, requests a year.[76]

As with immigration attorneys, however, employment lawyers cited deep flaws associated with having to resort to FOIA to obtain their clients' own charge files. One attorney described the frequency with which potential clients come to him too late in their ninety-day window to obtain a response to a FOIA request, and he will simply decline to take their case as a result. Since he cannot see the EEOC's file without going through the FOIA process, he cannot evaluate the merits of a case and advise a client, and so bringing a lawsuit would simply be too risky.[77] Other attorneys cited similar problems, such as receiving key documents on the eve of the deadline for a lawsuit and having those documents change strategy or representation, leaving the client with few alternatives.[78]

At base, these disputes are between third parties, not between an individual and the agency, but there is certainly some blurring of the line with respect to the EEOC because of its unique role providing administrative remedies in some cases. As one attorney put it, the EEOC's finding of "cause" to believe discrimination occurred

[72] *Id.*

[73] *Freedom of Information Act*, *supra* note 70.

[74] Telephone Interview with Gerald Prada, Att'y, Law Firm 12 (Nov. 15, 2017); Telephone Interview with Stephanie Romo, Att'y, Law Firm 10 (Aug. 3, 2017); Telephone Interview with Carl Sapp, Att'y, Law Firm 13 (Nov. 15, 2017); Telephone Interview with Tony Schaver, Att'y, Law Firm 11 (Sept. 27, 2017).

[75] Telephone Interview with Stephanie Romo, *supra* note 74; Telephone Interview with Gerald Prada, *supra* note 74.

[76] For example, Ogletree, Deakins, Nash, Smoak & Stewart made 762 requests in FY 2015, Littler Mendelson, P.C. made 661, and Jackson & Associates Law Firm made 532. EEOC Data, *supra* note 69.

[77] Telephone Interview with Tony Schaver, *supra* note 74.

[78] Telephone Interview with Gerald Prada, *supra* note 74; Telephone Interview with Carl Sapp, *supra* note 74.

versus "no cause" changes the dynamics of the dispute considerably.[79] As such, the narrow FOIA access to the charge file records after the investigation is complete can thwart individuals' abilities to make their best case to the agency with the power to influence the outcome of the dispute. As one attorney said, "How in God's name are we supposed to substantively respond to something that we've only gotten a percentage of?"[80] FOIA is not adequately serving these individuals in their pursuit of private remedies, either.

The EEOC receives by far the largest volume of requests related to third-party disputes among the agencies included in this study, but several others display significant trends in this regard in their data. A notable example also involves employment disputes at the Wage and Hour Division (WHD) of the Department of Labor (DOL).[81] At WHD, lawyers are by far the most frequent requesters, and although some firms are corporate firms representing employers and defending against liability (a phenomenon discussed in greater detail in Chapter 6), most of them are plaintiff-side employment firms representing individuals.[82] For example, the top requester, Morgan & Morgan, is a national plaintiffs' firm that, among other areas, brings overtime and wage and hour claims,[83] and it alone made 210 requests out of WHD's total 2,569 requests in the study year.[84] To be sure, not all of plaintiffs' attorneys' requests will be directly about their own client. For example, one wage-and-hour lawyer who represents plaintiffs explained that he typically requests all records about his client's employer, even if they do not involve his client, because he may find evidence of wage and hour practices more generally that are helpful to the client's case.[85] Yet, even those requests could be more loosely defined as first-person in nature because they are about the represented party's own workplace.

Two other agencies – the Federal Trade Commission (FTC) and the Centers for Disease Control and Prevention (CDC) – included in this study engage in

79 Telephone Interview with Stephanie Romo, *supra* note 74; *see also* Equal Emp't Opportunity Comm., EEOC-NVTA-0000-21, What You Should Know: The EEOC, Conciliation, and Litigation (2015).

80 Telephone Interview with Stephanie Romo, *supra* note 74.

81 OSHA and MSHA, other divisions of DOL, also have some first-person requesting related to third-party litigation by plaintiffs' attorneys, but those represent a far smaller fraction than at WHD. OSHA and MSHA are mostly dominated by defense attorneys with business clients, discussed in greater detail *infra* Ch. 6.

82 For example, Morgan & Morgan (211 requests), Nichols Kaster (sixty-three requests), Dunham & Jones (thirty-one requests), Fitapelli & Schafferr LLP and (fifty-eight requests) are plaintiff-side employment firms in the top five organizational requesters. U.S. Dep't of Labor, Wage & Hour Div., Freedom of Information Act Response to Apr. 15, 2016 Request by Margaret B. Kwoka (on file with author) [hereinafter WHD Data].

83 *Overtime/ Wage & Hour Law*, Morgan & Morgan, www.forthepeople.com/overtime-attorneys (last visited Nov. 23, 2020).

84 WHD Data, *supra* note 82.

85 Telephone Interview with James Rodriguez, Att'y, Law Firm 6 (July 21, 2017).

some amount of enforcement or investigation of complaints from the public and receive third-party litigation related requests. At those agencies, first-person requesters or their representatives tend to request their own complaints and/or agency records relating to an investigation of an incident involving themselves, seemingly to arm themselves for private litigation against the allegedly offending regulated entity.

At the FTC, which received 1,538 in the data year obtained, 26 percent (or 408 requests) were first-person requests as indicated by the agency redacting the requester's name on the log.[86] Nearly all of these requests have the subject matter listed as "requester's complaint."[87] Consumer complaints concern fraud, identity theft, or unfair business practices, among others.[88] As the FTC explains, "[t]he FTC cannot resolve individual consumer complaints"[89] and typically a consumer receives no individual response from the agency. However, the agency does aggregate complaints and investigates on its own when it finds significant patterns of problems. As such, consumers may want copies of their own complaint and any related agency documents to collect any information that may help them in their bid to seek a remedy directly from the offending company.[90]

At the CDC, 188 of 998, or 18.8 percent of requests have a (b)(6) privacy redaction in the subject matter of the request, indicating they pertain to individuals and as such are likely to be first-person in nature. Most of them are for medical records pertaining to an individual, but unlike the other agencies where medical records are

86 Fed. Trade Comm'n, Freedom of Information Act Responses to Sept. 29, 2014 and Feb. 12, 2015 Requests by Margaret B. Kwoka (on file with author) [hereinafter FTC Data].

87 *Id.*

88 *Report Fraud to the FTC*, FED. TRADE COMM'N, www.ftc.gov/faq/consumer-protection/submit-consumer-complaint-ftc (last visited Nov. 23, 2020).

89 *Id.*

90 FTC Data, *supra* note 86. Interestingly, at the Federal Communications Commission, (FCC), where consumer complaints are also received, although 287 of 902 requests, or 31.8 percent, concerned a complaint, matters of public concern and oversight requesters played an outsized role, rather than first-person requesters. *See* Fed. Commc'ns Comm'n, Freedom of Information Act Response to March 6, 2018 Request by Margaret B. Kwoka (on file with author) [hereinafter FCC Data]; *see also Consumer Complaint Center*, FED. COMMC'NS COMM., https://consumercomplaints.fcc.gov/hc/en-us (last visited Nov. 23, 2020). For example, there were many requests for complaints received about the presidential debates or candidates during the then-ongoing election cycle, mostly submitted by reporters. *See, e.g.*, FCC Data, supra, at Request Nos. FCC-2017-000001, FCC-2017-000016, FCC-2017-000027. Reporters also requested complaints about companies that were subject to public scrutiny at the time, such as DirectTV. *See, e.g.*, *id.* at Request Nos. FCC-2017-000273, FCC-2017-000282. That said, there are clearly some first-person requests among them, for example, a request that starts, "I filed an informal complaint with the FCC ..." and goes on to request records about the FCC's response. *See id.* at Request No. FCC-2017-000037. However, these are relatively rare in this data set. There are also some clearly commercial requests from corporate law firms representing companies that might be subject to complaints, discussed in greater detail *infra* Chapter 6.

often requested in a first-person manner, these medical records are clearly related to CDC investigations of disease outbreak incidents, not medical records held in the normal course of an agency providing direct medical services to a population.[91] Moreover, the requesters are nearly all represented by personal injury and workplace injury law firms – two of which specialize in food borne illness injuries[92] – indicating the purpose behind these requests is to advance the individual's interest vis-à-vis third-party liability.[93]

Finally, first-person FOIA requesting pertaining to a third-party dispute is evident at FEMA, albeit not concerning any enforcement or oversight activity FEMA engages in. To be sure, at FEMA, individuals make claims for benefits and some amount of first-person requesting clearly pertains to their efforts to challenge the agency's denial or determination of benefits, as discussed above. But in addition to that, individuals also request FEMA records for documentation they believe would assist them in their parallel disputes with private insurance companies. This practice is evident in the law firms that are frequent requesters at FEMA.[94] For example, Weisbroad Matteis & Copley PLLC submitted 689 requests alone in the studied year,[95] and one of their specialties is disaster recovery against insurance companies that underpay, engage in fraud, or other misconduct with respect to a disaster claim.[96] Nearly all of their requests are for a claim file (almost certainly their client's).[97] Several other law firms are similar frequent filers, indicating a very substantial number of requests that pertain to third-party disputes.[98]

[91] U.S. Dep't of Health & Human Servs., Ctrs. for Disease Control, Freedom of Information Act Response to Feb. 24, 2018 Request by Margaret B. Kwoka (on file with author) [hereinafter CDC Data]. Subject matters make clear that these medical records were obtained in the course of a CDC investigation, such as a request for a "copy of any and all reports or other material generated regarding an E.coli investigation pertaining to (b)(6)" *Id.* at Request No. 2017-01-04 or "medical records for (b)(6), pertaining to the nationwide Legionella outbreak of 2016 in Hopkins Minnesota involving Citrus System's cooling towers." *Id.* at Request No. 2016-12-14.

[92] *See generally* Marler Clark LLP, PS, https://marlerclark.com (last visited Nov. 23, 2020) (6 requests); Ron Simon & Assocs., www.ronsimonassociates.com (last visited Nov. 23, 2020) (5 requests).

[93] For example, Killian, Davis, Richter & Mayle PC, a personal injury firm, submitted 43 requests, almost all of which were listed as for "records pertaining to (b)(6)." CDC Data, *supra* note 91; Killian, Davis, Richter & Mayle PC www.killianlaw.com (last visited Nov. 23, 2020).

[94] FEMA Data, *supra* note 32.

[95] *Id.*

[96] *See generally* Weisbrod, Matteis & Copley, www.wmclaw.com (last visited Nov. 23, 2020).

[97] FEMA Data, *supra* note 32.

[98] For example, Gauthier, Murphy & Houghtaling made 279 requests, Mostyn Law Firm made 203, and Wilton & Pandit made 109. FEMA Data *supra* note 32. All similarly specialize in insurance claims and disasters. *See generally* Gauthier, Murphy & Houghtaling LLC, https://gmhatlaw.com (last visited Nov. 23, 2020); Mostyn Law, https://mostynlaw.com (last visited Nov. 23, 2020); Pandit Law, www.panditlaw.com (last visited Nov. 23, 2020).

G. ACCESS TO PRIVATE SERVICES

A final use for first-person requests for agency records is the need to obtain certain records to access private services. These do not, as in the last category, necessarily involve private disputes or litigation, but rather simply the need for documentation the government has about the requester. This dynamic is most apparent with respect to the Federal Aviation Administration (FAA), and is also significant at two other agencies previously discussed as having other types of first-person FOIA use: the VHA and the PBCG.

The FAA receives a large volume of FOIA requests, numbering 11,414 in the year for which data was obtained for this study.[99] Of these requests, 6,609 (57.9 percent) have a (b)(6) privacy redaction in the subject matter of the request, indicating the first-person nature of the request. To be sure, most of the requests are made by the first-party subject's representatives, in this case not lawyers but employers or companies performing background checks. Frequent requesters, some of whom are very frequent, include airlines themselves and large background check companies, such as HireRight (which submitted 1,069 requests in the study year) and Accurate Background, LLC (which submitted 767). Most of these requests target the "airman" file or disapproved airman certificates,[100] the license needed to pilot an aircraft. Indeed, the single dominant force behind this volume of requests is most apparently background checks for employment of pilots. In this way, FOIA facilitates those pilots' access to private employment.

At the VHA, while requests designed to access private market services certainly constitute a subset of requests (and one that is difficult to precisely quantify), they are nonetheless apparent in the logs. Most obvious, some frequent requesters at VHA are records retrieval services that serve insurance companies for underwriting purposes.[101] For example, EMSI made 627 requests in the study year, making it the highest-volume requester, while Source Access, Inc., made 158, and PDC Retrievals made 107.[102] It appears these companies, with the consent of the individual, request records for the insurance companies from which the individuals want insurance products, thereby facilitating the individual's access to private market benefits.[103]

[99] FOIA Library, FED. AVIATION ADMIN., www.faa.gov/foia/electronic_reading_room/ (select FY 2018 items).

[100] For example, a full 1,087 requests have subject matters that read identically: "copies of complete airman file, including disapproved applications for airman [exemption 6]." *Id.*

[101] VHA Data, *supra* note 19.

[102] *Id.*

[103] *See Source Access, Inc.*, LINKEDIN, www.linkedin.com/company/source-access-inc- (last visited Nov. 23, 2020); *APS Retrievals and Summaries*, PARAMEDS.COM, www.parameds.com/aps.html (last visited Nov. 23, 2020). EMSI was a leading medical records retrieval company that went out of business as a result of the 2020 coronavirus pandemic. *See Your Path to Medical Record Retrieval after EMSI Closing*, AM. MED. SOLS., https://amsemr.com/service/emsi-medical-record-retrieval (last visited Nov. 23, 2020).

In fact, insurance companies make two different kinds of appearances in the logs. Underwriting is certainly one of them, but claims adjusting is another way insurance companies use FOIA. At VHA for example, at least 480 requests were made directly by insurance companies,[104] most of which appear to be made by life insurance companies for deceased veterans' medical records,[105] with some others coming from insurance companies for police/uniform offense reports which are created by the VA police for accidents or incidents on VA property.[106] These requests clearly seem to be about documentation regarding claims made on policies, whether vehicular accidents or claims on a life insurance policy, which would be used in the claims adjusting process.

Similarly, at DOL's Occupational Safety and Health Administration (OSHA), insurance companies request records about a particular accident or a particular company on a routine basis, some 267 times in the study year.[107] At OSHA, Travelers Insurance was the third most frequent requester, with forty-five requests alone, and Liberty Mutual Insurance Co. was twelfth, having made twenty-nine requests. Meanwhile, the second most frequent requester – not counted among insurance companies generally – was the Metropolitan Report Bureau, a records retrieval company "serving the claims industry since 1957."[108]

While claims adjusting – as opposed to policy underwriting – may be on average more adversarial between the insurance company and the insured, it seems to largely fall in the same category of first-person requests made by the insured's representative – the insurance company – as part of a process for accessing the insured's insurance benefits. That said, some number of these requests will form the basis for disputes, and may end up crossing over into third-party litigation style claims, and insurance companies in those instances are acting more like a commercial requester. Despite ambiguity, however, these seem to largely be first-person in nature. In fact, some such claims are actually made by individuals themselves, specifying they are requesting records so they can provide them to their insurer.[109]

[104] VHA Data, *supra* note 19 (counting all requests with an organizational affiliation including the word "insurance").

[105] A full 265 of the insurance requests are for "deceased veterans' medical records," and 154 of those requests are from companies with "life insurance" specified in the name of the company. *See id.*

[106] Of the insurance requests there were forty-nine for these types of records. *Id.*

[107] U.S. Dep't of Labor, Occupational Safety & Health Admin., Freedom of Information Act Response to April 19, 2016 Request by Margaret B. Kwoka (on file with author) (counting all requests with an organizational affiliation including the word "insurance").

[108] *See generally* Metro. Reporting Bureau, www.metroreporting.com (last visited Nov. 23, 2020).

[109] For example, at the Defense Logistics Agency an individual requester stated, "My insurance is requesting the police report that Lt. Ali wrote last year." U.S. Dep't of Def., Def. Logistics Agency, Freedom of Information Act Responses to Oct. 6, 2014 and Feb. 12, 2015 Requests by Margaret B. Kwoka (on file with author).

Finally, at PBGC, 396 requests submitted (equaling 24 percent of the agency's total requests) were for income verification records.[110] The agency explains such requests can only be made by the individuals or their representatives, and any third-party requesting income verification (such as another government agency, housing authority, bank, residential care facility) must be doing so on behalf of the PBGC customer with the customer's consent.[111] These types of requests plainly facilitate the first-person requester's access to various private market benefits such as banking products or housing opportunities.

H. OTHER FIRST-PERSON USES

At another ten agencies, first-person requesters are evident in the FOIA logs, but for varying reasons, the likely purpose behind individuals' requests for their own information have not been able to be ascertained. Sometimes the kinds of records requested are clear, but the purpose behind the request is not. Other times, the nature of the request as being first-person is clear, but even the kinds of records being requested is not. This group of agencies is sort of a catchall category of agencies discussed in this section.

The FBI tops the list. It received 20,638 requests in the study year.[112] However, curiously, only 396, or 1.9 percent, appeared to be first-person in nature.[113] Because most requests to the FBI are simply listed as pertaining to a person's name, first-person requests were identified by requests for which the name of the requester matched the subject matter of the request.[114] There is good reason to believe there must be many more first-person requests at the FBI, as requesting one's own FBI file is practically a national pass-time if judged by the number of websites encouraging just about anyone to ask for theirs. For example, www.getmyfbifile.com helps members of the public do just that.[115] While the FBI has not responded to multiple inquiries asking for confirmation, I strongly suspect the FBI keeps first-person requests on a separate log by segregating Privacy Act requests from FOIA requests.[116] As a result, this count likely (vastly) undercounts first-person requests. Most requesting of one's own FBI file is likely motivated by pure curiosity.

[110] PBGC Data, *supra* note 27.

[111] *Income Verification Request Procedures*, PENSION BENEFIT GUAR. CORP., www.pbgc.gov/about/pg/footer/foia/income-verification-request-procedures (last visited Nov. 23, 2020).

[112] U.S. Dep't of Justice, Fed. Bureau of Investigations, Freedom of Information Act Responses to April. 14, 2016 Request and Feb. 8, 2018 Administrative Appeal by Margaret B. Kwoka, and (on file with author).

[113] *Id.*

[114] *Id.*

[115] GET MY FBI FILE, www.getmyfbifile.com (last visited Nov. 23, 2020).

[116] *See* Max Galka, *How to Request Your FBI File*, FOIA MAPPER (July 13, 2016), https://foiamapper.com/how-to-request-your-fbi-file (explaining that technically a request for one's own FBI file is a Privacy Act request).

Next, at three agencies, when the requester's name is redacted for privacy reasons, presumptively a first-person request, the subject matter of that request is also redacted, rendering it impossible to tell the nature of the inquiry. First, at the Bureau of Indian Affairs, a division of the Department of Interior, which received 1,553 total requests, a full 987 of those had both the requester and description categories redacted, indicating a 63.5 percent first-person request rate.[117] The nature of these requests is entirely unclear. Likewise, at the National Parks Service, which received a total of 1,224 requests, ninety-six or 7.8 percent of requests were listed as joint FOIA and Privacy Act requests and thus presumptively are first-person, but for all of those the subject matters have been redacted and thus the purpose behind or even kinds of records sought by the request is unknown.[118] And finally, at the Federal Reserve, which received 678 total requests, fifty-eight or 8.5 percent of requests had names and subject matters redacted under (b)(6).[119] At this group of agencies, when subject matters are categorically withheld for first-person requesters, it is impossible to ascertain even the kinds of records sought, much less the motivations behind those requests.

With similar effects, DOJ's Criminal Division released logs that do not contain a requester name field, but rather simply designate as one of the options in the subject matter field "first party request." Thus, it is easy to ascertain that 289 (29 percent) of the 996 requests in the study year are first-person. Regrettably, though, it is opaque what the requested records are or why the requester might want them. At two additional law enforcement agencies there are more clues, but not enough to tell a meaningful story. The Bureau of Alcohol, Tobacco, Firearms and Explosives (ATF), a component of DOJ, has first-party requesters that appear to be dominated by prisoners. Of 1,170 requests in the study year, 215 (18.4 percent) are affiliated with a penal institution but the request subject matter is listed as "self," making it almost certain prisoners are making the requests.[120] However, the reasons for the request or the records sought remains unknown. Similarly, at the US Marshals Service, the logs contain both a "description" field,

[117] U.S. Dep't of Interior, Bureau of Indian Affairs, Freedom of Information Act Response to Mar. 6, 2018 Request by Margaret B. Kwoka (on file with author).

[118] U.S. Dep't of Interior, Nat'l Park Serv., Freedom of Information Act Response to Mar. 6, 2018 Request by Margaret B. Kwoka (on file with author).

[119] Fed. Reserve, Freedom of Information Act Response to Mar. 6, 2018 Request by Margaret B. Kwoka (on file with author).

[120] U.S. Dep't of Justice, Bureau of Alcohol, Tobacco, Firearms & Explosives, Freedom of Information Act Response to Feb. 12, 2019 Request by Margaret B. Kwoka (on file with author). Although the ATF logs show requester names that are redacted under (b)(6), unlike with logs at other agencies, this designation in the ATF logs does not appear to indicate requests that are first-person in nature. Rather, because practically all requester names are redacted under this exemption (1,159 of 1,170), including those that are clearly not first-person requests, it appears this agency simply does not release requester names as a matter of course.

for which a privacy redaction is included in 201 of a total 590 requests, or 34 percent, thus probably indicating first-person requests.[121] But these logs also curiously contain a "subject" field which appears to be the agency's own description categories for requests.[122] Of the 201 requests with descriptions redacted, seventy-seven are for mug shots, nearly all of the remainder are listed simply as "other."[123] Thus, no more clues are given as to the purpose behind first-person requesting at the Marshals Service.

Finally, at three more agencies the subject matter of first-person requests is clear, but reasons or patterns are hard to find. To begin, at the Secret Service, a division of the Department of Homeland Security, the problem is not that subject matters are redacted, but that they reveal no actual pattern among them. The Secret Service received 1,400 requests in the study year, 466 or 33.3 percent were first-person as indicated by redacted requester names.[124] Of these, some subject matters were redacted,[125] others concerned employment matters,[126] others criminal histories,[127] and many were simply one-off types of requests for, say, a polygraph,[128] or denial of access to a White House tour.[129] There is no conclusion to be drawn about what motivates first-person requesters at the Secret Service overall.

Next, at the Defense Information Systems Agency (DISA), which received only 279 requests, fifty-two requests had the name of the requester redacted for privacy reasons, but an additional sixty-three requests with requester names released are also evidently first-person requests, for a total of 115 or 41.2 percent of requests.[130] Those sixty-three requests are for SF 61 or SF 61B forms, which are employment appointment affidavits (or the older version, a declaration of appointment) for federal employees.[131] But while the records sought are more clear and are employment related, the reasons behind the requests for these forms are not, since they do not clearly relate to an employment dispute.

[121] U.S. Dep't of Justice, Marshals Serv., Freedom of Information Act Response to Apr. 15, 2016 Request by Margaret B. Kwoka (on file with author).

[122] *Id.*

[123] *Id.*

[124] FOIA Logs 2018, U.S. SECRET SERV., www.secretservice.gov/press/foia/library.

[125] One hundred and forty were redacted in their entirety under (b)(6). *See id.*

[126] For example, one request was for "disciplinary and personnel files for your time as a uniformed division officer." *Id.* at Request No.20180056.

[127] For example, one request was for "a copy of any arrest report" and disposition. *Id.* at Request No. 20180227.

[128] For example, one request was for "your polygraph examination results taken on March 16, 2017." *Id.* at Request No. 20180453.

[129] *See, e.g., id.* at Request No. 20181064.

[130] 2018 FOIA Log, FOIA Reading Room, DEF. INFO. SYS. AGENCY, www.disa.mil/About/Legal-and-Regulatory/Accessibility/FOIA-Reading-Room.

[131] *Id.; see also Freedom of Information Act Program,* DEF. INFO. SYS. AGENCY, www.disa.mil/about/legal-and-regulatory/freedom-of-info-act-program (last visited Nov. 23, 2020) (making clear that Form SF 61 or SF 61B would be requested by a former employee of DISA).

Finally, and similar to DISA, at the Employee Benefits Security Administration of the Department of Labor, of 348 total requests, seventeen or 4.9 percent were related to the Technical Assistance and Inquiries System (TAIS), which is a tracking system of sorts for members of the public who make inquiries.[132] As the agency explains, TAIS collects personally identifiable information, for which public access is not available, thus making first-person requests for this information the only likely possibility.[133] Yet, why individuals need these records remains unexplained.

* * *

First-person FOIA requesting is a varied phenomenon. Beyond the immigration context, the motivations for asking for one's own records or one's own file can differ greatly between agencies. Yet, in many contexts, it appears similarly inefficient or odd that FOIA is the only way for individuals to access their own documents. Sometimes, it even appears prejudicial to the interests of the requester that FOIA is their only option. In all cases, it is clear that FOIA is an option of last resort. When someone has a dispute with an employer or insurance company, needs their documentation, wants to learn about their family, gets rejected from a government job, or needs to prove their eligibility for benefits, they turn to FOIA.

[132] U.S. Dep't of Labor, Emp. Benefits Sec. Admin., Freedom of Information Act Response to Feb. 25, 2018 Request by Margaret B. Kwoka (on file with author).

[133] *Privacy Impact Assessment – EBSA – Technical Assistance and Inquiries System (TAIS)*, U.S. Dep't of Labor, www.dol.gov/agencies/oasam/centers-offices/ocio/privacy/ebsa/tais (last visited Nov. 23, 2020).

6

FOIA, Inc.

Businesses have a broad range of uses for FOIA. Considering the vast wealth of regulatory, industry, and government transaction-related information held by federal agencies, it should come as no surprise that for-profit enterprises have found great utility in obtaining government information. This is particularly true at large regulatory agencies. While some public and private oversight uses occasionally crop up, discussed in greater detail in Chapter 3, this chapter will demonstrate that the vast majority of commercial requesters are seeking records for private purposes, that is to directly feed into their profit-making activities.

Regulated businesses, for example, are often seeking records to learn more about their competitors' activities and industry trends. Some businesses make use of federal records as part of the consulting, due diligence, or compliance services that they offer to other businesses. Another set of commercial users are seeking information about the government's own business activity as it relates to contracts, grants, or leases; often, it seems, to find out how to win those government awards or position themselves advantageously with respect to them. A huge set of businesses using FOIA are corporate and commercial lawyers seeking to defend their clients or otherwise represent them in the regulatory landscape. And finally, there is a group of businesses that make FOIA their actual business model: these are information resellers, or businesses whose business model is to request federal records under FOIA and resell them (usually to other businesses) at a profit.

These uses serve purposes that are potentially very important. They may increase business compliance with regulation; promote better market competition; or result in improved products, pricing, or services. Indeed, businesses need good information about the environment in which they operate to successfully meet market demand. But these uses do not advance the primary aim of FOIA: to inform the public about the operations of government. In fact, businesses are incentivized to keep information they obtain closely held and secret, so as to maintain any competitive advantage it might confer. Moreover, FOIA, not designed for the sort of en masse, routinized document production businesses want, is an inefficient and deeply imperfect delivery tool for commercial users. Indeed, this chapter lays bare that, especially at the agencies where commercial requesters are driving request volume, FOIA is ill-suited to the task.

A. REGULATED ENTITIES

Given that regulatory agencies are those at which commercial requesting is most consistently dominant, one might expect a strong presence of regulated entities since they have the most apparent interest in agency records. And, indeed, at several agencies regulated companies make significant numbers of requests to their regulator. Before detailing these examples, however, it is worth noting that the presence of regulated entity requests is not nearly as prominent as one might think. As it happens, many – if not most – regulated entity requests are masked by intermediaries. Regulated entities make heavy use of what I call information resellers, or businesses that request federal records under FOIA and resell them at a profit. As a result, the regulated businesses' names do not appear on the FOIA logs, because companies requesting records and reselling them to those businesses are the requesters of record. This phenomenon is discussed in much greater detail in Chapter 7. That said, regulated entities certainly do make appearances. Such examples are particularly apparent at the Food and Drug Administration (FDA) and the Mine Safety and Health Administration (MSHA).

At the FDA, where 74.5 percent of its 10,167 requests in the study year were from commercial organizations, one of the primary regulated industries is the pharmaceutical industry.[1] Pharmaceutical giants, therefore, unsurprisingly play a role in FDA requesting. Merck & Co., Inc., a large pharmaceutical company, filed 373 requests that year, and Eli Lilly & Co., another pharmaceutical company, made fifty-six requests.[2] Each of these companies had a distinct manner of using FOIA. For Merck, the vast majority of its requests (318 of 373) were for copies of other FOIA requests filed in the past; records produced in response to previously filed requests by others; or logs of FOIA requests filed over particular periods of time.[3] A sample of these request letters suggests that the purpose of the requests was to find out what documents others are requesting (and obtaining) about Merck itself.[4] Eli Lilly, for its

1 U.S. Dep't of Health & Human Servs., Food & Drug Admin. Freedom of Information Act Response to June 24, 2014 Requests by Margaret B. Kwoka (on file with author) [hereinafter FDA Data].

2 *Id.*

3 *Id.*

4 *See, e.g.*, *id.* at Request No. 2013-4755 (requesting Request No. 2013-3633, which is a law firm's request for information about clinical trials for a particular type of administration of a drug Merck manufactures, Temodar); *id.* at Request No. 2013-9340 (requesting Request No. 2013-8434, which is a request about adverse events reported for the drug Propecia, a Merck product); *id.* at Request No. 2013-2280 (requesting the request letter for Request No. 2013-1415, which is a request for information pertaining to Januvia, another Merck product).

part, mostly made requests for facilities inspection reports for companies with which it contracts, presumably as part of a due diligence accountability measure for the companies that produce and distribute its products.[5]

Yet, as with other regulatory agencies, regulated entities at FDA themselves do not make as dominant an appearance in the FOIA logs as one might imagine. Below, where FDA information resellers are discussed, it becomes apparent that these resellers request precisely the same kinds of documents that Merck and Eli Lilly are requesting individually, strongly suggesting (as would naturally be the case anyway) that regulated entities are their primary customers and that Merck and Eli Lilly's use of FDA records is representative of the industry as a whole. In addition, some regulated entity requests are masked by the fact that their attorneys make them on their behalf. These corporate law firm requests are also discussed in greater detail below.

At MSHA, 1,072 of the agency's total 1,265 requests in the year for which data was obtained were commercial in nature.[6] Among all requesters that made five or more requests that year, of which there were thirty-seven, fifteen are regulated entities. Of those, three are mining equipment companies, one is a mining training company, and one is an asphalt manufacturer.[7] The remainder are mining companies, including Armstrong Coal Co. (sixty-nine requests), XMV Inc. (fourteen), Fisher Sand & Gravel (nine), Hanson Aggregates (seven), Nally & Hamilton (seven), Hubble Mining Company, LLC (six), Lhoist North America (six), Thoroughfare Mining LLC (six), Clintwood Elkhorn Mining Company (five), and Pinnacle Mining Co. (five).[8]

Interestingly, the regulated entities filing requests at MSHA are mostly not seeking records about other companies, but about themselves. Specifically, the dominant type of request appears to be records concerning particular inspections or resulting citations or violations at the companies' own facilities. For example, Armstrong Coal's requests are typically formulated as "info on [a number of] violations at

[5] *See, e.g., id.* at Request No. 2013-7592 (requesting inspection records related to Dyax Corp., a company that has publicly announced joint ventures with Eli Lilly); *see id.* at Request Nos. 2013-766, 2013-898, 2013-899, 2103-900 (concerning PETNET facilities, which have been reported to be manufacturing and distributing contractors for Eli Lilly); *see id.* at Request Nos. 2013-4011, 2013-4012, 2013-4013, 2013-4014 (concerning Fisher Clinical Services, which is publicly linked to Eli Lilly as a distributor of clinical trial materials).

[6] U.S. Dep't of Labor, Mine Safety & Health Admin., Freedom of Information Act Response to April 15, 2016 Request by Margaret B. Kwoka (on file with author) [hereinafter MSHA Data].

[7] The equipment companies are JH Fletcher & Co. (mining equipment), Environmental Commodities Corp. (environmental equipment for mines), A&B Fire Services Inc. (fire suppression equipment for mines); the training company is Tri State Geologic & Mine Services, LLC; and the asphalt manufacturer is Bettis Asphalt.

[8] MSHA Data, *supra* note 6.

[a particular Armstrong mine]."[9] Pinnacle Mining specifies particular facilities about which it wants records, most of which are identified as Pinnacle-owned locations.[10] All of Thoroughfare Mining LLC's requests centered on violations at a particular facility it owns.[11] And XMV's requests appear to be about their own facilities, too.[12]

While for a few industry requesters it was not possible to ascertain whether the requests concerned their own facilities, all but one similarly requested records about a particular inspection, citation, violation or facility. For example, Fisher Sand & Gravel specifies a mine number and inspector or inspection event, and then asks for: "All inspection field notes and colored photos generated" by that inspection.[13] Hubble Mining Company is the only industry requester that deviates from this pattern. Rather than violation or inspection records, it appears to be requesting about the rest of the industry. During this period, it appears Hubble was interested in the use of compressed air in underground mines, having made requests about various geographic regions in this regard; for example, it requested records about: "All the mines in the district using compressed air underground"[14] and "List of underground mines in District 11 using compressed air."[15]

At MSHA, as at many other regulatory agencies, corporate attorneys representing regulated industry also have a heavy presence, an aspect of commercial requesting that is discussed in greater detail below. But regulated industry's own use of FOIA offers a glimpse into the needs of regulated entities for information held by the government, both to learn more about their own regulatory requirements and predicaments and to learn about the practices of their competitors.

B. DUE DILIGENCE SERVICES

Beyond the regulated entities themselves, businesses also rely heavily on FOIA for various services they offer to regulated companies. One such set of services is due diligence services, which are services rendered to investigate a risk associated with a particular proposed or anticipated commercial transaction prior to finalizing the transaction. Pockets of these commercial requesters can be found across the federal government, but, again, at some agencies – particularly those related to financial

9 *See, e.g.*, *id.* at Request No. 113 (requesting "info on 26 violations @ Parkway 10/27/2014 20/28/2014"); *Id.* at Request No. 218 (requesting "info on 2 violations at Midway"); *Id.* at Request No. 401 (requesting "info on 3 violations at Equality").

10 *See, e.g.*, *id.* at Request No. 131 (requesting records about "Pinnacle Preparation Plant, I.D.: 46-05868 (9/2014)"); *Id.* at Request No. 409 (requesting records about "Pinnacle Mine, I.D.: 46-01816 (1/2015)").

11 *Id.* at Request Nos. 732, 927, 1276, 1442, 1443, 1444 (all concerning violations at Thoroughfare's Survant Mine).

12 *See, e.g.*, *id.* at Request No. 976 (requesting records about "XMV Inc., #35 Mine").

13 *Id.* at Request Nos. 32, 148, 150, 170, 171, 385, 891, 336, 337.

14 *Id.* at Request No. 200.

15 *Id.* at Request No. 195.

due diligence and environmental due diligence – these requesters have an overwhelming presence.

Starting with financial due diligence, at the Securities and Exchange Commission (SEC), out of 12,091 total requests in the study year, it reported 8,292, or 68.6 percent, as commercial.[16] However, in the sole instance in which this study has redesignated a requester from the agency's own designation, I count a single requester who made 2,498 requests that year as a commercial requester, rather than the agency's classification as news media. That requester, SECProbes.com, is properly counted as an information reseller, and discussed in detail in Chapter 7. This reclassification brings the total to 10,790 commercial requests, or 89.2 percent of requests made to the SEC.[17]

Of these commercial requests, due diligence-oriented requests are one of two principal types of requests. Because the SEC regulates publicly-traded companies, it investigates those companies' violations of securities laws, and thus naturally holds important information about the legal risk of doing any business with those companies.[18] Thus, other companies looking to contract with, merge with, acquire, or otherwise do business with a publicly traded company will want SEC records. Moreover, investors will want to know if there is legal risk before investing, as that will affect a company's value.

Companies that provide due diligence services are prominent. For example, International Business Research (IBR) made 2,155 requests, each with a particular company name as the subject of the request, and with formulaic request letters asking for all investigative records for the past twenty-five years involving that company.[19] IBR describes its services as providing information to clients prior to initial public offerings, mergers and acquisitions, and other types of corporate deals for which due diligence services are essential.[20] Check Fund Manager, LLC, does precisely the same, and it submitted 1,820 requests that year, a sample of which reveals a formulaic recitation asking for "records of consumer complaints, civil

[16] U.S. Sec. & Exch. Comm'n, Freedom of Information Act Response to Sept. 5, 2014 Request by Margaret B. Kwoka (on file with author); FOIA Logs, U.S. Sec. & Exch. Comm'n, www.sec.gov/foia/docs/foia-logs.htm (select "2013" and "2014") [hereinafter SEC Data]. The dataset compiled includes the months between January 2013 and December 2013, representing CY 2013.

[17] *Id.*

[18] *See How Investigations Work*, U.S. Sec. & Exch. Comm'n (Jan. 27, 2017), www.sec.gov/enforce/how-investigations-work.html (describing SEC investigations).

[19] SEC Data, *supra* note 16. *See, e.g.*, *id.* at Request Nos. 13-03098-FOIA (concerning Jolson Merchant Partners, Inc.), 13-03655-FOIA (Dimitrios Raptis), 13-05167-FOIA (Corinne H. Lyle a/k/a Nin Lyle), 13-08247-FOIA (Matthew L. Sherman), 13-09170-FOIA (MigraTEC, Inc.), 13-10997-FOIA (G-Force 1 LLC), 13-11466-FOIA (Brentwood Beauty Labs. Int'l Inc.), 14-00256-FOIA (Mac Motors Inc.), 14-00365-FOIA (Corbin Capital Partners).

[20] *About IBR*, Int'l Bus. Research, ibrusa.com/#about.

complaints, investigations, or preliminary inquiries" regarding a particular company.[21]

Due diligence requests are also made by investment firms, presumably as part of their decision to invest, or not, in a particular company. For example, EACM Advisors, LLC, a now-shuttered wholly owned subsidiary of BNY Mellon, a large investment firm, made 726 requests that year.[22] And finally, information resellers, discussed in greater detail in Chapter 7, also make significant numbers of due diligence requests at the SEC (most notably the reclassified requester, SECProbes.com, mentioned above). Overall, FOIA officials at the SEC estimate that about two-thirds of SEC requests are due diligence related.[23]

Beyond the SEC, due diligence requesters appear at other financial regulators as well. For example, at the Comptroller of the Currency, which received 1,606 requests in the study year, nearly all top requesters are commercial in nature, though the agency's data do not have official designations for commercial requesters on their logs and thus no count is reported in this study. Fully half of all requests – 807 to be precise – were for a "certificate of corporate existence," which this agency issues to banks certifying that they are authorized to transact business. Many of the requests for these certificates were made by due diligence services companies, such as Wolters Kluwer (152), Corporate Service Company (134), and Cogency Global (fifty-five).[24] Similarly, at the Federal Reserve, the Corporation Service Company is the single highest volume requester, having filed thirty-six of the agency's 678 in the study year,[25] and its requests are nearly all for certificates of corporate name verification or certificates of good standing for particular businesses.[26]

The other significant category of due diligence requesters is not seeking financial information about target companies or commercial transactions, but rather

[21] *About Us*, Check Fund Manager, www.checkfundmanager.com/aboutus.html. A sampling of Check Fund Manager's requests reveals a pattern of requesting "records of consumer complaints, civil complaints, investigations, or preliminary inquiries" regarding the subject of the request. *See* SEC Data, *supra* note 16, at Request Nos. 13-03997-FOIA, 13-04856-FOIA, 13-06060-FOIA, 13-10123-FOIA, 13-10555-FOIA, 14-01130-FOIA, 14-01414-FOIA, 14-01475-FOIA, 14-02693-FOIA, 13-03328-FOIA, 13-03893-FOIA, 13-04578-FOIA, 13-05608-FOIA, 13-05743-FOIA, 13-06921-FOIA, 13-08874-FOIA, 13-09586-FOIA, 13-09804-FOIA, 14-01302-FOIA, 14-01705-FOIA, 14-02279-FOIA, 13-03058-FOIA, 13-03411-FOIA, 13-04378-FOIA.

[22] SEC Data *supra* note 16. James Comtois, *BNY Mellon to Shutter EACM Advisors Hedge Funds-of-Funds Business*, Pensions & Invs. (Sept. 25, 2018), www.pionline.com/article/20180925/ONLINE/180929937/bny-mellon-to-shutter-eacm-advisors-hedge-funds-of-funds-business.

[23] Interview with Barry Walters, Chief FOIA Officer, John Livornese, FOIA/PA Officer & Mark Siford, Counsel to the Dir./Chief FOIA Officer, U.S. Sec. & Exch. Comm'n, in Wash. D.C. (Jul. 24, 2019).

[24] U.S. Dep't of Treasury, Office of the Comptroller of the Currency, Freedom of Information Act Response to Mar. 13, 2018 Request by Margaret B. Kwoka (on file with author).

[25] Fed. Reserve, Freedom of Information Act Response to Mar. 6, 2018 Request by Margaret B. Kwoka (on file with author) [hereinafter Federal Reserve Data].

[26] Corp. Serv. Co., www.cscglobal.com (last visited Oct. 2, 2020). *See, e.g.*, Federal Reserve Data, *supra* note 24, at Request Nos. G-2017-00187 (Certificate of Good Standing), G-201700297 (Certificate of Corporate Name Verification).

environmental information about commercial real estate. At the Environmental Protection Agency (EPA), there is a similarly dominant presence of due diligence requests, usually made by environmental due diligence firms. These requests are related to Phase I Environmental Site Assessments (ESAs), which are due diligence searches about environmental hazards on commercial property a business seeks to acquire or finance. This due diligence process limits the company's liability if it purchases property and a problem is later discovered.[27] Of the six commercial requesters that submitted more than 100 requests in the study year, five of them used FOIA in this manner.[28] ECC, Inc. submitted 180 requests,[29] Hillman Consulting submitted 172,[30] REPSG, Inc. submitted 170,[31] Environmental Operations submitted 129,[32] and Brinkerhoff Environmental Services, Inc. submitted 101.[33] By EPA's own estimate, 80 percent of the FOIA requests it received around this time period were for environmental records pertaining to a particular address.[34]

Beyond EPA, it appears Phase I ESAs may prompt some FOIA requests at other agencies as well. For example, at the Coast Guard, the single highest volume requester is LaBella Associates, which made 657 of the agency's 1,450 commercial requests, where commercial requests constituted 44.6 percent of the agency's total 3,248 requests that year. LaBella is an environmental consulting firm,[35] and their

[27] *Brownfields All Appropriate Inquiries*, U.S. ENVTL. PROT. AGENCY (Dec. 19, 2019), www.epa.gov/brownfields/brownfields-all-appropriate-inquiries.

[28] U.S. Envtl. Prot. Agency, Freedom of Information Act Response to June 9, 2015 Request by Margaret B. Kwoka (on file with author); FOIAOnline, foiaonline.gov/foiaonline/action/public/search/advancedSearch (under "Look Up By" select "agency" then search for "EPA – Envrionmental Protection Agency") [hereinafter EPA Data].

[29] *See, e.g., id.* (specifying, as do nearly all of ECC's requests, that "ECC is currently performing a Phase I Environmental Site Assessment for the above-referenced location").

[30] *See, e.g., id.* (enumerating Hillman Consulting requests as all concerning a particular property); *see also Real Estate Due Diligence*, HILLMAN CONSULTING LLC, hillmannconsulting.com/services/real-estate-due-diligence (last visited Nov. 23, 2020) (specifying services that include Phase I ESA's as part of their "Real Estate Due Diligence" services).

[31] *See* EPA Data, *supra* note 28 (enumerating REPSG requests as concerning various environmental aspects about a particular property); *see also Property Assessment*, REACT ENVTL. PROF'L SERVS. GRP., INC., www.repsg.com/propertyassessment (last visited Nov. 23, 2020) (specifying that REPSG's services include government records search as part of its property assessment and investigation services).

[32] *See* EPA Data, *supra* note 28 (enumerating Environmental Operations requests, which specifies that it is conducting Phase I ESA in its requests).

[33] Because the company submitted most of its requests as attachments to e-mails, descriptions of most requests are not present in the EPA's FOIA logs. A random sample of ten of the attached request letters is available online, though, and all made reference to a Phase I ESA. *Id.*; *see Advanced Search*, FOIA ONLINE, foiaonline.gov/foiaonline/action/public/search/advancedSearch (select "Agency" as "EPA," and type in the desired request number) (last visited Nov. 23, 2020).

[34] Larry Gottesman, Chief, FOIA & Privacy Act Branch, U.S. Envtl. Prot. Agency, Remarks at the Freedom of Information Act Advisory Committee Meeting (Apr. 19, 2016), ogis.archives.gov/foia-advisory-committee/2014-2016-term/documents/04-19-2016-meeting-transcript.htm.

[35] U.S. Dep't of Homeland Sec., U.S. Coast Guard, Freedom of Information Act Response to Oct. 2, 2014 Request by Margaret B. Kwoka, as modified by email on Mar. 19, 2018 (on file with author) [hereinafter Coast Guard Data]; *see* LABELLA PC, www.labellapc.com (last visited Oct. 5, 2020).

requests all pertain to particular addresses, sometimes formulated as simply records about the address, sometimes specifying incident reports related to the address.[36] It may not be that all such requests are for Phase I ESAs, but the nature of the requests certainly suggests that many of them likely are.

Due diligence in both the financial and environmental contexts prompts thousands of requests a year aimed at verifying the status and uncovering any risks associated with a particular company or particular commercial property. These requests are routine, and the requesters are usually companies making dozens, if not hundreds – sometimes thousands – of requests a year. They serve a valuable purpose, and the information is important to the requesting parties. They also may secondarily promote the public interest in improving the market and assigning environmental responsibility. But the information does not usually get publicized for general consumption, nor is it of general interest. It does not inform the public about government activities or help the public hold officials accountable. It is a largely private good.

C. CONSULTING AND COMPLIANCE

Beyond strict due diligence, a variety of other consulting and compliance companies make strong appearances across agencies as well. These companies typically offer market or regulatory research and strategic business advice. They appear across a wide variety of mostly health and safety-oriented agencies.

For example, at FDA, which regulates food and drug safety, there are multiple frequent requesters that are consulting firms. INC Research, a consulting firm, made 139 requests, about half of which were for records related to facilities inspections, and the other half of which pertained to FDA approval of particular drugs.[37] In addition, EAS Consulting, which specializes in "FDA [r]egulatory [m]atters,"[38] submitted sixty-one requests, and Favus Institutional Research LLC, a healthcare consultant,[39] made forty-four requests that year.[40]

At the Federal Trade Commission (FTC), which regulates fair marketplaces, Height Analytics was the third highest volume requester, with twenty-four requests in the study year, and it markets research-consulting services to corporate boards, industry associations, and other commercial organizations.[41] At the Federal

36 *See* Coast Guard Data, *supra* note 35.

37 FDA Data, *supra* note 1.

38 *Id.*; *see* EAS Consulting Grp., easconsultinggroup.com (last visited Oct. 5, 2020).

39 Favus Institutional Research, favusinstitutionalresearch.com (last visited Oct. 5, 2020).

40 FDA Data, *supra* note 1.

41 Fed. Trade Comm'n, Freedom of Information Act Responses to Sept. 29, 2014 and Feb. 12, 2015 Requests by Margaret B. Kwoka (on file with author) [hereinafter FTC Data]; *see Our Services*, Height Sec. LLC, www.heightllc.com/our-services (the requester's name is Christine Muchanic, who works at Height Analytics); *see also* FTC Data, *supra*, at Request

Motor Carrier Safety Administration, which regulates commercial trucking, a consultant appears among the top requesters. Fleet Safety Services, LLC, was the fifth-highest requester by volume, making seventeen requests in the study year, and it is a management and compliance consulting company.[42] At the Consumer Product Safety Commission (CPSC), Safety Research & Strategies, a safety consultant for other companies,[43] filed ninety-one of the total 525 requests in the study year, making it the most frequent requester at the agency.[44]

Two agencies that are not primarily regulators also have a consulting requester presence in their logs, even if these companies do not dominate the list of top requesters. At the Department of Housing and Urban Development (HUD), Torres Consulting & Law Group was the seventh highest requester by volume, with thirteen requests in the study year,[45] and is a government affairs and regulatory compliance firm.[46] And at the National Labor Relations Board (NLRB), with its total 4,392 requests, the Labor Relations Institute (ninety-six requests)[47] and PTI Labor Research (twenty-nine requests)[48] are both management-oriented labor relations consultants that are among the top-fifteen requesters.[49]

Nos. FOIA-2013-00918, FOIA-2013-00913, FOIA-2013-00922, FOIA-2013-00916 (affiliating Christine Muchanic with Height Analytics).

42 U.S. Dep't of Transp., Fed. Motor Carrier Safety Admin., Freedom of Information Act Response to Mar. 6, 2018 Request by Margaret B. Kwoka (on file with author). The logs reveal that about half of these requests are for documents related to a compliance review of particular company, and the other half are for motor carrier records about a particular company. Almost certainly these are client companies of this consulting firm. *See* Fleet Safety Servs., LLC, www.fleetsafetyservices.com/ (last visited Oct. 5, 2020).

43 *Biomechanical Analysis & Injury Review*, Safety Research & Strategies, Inc., www.safetyresearch.net/biomechanical-analysis-and-injury-review (last visited Nov. 23, 2020).

44 FOIA Request Logs, Consumer Product Safety Comm'n., www.cpsc.gov/Newsroom/FOIA/FOIA-Request-Logs (select FY 2018 items). The logs reveal that many of these requests seek records released in response to prior FOIA requests, and others are related to particular safety investigations or recalls.

45 *See* U.S. Dep't of Hous. & Urban Dev., Freedom of Information Act Response to Sept. 29, 2014 Request by Margaret B. Kwoka (on file with author). Oddly, HUD inconsistently classified Torres Consulting, sometimes as a commercial requester, sometimes as a news media/educational requester, and sometimes as "other." *See id.*

46 Torres Consulting & Law Grp., thetorresfirm.com (last visited Oct. 5, 2020).

47 Labor Relations Inst., Inc., lrionline.com (last visited Oct. 5, 2020).

48 PTI Labor Research & Media Sols., www.ptilaborresearch.com (last visited Oct. 5, 2020).

49 Nat'l Labor Relations Bd., Freedom of Information Act Response to Apr. 15, 2016 Request by Margaret B. Kwoka (on file with author) [hereinafter NLRB Data]. Because this data did not contain an organizational field, the top requesters are listed by name rather than organization, and independent research was required to connect the requester to their employer. In these cases, Erin Lormer is a Data Specialist at the Labor Relations Institute, and Susan Connelly is the Executive Director at PTI Labor Research. *See Erin Lormer*, ZoomInfo, www.zoominfo.com/p/Erin-Lormer/-907337740 (last visited Nov. 23, 2020); *Susan Connelly*, ZoomInfo, www.zoominfo.com/p/Susan-Connelly/14063371 (last visited Nov. 23, 2020).

D. CONTRACTS, GRANTS, AND LEASES

Beyond regulated businesses and the businesses that serve those regulated entities with auxiliary services, companies that do business with the government by contract are also deeply interested in government held information. Rather than regulatory agencies, these requesters tend to dominate at agencies that manage property, produce scientific innovation, or operate arms of the military or foreign aid. For the most part, it appears that contracting companies (or aspiring contractors) seek information about competitors' bids or awarded contracts. For a small subset, information resellers play an intermediary role. But nearly all the requests for contracts and contract-related information come from commercial requesters. The agencies included in this study at which significant contract-related requests are evident are the Defense Logistics Agency (DLA), Army, Navy, Veterans Health Administration (VHA), General Services Administration (GSA), US Agency for International Development (USAID), National Institutes of Health (NIH), and National Aeronautics and Space Administration (NASA).

Nowhere is the demand for contract-related information as evident as it is at DLA, where 4,226 of its 4,420 requests in the study year, or 95.6 percent, were commercial requests.[50] Nearly all of those, in turn, are for requests for particular awarded contracts, bids for contracts, and abstracts pertaining to the bids – which is essentially summary data about the bid – for particular contracts.[51] That DLA receives so many requests for contract information makes sense; it is the agency that, in its words, "manages the global supply chain" for every branch of the military,[52] supplying "86% of the military's spare parts and nearly 100% of fuel and troop support consumables," among other things.[53]

With a single exception of an information reseller discussed below, these commercial requesters are businesses that regularly contract with DLA to provide goods and services. For example, Polytechnic Industries, Inc., which was the highest volume requester that year having filed 246 requests,[54] manufactures various metal components it sells to the military.[55] It requests, over and over again, "The ABVS summary data information (or bid abstract)" for particular contracts identified by

[50] U.S. Dep't of Def., Def. Logistics Agency, Freedom of Information Act Responses to Oct. 6, 2014 and Feb. 12, 2015 Requests by Margaret B. Kwoka (on file with author) [hereinafter DLA Data].

[51] *Id.*

[52] *About DLA*, Def. Logistics Agency, www.dla.mil/AboutDLA (last visited Nov. 23, 2020).

[53] *DLA at a Glance*, Def. Logistics Agency, www.dla.mil/AtaGlance (last visited Nov. 23, 2020).

[54] DLA Data, *supra* note 50.

[55] *About Us*, Polytechnic Indus., Inc., www.polytechnicind.com/index_files/Page366.htm (last visited Nov. 23, 2020).

number.[56] Similarly, JGB Enterprises, Inc., filed 221 requests, and it specializes in manufacturing hydraulic hoses, boasting "[o]ver 5,000 military contracts pass through our doors annually."[57] JGB's requests appear to target bid abstracts from other companies pertaining to contracts that JGB itself was eventually awarded.[58] In another example, BEC Machine Products filed 208 requests for particular contract-related information identified by contract number,[59] and it "produce[s] precision machine parts for military systems."[60]

The list of requesters who are themselves defense contractors asking for information pertaining to particular DLA contracts goes on and on. Indeed, it occupies nearly the entirety of the FOIA office's business at DLA. It is apparent from some of the requests, and easy to infer regarding the others, that contracting businesses are looking for information about their competitors. The bid, abstract, and contract information these businesses seek would hold details about their competitors' operations, capabilities, and strategies for winning DLA contracts. This information may help businesses be more successful in the marketplace for government work.

While DLA is the starkest example of this use of FOIA, contract-related information is routinely sought from branches of the military and the VHA. At the Army, for example, while commercial requesters are not separately identified and thus not able to be precisely counted, a minimum of around one thousand requests (of the total 16,828 that year) were related to particular contracts.[61] These are most likely to be requested by businesses, for precisely the reasons identified at the DLA. Similarly, though the Navy does not identify commercial requesters and thus no total count is reported in this volume, contracts make a strong appearance in the descriptions of the requests received and contracting entities are among the requesters.[62] For example, Lockheed Martin

[56] *See, e.g.*, DLA Data, *supra* note 50, at Request Nos. DSCR-13-RFOI 13-00874, DSCR-13-RFOI 13-00468; DSCR-13-RFOI 13-00616.

[57] JGB Enters., Inc., www.militarysupplier.com (last visited Oct. 5, 2020).

[58] *See* DLA Data, *supra* note 50, at Request Nos. DSCR-13-RFOI 13-00286, DSCR-13-RFOI 13-00364, DSCR-13-RFOI 13-00619.

[59] *Id.*

[60] BEC Mach. Prods., becmachine.com (last visited Oct. 5, 2020).

[61] *See* U.S. Dep't of Def., U.S. Army, Freedom of Information Act Response to Oct. 6, 2014 Request by Margaret B. Kwoka (on file with author). There were 929 requests that had the word "contract" in the subject matter, typically accompanied by a long number appearing to be attached to a particular contract. Many other requests, however, had a similarly formatted long number without the word "contract," but likely also being related to contracts. These number in the hundreds, or maybe more than 1,000, but are difficult to count because of the formatting discrepancies.

[62] *See, e.g.*, U.S. Dep't of Def., U.S. Navy, Freedom of Information Act Response to Apr. 18, 2016 Request and Nov. 1, 2016 Administrative Appeal by Margaret B. Kwoka (on file with author) [hereinafter Navy Data], at Request No. DON-NAVY-20154-009720 (Harry Pritchett of AOC Key Solutions requested a copy of a contract with KBR, Inc.). AOC Key Solutions is a consulting company that assists companies with bidding and winning government contracts. *See* AOC Key Sols., www.aockeysolutions.com (last visited Oct. 5, 2020).

made thirteen requests concerning contract information.[63] Moreover, resellers, discussed in Chapter Seven, made many such requests and are likely supplying that information to contracting businesses.

At the VHA, while commercial requesters only account for just shy of 5 percent of all requesters, their requests still number 1,291 in the study year and nearly half of those, or 525, were for contracts or business information as designated by the agency itself.[64] Among them are examples of contractors clearly seeking information about their competitors. For example, that year Economy Linen and Towel Service, Inc., which provides medical linen services,[65] made five requests for "contract bid award information for commercial services for laundry and linen services"[66] at various VA medical facilities, in which it specifies various pieces of information sought such as "pricing per piece or pound, allowed charges for linen loss, damage or replacement, delivery charges and energy surcharges," and more.[67] Other similar requests by contracting (or aspiring-to-be-contracting) businesses are scattered throughout the logs.[68]

Two non-military agencies engage in frequent contracting and thus evidence substantial requests for contract-related information. First, USAID, like the military, depends heavily on contractors to provide goods and services related to its foreign aid and development missions.[69] USAID has a small FOIA operation, receiving only 326 requests in the study year, but forty-nine of those requests contained the word "contract" in the subject matter term.[70] Second, the GSA received 1,442 requests in the study year, 41.7 percent of which were from commercial requesters. The GSA owns and leases all federal government properties, such as courts, post offices, and office spaces,[71] and thus engages in substantial lease agreements and other contractual arrangements. Requests that mentioned a lease, or a contract, or both totaled 674 that year; 337 were submitted by commercial requesters.[72]

63 Navy Data, *supra* note 62.

64 U.S. Dep't of Veterans Affairs, Veterans Health Admin., Freedom of Information Act Response to Apr. 15, 2016 Request by Margaret B. Kwoka (on file with author) [hereinafter VHA Data].

65 Economy Linen & Towel Service, www.economylinen.com (last visited Oct. 5, 2020).

66 *See* VHA Data, *supra* note 64.

67 *See, e.g., id.* at Request No. 15-07708-F.

68 *See, e.g., id.* at Request Nos. 15-07701-F (request from Gold Coast Medical Supply, which made two requests that year), 15-00757 (request from KPaul, which made sixty requests that year), 15-01835-F (request from Lockheed Martin, which made two requests that year), 15-07055-F (request from Medical Equipment and Supplies LLC, which made three requests that year), 15-01627-F (request from QB Medical, which made forty-one requests that year).

69 *See Grant and Contract Process*, U.S. Agency for Int'l Dev. (Aug. 14, 2020), www.usaid.gov/work-usaid/get-grant-or-contract/grant-and-contract-process.

70 U.S. Agency for Int'l Dev., Freedom of Information Act Response to April 15, 2016 Request by Margaret B. Kwoka (on file with author).

71 *GSA Properties*, U.S. Gen. Servs. Admin. (Oct. 11, 2017), www.gsa.gov/real-estate/gsa-properties.

72 Gen. Servs. Admin., Freedom of Information Act Response to Mar. 6, 2018 Request by Margaret B. Kwoka (on file with author).

Finally, the government's scientific arms receive requests for similar information they hold. At NASA, contracting is a key component of how the agency accomplishes its mission.[73] Out of a total 342 commercial requests (representing 38.6 percent of the agency's total), at least 185 are concerning contracting.[74] That is, a majority of commercial requests at NASA sought contract-related information. Similarly, at NIH, though contracts are not the means of operations, grants to particular scientists and scientific institutions are the mission of the agency. Of the agency's 1,198 total requests, 436 (or 36.4 percent) were commercial, and of those, 190 (or 43.6 percent) were about grant-related information.[75]

In all, businesses have a great interest in obtaining documents about the government's own contracting process, whether it be procurement, collaboration, or funding opportunities. Contract, lease, and grant-related requests flood certain FOIA offices, mostly from businesses seeking to place themselves in a better position to obtain key government opportunities. No doubt, there is a public benefit to increased competition in the government contracting process, as it may produce better goods or services or pricing for the public. Moreover, some grant, license, lease, or contract information may be sought for more oversight or anti-corruption purposes. But this data reveals the vast glut of these requests are primarily for private use, not to publicize the activities or operations of government for all to see.

E. CORPORATE LAWYERS

Lawyers featured prominently in first-person uses of FOIA,[76] discussed at length in Chapters 4 and 5. But lawyers make a distinct and also prominent appearance among commercial requesters, and these are lawyers representing businesses. Corporate lawyers make heavy use of FOIA in many corners of the federal government. The uses are varied, and sometimes difficult to ascertain, but reflect corporate and commercial concerns and largely appear to advance the private interests of these lawyers' business clients and not public knowledge and oversight of agency activity.

At many health, safety, and consumer protection agencies, corporate lawyers use FOIA to gather information to defend their clients against liability. Sometimes attorneys are assisting clients in navigating investigations or defending against

[73] *Contracts*, Nat'l Aeronautics & Space Admin. (May 2, 2018), www.nasa.gov/centers/johnson/news/contracts/index.html.

[74] Nat'l Space & Aeronautics Admin., Freedom of Information Act Response to Mar. 6, 2018 Request by Margaret B. Kwoka (on file with author). This count includes both those requests that mention "contract" as a term, and those that specify a particular "NN" number which is the designation for a NASA contract.

[75] U.S. Dep't of Health & Human Servs., Nat'l Insts. of Health, Freedom of Information Act Responses to Sept. 29, 2014 and Feb. 12, 2015, Requests by Margaret B. Kwoka (on file with author).

[76] First-person FOIA requests refer to the use of FOIA by individuals to secure their own government files. *See supra* Ch. 3, pt. C(1) for a detailed discussion.

enforcement actions initiated by the agency itself. Other times attorneys are protecting clients from third parties such as employees or consumers who have brought or may bring a civil suit. Between agencies, the balance between defense against public enforcement and private enforcement differs based on a variety of factors, such as the strength of the agency's enforcement practices, the availability of a private right of action against the regulated entity, and the various incentives involved.

For example, most of the largest FOIA operations at the Department of Labor (DOL) – including the Occupational Safety and Health Administration (OSHA), MSHA, and Wage and Hour Division (WHD) – receive significant numbers of requests from corporate lawyers. These requests appear mostly aimed at potential or actual third-party workplace litigation in which their clients are defendants. However, in each instance, it is also possible that requests relate to agency enforcement proceedings instead of or in addition to private litigation.

For example, at OSHA, where 6,107 of its 8,724 requests were commercial in nature, corporate lawyers play a very prominent role.[77] Among the top fifteen requesters at OSHA,[78] law firms accounted for nine, with six of those nine qualifying as corporate or commercial law firms with mainly business clients. To be sure, three are plaintiff-side personal injury law firms representing individuals,[79] for whom requests are much more likely to qualify as first-person requests, but these firms are squarely outnumbered by corporate law firms in the FOIA logs.

Several of these top law firm requesters are likely looking for records about their own clients' interactions with the agency. One attorney at Ogletree who made many of that law firm's thirty-seven requests represents employers in OSHA enforcement matters,[80] and made requests for records about particular companies, or particular inspections or OSHA investigations.[81] Similarly, an attorney at Jackson Lewis who

77 U.S. Dep't of Labor, Occupational Safety & Health Admin., Freedom of Information Act Response to April 19, 2016 Request by Margaret B. Kwoka (on file with author) [hereinafter OSHA Data].

78 Notable exceptions include some insurance industry requesters, presumably engaged in claims adjusting. *See id.* (Travelers Insurance & Metropolitan Reporting Bureau). In addition, the third most frequent requester, the Hubble Foundation, is inconsistently categorized as commercial and non-commercial, but is a non-profit organization dedicating to supporting families of workers who work at heights and who are injured or killed by workplace falls. *See Who We Are*, Hubble Found., www.hubblefoundation.org/who-we-are (last visited Nov. 23, 2020). Finally, lower on the list is the Service Employees International Union.

79 OSHA Data, supra note 77; Saltz, Mongeluzzi & Bendesky, www.smbb.com (last visited Oct. 5, 2020) (tied for ninth most frequent requester at OSHA, having submitted twenty-five requests); Domingo Garcia Law Office, domingogarcia.com (last visited Oct. 5, 2020) (tied for ninth); Marsh, Rickard & Bryan, P.C., www.mrblaw.com (last visited Oct. 5, 2020) (twelfth most frequent requester at OSHA with twenty-two requests).

80 *Shontell Powell: Professional Biography*, Nat'l L. R., www.natlawreview.com/author/shontell-powell (last visited Nov. 23, 2020) (confirming Ms. Powell's employment at Ogletree Deakins in 2017).

81 OSHA Data, *supra* note 77.

made most of that firm's twenty-three requests[82] specializes in representing employers in health and safety compliance, inspections, and investigations.[83] A third law firm, which submitted nineteen requests for specific company or job site information, similarly does general employer compliance and defense work.[84] At firms such as these, the requests are likely about the attorney's own clients and the records the agency holds about them, akin to first-person requests on behalf of their business clients. They may be used to defend against agency enforcement or advocate before the agency, and/or to defend against third party litigation brought by injured employees.

Another group of top-requesting law firms specializes in asbestos defense. At Foley & Mansfield (thirty-five requests), Hawkins Parnell Thackson & Young (thirty-two requests), and Pond North LLP (twenty requests), the requesting attorneys appear to focus on this practice in particular and their requests often seek asbestos-related information at particular job sites.[85] Attorneys who practice in this line of work explained to me that asbestos defense litigators often use FOIA to find evidence of alternative sources of asbestos exposure, and thus that these requests are about documented asbestos at other employers' workplaces, not their own client's.[86] These, too, aid the attorneys in defending their clients against workplace related claims brought against them arising out of asbestos exposure.

At MSHA the situation is similar. Apart from regulated entities requesting directly, discussed above, corporate attorneys are the next most represented frequent requesters, with fourteen such requesters who made more than five requests that year.[87] In fact, corporate attorneys average a higher volume of requests, and thus may be slightly fewer in number but are likely responsible for a greater proportion of requests at MSHA than regulated entities.

Many of the same firms appear on the list of frequent requesters at MSHA as appeared in OSHA's logs, including Ogletree Deakins (twenty-two requests, fourth highest) and Jackson Lewis (fourteen requests, ninth most-frequent requester). Others appear to focus in particular on representing mining companies. For example, Jackson Kelly, which rang in a whopping 155 requests out of 1,265 in the study year, constituting 12.2 percent of all MSHA requests alone, lists mining

[82] *Id.*

[83] *Pedro P. Forment*, Jackson Lewis, www.jacksonlewis.com/people/pedro-p-forment (last visited Nov. 23, 2020).

[84] Marshall Dennehey, marshalldennehey.com (last visited Oct. 5, 2020).

[85] *Jennifer A. Cecil*, Foley & Mansfield, www.foleymansfield.com/professionals/jcecil (practicing toxic tort law and making OSHA requests concerning asbestos); *Ana T. Portillo*, Hawkins Parnell Thackston & Young LLP, www.hptylaw.com/attorneys-ana-portillo.html (specializing in toxic tort product liability defense and making OSHA requests concerning asbestos); Pond North LLP, www.pondnorth.com/about (last visited Oct. 5, 2020).

[86] *See, e.g.*, Telephone Interview with Theresa Queen, Att'y, Law Firm 7 (July 21, 2017); Telephone Interview with Laura Davis, Att'y, Law Firm 8 (July 25, 2017).

[87] MSHA Data, *supra* note 6.

companies as one of its areas of focus.[88] Other law firms that appear on the list similarly seem to represent business interests including in energy and mining, suggesting they are requesting on behalf of their regulated entity clients.[89] The subject matters of these requests, just like the regulated entities themselves, specify particular mines, inspections, or incidents.[90]

To round out DOL's requesting, WHD also shows high levels of corporate law firm requesting. There, among the 131 requesters who made three or more requests, 88 percent came from law firms.[91] Those firms, however, were more mixed in their representation. Many of the most frequent requesters are plaintiff-side employment lawyers, not corporate defense attorneys. These plaintiff-side lawyers again are much more likely to be engaged in what this study classifies as first-person requesting, and is discussed as such. But those corporate defense attorneys that are present fall squarely in the commercial category. For instance, Littler Mendelson made forty-seven requests, and it represents companies in a variety of matters, including employment disputes.[92] Jackson Lewis makes another appearance, having filed nineteen requests in the study year. And Pechman Law Group, PLLC, which made fourteen requests, uniquely represents both plaintiffs and defendants in employment disputes.[93]

Beyond DOL, however, similar dynamics are at play at FTC, where attorneys are using FOIA in defense of their clients with respect to both public and private enforcement. Because this agency breaks down its requester categories with more specificity, law firms are identified separately and constitute 296 of the agency's total 1,538 requests in the study year, or 19.2 percent.[94] Other commercial requesters made 232 requests, or 15.8 percent of FTC's total, meaning that law firms are the (narrow) majority of commercial requesters at FTC. The top law firm requester is an attorney at Bryan Cave who specializes in data privacy regulations and "assist[s] clients in responding to investigations conducted by the FTC."[95] Of his seventy

88 *Id.*; *Denver*, Jackson Kelly PLLC, www.jacksonkelly.com/offices/denver (last visited Nov. 23, 2020).

89 MSHA Data, supra note 6; *see, e.g.*, Dinsmore & Shohl, www.dinsmore.com (last visited Oct. 5, 2020) (thirty requests); Steptoe & Johnson, www.steptoe-johnson.com (last visited Oct. 5, 2020) (twenty-two requests); *Regulatory*, Flaherty Sensabaugh, flahertylegal.com/practice-area/regulatory (last visited Oct. 5, 2020) (sixteen requests), Maynard Cooper, www.maynardcooper.com (last visited Oct. 5, 2020) (fifteen requests).

90 MSHA Data, *supra* note 6, at Request Nos. 441-768920.0 (request by Steptoe & Johnson re: July 13, 2014 incident at Camp 9 Prep Plant), 1079-780894.0 (request by Ogletree Deakins re: Meile Mine, Event No. 6597539), 800-775339.0 (request from Jackson Kelly re: Sumitomo Metal Mining LLC, Event No. 6598045).

91 U.S. Dep't of Labor, Wage & Hour Div., Freedom of Information Act Response to Apr. 15, 2016 Request by Margaret B. Kwoka (on file with author).

92 *Id.*; Littler Mendelson PC, www.littler.com (last visited Oct. 5, 2020).

93 Pechman Law Group PLLC, pechmanlaw.com (last visited Oct. 5, 2020).

94 FTC Data, *supra* 41.

95 *Joshua A. James*, Bryan Cave, www.bryancave.com/joshjames.

requests, forty-seven were for information about particular companies or sets of particular consumer complaints, and the remaining twenty-three were for FTC's own FOIA logs.[96] Two other lawyers at the same firm made significant numbers of requests to the FTC, and their practices involve compliance with FTC regulations, defending against FTC investigations, and/or defending data privacy class action lawsuits.[97]

Two other health and safety agencies experience significant attorney requesting, though at these agencies the attorneys are thoroughly mixed between plaintiff-side tort lawyers and defense-side corporate attorneys. First, at the Centers for Disease Control and Prevention (CDC), while some attorneys are requesting records about a specific person, almost certainly their client, and thus are first-person in nature (discussed in Chapter 5), other attorneys are corporate lawyers acting in a defense capacity and are requesting records to defend their business clients in investigations or lawsuits. Roetzel & Andress, which submitted seven requests, making it the ninth most frequent requester at the CDC, represents companies across a variety of areas,[98] and its requests are generally about research, recommendations, or investigations about a particular company conducted by the National Institute of Occupational Safety and Health, a division of the CDC. These subject matters suggest the requests relate to workplace injuries or employer liability.[99] Two other corporate defense firms make the frequent requester list, generally submitting requests concerning CDC investigation of particular disease outbreak incidents.[100]

Next, at the CPSC, attorneys similarly use FOIA on both sides of the "v." Law firms submitted 188 of 525 requests received by CPSC in the study year, or 35.8 percent, but are fully mixed between plaintiff-side personal injury attorneys and corporate defense attorneys.[101] In this case, however, lawyers on both sides tend to be asking about records concerning particular products' safety records, rather than pertaining to an individual, and thus the plaintiff-side attorneys were not included in the discussion of first-person requesting in Chapter 5.

Beyond the regulatory context, some other agencies experience significant corporate attorney requesting for idiosyncratic reasons. At the Internal Revenue Service (IRS), tax attorneys dominate the frequent requester list. For example, of the IRS's

96 FTC Data, *supra* 41.

97 *See id.*; *David A. Zetoony*, Bryan Cave, www.bryancave.com/davidzetoony (last visited Oct. 5, 2020) (eighteen requests); *Kristin Robinson*, Bryan Cave, www.bryancave.com/kristinrobinson (last visited Oct. 5, 2020) (eight requests).

98 Roetzel & Andress, www.ralaw.com (last visited Oct. 5, 2020).

99 U.S. Dep't of Health & Human Servs., Ctrs. for Disease Control, Freedom of Information Act Response to Feb. 24, 2018 Request by Margaret B. Kwoka (on file with author).

100 *See id.* (indicating that Faegre Baker Daniels, submitted six requests and Balch & Bingham LLP submitted four).

101 *Id.* (showing Martin, Hardin & Mazzotti LLP, a plaintiff-side law firm, made fifteen requests, Schiffmann Firm LLC, another plaintiff-side law firm, made three requests, Munger Tolles & Olson LLP, a defense-side law firm, made one request, and Mintz Levin, a defense-side law firm, made one request).

7,913 requests, the Bryson Law Firm[102] made 174, Len W Stauffenger Attorney and Counselor at Law[103] made 134, the Alliant Group[104] made 119, and the Law Offices of Nick Nemeth[105] made 112. While interviews with some tax attorneys suggest that a majority of these requests are likely made on behalf of invidual clients, all of the lawyers I spoke with also represented business clients, and thus business interests are also driving FOIA requests to the IRS as well.[106]

At the US Postal Service, lawyers use FOIA in droves looking for the addresses for individuals. Some of the law firm requests indicate that service of process – the formal step to notify someone that they are being sued – is the motivating force, such as one for change of address orders filed by a particular person that specifies the request is "related to service of process on this individual."[107] Of the 675 commercial requests, the word "address" appeared in the subject matter 275 times.[108]

At the NLRB, attorneys representing both employers and unions are some of the top requesters, though for various reasons concerning the NLRB charge process, it is unlikely these are either regarding agency enforcement or third-party liability. The NLRB process for investigating a charge of unfair labor practice is an internal one, the result of which is either for the agency to decide not to issue a formal complaint before the administrative law judge or to file such a complaint.[109] Either way, the final determination is released to the charging and charged parties, and the Administrative Law Judge process (if it moves forward) has a discovery mechanism.[110] But there is no private cause of action for the charging party to sue the charged party, and so the only remedy is through the agency.[111] Because private litigation over these claims is non-existent, FOIA does not serve as a discovery workaround at the NLRB. Rather, lawyers must be using FOIA for other reasons, even though most still request some case related information.

[102] Bryson Law Firm LLC, www.brysonlawfirm.com (last visited Oct. 5, 2020).

[103] IRS Help LLC, www.fixtaxproblemsnow.com (last visited Oct. 5, 2020).

[104] AlliantGroup LP, www.alliantgroup.com/2017/08/23/strengthening-american-businesses (last visited Nov. 23, 2020).

[105] Law Offices of Nick Nemeth LLC, www.myirsteam.com (last visited Oct. 5, 2020).

[106] *See, e.g.*, Telephone Interview with Gideon Price, Att'y, Law Firm 14 (Jan. 12, 2021) (estimating that about thirty percent of clients are business clients); Telephone Interview with Chandler Soto, Att'y, Law Firm 17 (Feb. 4, 2021) (same).

[107] U.S. Postal Serv., Freedom of Information Act Response to March 13, 2018 Request by Margaret B. Kwoka (on file with author), at Request No. 2017-FRPO-00096.

[108] *Id.*

[109] *Unfair Labor Practice Process Chart*, Nat'l Labor Relations Bd., www.nlrb.gov/resources/nlrb-process/unfair-labor-practice-process-chart (last visited Nov. 23, 2020).

[110] *Id.*

[111] *The NLRB Process*, Nat'l Labor Relations Bd., www.nlrb.gov/resources/nlrb-process (last visited Nov. 23, 2020).

For example, employer-side firm Ogletree Deakins made ninety-six requests to NLRB, mostly for past-filed charges and petitions,[112] union-side firm Weinberg, Roger & Rosenfeld made twenty-eight requests, mostly for certain documents filed with respect to particular cases,[113] employer-side firm Jackson Lewis made twenty-eight requests, mostly for past-filed charges,[114] and employer-side firm Perez Vaughn Feasby made twenty-one requests, mostly for employee handbooks and manuals for NLRB employees themselves.[115] Union-side requests would not have the profit motive of corporate requesters, but the employer-side firms would fall squarely in the commercial requesting category.

Finally, two agencies that manage public lands – the National Park Service (NPS) and the Bureau of Land Management (BLM) – receive corporate law firm requests as well. At BLM, 108 of their 734 requests were commercial.[116] While no single firm submitted substantial numbers of requests, the most frequent type of commercial requester was a law firm.[117] The topics of the requests varied from incident investigations to correspondence to rulemaking records.[118] And at NPS, 179 of the 1,224 requests received in the study year were commercial requests, and a majority of those were law firms.[119] Again, no one firm dominated the requesting, but the requests tended to be about incidents on National Park property, agency communications and correspondence, or records about agency actions.[120]

To be sure, it may seem like corporate attorneys as a group do not hang together very well. They are worthy of a collective discussion, however, in part because they touch so many areas of government. Moreover, they represent the interests of their clients, for the most part, and thus act as a proxy for other kinds of requesting: regulated party requesting, end-runs around discovery, inquiries into competitor

[112] *Vivian Whitmire*, LinkedIn, www.linkedin.com/in/vivian-whitmire-96829417a (last visited Nov. 23, 2020).

[113] NLRB Data, supra note 49; *David A Rosenfeld*, Weinberg, Roger & Rosenfeld P.C., unioncounsel.net/attorneys/D_Rosenfeld.html (last visited Nov. 23, 2020).

[114] NLRB Data, *supra* note 49; *Paul T. Trimmer*, Jackson Lewis P.C., www.jacksonlewis.com/people/paul-t-trimmer (last visited Nov. 23, 2020).

[115] NLRB Data, *supra* note 49; *Christopher W. Rowlett*, Perez, Vaughn & Feasby, Inc., pvflaw.com/our-partners/christopher-rowlett/christopher-w-rowlett (last visited Nov. 23, 2020).

[116] U.S. Dep't of Interior, Bureau of Land Mgmt., Freedom of Information Act Response to Mar. 6, 2018 Request by Margaret B. Kwoka (on file with author).

[117] *Id.*

[118] *Id.* at Request Nos. BLM-2017-00829 (requesting records regarding OHV Incident on Sand Mountain from Bowman & Brooke), BLM-2017-00547 (requesting correspondence between BLM and NM Environmental Department regarding Mosaic Mine from Miller Stratvert), BLM-2017-00498 (requesting records regarding Colorado River Valley Field Office Proposed Decision from Hageman Law P.C.).

[119] U.S. Dep't of Interior, Nat'l Park Serv., Freedom of Information Act Response to Mar. 6, 2018 Request by Margaret B. Kwoka (on file with author).

[120] *Id.* at Request Nos. NPS-2017-00026 (requesting an Incident Report for Yellowstone Kayak Guide Fatality Case from Caesar & Napoli P.C), NPS-2017-00700 (requesting correspondence on labor guidelines from Kippes & Bergin, Attorneys at Law PLLC), NPS-2017-00154 (requesting copy of EEO Report from Decolator, Cohen & Diprisco LLP).

businesses, and more. Yet, in many of these instances, the information constituents – the represented parties – may not be particularly well-served by FOIA, except as a last resort. And most importantly, as this discussion highlights, lawyers' use of FOIA in this regard largely serves the private interests of their clients, not the public's interest in knowing what its government is up to.

* * *

Commercial uses of FOIA are wide-ranging, and touch on huge swaths of federal agencies' FOIA practices. At many, many agencies, commercial FOIA requesting dominates. Businesses may, on occasion, request information so they can better participate in or facilitate democratic decision-making and agency accountability to the public. But this Chapter documents how, by and large, businesses use information they obtain under FOIA privately, for their own profit-making purposes. Any public benefit is incidental and, in any case, does not specifically advance the public's knowledge of government operations or activities. In fact, the information businesses receive is often useful precisely because it is not generally known, and, as a result, is closely held by the requesting business. Rather than promoting public transparency, commercial requesting often leads to private secret-keeping. Secret-keeping is fine, in business, but it is not the business FOIA is designed to promote.

7

Information Resellers

There is a group of commercial requesters distinct from the various types of businesses discussed in Chapter 6 that are using FOIA to retrieve records as part of their other profit-making enterprises. Indeed, this group of commercial requesters is the one that, in many ways, is most telling about businesses' information constituencies and the value of federal records to commercial enterprises. They also tell us much about FOIA, and for this reason are worthy of separate examination. These requesters are what I call information resellers.

Information resellers' business model is to request records under FOIA and to resell those records at a profit. Information resellers tend to submit large volumes of requests. They sometimes warehouse federal records in databases or repositories, selling them off to interested buyers one at a time or marketing access to their accumulated databases for a subscription fee. Sometimes they make custom requests on behalf of a client and charge the client for the service of retrieving federal records under FOIA on their behalf.[1] Either way, they trade in public records obtained under FOIA.

To be clear, there is nothing unseemly, unethical, inappropriate, or illegal about this line of business. Nothing in FOIA prohibits the practice. To the extent they are offering a service that businesses are willing to pay for, it is a legitimate enterprise. And, indeed, resellers do offer services of value, which is precisely why businesses turn to these resellers in droves rather than simply filing FOIA requests themselves.

The reasons for using a reseller can vary. Sometimes the value of the reseller is a comprehensible database: resellers have already compiled, indexed, or otherwise made more searchable or more accessible certain federal records. Sometimes it is a

[1] DOJ first identified these two methods of reselling in a 1986 issue of its FOIA Update. U.S. Dep't of Justice, Office of Info. Policy, *Surrogate FOIA Requests Increasing*, 7 FOIA Update 1 (Jan. 1, 1986), www.justice.gov/oip/blog/foia-update-surrogate-foia-requests-increasing [hereinafter *DOJ 1986 FOIA Update*] (describing "clearinghouse" and "surrogate" requesters).

question of speed: a reseller may be able to provide faster access to public records than the federal government can, because the reseller already requested and warehoused the records. Sometimes businesses are looking for an intermediary with expertise in the requesting process, or they simply prefer to outsource the time and resources this process takes. Sometimes it is anonymity the client seeks, and they are using an information reseller to mask the identity of the requesting party. Regardless, there is no question that these companies add value for which the market is willing to compensate them.

There is also a grey area in defining information resellers. One could conceive of a pure information reseller as a company that requests records and simply resells those exact records at a markup. Here, the added value may be speed, time, anonymity, or expertise in navigating the FOIA process on behalf of the client. Another kind of reseller is one that adds value by, say, indexing the records so they are more easily identifiable. Thus, the sold product is more akin to a nicely organized library, or a great Google search engine. After all, Westlaw and Lexis are built off the same premise: they sell better organized and more efficient access to what are inherently public court documents. A step further than that would be an industry or trade newsletter, or some other compilation of information from the public documents. Many of these are little more than summaries of the records – short of what most of us consider to be journalistic activity – but original in content rather than simply reselling the underlying records. To round it out, one could take it a step farther and say that due diligence or consulting firms are a form of reseller; after all, they are mostly just conveying the information that they obtain from FOIA requests to their client. This study does not go so far as to define that last category of businesses as resellers, but ambiguity certainly exists as to where to draw the line.

A. RESELLERS ARE LONG-STANDING REQUESTERS

The existence of information resellers as a requester category has been acknowledged, albeit sporadically, for more than three decades. As early as 1986, the US Department of Justice (DOJ) asserted a "growing trend toward 'surrogate' Freedom of Information Act requests," which it defined as requests that are "made by persons or entities seeking federal records on behalf of others." DOJ went on: "Perhaps the best known surrogate requesters are the commercial enterprises that have sprung up in the Washington, D.C. area to engage in the business of information acquisition and sale. Referred to by some as "cottage industries," these business entities serve a nationwide clientele consisting of any corporate or other type of customer willing to pay for compiled government information."[2]

The DOJ flagged the Food and Drug Administration (FDA) and the US Department of Defense (DoD) as targets for these high-volume business requesters,

[2] *Id.*

something that continues to be true today and is detailed in this volume. It also included a requester in this category that I classify differently: the National Security Archive, which is a non-profit research institute at George Washington University, but the DOJ's report emphasized the burden that requester placed on agencies as similar in kind.[3]

Fast forward twenty years, in 2006, the now-defunct Coalition of Journalists for Open Government (CJOG) analyzed about 6,000 FOIA requests for seventeen different agencies, and found that 60 percent were commercial, with a quarter of commercial requests coming from "data brokers working on behalf of clients."[4] The study further declares that "FOIA Requesting Becomes a Cottage Industry," with professional requesters submitting requests and reselling data to other businesses. The group concluded that, "professional requesters are the second-largest subcategory of FOIA users, after law firms."[5] Particular examples were cited, including Input and Centurion Research, which provide access to information about government contracting; SEC Insight, which gathers documents about US Securities and Exchange Commission (SEC) investigations; and Adams, Nash, Haskell & Sheridan, which helps employers fight unions by obtaining records from the National Labor Relations Board.[6]

The data gathered for this study does not suggest, as these previous reports do, that information resellers are dominating the FOIA landscape as a whole. Indeed, as described in the chapters above, first-person requesting[7] outpaces commercial requesting by a factor of ten, and certainly information resellers are only a fraction of commercial requesting. That said, at some agencies commercial requesting constitutes *nearly all* of the agency's total requests; and at many of those agencies, information resellers play a very significant role. Remarkably, some of the same resellers identified by the DOJ in 1986 and the CJOG in 2006 are still active in this field. The significant numbers of requests by these businesses offer a particularly interesting glimpse into business information constituencies.

B. FDA INSPECTION RECORDS

The FDA is a natural place to begin, both because it was identified early by the DOJ as the recipient of reseller requests and because its logs reveal multiple resellers that compete against one another. The FDA received 10,167 requests in the study year,

3 *Id.*

4 COAL. OF JOURNALISTS FOR OPEN GOV'T, FREQUENT FILERS: BUSINESSES MAKE FOIA THEIR BUSINESS 1 (July 3, 2006), available at www.humanrightsinitiative.org/programs/ai/rti/international/laws_papers/intl/businesses_make_foia_their_business.pdf [hereinafter CJOG STUDY].

5 *Id.* at 6.

6 *Id.* at 7.

7 "First-person FOIA requesting" refers to the use of FOIA by individuals to secure their own government files. *See supra* Ch. 3, pt. C(1) for a detailed discussion.

74.9 percent of which were from commercial requesters.[8] At the FDA, resellers dominate the frequent requester list. The single highest volume requester – having submitted 571 requests that year – was FOI Services, Inc., a company that is dedicated to warehousing FDA records in a database for which it sells subscription access.[9] It also files some custom FOIA requests on behalf of particular clients.[10] FOI Services was one of the original companies identified by the DOJ as a reseller: in 1986 the DOJ noted that the FOI Services's "request load is so great at the FDA that that agency bills it on a monthly basis, rather than for individual requests, and its monthly FOIA bill is sometimes as high as $4,000."[11] A majority of its requests were for facilities inspection reports, or Form 483s, which document the details of FDA inspection events.[12]

FDA News is another reseller, which submitted 237 requests in the study year.[13] While it does produce some newsletters and other editorialized content, FDA News also runs a database service for facilities inspection reports called 483sOnline.com, which advertises "instant, unlimited access to more than 7,200 Form 483s."[14] An annual subscription is $1,297, or individual 483 Forms can be purchased for $117 a piece.[15] Unsurprisingly, nearly all of its requests are for Form 483s.[16]

Another frequently requesting reseller is Washington Information Source (WIS), which made 344 requests in the study year.[17] Strangely, the agency more often categorized this requester as news media, rather than commercial (though it was inconsistent),[18] but its business model is essentially the same as FOI Services Inc.

8 U.S. Dep't of Health & Human Servs., Food & Drug Admin. Freedom of Information Act Response to June 24, 2014 Request by Margaret B. Kwoka (on file with author) [hereinafter FDA Data].

9 *Id.*; *About Us*, FOI Servs., Inc., www.foiservices.com/brochure/about.cfm.

10 *Document Retrieval*, FOI Servs., Inc., www.foiservices.com/brochure/docretrieval.cfm.

11 *DOJ 1986 FOIA Update*, *supra* note 1.

12 FDA Data, *supra* note 8. Other requests that were frequent were premarket notifications for medical devices, new drug applications, and the FOIA logs themselves. *See, e.g.*, *id.* at Request Nos. 2013-2452 (premarket notification), 2013-2225 (new drug application), 2013-2664 (FOIA log). *See FDA Form 483 Frequently Asked Questions*, U.S. Food & Drug Admin. (Jan. 9, 2020), www.fda.gov/ICECI/Inspections/ucm256377.htm.

13 FDA Data, *supra* note 8.

14 *Form 483s Database*, FDA News, www.fdanews.com/form483 (last visited Nov. 23, 2020). The remaining FOIA requests were mostly requests for FDA's FOIA logs. *See, e.g.*, FDA Data, *supra* note 8, at Request No. 2013-2313 (requesting "FOIA Request Log (03/18/2013 – 03/22/2013)").

15 *Form 483s Database*, *supra* note 14.

16 *See, e.g.*, FDA Data *supra* note 8, at Request Nos. 2013-23 (request for "all notices to pharmaceuticals – 483s 11/12"), 2013-264 (request for "Aptuit, LLC Harrsonville, MO-483 11/12").

17 FDA Data, *supra* note 8.

18 *Id.* Out of 344 total requests by WIS, 269 were designated news media and seventy-five were designated commercial requests. Again, from looking at a sample, it was not possible to identify differences in content that would explain differing categorizations. For example, two requests contained identical language requesting news media status, and one was granted and another was not. *Compare id.* at Request No. 2013-7573 (news media), *with id.* at Request No. 2013-7962 (commercial).

and FDA News. It has a database of "all the critical inspection records you need . . . in one handy source," access to which can be purchased for around $1,000.[19] And, correspondingly, the vast majority of its requests are for inspection-related records.[20] WIS also synthesizes information from these records into various industry newsletter products.[21]

Notably, these three dominant players, each engaging in relatively pure information reselling, are all selling essentially the same thing: FDA documents pertaining to agency inspections of regulated facilities. These three resellers also routinely request, albeit in smaller numbers than inspection reports, the agency's FOIA logs in various time periods. WIS's website suggests why: it advertises the ability to provide "[i]nformation on which firms are trying to get copies of the reports you filed with FDA."[22] That is, businesses are using information resellers to find out what information their competitors are trying to get about themselves.

C. SEC INVESTIGATIONS

The SEC is another agency where information resellers have a particularly strong presence. Its highest-volume requester in the study year, SECProbes.com, is an information reseller that submitted 2,498 requests, or 20.7 percent of SEC's total requests that year.[23] In fact, it is the latest of a series of reselling businesses founded

[19] *483s/EIRs on DVD*, Wash. Info. Source, fdadocuments.org/store/483s-EIRs-on-DVD-p237110260 (last visited Nov. 23, 2020). "FDADocuments.org" is the website for the RECORD-RETRIEVE Service, a subsidiary of Washington Information Source Company. Wash. Info. Source, www.fdadocuments.org (last visited Nov. 23, 2020) (describing Washington Information Source and its relationship to RECORD-RETRIEVE).

[20] It also sells individual records such as premarket notifications and approvals for medical devices. *See Rates and Policies*, Wash. Info. Source, fdadocuments.org/policies (last visited Nov. 23, 2020).

[21] *See Adverse Event Reporting News*, Wash. Info. Source, www.fdadocuments.org/store/adverse-event-reporting-news-p310115 (last visited Nov. 23, 2020) ("It's your best solution for avoiding problems with the FDA."); *see also GMP Validation Handbook*, Wash. Info. Source, www.fdadocuments.org/store/gmp-validation-handbook-p310113 (last visited Nov. 23, 2020) ("800 pages of importance guidance . . . documents that are vitally important to keep you in compliance with FDA and EMA inspections.").

[22] *Adverse Event Reporting News*, *supra* note 21.

[23] U.S. Sec. & Exch. Comm'n, Freedom of Information Act Response to Sept. 5, 2014 Request by Margaret B. Kwoka (on file with author); FOIA Logs, U.S. Sec. & Exch. Comm'n, www.sec.gov/foia/docs/foia-logs.htm (select "2013" and "2014") [hereinafter SEC Data]. The dataset compiled includes the months between January 2013 and December 2013, representing CY 2013. Over time the SEC changed its approach to categorizing John Gavin for fee purposes. It used to classify him as a commercial requester. Then, after the 2007 FOIA amendments broadening the definition of news media, it reclassified him as a news media requester at his request. Video Conference Call Interview with Barry Walters, Chief FOIA Officer, Olivier Girod, Deputy Chief FOIA Officer, Mark Siford, Counsel to the Dir./Chief FOIA Officer & John Livornese, FOIA/PA Officer, U.S. Sec. & Exch. Comm'n (July 21, 2016). This study, however, concludes that he is more properly classified as a commercial requester, indeed an information reseller, even if SEC has decided to provide a more favorable fee status.

by John Gavin that are dedicated to providing due diligence records related to SEC investigations.[24] At one point, the business was called SEC Insight, one of the resellers identified by CJOG. SEC Insight's motto was: "Just because it's public information … doesn't mean it's public knowledge."[25] Access to the watchlist it produced with these records sold for as much as $50,000 a year to hedge funds and other investment firms.[26] SECProbes.com never materialized as a functioning website, but Probes Reporter appears to have taken its place.[27] Probes Reporter offers the same kind of information at subscription prices, starting at $1,200 for individuals, and offers customized services for institutional customers.[28] Indeed, it advertises that, "each year, we file about 2,500 [FOIA] requests" to the SEC, beginning in the year 2000.[29] In essence, this reseller is providing records for due diligence purposes, but instead of acting as a due diligence company itself, it warehouses the records and lets elite business clients peruse them on their own.

D. PUBLICLY FILED COMMERCIAL AGREEMENTS

Two other information resellers market databases filled with corporate contracts that were filed with the SEC. While the SEC filings by publicly traded companies are typically immediately public, certain exhibits are filed under a confidential treatment rule. Resellers typically file a request for these contract-containing records immediately upon expiration of the confidentiality time period.[30] These contracts contain information that is potentially commercially valuable for competitors and other industry actors.

BioScience Advisors, which filed 1,323 requests in the study year for particular exhibits to public filings, offers a signature database product containing copies of "10,900 unredacted contracts obtained through Freedom of Information Act (FOIA) disclosures."[31] Access to the database costs nearly $10,000 a year.[32] Similarly, RoyaltyStat LLC, which submitted 548 requests for exhibits to public filings in the study year, offers a database product containing "royalty rates and profit indicators" useful for businesses in a variety of regulatory, enforcement, and commercial negotiations.[33]

24 Gretchen Morgenson, *Deafened by the S.E.C.'s Silence, He Sued*, N.Y. TIMES (May 28, 2006), www.nytimes.com/2006/05/28/business/yourmoney/28gavin.html.
25 CJOG STUDY, *supra* note 4, at 6.
26 *Id.* at 7.
27 PROBE'S REPORTER, probesreporter.com (last visited Oct. 25, 2020).
28 *Service Levels*, PROBE'S REPORTER, probesreporter.com/service-levels (last visited Oct. 25, 2020).
29 *About Us*, PROBE'S REPORTER, probesreporter.com/about-us (last visited Oct. 25, 2020).
30 *See* SEC Data, *supra* note 23.
31 *Id.*; BIOSCIDB, www.bioscidb.com (last visited Oct. 25, 2020).
32 *Pricing*, BIOSCIDB, www.bioscidb.com/pricing (last visited Oct. 25, 2020).
33 SEC Data, *supra* note 23; ROYALTYSTAT, www.royaltystat.com/royaltystat.cfm (last visited Oct. 25, 2020).

These agreements and exhibits to public filings are mostly useful to competitors looking for insights into the target business's commercial practices, intellectual property, or competitive advantages. But the value is a private, commercial one, not a public one. Moreover, these agreements typically show very little about government itself; rather, this is a form of routine corporate espionage. There may be end benefits to consumers or the public in the marketplace, but the values advanced are not ones of public oversight.

E. DEFENSE CONTRACTING

Defense contracting is another area where information reseller requests are significant. In its 1986 report, the DOJ (with some apparent disdain) labeled these resellers in particular as "'data brokers,' because they do little more than compile publicly available information pertaining to the defense procurement process and then sell it, at considerable profit, to potential government contract bidders."[34] One such business now dominates the field: Day & Day, Inc., which made 224 requests to the Defense Logistics Agency (DLA), all for information about particular bids or contracts awarded.[35] In turn, Day & Day markets an online database of DLA procurements, contracts, and contractors, advertised as "the most comprehensive collection of cross-referenced information" about defense contracts.[36] The company offers annual, monthly, or per minute access for various fees.[37] Day & Day is using FOIA precisely the way other industry players – contractors or aspiring defense contractors – are doing on their own in droves, but is charging for the service of making FOIA requests and providing database access.

Information resellers are also actively requesting defense contracting information at the US Army. Centurion Research, one of the firms identified by the Society for Professional Journalists study, has a significant presence in the Army's FOIA logs.[38] One of their employees made at least 189 requests in the study year; the subjects of which were all contracts.[39] His online profile suggests that this particular employee's

[34] *DOJ 1986 FOIA Update*, *supra* note 1.

[35] U.S. Dep't of Def., Def. Logistics Agency, Freedom of Information Act Responses to Oct. 6, 2014 and Feb. 12, 2015 Requests by Margaret B. Kwoka (on file with author) [hereinafter DLA Data].

[36] *Online Database*, Day & Day, Inc., www.dayandday.com/dla-database.html (last visited Oct. 25, 2020). It also offers various other services based on these records, in addition to raw access. *Id.*

[37] *Defense Procurement Services Pricing*, Day & Day, Inc., www.dayandday.com/dla-servicespricing.html (last visited Oct. 25, 2020).

[38] Centurion Research is the second-most-frequent requester at the Army. U.S. Dep't of Def., U.S. Army, Freedom of Information Act Responses to Oct. 6, 2014 Request by Margaret B. Kwoka (on file with author) [hereinafter Army Data].

[39] *Id.* The requester name associated with Centurion is Frank Chilli. *See, e.g.*, *id.* at Request Nos. FP-13-009384, (request for "Contract W900KK-09-D-0006 awarded to ECS"), FP-13-010173 (request for "Contract w9124A-13-C-001").

job title was "FOIA Analyst," and explained that the position "is responsible for maintaining the FOIA log, updating clients (internal & external) on recent FOIA activities, [and] adding content to the Centurion Business Intelligence NOW™ (biNOW) product."[40]

Again, like with the contract-related requests made directly by government contractors, these requests are most valuable for competitors to learn about the contours of bids submitted by others. Indeed, the clientele for these resellers is likely precisely the same type of business – those that contract to provide goods and services to the government – as are submitting requests on their own. Some businesses may simply prefer, for confidentiality or efficiency reasons, to outsource the work of requesting these contracts under FOIA.

F. LAND USE RECORDS

An information reseller also appears among top requesters – fourth by volume – at the Environmental Protection Agency (EPA).[41] EDR, Inc., which submitted 160 requests in the study year, requested whole categories of EPA records rather than, as most other frequent requesters did, records about a specific property by address.[42] For example, it requested all enforcement and violation data regarding groundwater and drinking water safety for each of the ten EPA regions for a period of more than two years.[43] In another example, it requested, region by region, all underground storage tank site locations on Native American lands.[44] In turn, it markets various sets of EPA records to its clients, advertising them as a "comprehensive look at current government environmental filings."[45] EDR's clients appear to be commercial property owners and investors, and it promises that it "delivers the most comprehensive, trusted property data, maps and reports available across billions of records."[46]

While EDR is the only apparent reseller at the EPA, it is similar to the resellers described in other arenas insofar as it warehouses vast amounts of government data

40 *Frank Chilli*, LinkedIn, www.linkedin.com/in/frank-chilli-4962b951/ (last visited Oct. 25, 2020).

41 U.S. Envtl. Prot. Agency, Freedom of Information Act Response to June 9, 2015 Request by Margaret B. Kwoka (on file with author); FOIAOnline, foiaonline.gov/foiaonline/action/public/search/advancedSearch (under "Look Up By" select "Agency" then search for "EPA – Environmental Protection Agency").

42 *Id.*

43 *Id.* at Request No. EPA-HQ-2013-002738.

44 *Id.* at Request Nos. EPA-R4–2013-008495, EPA-R5–2013-008496, EPA-R5–2013-008497, EPA-R6–2013-008498, EPA-R6–2013-008499, EPA-R7–2013-008500, EPA-R7–2013-008501, EPA-R8–2013-008502, EPA-R8–2013-008503, EPA-R9–2013-008504, EPA-R9–2013-008505, EPA-R10–2013-008507, EPA-R10–2013-008508.

45 *Environmental Compliance Offerings*, EDR, Inc., edrnet.com/prods/environmental-compliance-reports.

46 *About EDR*, EDR, Inc., edrnet.com/edr (last visited Oct. 25, 2020).

and records and sells that access to a client base for profit. Moreover, like the other resellers, it specializes and focuses its efforts on a particular agency's records. That is, resellers tend to find business not in dealing in government records generally, but rather in finding a niche set of information constituents who can benefit from or are seeking government records but who, for whatever reason, do not want to or are not in the position to themselves use FOIA as a primary records gathering tool.

G. CUSTOM REQUESTING

There is an entirely different kind of information reseller at play as well. This type of reseller is one who primarily makes custom requests on behalf of clients, rather than storing and selling databases of records pre-requested and warehoused. The DOJ first identified this type of requester in its 1986 FOIA Update, calling them "individual surrogates."[47] It identified Michael C. Antonelli, as a traditional jailhouse lawyer, and the "most ubiquitous such surrogate," who had submitted hundreds of requests on behalf of other inmates.[48] While this study did not unearth jailhouse lawyers acting as surrogates, there are nonetheless information resellers performing this same sort of custom requesting as an intermediary for someone else.

The dominant player in this regard is, no doubt, The FOIA Group. Established in 1988, The FOIA Group is primarily a requesting service that will draft and file a FOIA request for the customer, navigate the process and negotiate with the agency, and file administrative appeals of denials.[49] It brags that its clients "include the 'Who's – Who' of government contractors, major corporations, law firms and new media – but you will never see their identities disclosed in our marketing brochures or in any other manner."[50] It describes itself as "very aggressive" and "brings results for our customers that other vendors can't compare."[51] The FOIA Group charges $125 per request and up.[52] As is suggested by the domain name it managed to snag – foia.com – this appears to be the first generalist custom information reseller.

The FOIA logs confirm as much. Unlike the other resellers identified in this study, The FOIA Group does not specialize in the records of a particular agency. Rather, it ranks among top requesters across many agencies. Indeed, in a previous study by Max Galka at the FOIA Mapper – one that admittedly reached a more

47 *DOJ 1986 FOIA Update*, *supra* note 1.

48 *Id.* Indeed, he so often sued over the denials of these requests (in his own name) that DOJ referred to them collectively as "'Antonelli' FOIA cases," though the revelation that he was being compensated by some of his clients led to sanctions for his misrepresentations in court that he should receive *in forma pauperis* personal indigency filing status. *Id.*

49 *About*, FOIA Grp., Inc., foia.com/about.aspx (last visited Oct. 25, 2020).

50 FOIA Grp., Inc., foia.com (last visited Oct. 25, 2020).

51 *Id.*

52 *FOIA Requests & Consult*, FOIA Grp., Inc., foia.com/foia.aspx (last visited Oct. 25, 2020).

limited slice of government FOIA activity – The FOIA Group is listed as the eighth most frequent commercial requester government-wide.[53]

The FOIA Group – and its ubiquitously named FOIA requester Rose Santos – are most often looking for government contracting information.[54] In this realm, too, government contracts yet again drive a significant wave of FOIA requesting. Unsurprisingly, then, this requester has a significant presence at DoD components included in this study, including its 390 requests to the Navy, 230 requests to the US Army, fifty-three requests to the Office of the Secretary, forty-six requests to DLA, and nine requests to the Defense Information Systems Agency.[55] In the same vein, it also makes an appearance on the top requester list at some components of the Department of Homeland Security, including the Coast Guard, with twelve requests to that agency, and the Transportation Security Administration, with six requests.[56]

The FOIA Group submits significant numbers of requests at most of the same agencies as this study identified as receiving substantial numbers of requests for government contracts. First, the government's scientific arms receive requests from The FOIA Group. It submitted thirty-eight requests to the National Aeronautics and Space Administration, thirty-seven requests to the EPA, twenty-five requests to the National Institutes of Health, and nine requests to the Centers for Disease Control and Prevention.[57] Second, The FOIA Group also does business with arms of the government involved in administering aid; it submitted eleven requests to the Federal Emergency Management Agency and six to the US

[53] Max Galka, *Who Uses FOIA? – An Analysis of 229,000 Requests to 85 Agencies*, FOIA Mapper (Mar. 13, 2017), foiamapper.com/who-uses-foia.

[54] Army Data, *supra* note 38, at Request No. FR-13-010503 (requesting specific contracts); FDA Data, *supra* note 8, at Request No. 2013-1636 (requesting specific contract and modifications); SEC Data, *supra* note 23, at Request No. 13-06332 (requesting specific contract).

[55] U.S. Dep't of Def., U.S. Navy, Freedom of Information Act Response to Apr. 18, 2016 Request and Nov. 1, 2016 Administrative Appeal by Margaret B. Kwoka (on file with author) [hereinafter Navy Data]; Army Data, *supra* note 38; U.S. Dep't of Def., Office of the Sec'y/Joint Chiefs of Staff, Freedom of Information Act Response to Mar. 20, 2018 Request by Margaret B. Kwoka (on file with author); DLA Data, *supra* note 35; 2018 FOIA Log, FOIA Reading Room, Def. Info. Sys. Agency, www.disa.mil/About/Legal-and-Regulatory/Accessibility/FOIA-Reading-Room.

[56] U.S. Dep't of Homeland Sec., U.S. Coast Guard, Freedom of Information Act Response to Oct. 2, 2014 Request by Margaret B. Kwoka, as modified by email on Mar. 19, 2018 (on file with author) [hereinafter Coast Guard Data]; U.S. Dep't of Homeland Sec., Transp. Security Admin., Freedom of Information Act Response to Feb. 26, 2018 Request by Margaret B. Kwoka (on file with author), *and* U.S. Dep't of Homeland Sec., Transp. Security Admin., FOIA Reading Room, www.tsa.gov/foia/readingroom (search for FOIA Logs - FY 2017).

[57] Nat'l Space & Aeronautics Admin., Freedom of Information Act Response to Mar. 6, 2018 Request by Margaret B. Kwoka (on file with author); U.S. Dep't of Health & Human Servs., Nat'l Insts. of Health, Freedom of Information Act Responses to Sept. 29, 2014 and Feb. 12, 2015 Requests by Margaret B. Kwoka (on file with author); U.S. Dep't of Health & Human Servs., Ctrs. for Disease Control, Freedom of Information Act Response to Feb. 24, 2018 Request by Margaret B. Kwoka (on file with author).

Agency for International Development.[58] Third, when the government is managing property as a landlord, contracting requests are present and The FOIA Group is no exception. It submitted seventy-one requests to the General Services Administration, and eleven to Department of Housing and Urban Development.[59] And finally, it makes appearances at some other agencies with less clear patterns. For example, it submitted seven requests to the Federal Communications Commission, five requests to the Federal Deposit Insurance Corporation (FDIC), four requests to the US Census Bureau, and three requests to the SEC.[60]

H. THE DIFFICULT CASES

The resellers previously discussed act in a relatively pure reselling capacity. They do not provide a lot of editorial content, consulting services, or other original material beyond the records themselves. Their primary added value comes from handling the document retrieval and organizing and indexing documents. That said, it is worth understanding how grey this area can be. This last section will explore three requesters who operate across the federal government and the ambiguity in their classification. In some ways, these companies act as information resellers. In other ways, their services go far beyond document retrieval and resale. Regardless of whether they are properly classified as regular commercial requesters or information reseller requesters, these companies are significant players in the FOIA requesting world.

LexisNexis and Thomson Reuters are the two most prominent companies across the federal government in this ambiguous category. Thomson Reuters was also identified as one of the top-ten commercial requesters government wide by the FOIA Mapper study mentioned above.[61] Thomson Reuters does more FOIA business with financial and regulatory agencies, whereas LexisNexis does more requesting with defense and land use agencies. A third similar company, Wolters Kluwer, makes a strong appearance only at the US Department of the Treasury. All, however, use FOIA to feed their various databases, along with attendant

58 U.S. Dep't of Homeland Sec., Fed. Emergency Mgmt. Agency, Freedom of Information Act Response to Apr. 13, 2018 Request by Margaret B. Kwoka (on file with author); U.S. Agency for Int'l Dev., Freedom of Information Act Response to Mar. 6, 2018 Request by Margaret B. Kwoka (on file with author).

59 Gen. Servs. Admin., Freedom of Information Act Responses to Mar. 6, 2018 Request by Margaret B. Kwoka (on file with author).

60 Fed. Commc'ns Comm'n, Freedom of Information Act Response to Mar. 6, 2018 Request by Margaret B. Kwoka (on file with author); FOIA Logs, Fiscal Year 2013, U.S. Census Bureau, www.census.gov/about/policies/foia/foia_library/foia_logs.html; SEC Data *supra* note 23.

61 Galka, *supra* note 53.

publications, research, and other information services provided to all manner of clients from private citizens to law firms to investment firms to law enforcement.[62]

Thomson Reuters advertises itself as a company providing "intelligence, technology, and human expertise."[63] It is the second-highest-volume requester at the FDA, for example, which classifies it as a commercial requester.[64] Its more than 527 requests that year likely sought documents to feed its Cortellis life sciences industries database products, including, for example, Cortellis Regulatory Intelligence, which provides information about drug and medical device regulatory compliance,[65] or Cortellis Competitive Intelligence, which is marketed to pharmaceutical companies as a way to "[t]rack your closest competitors."[66] It also submitted seventy-five requests to the SEC, thirty-one requests to the Federal Reserve, and four requests to the FDIC, which likely seek documents to fuel its various business information products.[67]

LexisNexis, probably more well known for its legal resources and indexing of judicial opinions, court-filed documents, and secondary sources, has another side of its business aimed at data and information provision to companies and government agencies for risk management across a variety of dimensions, including financial, regulatory, health, and public safety.[68] One of the products it offers is a public records database search, in which it amalgamates public records across a huge number of areas and government agencies.[69] The FOIA requests that Lexis makes may serve this database or other information products it markets. For example,

[62] *See Success Stories*, Counsel Link, counsellink.com/success-stories (last visited Oct. 25, 2020) (Lexis Nexis product marketed toward insurance companies and law firms); *Government Legal Solutions*, LexisNexis, www.lexisnexis.com/en-us/government/default.page (last visited Oct. 25, 2020) (Lexis Nexis marketing page for government agencies); *Accurint for Law Enforcement*, LexisNexis Risk Sols., risk.lexisnexis.com/products/accurint-for-law-enforcement (last visited Oct. 25, 2020) (Lexis Nexis product marketed toward law enforcement); *FP Solutions*, Wolters Kluwer, www.wolterskluwer.com/en-ca/solutions/fp-solutions (last visited Oct. 25, 2020) (Wolters Kluwer product marketed toward investment firms and financial services providers).

[63] *About Us*, Thomson Reuters, www.thomsonreuters.com/en/about-us.html (last visited Oct. 25, 2020).

[64] FDA Data, *supra* note 8.

[65] *Id. Cortellis Regulatory Intelligence: Features & Benefits*, Thomson Reuters, thomsonreuters.com/en/products-services/pharma-life-sciences/regulatory-affairs/productoverview/features-benefits.html.

[66] *Pharma Competitive Intelligence*, Thomson Reuters, thomsonreuters.com/pharma-life-sciences/pharma-competitive-intelligence.

[67] SEC Data, *supra* note 23; Fed. Reserve, Freedom of Information Act Responses to Mar. 6, 2018 Request by Margaret B. Kwoka (on file with author); Fed. Deposit Ins. Corp., Freedom of Information Act Response to Mar. 6, 2018 Request by Margaret B. Kwoka (on file with author); *see Corporate Solutions*, Thomson Reuters, www.thomsonreuters.com/en/products-services/corporate-solutions.html (last visited Oct. 25, 2020).

[68] LexisNexis Risk Sols., https://risk.lexisnexis.com (last visited Oct. 25, 2020).

[69] *Powerful Public Records Search*, LexisNexis, www.lexisnexis.com/en-us/products/public-records/powerful-public-records-search.page (last visited Oct. 25, 2020).

evidenced in this study, LexisNexis made ninety-five requests to the Army in the study year; another twenty-seven requests to the Navy, and eleven requests to the Coast Guard, nearly all for accident, incident, or police reports created by those agencies.[70]

* * *

Information resellers are revealing of commercial information constituencies writ large. They show a substantial private need for information across a variety of business industries, information that helps fuel those businesses success in the private market. The government should facilitate good information for business to ensure a healthy marketplace. But having cottage industries dedicated to requesting, one at a time, whole categories of federal records just to recreate a private database for sale to industry players is not a sensible use of FOIA. Indeed, these players indicate obvious opportunities for government to do a better job meeting the needs of these information constituents outside of FOIA. These are almost by definition requests that are fueling a private, not public, interest and for which FOIA was never designed.

[70] Coast Guard Data, *supra* note 56, at Request No. 2017-CGFO-00065 (Requesting "Report of overturned vessel on June 25, 2016 in Long Beach, CA"); Navy Data, *supra* note 55, at Request No. DON-USMC-2015-009707 (Requesting an Accident Report for 11/12/2014), Army Data, *supra* note 38, at Request No. FP-13-012131 (Requesting "MPR [military police report] occurred 12-1-2012 involving Kristina Denbo").

8

Idiosyncratic Requesters

There are some requesters – even frequent requesters – that defy easy categorization. After all, FOIA's design is to open up government for all to see, regardless of the reasons for the request, the value of the records, or the likely effect of disclosure, except where relevant to determining an exemption to mandatory production or fee category.[1] As a result, it attracts all manner of requesters. First-person requesting largely reflects the fact that people who have no other way of obtaining their own file use FOIA as a last resort. Commercial requesting merely represents data on what information companies actually need and want from the government and may provide insights into how government can better manage its information flow. These information constituents are certainly dominant across government agencies.

Other significant pockets of requesting are interesting, though. While none may provide a clear path toward reforms per se, they each demonstrate the idiosyncrasy of FOIA users. It is this feature, perhaps, that has made FOIA stubbornly resistant to effective reform. Some of these users demonstrate FOIA's powerful opportunities. Some of them exploit FOIA's deepest weaknesses. Some are merely interesting curiosities in the world of FOIA's largely unknown requester community. Some of these requesters tell us a little bit about humanity, and what it is we really want to know. But it is worth seeing this side of FOIA for what it is: a feature, not a bug, of the FOIA system.

A. PUBLIC GOOD DATABASES

One interesting set of requesters is not quite news media, not quite academic, not quite commercial. These are independent research institutes affiliated with universities that, somewhat like information resellers, warehouse federal records in

[1] *See*, Milner v. Navy, 562 U.S. 562, 564 (2011); U.S. Dep't of Justice v. Reporters Comm. for Freedom of the Press, 489 U.S. 749, 762 (1989); 5 U.S.C. § 552(a)(4)(A)(ii) (2018).

database form. In fact, they sometimes charge for access to the records, but they are nonprofit and public interest–oriented for use in research. Two such institutes stand out in prominence in the FOIA community and also make significant appearances in the data included in this study: the National Security Archive, housed at George Washington University, and the Transactional Records Access Clearinghouse, housed at Syracuse University.

The National Security Archive (the "Archive") admits to its ambiguous role:

> Founded in 1985 by journalists and scholars to check rising government secrecy, the National Security Archive combines a unique range of functions: investigative journalism center, research institute on international affairs, library and archive of declassified US documents ("the world's largest nongovernmental collection" according to the Los Angeles Times), leading non-profit user of the US Freedom of Information Act, public interest law firm defending and expanding public access to government information, global advocate of open government, and indexer and publisher of former secrets.[2]

Early in its history, the Department of Justice (DOJ) took the position that the Archive was an information reseller (or in its words, a surrogate requester), calling it an "unprecedented enterprise" with an "extraordinary goal of obtaining and compiling federal records on matters of national security and foreign policy decision-making."[3] The DOJ concluded the Archive was akin to other information resellers because it planned to offer subscriptions to major research libraries and various document sets, and planned to be financially self-sufficient by selling access to these various records databases.[4] Whether or not that would qualify the Archive as a surrogate or reseller of government records, it did not materialize as the organization's funding model. Now, the Archive's materials are freely available, with limited publications available for sale.[5] In turn, its funding appears to largely come from foundations and other charitable giving.[6]

Moreover, the Archive is undoubtedly serving primarily public education and research aims. For example, in its 2019 Annual Report, it detailed an astonishing number of record requests filed and pages of material received, but also some forty-five national news stories based on records they pried loose, thirty-six e-books or briefing books published by the Archive on discrete topics based on those records,

[2] *About the National Security Archive*, Nat'l Sec. Archive, nsarchive.gwu.edu/about (last visited Nov. 23, 2020).

[3] U.S. Dep't of Justice, Office of Info. Policy, *Surrogate FOIA Requests Increasing*, 7 FOIA Update 1 (Jan. 1, 1986), www.justice.gov/oip/blog/foia-update-surrogate-foia-requests-increasing [hereinafter *DOJ 1986 FOIA Update*].

[4] *Id.*

[5] *Guide for Researchers*, Nat'l Sec. Archive, nsarchive.gwu.edu/guide-researchers (last visited Nov. 23, 2020).

[6] Funders and Supporters, Nat'l Sec. Archive, nsarchive.gwu.edu/funders-supporters (last visited Nov. 23, 2020).

some 3,800 research requests to the Archive from outsiders along with 262 in-person visits to their document library, and various other forms of digital delivery of information contained therein. That same year, they also filed three new FOIA lawsuits and participated as Amicus Curiae[7] in two other lawsuits.[8] That its model is unique does not undermine its status as a requester acting to inform the public about governmental activities.

In the data included in this study, the Archive makes regular appearances at many expected places. For example, it made forty-one requests to the Office of the Secretary at the Department of Defense, seventeen requests to the DOJ's Criminal Division, and, at a very minimum, 199 requests to the Department of State.[9] Isolated Archive requests appeared at other agencies as well.[10]

The Transactions Records Access Clearinghouse (TRAC) at Syracuse University is not unlike the Archive – indeed it was founded around the same time in 1989 – but with a different substantive focus. As it describes itself, it is "[y]our source for comprehensive, independent and nonpartisan information about federal enforcement, staffing and spending."[11] It offers a subscription site for its "data warehouse," as well as public website pages dedicated to providing easily digestible information on selected federal enforcement agencies, including the Department of Homeland Security (DHS), the Federal Bureau of Investigations (FBI), the Internal Revenue Service (IRS), the Drug Enforcement Administration, and the Bureau of Alcohol,

7 The term "Amicus Curiae" means friend of the court, not friend of a party. The courts are beyond the original meaning now; an adversary role of an amicus curiae has become accepted. Weininger v. Castro, 462 F. Supp. 2d 457, 473 n.12 (S.D.N.Y. 2006) (citing Ryan v. Commodity Futures Trading Comm'n, 125 F.3d 1062, 1063 (7th Cir. 1997) (Posner, J. in chambers).

8 Nat'l Sec. Archive, Annual Report 1 (2019).

9 U.S. Dep't of Def., Office of the Sec'y/Joint Chiefs of Staff, Freedom of Information Act Response to Mar. 20, 2018 Request by Margaret B. Kwoka (on file with author) [hereinafter Sec'y of Def. Data]; U.S. Dep't of Justice, Criminal Div., Freedom of Information Act Response to Feb. 21, 2018 Request by Margaret B. Kwoka (on file with author) [hereinafter Criminal Division Data]; Virtual Reading Room, U.S. Dep't of State, foia.state.gov/Search/Search.aspx (search for "FOIA Log" select "FOIA LOG - CASES RECEIVED BETWEEN 1/1/2014 AND 12/31/2014". The Department of State FOIA logs do not contain organizational affiliations, therefore 199 requests were able to be connected to the Archive by the name of the requester, though there are likely many more unidentifiable affiliated requests.

10 For example, the DOD's Defense Information Systems Agency received two requests from the Archive in the study year, the Coast Guard received one, ATF received three, and ICE received eleven. *See* 2018 FOIA Log, FOIA Reading Room, Def. Info. Sys. Agency, www.disa.mil/About/Legal-and-Regulatory/Accessibility/FOIA-Reading-Room [hereinafter DISA Data]; U.S. Dep't of Justice, Bureau of Alcohol, Tobacco, Firearms & Explosives, Freedom of Information Act Response to Feb. 12, 2019 Request by Margaret B. Kwoka (on file with author) [hereinafter ATF Data]; FOIA Library, U.S. Immigration & Customs Enf't (Oct. 3, 2017), www.ice.gov/foia/library (follow "ICE FOIA Logs" tab) [hereinafter ICE Data] (the dataset compiled included the months between October 2014 and September 2015, representing FY 2015).

11 Transactional Records Access Clearinghouse, trac.syr.edu (last visited Nov. 23, 2020).

Tobacco, Firearms, and Explosives.[12] TRAC focuses on enforcement agencies. In the data included in this study, TRAC submitted 215 requests to the FBI, eighty-two requests to Immigration and Customs Enforcements, and a smattering of requests to other agencies.[13]

Like the Archive, TRAC's website documents how its data has been used by the media, Congress, and in public interest advocacy work.[14] Interestingly, and in the kind of meta-irony I particular appreciate as a FOIA requester who requests information about FOIA activities using FOIA itself, TRAC also runs The FOIA Project, a tracker designed to monitor the federal government's FOIA performance.[15]

These nonprofit research institutes that morph into public-interest databases are clearly providing a public good. They are warehousing records, not for profit, but for researchers, journalists, and others to harvest for public consumption. Moreover, when they do charge fees, it appears to be in an attempt to cover costs; much of their content is available free of charge. They also perform some journalistic functions in publishing original content based on the records they receive. They defy easy categorization, but no doubt exist because of FOIA's very existence. Without FOIA, these institutes would vanish.

B. POLITICAL OPPOSITION RESEARCH

Another fascinating group of FOIA requesters are political campaign committees. These requesters appear to be using FOIA for opposition research, capitalizing on the fact that opposing political candidates often have relatively public lives before running for office. These requests often seek the communication record between the opposing candidate and the agency, either because the opposing candidate was previously in a different elective office and had dealings with the agency or because the candidate was operating as a lobbyist, industry representative, or business leader that had dealings with the agency. Other requests target candidates who previously

[12] *About Us*, Transactional Records Access Clearinghouse, trac.syr.edu/aboutTRACgeneral.html (last visited Nov. 23, 2020).

[13] U.S. Dep't of Justice, Fed. Bureau of Investigations, Freedom of Information Act Response to Apr. 15, 2016 Request and Jan. 23, 2017 Administrative Appeal by Margaret B. Kwoka, and (on file with author) [hereinafter FBI Data]; ICE Data, *supra* note 10. For example, DOJ's Criminal Division received eight TRAC requests, ATF received one, and USCIS received one request under the name of David Burnham, co-director of TRAC. *See* Criminal Division Data, *supra* note 9; ATF Data, *supra* note 10; Electronic Reading Room, U.S. Citizenship & Immigration Servs., www.uscis.gov/about-us/electronic-reading-room (filter by "FOIA Logs") (The dataset compiled includes the months between October 2014 and September 2015, representing FY 2015, and USCIS FOIA logs do not provide organizational affiliations).

[14] *Putting TRAC to Work*, Transactional Records Access Clearinghouse, trac.syr.edu/tracatwork (last visited Nov. 23, 2020).

[15] *About the Project*, The FOIA Project, foiaproject.org/about-the-project (last visited Nov. 23, 2020).

served as political appointees at a federal agency, seeking records on their various actions taken in that capacity for use in the political arena.

The FOIA Mapper previously documented this trend, noting "the request volume of the top political committees is comparable in size to that of the top news outlets," and that Democrats appear to use FOIA in this manner more than Republicans.[16] That study identified the top political campaign committee requesters as, on the Democratic side, the Democratic Senatorial Campaign Committee (DSCC), the Democratic Congressional Campaign Committee (DCCC), the Democratic National Committee (DNC), and American Bridge 21st Century; and, on the Republican side, America Rising, America First, and the Republican National Committee (RNC).

Those same campaign committees make significant appearances in this study as well. Collectively, political committees submitted over 550 requests easily identified in the databases included in this study. Of those, a back-of-the-envelope count across agencies revealed that American Bridge 21st Century topped the list with 157, then came the DSCC with 150, the DNC at 121, then America Rising with sixty-eight, the DCCC with twenty-two, and then the National Republican Senatorial Committee, with two. Like the FOIA Mapper study, this study's data suggests Democrats are using FOIA in this manner far more frequently than Republicans.

Some agencies in particular received substantial requests from the major political action committees, including the DOJ's Office of Information Policy (sixty-three), the Environmental Protection Agency (EPA) (fifty-one), the FBI (forty-five), the General Services Administration (thirty-nine), and the Federal Aviation Administration (FAA) (thirty-four).[17] Sometimes, individual committees were responsible for many requests at a single agency, such as American Bridge 21st Century's thirty-eight requests to the FBI, the Democratic National Committee's twelve requests to the Mining Safety and Health Administration (MSHA) and twenty-two requests to the Department of Treasury Departmental Offices, the Democratic Senatorial Campaign Committee's eleven requests to the Securities and Exchange Commission, and the DSCC's fifteen requests to the DoD's Office of the Secretary.[18]

[16] Max Galka, *Who Uses FOIA? – An Analysis of 229,000 Requests to 85 Government Agencies*, FOIA Mapper (March 13, 2017), foiamapper.com/who-uses-foia.

[17] U.S. Dep't of Justice, Office of Info. Policy, Freedom of Information Act Responses to Feb. 24, 2018 Request by Margaret B. Kwoka (on file with author); U.S. Envtl. Prot. Agency, Freedom of Information Act Response to June 9, 2015 Request by Margaret B. Kwoka (on file with author); FOIAONline, foiaonline.gov/foiaonline/action/public/search/advancedSearch (under "Look Up By" select "Agency" then search for "EPA – Environmental Protection Agency"); FBI Data, *supra* note 13; Gen. Servs. Admin., Freedom of Information Act Response to Mar. 6, 2018 Request by Margaret B. Kwoka (on file with author) [hereinafter GSA Data]; FOIA Library, Fed. Aviation Admin., www.faa.gov/foia/electronic_reading_room/ (select FY 2018 items) [hereinafter FAA Data].

[18] FBI Data, *supra* note 13; U.S. Dep't of Labor, Mine Safety & Health Admin., Freedom of Information Act Response to Apr. 16, 2016 Request by Margaret B. Kwoka (on file with author); Other Frequently Requested FOIA Records, Log of FOIA Requests, U.S. Dep't of the

Examples of this use of FOIA illustrate how political committees are gathering information that might be helpful to campaigns. For example, some requests broadly ask for categories of correspondence, such as congressional correspondence with the agency, which presumably could reveal the actions or statements of current members of Congress who may be up for re-election or election for another office.[19] Others request correspondence to or from a particular representative.[20] Indeed, correspondence is the dominant theme of these requests.

A few exceptions to that rule prove interesting. For example, at the FAA, flight history is often the subject of requests, presumably to uncover travel of political candidates by private aircraft.[21] At a few agencies, requests for the FOIA logs appear,[22] or sometimes requests for any FOIA requests about a particular person,

Treasury, home.treasury.gov/footer/freedom-of-information-act/electronic-read-room/other-frequently-requested-foia-records (select FY 2018); U.S. Sec. & Exch. Comm'n, Freedom of Information Act Response to Sept. 5, 2014 Request by Margaret B. Kwoka (on file with author); FOIA Logs, U.S. Sec. & Exch. Comm'n, www.sec.gov/foia/docs/foia-logs.htm (select "2013" and "2014") (The dataset compiled includes the months between January 2013 and December 2013, representing CY 2013) [hereinafter SEC Data]; Sec'y of Def. Data, *supra* note 9.

19 *See, e.g.*, U.S. Dep't of Homeland Sec., U.S. Coast Guard, Freedom of Information Act Response to Oct. 2, 2014 Request by Margaret B. Kwoka, as modified by email on Mar. 19, 2018 (on file with author) [hereinafter Coast Guard Data], at Request No. 2016-CGFO-01337 (DNC request for "all records pertaining to TRUMP PRINCESS").

20 *See, e.g.*, FAA Data, *supra* note 17, at Request No. 2018-002631 (DSCC request for "any correspondence with Martha McSally, or the staff or representatives of Martha McSally, in her capacity as United States Congresswoman from January 1, 2015 to present"); Coast Guard Data, *supra* note 19, at Request No. 2017-CGFO-03089 (DCCC's request "seeking records on all logs of congressional correspondence regarding Coast Guard officials and Rep. Martha McSally between January 6 2015 to the present day"); SEC Data, *supra* note 18, at Request No. 13-09344-FOIA (America Rising's Request for "Senator Mitch McConnell correspondence").

21 *See e.g.*, FAA Data, *supra* note 17 at Request No. 2018-001293 (DSCC request for "any flight plan records for the aircraft with tail number N47347, owned by Hoosier Seneca LLC from January 2003 to present and correspondence between the FAA and U.S. Representative [Exemption 6] or staff members from January 2011 to present."); *Id.* at Request No. 2018-001827 (American Bridge request for "air traffic/flight records For aircraft With tail number N401AS from January 2017 through the present."); *Id.* at Request No. 2018-011348 (America Rising request for "records reflecting the flight of airplane that departed from Detroit on June 6, 2018, at 4:40 p.m. local time and arrived in Turin, Italy on June 7, 2018, at 6:10 a.m. local time").

22 *See, e.g.*, U.S. Agency for Int'l Dev., Freedom of Information Act Response to Mar. 6, 2018 Request by Margaret B. Kwoka (on file with author) [hereinafter USAID Data], at Request No. F-00179-17 (DSCC "Request FOIA requests/responses filed regarding Joe Manchin/staff as US Senator and private citizen. (Date Range for Record Search: From 11/01/2012 To 05/01/2017)"); U.S. Dep't of Homeland Sec., Fed. Emergency Mgmt. Agency, Freedom of Information Act Responses to Apr. 13, 2018 Request by Margaret B. Kwoka (on file with author), at Request No. 2017-FEFO-02243 (DNC request "seeking a log of all FOIA requests received by the Federal Emergency Management Agency (and all agencies, offices, and components within FEMA) from January 1, 2017 to the present. For each FOIA request, please specify the tracking number, the requester's name, the requester's organization, the request date, a description of the records requested, and the status of the request. (Date Range for Record Search: From 1/1/2017 To 9/1/2017)").

suggesting the committee is looking to find out what others are requesting about their own candidates.[23] Finally, a group of requests targets the agency's job vacancies or appointments to agency jobs.[24]

It is thus clear that political opposition research, or research feeding political campaigns, is a consistent use of FOIA across agencies and the political divide. Without doubt, one can conceive of this use as a form of oversight – maybe even the strongest form of oversight – as voters will learn about candidates from this information and be able to act on that information at the ballot box.[25] It can also be seen as a private political use whose beneficiary is the candidate trying to win the election. Regardless, information about government actors are revealed to the public through FOIA and, while not a purely oversight motivation, these requests have a sort of hybrid private/public purpose.

C. INTER-GOVERNMENTAL REQUESTING

One nonintuitive group of FOIA requesters appeared throughout the logs: other government agencies. Sometimes, these other agencies were state or local government agencies looking for federal information. Often though, it is other federal agencies that are using FOIA to gain information from another federal agency, and sometimes even other components of the same Department requesting among themselves. The underlying purpose of these requests was much harder to glean, but their consistent appearance in the logs is striking.

To be sure, some agencies see much more of this type of requester than others. The FBI, the IRS, the Veterans Health Administration (VHA), and components of

23 *See, e.g.*, Fed. Reserve, Freedom of Information Act Response to Mar. 6, 2018 Request by Margaret B. Kwoka (on file with author) [hereinafter Federal Reserve Data], at Request No. G-2017-00139 (DSCC request for "Any Freedom of Information Act (FOIA) requests filed January 2016 to present regarding Senator Sherrod Brown or the staff or representatives of Senator Sherrod Brown, in both his capacity as a U.S. Senator and as a private citizen; and any responsive documents sent out by your agency in response to the above Freedom of Information Act (FOIA) requests"); USAID Data, *supra* note 22, at Request No. F-00152-17 (DSCC "Request FOIA requests/responses filed 1/2011 to 3/2/2017 regarding Senator Elizabeth Warren/staff in her capacity as U.S. Senator and private citizen").

24 *See, e.g.*, Sec'y of Def. Data, *supra* note 9, at Request No. 17-F-1070 (American Bridge request for "Congressional And Governmental Correspondence Logs For The Public Officials Listed Below. I am requesting copies of the Congressional Correspondence logs that are maintained by the Department of Defense that lists congressional and/or governmental correspondence between the Department and Congressional officials listed below with the years to search in parenthesis."); ATF Data, *supra* note 10, at Request No. 2017-0762 (American Bridge request for "list of presidential appointed positions").

25 For example, American Bridge 21st Century's mission is: "We find what Republicans are hiding and make sure voters hear about it." *About Us*, Am. Bridge PAC, americanbridgepac.org/about-us (last visited Nov. 23, 2020).

the DoD were the most prominent agencies to whom requests from other government bodies were made. At the FBI, most such requesters were state police departments, such as the New York City Police Department with twenty-two requests, Smithfield Police Department with twenty-four requests, or the Warwick Police Department with nineteen requests.[26] Beyond those law enforcement agencies, though, the FBI also received a whopping 342 requests from the Pennsylvania Gaming Control Board, and a few isolated requests from other federal agencies.[27] Similarly, the Secret Service received routine requests from local law enforcement.[28]

Similarly, the VHA receives a huge number of requests from local agencies – except at this agency, the list is dominated by coroners and medical examiners. They accounted for a full 1,667 requests in the study year, which is 6.3 percent of the agency's total requests.[29] These requesters can receive deceased individuals' health records without violating HIPPA or submitting a privacy waiver, and are presumably attempting to verify or investigate cause of death.[30] Local law enforcement also has some presence in the requester list at the VHA, but so do federal agencies, such as the Social Security Administration with thirty-seven requests, among a few others.[31]

The other agencies with large numbers of inter-governmental requests evidenced far more requests from other federal agencies, rather than state or local agencies. The IRS, for example, received at least fifty-five such requests, including a full thirty from the FBI, another nine from the Office of Personnel Management, seven from DOJ, and scattered requests from assorted other agencies.[32] And, several

26 FBI Data, *supra* note 13.

27 *Id.* For example, it received three requests from the Department of Corrections and one from the Department of Health and Human Services. *Id.*

28 FOIA Logs 2018, U.S. SECRET SERV., www.secretservice.gov/press/foia/library [hereinafter Secret Service Data] (For example, the Secret Service received at least sixteen requests from police departments alone, including two requests from the Tucson Police Department, two from the Colorado Springs Police Department, and two from the New Jersey State Police).

29 U.S. Dep't of Veterans Affairs, Veterans Health Admin., Freedom of Information Act Response to Apr. 15, 2016 Request by Margaret B. Kwoka (on file with author) [hereinafter VHA Data] (counting the number of requesters with names that include "exami" or "coron").

30 *Health Information of Deceased Individuals*, U.S. DEP'T OF HEALTH & HUMAN SERVS. (Sept. 19, 2013), www.hhs.gov/hipaa/for-professionals/privacy/guidance/health-information-of-deceased-individuals/index.html.

31 VHA Data, *supra* note 29. For example, for veterans' medical records alone, the VHA received three requests from the Army including the Army Reserve Medical Management Center and Army Review Board, seven from the Department of Health and Human Services, and four from the CDC, specifically for deceased veterans' medical records. Additionally, the VHA received 200 requests from other veterans-oriented organizations or agencies including the U.S. Department of Labor Veterans Employment and Training Service, the U.S. Senate Veterans Affairs Committee, National Veterans Disability Advocates, and the Veterans Law Group.

32 U.S. Dep't of Treasury, Internal Revenue Serv., Freedom of Information Act Response to order in *Kwoka v. Internal Revenue Serv.*, 1:17-cv-1157-DLF, 2018 U.S. Dist. LEXIS 167547 (D.D.C. Sept. 28, 2018); IRS FOIA Logs, Internal Revenue Serv., www.irs.gov/privacy-disclosure/irs-foia-

components of the DoD evidence significant federal agency requesting, including intra-DoD requesting between components within the Department. For example, the Navy received ninety-five requests from the US Marine Corps, and fifteen requests from Veterans Affairs.[33] The Army received thirty-three requests from the FBI, as well as another sixty-four from an official in the New York state government.[34] The Defense Logistics Agency (DLA), the FAA, the GSA, and the Defense Information Systems Agency (DISA) also exhibited inter-agency requesting in smaller numbers.[35]

It is striking that federal and state or local agencies have routine use for federally controlled information but evidently have no other means of access but FOIA. Among the contemplated uses of FOIA, inter-governmental information sharing seemingly never makes the list. Indeed, data-sharing efforts between federal authorities as well as between federal and state or local authorities are commonly touted, especially in the area of law enforcement.[36] That the information needs of agencies are not being met turns the objects of FOIA requests – the agencies themselves – into FOIA users and information constituents.

D. CURIOSITY

Another set of requesters appears to be those requesting out of sheer curiosity. FOIA is actually designed almost perfectly for the curiosity requester. And curiosity can be quite a powerful motivator, as well as the driving force behind requests that sometimes unearth important information about government for public consumption. These requesters can take many forms: Sometimes they are quasi journalistic in nature, though many also appear to be for private consumption, and other times

logs (For example, DHS made four requests, Department of State made four requests, and the Department of Veterans Affairs made one).

33 U.S. Dep't of Def., U.S. Navy, Freedom of Information Act Response to Apr. 18, 2016 Request and Nov. 1, 2016 Administrative Appeal by Margaret B. Kwoka (on file with author).

34 U.S. Dep't of Def., U.S. Army, Freedom of Information Act Response to Oct. 6, 2014 Request by Margaret B. Kwoka (on file with author).

35 U.S. Dep't of Def., Def. Logistics Agency, Freedom of Information Act Responses to Oct. 6, 2014 and Feb. 12, 2015 Requests by Margaret B. Kwoka (on file with author); DISA Data, *supra* note 10; FAA Data, *supra* note 17 (the FAA received one request from the Department of State, one request from the Department of Transportation, one request from the US Navy, one request from the NRC and one request from the US Attorneys Office); GSA Data, *supra* note 17 (GSA also received a small number of requests from the VA, US Treasury, and Department of Energy).

36 *Secure Communities*, U.S. Immigration & Customs Enf't (Mar. 20, 2018), www.ice.gov/secure-communities (stating that "Secure Communities is a simple and common-sense way to carry out ICE's enforcement priorities for those aliens detained in the custody of another law enforcement agency (LEA). It uses a federal information-sharing partnership between DHS and the Federal Bureau of Investigation (FBI)."); *The Secure Communities Illusion*, N.Y. Times, (Sep. 5, 2014), www.nytimes.com/2014/09/06/opinion/the-secure-communities-illusion.html (claiming that the Secured Communities program has had zero effect on crime).

they are driven by what most in society would consider somewhat extreme concerns about government conspiracies and cover-ups.

Michael Ravnitzky is the paradigm of the journalist/private citizen/curiosity requester hybrid. He is both a lawyer and a former journalist,[37] but he has developed a well-respected reputation as a FOIA expert from the perspective of the requester community and privately requesting citizenry. He routinely appears to comment before the FOIA Advisory Committee,[38] he has given FOIA trainings,[39] and his advice to requesters shows up all over the internet, from the website of the Bicycle Helmet Safety Institute[40] to the Aerosol Crimes (aka Chemtrails) Discussion Forum.[41]

He has occupied more formal journalistic roles at times, including a stint as editor at American Lawyer Media in the early 2000s,[42] and he has also published original content on other platforms.[43] He also previously held a formal role on the attorney side of his professional identity, as the chief counsel to the chairman of the Postal Regulatory Commission.[44] But, for the most part, he identifies as a "private citizen" vis-à-vis the FOIA process.[45]

[37] *See, e.g.*, Michael Ravnitzky, *The Directorate of Legal Research at the Library of Congress: A Treasure Hidden under a Bushel Basket*, Law & Tech. Resources for Legal Prof'ls (Nov. 22, 2006), www.llrx.com/2006/11/the-directorate-of-legal-research-at-the-library-of-congress-a-treasure-hidden-under-a-bushel-basket/ (identifying Ravnitsky as a "Washington, D.C. area attorney and journalist").

[38] *See, e.g.*, *Freedom of Information Act Advisory Committee Meeting Transcript*, Nat'l Archives (April 19, 2016), www.archives.gov/ogis/foia-advisory-committee/2014-2016-term/documents/04-19-2016-meeting-transcript (transcript of an Advisory Committee meeting at which Ravnitzky spoke during the public comments portion of the meeting); *see also*, Statement of Michael J. Ravnitzky, Nat'l Archives (September 27, 1999), www.archives.gov/iwg/research-papers/ravnitzky-statement-september-1999.html (Ravnitzky's statement to a previous working group on Nazi War Crimes).

[39] *See, e.g.*, Michael Morisy, *FOIA Expert Michael Ravnitzky Shares New Tactics to Obtain Useful Records from Agencies*, MuckRock News (July 18, 2017), www.muckrock.com/news/archives/2017/jul/18/spj-dc-event.

[40] Michael Ravnitzky, *FOIA Tips for Dealing with the Consumer Product Safety Commission*, Bicycle Helmet Safety Inst. (Feb. 24, 2019), helmets.org/foiatips.htm.

[41] Kim Weber (@kdw43215), *Info from Michael Ravnitzky re: FOIA Act*, Post on *Aerosol Operations Message Board: Top Level*, Tapatalk (Aug. 9, 2000), www.tapatalk.com/groups/chemtrails/info-from-michael-ravnitsky-re-foi-act-t865.html.

[42] *See, e.g.*, Va. Freedom of Info. Advisory Council, AO-07-03, Staff Advisory Opinion (April 3, 2003), foiacouncil.dls.virginia.gov/ops/03/AO_07_03.htm; Ravnitzky, 16 FCC Rcd. 21745 (30) (2001); Letter from Melanie Ann Pustay, Deputy Dir., Office of Info. & Privacy, U.S. Dep't of Justice, to Michael Ravnitzky, Re: OLA/02-R0174 (Jan. 15, 2002), cryptome.info/doj-footshot2.htm.

[43] *Author Archives: Michael Ravnitzky*, Law & Tech. Resources for Legal Prof'ls, www.llrx.com/author/ravnitzky-michael (last visited Nov. 24, 2020).

[44] Chase Gunter, *Can Agencies Build Greater Trust in the FOIA Process?*, Fed. Computer Week (July 28, 2017), fcw.com/articles/2017/07/28/foia-process.aspx.

[45] *See, e.g.*, *Freedom of Information Act Advisory Committee Meeting Transcript*, *supra* note 38 ("My name is Michael Ravnitzky, I'm speaking as a private individual."); Departmental Offices, FOIA Log January 1 - March 31, 2020, U.S. Dep't of the Treasury, at 2020-01-120, home

Back in 1999, Ravnitzky had already represented that he had filed more than 2,000 requests under FOIA, and also cited topics of research interest to him, suggesting a dual journalistic/curiosity motive underlying his requesting pattern. And, indeed, his requesting is wide ranging. While not exhaustive, a representative list of his requests identified in the data for this study include twenty-nine requests to the Nuclear Regulatory Commission (NRC), twenty-seven requests to the Federal Deposit Insurance Corporation, twenty-two requests to the Federal Reserve, twenty requests to the Centers for Disease Control, twelve requests to the US Agency for International Development, and five requests to the Transportation Security Administration.[46] The subject matters of his requests do not follow a clear pattern. For example, at the NRC, his requests range from a list of closed NRC Office of Inspector General investigations to records related to the Congressional Budget Justification to records documenting cyber vulnerabilities at a particular plant.[47]

Beyond the example of Mr. Ravnitzky, other curiosity requesters are easier to identify by subject matter, and one striking example is in FBI files. The FBI files of now-deceased famous people are the subject of frequent requests, although not obviously dominated by any particular requester. For example, in the study year there were thirty-seven requests to the FBI for the file of Benjamin Bradlee, who was a *Washington Post* reporter who oversaw the Watergate reporting. There were eighteen requests for the FBI file of Mario Cuomo, former governor of New York; seventeen for the file for Tupac Shakur (2Pac), a musician and actor, and fourteen for the file of Nelson Mandela, former President of South Africa and anti-apartheid revolutionary.

Certainly, some of these may be for research or journalistic purposes but many of them are likely to be curiosity requesters. Some evidence of this can be found in the various websites that explain how to obtain FBI files of deceased individuals or publicize the FBI files of deceased famous people. For example, FOIATheDead.org is an entire project that does nothing but "request information from the FBI about

.treasury.gov/system/files/236/2020-2nd-Quarter-Log-of-FOIA-Requests.pdf (Department of the Treasury Departmental Offices designating Michael Ravnitzky as a private citizen in its organizational affiliation category).

46 Nuclear Regulatory Comm'n, Freedom of Information Act Response to Mar. 6, 2018 Request by Margaret B. Kwoka (on file with author) [hereinafter NRC Data]; Fed. Deposit Ins. Corp., Freedom of Information Act Response to Mar. 6, 2018 Request by Margaret B. Kwoka (on file with author); Federal Reserve Data, *supra* note 23; U.S. Dep't of Health & Human Servs., Ctrs. for Disease Control, Freedom of Information Act Response to Feb. 24, 2018 Request by Margaret B. Kwoka (on file with author); USAID Data, *supra* note 22; U.S. Dep't of Homeland Sec., Transp. Sec. Admin., Freedom of Information Act Response to Feb. 26, 2018 Request by Margaret B. Kwoka (on file with author) *and* U.S. Dep't of Homeland Sec., Transp. Sec. Admin., FOIA Reading Room, www.tsa.gov/foia/readingroom (searching for FOIA Logs – FY 2017).

47 NRC Data, *supra* note 46, at Request Nos. FOIA/PA-2017-00209, FOIA/PA-2017-00398, FOIA/PA-2017-00615.

the recently deceased."[48] It has no other mission but to publish these files. Curiosity appears to be driving these requests.

And finally, there are requesters driven by somewhat fringe beliefs about government coverups. A previous study once found that at the National Security Agency (NSA), twelve percent of all requests concerned Unidentified Flying Objects, including requests for "information and research on nine flying saucers you have in an underground US Air Force hanger at Groom Air Force Base, Nevada," files on "extraterrestrials of Roswell and Men in Black," and "documents related to a near head-on collision between a helicopter and a UFO on 10/18/75 in Mansfield Ohio."[49] While this study did not manage to obtain data from the NSA, a substantial number of such requests were submitted to the National Aeronautics and Space Administration (NASA), which is included in this study. At NASA, at least twenty-one requests mentioned aliens or UFOs, such as a request for "All documented UFO sightings in the past decade" or one for "the existence of extraterrestrial presence [] within our atmosphere" or one for "Alien crash files."[50] A few such requests also appear in the FBI logs.[51]

Examples of other similarly skeptical requesters engaged in curiosity requesting appear in the logs in more isolated numbers. Some requests are still seeking information about John F. Kennedy's assassination or the person thought to have committed his assassination, Lee Harvey Oswald.[52] Others still seek information about the assassination of Martin Luther King, Jr., or the Nixon-era Watergate scandal.[53] Some of these requesters may be seeking to learn more about current events or they may be using FOIA to probe behind an event's official account, such as requests for information about the Sandy Hook Elementary School shooting or the 9/11 attacks, hijackers, or commission.[54]

That FOIA is used by folks who suspect government cover-ups on all manner of topics should not come as a surprise. Indeed, as described in some detail in

48 *About this Project*, FOIA THE DEAD, foiathedead.org/about (last visited Nov. 24, 2020).

49 Michael Doyle, The Freedom of Information Act: In Theory and Practice 95 (May 2001) (unpublished M.A. thesis, Johns Hopkins University) (on file with author).

50 Nat'l Space & Aeronautics Admin., Freedom of Information Act Response to Mar. 6, 2018 Request by Margaret B. Kwoka (on file with author) [hereinafter NASA Data], at Request Nos. 17-HQ-F-00827, 17-HQ-F-00131, 17-HQ-F-00773.

51 *See e.g.*, *id.* at Request Nos. 17-HQ-F-00775 (request for "Alien Files"), 17-HQ-F-00576 (request for "Intelligent Alien Life"), 17-HQ-F-00150 (request for "extraterrestrial life").

52 *See e.g.*, FBI Data, *supra* note 13, at Request Nos. 1326381-000 (request for "JFK Assassination"), 1329321-000 (request for "Lufthansa JFK Heist"); Secret Service Data, *supra* note 28, at Request No. 20181342 (request for "the entire Zapruder Film unedited of the November 22, 1963 assassination of JFK and the name of the California movie producer").

53 *See e.g.*, FBI Data, *supra* note 13, at Request Nos. 1318713-000 (request for "Assassination of Martin Luther King"), 1326067-000 (request for "Watergate Scanda"l), 1334797-000 (request for "Richard Nixon National Security Decision Memorandum 2").

54 *See e.g.*, NASA Data, *supra* note 50, at Request No. 17-HQ-F-01100 (request for "9/11 Documents and/or Photos"); FBI Data, *supra* note 13, at Request No. 1329735-000 (request for "9/11 Hijackers").

Chapter 2, FOIA has been a powerful tool in revealing government cover-ups in various areas.[55] The only thing distinguishing these requesters from the news media requesters central to those stories is that these curiosity requesters hold preconceived beliefs about what the government is covering up that often fall further outside societal norms. For all we know, we may learn more about extraterrestrial life in the future because of these requesters' curiosity.

E. HARASSMENT AND ABUSE

By this point in the recitation of who uses FOIA by the numbers and by the stories, it should be clear that most requesters have legitimate – sometimes even vital – interests in the records they seek, whether or not their purpose is aligned with Congress's vision for the statute. It should be acknowledged, however, that like with any broad right of access, abuse is not only possible but to some degree an almost inevitable cost. Sometimes, FOIA is used to harass government officials, or otherwise abused for nefarious purposes.

The most well-documented and cited instances of harassment involve academic institutions. Climate change researchers,[56] tax policy reform academics,[57] and researchers who have taken advocacy positions as public intellectuals[58] have all been targets under various state laws. Recently, a public records request from an opposition researcher sought nine months' worth of emails and text messages of a professor who studies the gig economy and was a vocal supporter of a piece of legislation in California seeking to regulate employment practices of companies like Uber.[59]

And, it is not just coming from the political right. For example, the left targeted the travel expenses and cell phone records of a University of Virginia law professor whose research on religious liberties was used to support state legislative efforts

[55] *See e.g.*, FBI Data, *supra* note 13, at Request Nos. 1330097-000 (request for "CIA Plan to Sabotage the Economy of the Soviet Union"), 1170912-002 (request for "Specov-sensitive Coverage Placed at the Request of the White House").

[56] *See, e.g.*, *Victory for Academic Freedom at University of Arizona*, Am. Assoc. of Univ. Professors (Apr. 8, 2015), www.aaup.org/news/victory-academic-freedom-university-arizona#.XvZGmfJ7nOQ; *see also* Kate Sheppard, *Climategate: What Really Happened?*, Mother Jones (Apr. 21, 2011), www.motherjones.com/environment/2011/04/history-of-climategate (documenting how although originally hacked, emails were later sought through public records statutes).

[57] *See, e.g.*, Elizabeth Williamson, *Industries Turn Freedom of Information Requests on Their Critics*, N.Y. Times (Nov. 5, 2018), www.nytimes.com/2018/11/05/us/politics/freedom-of-information-requests.html.

[58] *See* Andi Curcio, *Public Opposition to Jeff Sessions Results in an Open Records Request*, Soc'y of Am. Law Teachers (Jan. 18, 2017), www.saltlaw.org/public-opposition-jeff-sessions-prompts-open-records-request.

[59] Michael Hiltzik, *How Millions from Uber and Lyft Are Funding Harassment*, L.A. Times (Sept. 2, 2020), www.latimes.com/business/story/2020-09-02/uber-lyft-veena-dubal-twitter-bullying.

allowing discrimination against the LGBTQ community and curtailing access to contraception.[60] Similarly, requests for the personal information of researchers that use animals for scientific purposes were deemed so harassing that some states amended their public records laws to specifically protect them.[61] Indeed, the range of academic research targeted in this manner appears to be growing.[62] As a result of these instances, notable calls are being made for an academic freedom or researcher carve-out to state open records laws to protect individuals in academia.[63]

These high-profile instances of abuse and harassment predominantly happen at the state level, with university professors, researchers, and others affiliated with public academic institutions targeted because of ideological disagreements with their research. Because the federal government has no comparable institutions, an analogous use of the federal FOIA is not evident as a pattern. Indeed, the media coverage and opinion commentary concerning public records requests that are abusive, harassing, or vexatious all focus on the use of state laws.[64]

Yet, some such harassment and abuse of FOIA can be detected, albeit sporadically, at the federal level. Julian Tarver is a prisoner at Clallam Bay Correction Center in Washington.[65] He was convicted of third-degree child rape, first-degree extortion and unlawful imprisonment, and various other charges arising out of a 2010 incident in which he impersonated a police officer and sexually assaulted several women working in the sex trade industry.[66] Unrelated, but also interestingly, he is the son of Rob Tarver and Kristine Alles, former members of the California-based Peoples Temple religious group, which infamously established an

[60] Will Creeley, *FOIA Request for UVA Law Prof's Records Threatens Academic Freedom*, Found. for Individual Rights in Educ. (May 28, 2014), www.thefire.org/foia-request-for-uva-law-prof-records-threatens-academic-freedom.

[61] *See, e.g.*, Or. Rev. Stat. § 192.345(30) (2018) and Utah Code Ann. § 63G-2-305(52) (2017) (protecting state university personnel conducting animal research).

[62] *See* Claudia Polsky, *Open Records, Shuttered Labs: Ending Political Harassment*, 66 UCLA L. Rev. 208, 215–16 (2019).

[63] *See e.g.*, Zach Greenberg, *The Chilling Effect of Sunlight: Preserving Academic Freedom in the Face of Abusive Open Records Requests*, 29 Geo. Mason U. C.R.L.J. 145 (2019); Polsky, *supra* note 62.

[64] *See, e.g.*, Rob Jenkins, *FOIA Harassment: Because There's No Crime Like Thought Crime*, The Chronicle of Higher Educ.: Chron. Community (Sept. 25, 2014), community.chronicle.com/news/720-foia-harassment-because-there-s-no-crime-like-thought-crime; Michael Halpern, *Freedom to Bully: How Laws Intended to Free Information are Used to Harass Researchers*, Union of Concerned Scientists (Feb. 11, 2015), www.ucsusa.org/openrecordsabuse; Nat'l Freedom of Info. Coal., Beast or Burden: Nuisance, Vexatious, or Burdensome Public Records Requests (2018); Opinion, *Using Open-Records Laws to Harass Scholars*, Wash. Post (Apr. 1, 2011), www.washingtonpost.com/opinions/using-open-records-laws-to-harass-scholars/2011/04/01/AFLInHXC_story.html.

[65] *See* Letter from Darren B. Ash, Deputy Exec. Dir. for Corp. Mgmt., Office of Gov't Info. Servs., Nat'l Archives & Records Admin., to Julian Tarver, DOC 885530 (Jan. 28, 2015) (on file with author).

[66] Levi Pulkkinen, *Seattle Cop Impersonator Sentenced to 14 Years*, KOMO News (Feb. 3, 2012), komonews.com/news/local/seattle-cop-impersonator-sentenced-to-14-years.

agricultural project in Jonestown in Guyana, leading to the mass murder and suicide of over 900 people.[67]

In the study year, Julian Tarver submitted 320 requests to the NRC. His requests have little apparent rhyme or reason. Many requests target records released in response to other FOIA requests.[68] Others involve certain correspondence or communications, certain policies, or certain incident reports.[69] It is legitimately impossible to figure out what Mr. Tarver is trying to uncover, yet his name continues to appear on NRC logs years later.[70] Moreover, it is clear that he is a frequent requester beyond this particular agency. In 2018, Emma Best filed a request to the FBI for the most recent copy of the "vexsome filer list" aka "high-volume requesters" list or "serial filer list" or "nuisance filer list."[71] Julian Tarver was listed eleventh, having filed eighty-five requests for 7,120 pages in some unspecified period of time.[72]

Of course, just because Mr. Tarver is incarcerated, or just because his requesting is voluminous, does not render his use of FOIA automatically nefarious. However, other indicia suggest he may be engaged in some sort of FOIA abuse. At the state level, the state of Washington actually banned Mr. Tarver from filing more requests in two separate orders. The permanent injunction order detailed Mr. Tarver's use of the state open records law "to harass and intimidate the Department, the Washington State Patrol, the Attorney General's Office, and their employees."[73] From the order, it appears that many of Mr. Tarver's requests sought the home address of public employees.[74] This order, at the very least, suggests a pattern of using FOIA for the purpose of harassment and abuse of the public records process, which may well carry over to his requesting at the federal level.

Mr. Tarver cannot be the only such example at the federal level. But they are hard to identify in the logs. Some agency officials cite instances of using FOIA for harassment or abuse that may indeed fall in that category or, alternatively, may be more charitably categorized as vigorous use. For example, Ginger McCall, formerly

[67] *The Incarcerated: A Report*, ALTERNATIVE CONSIDERATIONS OF JONESTOWN & PEOPLES TEMPLE (Oct. 4, 2020), jonestown.sdsu.edu/?page_id=70317.

[68] *See, e.g.*, NRC Data, *supra* note 46, at Request Nos. FOIA/PA-2017-00046, FOIA/PA-2017-00056.

[69] *See, e.g.*, *id.* at Request Nos. FOIA/PA-2017-00077 (communications between NRC and Governor of Washington), FOIA/PA-2017-00084 (policy on radioactive shipments), FOIA/PA-2017-00088 (incident reports for a particular facility).

[70] *Recent FOIA Requests – February 2020*, U.S. NUCLEAR REGULATORY COMM'N, www.nrc.gov/reading-rm/foia/recent-requests/2020/foia-february.html (last visited Nov. 25, 2020).

[71] Emma North-Best, FBI Vexsome Filer List (2018 Pre-file) (Federal Bureau of Investigation) (Sept. 7, 2018), www.muckrock.com/foi/united-states-of-america-10/fbi-vexsome-filer-list-2018-pre-file-federal-bureau-of-investigation-60440/.

[72] *Id.* at www.muckrock.com/foi/united-states-of-america-10/fbi-vexsome-filer-list-2018-pre-file-federal-bureau-of-investigation-60440/#file-794469.

[73] *Washington v. Tarver*, No. 12-2-01779-1, at 2 (Wash. Super. Ct., Apr. 25, 2017) (order granting permanent injunction).

[74] *Id.* at 3.

a top FOIA official at the Department of Labor, lamented there are a few people making very broad requests "almost every day" and cited an example of once getting a request for "all of Secretary Acosta's emails" with no limitation whatsoever.[75] Clearly, these sorts of requests are burdensome, but, whether or not they constitute abuse or harassment is difficult to ascertain. In any event, overt attempts to harass federal government officials are not as apparent as they are at the state level. Nonetheless, this potential for abuse of the FOIA process is certainly more than theoretical and worth acknowledging.

* * *

Sometimes, requesters do not fit into neat categories. Even beyond these examples, it is easy to find completely idiosyncratic uses of FOIA. Eugene Baime, at the Bureau of Prisons (BOP), cited uses of FOIA that one would be hard pressed to imagine, such as inmates who routinely request menus, recipes, or nutritional information about meals served in their institutions.[76] One important aspect of this idiosyncrasy, however, is that it reveals a central problem in the decades-long effort to perfect FOIA reform: FOIA looks different at every agency. The information constituencies FOIA serves vary widely across the federal government. Best serving their needs is not a one-size-fits-all mission. What follows in Part III outlines a tailored approach to meeting the information needs of these constituencies without curtailing anyone's right to file a FOIA request, but reducing the need to resort to FOIA and thereby saving FOIA for predominantly oversight requesters.

[75] Telephone Interview with Ginger McCall, Former Att'y Advisor, Office of the Solicitor, U.S. Dep't of Labor (May 10, 2019).

[76] Telephone Interview with Eugene Baime, Supervisory Att'y, FOIA/PA Section, Office of the Gen. Counsel, Fed. Bureau of Prisons, U.S. Dep't of Justice (Mar. 3, 2020).

PART III

Let Oversight Reign

9

The Problem with Repurposing FOIA

As you pull up to the National Records Center outside of Kansas City, Missouri, you realize why everyone keeps referring to it as "the Cave." It is, quite literally, a cave. Your car enters a subterranean parking lot, the walls and columns of which are formed by rocky limestone outcroppings. The entrance is noticeable only because it is brightly lit, tucked deep within the parking area. After passing through a modest, though tightly controlled, security screening, you enter what could be any windowless office space filled with cubicles and specially reserved private offices, except that the same limestone rock occasionally intrudes, protrudes, or forms the walls of the areas through which you traverse.

It becomes clear immediately that the Cave is immense. I am told that, although it has dropped ceiling tiles, the Cave itself forms the cavernous ceiling above it, occasionally letting loose a piece of rock that drops with a dramatic crash onto the ceiling above the office space. The Cave is privately owned by a company called the Space Center, but it is leased to various tenants. One is Hanna's Handiworks, a leading wholesaler of holiday trinkets and kitschy home decor. Another is US Citizenship and Immigration Services, which operates the National Records Center.

While touring the Cave, you notice one person who is individually stuffing CD mailers from stacks upon stacks of CDs. Several others huddle over scanners. Many more push carts of records around. And then you come upon one of the four unthinkably large "stack" rooms. These rooms collectively house more than twenty million paper A-Files, each containing the single official record documenting the immigration history of a particular noncitizen. Another twenty million such files are in the custody of the National Archives, transferred there after 100 years. The stack rooms contain enough records to fill four football fields, all held in the relatively cheap, relatively secure, relatively climate-insulated cave. And each day, multiple semitrailer trucks pull up full of files to be newly deposited in or returned to the Cave.

It is because of the A-Files that the Cave is the single largest FOIA processing center in the country. Two hundred and fifty employees do nothing but process FOIA requests at the facility. Another 500 contracted staff do nothing but file management – tracking, sorting, pulling, refiling, scanning, mailing, and otherwise managing the records kept in the facility. The Cave now processes upwards of 200,000 FOIA requests a year.

A. FOIA IS EXPENSIVE

Federal agencies are overwhelmed by their obligations under FOIA. Year-over-year increases in the number of requests made to the federal government are staggering. In Fiscal Year (FY) 2018, the federal government received 863,729 requests, compared to 818,271 in FY 2017, 788,769 in FY 2016, and 713,168 in FY 2015.[1] That is, the total number submitted has jumped more than 100,000 in the span of three years, and the trend shows no sign of abating. As a result, agency resource concerns play a perennial role in FOIA debates.

This phenomenon is nothing new. As Sam Lebovic documented, before FOIA was even passed, twelve of the twenty-seven agencies testifying against the law protested the administrative cost and burden it would impose. Lebovic cites as illustrative one agency's contention that FOIA would impose "inestimable costs and manpower burden."[2] The concerns today are not measurably different. Agencies routinely testify in FOIA oversight hearings regarding the resources necessary to fulfill FOIA obligations and the difficulty in meeting an ever-growing demand.[3]

Today the costs of FOIA are undoubtedly high, much higher than Congress ever anticipated. When Congress passed the 1974 amendments to FOIA that morphed the law into the form in which it substantially remains today, it estimated the costs of government compliance would be $100,000 a year,[4] roughly $500,000 in today's dollars. By contrast, in Fiscal Year 2019, agencies spent an estimated $525 million processing FOIA requests and appeals and litigating FOIA cases.[5] That is, FOIA

1 Office of Info. Policy, U.S. Dep't of Justice, Summary of Annual FOIA Reports for Fiscal Year 2018, at 2 (2018) [hereinafter 2018 FOIA Reports Summary].

2 Sam Lebovic, *How Administrative Opposition Shaped the Freedom of Information Act*, *in* Troubling Transparency: The History and Future of Freedom of Information 13, 23 (David E. Pozen & Michael Schudson eds., 2018).

3 *See, e.g.*, *FOIA: Examining Transparency under the Trump Administration before the H.R. Comm. on Oversight & Reform*, 116th Cong. 18–19 (2019) (statement of Tim Epp, Acting Dir., Nat'l FOIA Office, Envtl. Prot. Agency) (explaining the agency increased resource allocation to FOIA processing in response to request backlog, including increased hiring to process FOIA requests).

4 H. R. Rep. No. 93-876, at 130 (1974).

5 Office of Info. Policy, U.S. Dep't of Justice, Summary of Annual FOIA Reports for Fiscal Year 2019 (2019) [hereinafter 2019 FOIA Reports Summary].

costs more than one thousand times as much as Congress envisioned. Moreover, less than one percent of those costs are recouped in fees charged to requesters.[6]

And the costs are substantially underestimated. As US Citizenship and Immigration Services (USCIS) FOIA director Jill Eggleston explained, not captured in that number are the hours that non-FOIA personnel or program staff spend searching their records and assisting FOIA staff in complying with requests.[7] That time can be significant. Professor David Pozen has noted that non-salary costs associated with FOIA personnel are also often not counted, as well as opportunity costs and diversion costs associated with appropriating non-FOIA personnel time for FOIA matters.[8] Moreover, Pozen notes, "As the volume of FOIA requests rises, then, so will the drain on non-FOIA employees' time, resources, and focus."[9] For her part, Eggleston believes that if the public really understood the taxpayer cost of FOIA, there would be a more significant conversation about whether the money is well spent.[10] It is hard not to take that concern seriously, since she is the one overseeing the Cave.

Worse yet, regardless of how much money agencies throw at FOIA, they are hardpressed to keep up with the public's insatiable demand for records. The Department of Justice's (DOJ) most recent annual summary of agency FOIA reports explains that, while the federal government overall increased its backlog of requests because it did not process as many as it received in FY 2018, "the 830,060 requests processed . . . is also more than the number of requests agencies received in the prior fiscal year."[11] That is, agencies increased their processing capacities, just not as fast as the increase in requests being made. As a result, the total number of backlogged requests at the end of the fiscal year was still a staggering 130,718 requests, representing a 17.4 percent increase from the previous year.[12]

A 2016 US House of Representatives Committee on Oversight and Government Reform report dramatically entitled "FOIA Is Broken" declares, as its ultimate subheading "The Biggest Barrier of All: Delay, Delay, Delay." The report noted various instances in which it took years to reach a resolution of a request, or in which the timeframe led to ineffectual results, or in which agencies simply never responded.

While the sheer volume of requests is not always the reason for agency obstruction, it cannot help that agencies are overwhelmed by requests. As the House

6 *Id.*

7 Interview with Jill Eggleston, Assistant Ctr. Dir., Freedom of Info. & Privacy Act Unit, Nat'l Records Ctr., U.S. Citizenship & Immigration Servs., U.S. Dep't of Homeland Sec., in Lee's Summit, Mo. (June 12, 2019).

8 David E. Pozen, *Freedom of Information beyond the Freedom of Information Act*, 165 U. Pa. L. Rev. 1097, 1123–25 (2017).

9 *Id.* at 1125.

10 Interview with Jill Eggleston, *supra* note 7.

11 2018 FOIA Reports Summary, *supra* note 1, at 21.

12 *Id.* at 9.

Committee said, "[i]t is unreasonable to expect citizens to maintain trust in a government that simply ignores them when they make requests for information. The consequences of these extreme delays could have serious and far reaching effects."[13]

B. UNINTENDED FOIA USERS UNDERMINE ITS JUSTIFICATION

Then-Professor Antonin Scalia's famous declaration about FOIA still reverberates in conversations about the law in practice. In an essay entitled "The Freedom of Information Act Has No Clothes," he proclaimed that FOIA "is the Taj Mahal of the Doctrine of Unanticipated Consequences, the Sistine Chapel of Cost-Benefit Analysis Ignored."[14] Interestingly, he notes the disconnect between the law's purpose and its broad reach: "The question, of course, is whether this public expense is worth it, bearing in mind that the FOIA requester is not required to have any particular 'need to know.'"[15]

From the very outset, agencies voiced concerns over who would use the law, anticipating that many uses would not align with Congress's oversight vision. Commercial requesters were featured in these comments, with some agencies citing possibilities that private profitmaking rather than public good could motivate requests. As Lebovic details, however, the more prevalent worry among agencies was the imagined "parade of irresponsible troublemakers," or people seeking to harass agency officials, pursue fringe conspiracy theories, obtain revenge or just desserts, or otherwise produce little-value gossip or dirt.[16]

Interestingly, though the general worry about a flood of non-oversight-minded requesters was articulated, first-person uses of the law were not among the commonly cited concerns. Nonetheless, Lebovic concluded that "[t]he concerns of the administration foreshadowed the uneven effectiveness of FOIA in its first half-century," including that FOIA has been more often used by nonoversight requesters (Lebovic specifically cites commercial requesters) than by news media or their proxies.[17]

Others have taken this observation one step further arguing that FOIA may in fact be more regressive than progressive; that is, the law may be detracting from the democratic project rather than advancing it. David Pozen is a leader of this view, arguing that FOIA "saps regulatory capacity; distributes government goods in an inegalitarian fashion; and contributes to a culture of adversarialism and derision

[13] Staff of H.R. Comm. on Oversight and Gov't Reform, 114th Cong., FOIA is Broken: A Report 39 (2016) [hereinafter FOIA is Broken].

[14] Antonin Scalia, *The Freedom of Information Act Has No Clothes*, Reg.: AEI J. on Gov't & Soc'y, Mar./Apr. 1982, at 14, 15.

[15] *Id.* at 17.

[16] Lebovic, *supra* note 2, at 27.

[17] *Id.* at 28.

surrounding the domestic policy bureaucracy while insulating the far more secretive national security agencies, as well as corporations, from similar scrutiny."[18]

Behind some of these claims is support in the data on who uses FOIA. For example, Pozen cites the volume of commercial requesters, lawyers, and contractors as evidence that they constitute a set of "FOIA Winners." They routinely take advantage of the law's provisions to obtain commercially valuable information, but they are also highly effective in protecting their own information through so-called reverse-FOIA lawsuits to prevent agencies from disclosing their submissions in response to others' requests. This, Pozen, says, has meant that agencies have been reticent to release information that touches on private enterprise, much to the frustration of consumer advocates and other public interest minded requesters.[19] Moreover, Pozen cites my own previous work for the proposition that FOIA operates as a form of corporate subsidy.[20]

The "FOIA Losers," on the other hand, include the agencies, which are saddled with bureaucratic cost, are hindered in their mission by diversion of resources, and suffer diminished public standing because FOIA becomes a tool to uncover any dirt by a political opponent interested in either shaming the administrative state generally or a particular agency and its mission specifically.[21] He uses these examples and others to support his overall view that "FOIA does the least work where it is most needed and, at least from a normative standpoint that values effective and egalitarian governance above transparency per se, does too much work everywhere else."[22]

A recent volume published on the fiftieth anniversary of FOIA's enactment is far from celebratory. As the introduction declares, "a growing number of scholars, advocates, and regulators have begun to raise hard questions about the costs and limits of the transparency movement."[23] It goes on to describe the collective effects of these critiques as not having dampened civil society's enthusiasm for promoting government transparency, but arrestingly states that the critiques have "developed to the point where we might say that government transparency, as a democratic ideal, is contested not only in practice but in theory."[24] Viewed in this light, these critiques verge on advocating for FOIA's demise.[25]

To be sure, there are no credible efforts at repeal in play, nor are policy debates shifting toward such measures. Indeed, others have described FOIA as "quasi-constitutional," "entrenched" and a "super statute," precisely because it has created a

[18] Pozen, *supra* note 8, at 1097.
[19] *Id.* at 1115.
[20] *Id.* at 1116–17.
[21] *Id.* at 1123–28.
[22] *Id.* at 1111.
[23] David E. Pozen & Michael Schudson, *Introduction* to TROUBLING TRANSPARENCY: THE HISTORY AND FUTURE OF FREEDOM OF INFORMATION, *supra* note 2, at 1, 1.
[24] *Id.*
[25] Pozen, *supra* note 8, at 1123–1128.

difficult to uproot set of rights, expectations, and norms.[26] Seth Kreimer explains that "[w]hat the Constitution's text omits, the last two generations have embedded in 'small-c' constitutional law and practice," including FOIA.[27]

For all of the many reasons described in detail in Part I of this volume, including Kreimer's own piercing analysis of how FOIA fits into an "ecology" of transparency, the benefits of which may be even harder to quantify than the costs, it would be a grave mistake to conclude that the glut of nonoversight requesters is a reason to repeal or even narrow the law. As Kreimer recently wrote in response to this line of critique, the "virtues of the current system reside precisely in the characteristics that generate critique. The breadth of the FOIA gives it robustness . . . ."[28]

Importantly, however, even though narrowing FOIA is not the answer in my view, this does not mean that we should not pay attention to the vast majority of FOIA users. They are what gives the vociferous critiques of FOIA legs to stand on. They are what detracts from the ability to clearly state that FOIA is worth its considerable costs. And they are what leads to questioning about whether FOIA is accomplishing its goal.

C. AGENCIES SPECIALIZE IN NON-OVERSIGHT RECORDS

Given that agencies are overwhelmed by requests, they necessarily engage in triage. Rational responses to volumes of non-oversight requesters include creating processes, systems, and specialists who speak to the volume of routine requests, not one-off media requests about a pressing timely topic. In fact, agencies often do not have the resources or technology to best serve the specialized interests of news media.

Visits to agency offices confirm the same. In a conversation with me, James Holzer, the Deputy Chief FOIA Officer at the Department of Homeland Security's (DHS) Privacy Office, repeatedly referenced "real" FOIA requests or "true" FOIA requests as a way of differentiating the tiny fraction of requests made to DHS that are about policy, decision-making, agency contracting, events of public importance and the like. The reason this distinction is salient is that, according to Holzer, ninety-six percent of DHS's overall requests are first-person in nature.[29]

Importantly, however, Holzer confirmed the entirely rational approach the agency takes to managing the enormity of its FOIA task: DHS is "trying to build a

[26] Mark Fenster, *FOIA as an Administrative Law*, *in* TROUBLING TRANSPARENCY: THE HISTORY AND FUTURE OF FREEDOM OF INFORMATION, *supra* note 2, at 52, 62–63.

[27] Seth F. Kreimer, *The Ecology of Transparency Reloaded*, *in* TROUBLING TRANSPARENCY: THE HISTORY AND FUTURE OF FREEDOM OF INFORMATION, *supra* note 2, at 135, 135.

[28] *Id.* at 153.

[29] Interview with Dr. James V.M.L. Holzer, Deputy Chief FOIA Officer, Jimmy Wolfrey, Senior Dir., FOIA Operations and Mgmt. & Amy Bennett, Public Liaison, U.S. Dep't of Homeland Sec., in Wash. D.C. (June 5, 2019). He referred to these as Privacy Act requests.

system that speaks to ninety percent of the requests that we get." As to the bulk of requests, they are "trying to drive down the response time for routine requests as far as possible."[30] Similarly, at the Bureau of Prisons (BOP), Eugene Baime explained: "I put a lot of emphasis in processing simple requests quickly because it is one of the few things we have a lot of control with our metrics."[31] If I were a Chief FOIA Officer, I would do the very same thing. The key to getting numbers under control is to make sure you can handle the vast majority of your requests in a routine, streamlined, and efficient fashion.

But where does that leave the others? At DHS, at least, as a general matter Holzer thinks that "true" FOIA requests mostly go into the backlog, and "the backlog is masked with routine requests."[32] To be clear, these "true" requests truly are more difficult and take more resources. Jimmy Wolfery, Acting Senior Director of FOIA Operations at DHS, has had to personally handle some of the most uniquely complex cases, such as requests about the shoe bomber, the Boston Marathon bomber, and the BP oil spill. It basically requires the agency to "create a new expert on that topic each time."[33]

Jill Eggleston, Associate Center Director of the FOIA/Privacy Act Branch of the National Records Center (the Cave) for USCIS, spoke to the division of labor and specialization of her 250 FOIA employees. The vast majority of those employees process nothing but A-Files. A separate unit with eleven employees within the FOIA branch is named the Significant Interest Group and all non-A-File requests are directed to them. The positions have a higher grade, they deal with any requests from media, anything with high visibility, and anything that involves program staff. Notably, the unit only processes about two thousand of USCIS's nearly 200,000 requests per year.[34]

Those requests clearly take special expertise, and to USCIS's credit, the agency has devoted a separate unit to processing them. But SIG's existence demonstrates that, overall, most of the agency's FOIA resources expressly do not serve media requests. SIG's requests, in the words of one senior government information specialist working in SIG, "are much more complex and take much more time and resources."[35] Tellingly, it was only in 2018 that SIG obtained e-discovery tools, computer software that has existed for decades that makes records search and identification much more streamlined. The unit with the most complex job simply did not, until recently, have the best tools available for fulfilling those requests. One

[30] *Id.*

[31] Telephone Interview with Eugene Baime, Supervisory Att'y., FOIA/PA Section, Office of the Gen. Counsel, Fed. Bureau of Prisons, U.S. Dep't of Justice (Mar. 3, 2020).

[32] Interview with Dr. James V. M. L. Holzer, Jimmy Wolfrey & Amy Bennett, *supra* note 29.

[33] *Id.*

[34] Interview with Jill Eggleston, *supra* note 7.

[35] Interview with Jarrod T. Panter, Significant Interest Grp. Processor, U.S. Citizenship & Immigration Servs., in Lee's Summit, Mo. (June 12, 2019).

can imagine that the resources required to address to the bulk of USCIS requests – again, a completely rational agency response – may well preclude or delay obtaining other admittedly expensive tools that are designed to best serve media interests under FOIA.

E-Discovery tools for FOIA offices also came up in a telephone conversation with Ginger McCall, former Attorney Advisory at the Department of Labor who worked on FOIA. She said that one of the things she was most surprised about when she moved into government was the lack of technology.[36] A former Department of Housing and Urban Development (HUD) Executive Secretary who oversaw FOIA for the agency put it simply: "People don't understand that it's impossible . . . . The system is set up to fail." After describing the enormity of the task and the many obstacles FOIA offices face, she summed up the situation as: "FOIA is the Titanic. It sank years ago. We are trying to make it float again."[37]

D. NEWS MEDIA ARE HINDERED IN USING FOIA

Evidence suggests that these very real resource challenges agencies face do have an effect on media requesters' ability to use the law effectively. Certainly, the impact on the news media of the glut of other FOIA requesters cannot be precisely quantified. Nonetheless, delay and administrative burden are by far the biggest complaints journalists raise about the law, and those concerns are directly related to agencies' resource constraints, which are strained under the weight of non-oversight requesters. Moreover, the changing nature of the news media and the economics of its business are only exacerbating the challenges journalists face when using the law.

Hamilton's study of investigative journalists' successful use of FOIA was paired with a second dataset demonstrating that news media requests overall have declined over a five-year period by twenty-five percent.[38] Moreover, the types of media requesters changed over time, shifting from local newspapers as the dominant media category to what he describes as "other media," which includes the *Associated Press* (AP), *Bloomberg*, and various specialty publications.[39]

Most interestingly, Hamilton concludes that the publications that use FOIA the most have unique funding models, whereas local papers were unable to sustain the costs of investigative journalism to the same degree. For example, the three media outlets in his study that filed over 100 requests each were *The New York Times*, which

36 Telephone Interview with Ginger McCall, Former Att'y Advisor, Office of the Solicitor, U.S. Dep't of Labor (May 10, 2019).

37 Telephone Interview with Helen Foster, Former Chief Privacy and FOIA Officer & Chief Administrative Officer, U.S. Dep't of Housing and Urban Development (May 14, 2019).

38 James T. Hamilton, *FOIA and Investigative Reporting: Who's Asking What, Where, When—And Why It Matters*, *in* TROUBLING TRANSPARENCY: THE HISTORY AND FUTURE OF FREEDOM OF INFORMATION, *supra* note 2, at 116, 121.

39 *Id.* at 121.

can "spread costs across a national or international audience," AP, which can fund its reporting from its variety of outlets to whom it provides content, and the Center for Public Integrity, which is funded through donations as a nonprofit.[40]

My own interviews with journalists – even those using FOIA to great effect as documented in Chapter Two – confirm the ways in which delay and administrative burden in using FOIA are hindering full realization of FOIA's goals. Notably, every journalist I spoke to listed delay among top concerns.

Many told me of particularly frustrating instances where delay in a FOIA response hindered reporting. For example, Zach Mider of *Bloomberg* recounted: "I just got one yesterday that was from a story – I requested the documents, in, I think, February or March – March of 2017 . . . . And I wrote this story in like, late April, and I just got the documents yesterday . . . . [The documents are] not helpful at all now."[41] I spoke with Mider in the spring of 2019, so "yesterday" represented a two-year wait for the records he requested.

Justin Elliot of *ProPublica* similarly lamented that "delay in many cases is effectively denial, because stuff just stops being interesting and newsworthy."[42] The delay is directly related to the news media's ability to promote government accountability in his mind: "[Y]ou're robbing the public of information while it's relevant."[43]

At one point, Elliot was so frustrated with the delay he experienced waiting for responses to FOIA requests about relief efforts for Hurricane Sandy he wrote a column about it in the *Washington Post.* His column, entitled "The Federal Government No Longer Cares About Disclosing Public Information," is blistering. He published his investigation on the Sandy response eight months after filing his initial request to the Federal Emergency Management Agency for relevant records, but without any of the records because there had been no response. Four hundred and ninety-two business days after FOIA's deadline, he finally heard that the agency was starting over in processing his request because mistakes had been made. His further probing revealed understaffing, inadequate training, and mismanagement, all traceable in some way to lack of resources. Elliot recounted similar experiences of his colleagues; for one of them, it took more than seven years to obtain TSA records, and the "latest contact in the FOIA office was still in high school when [the reporter] filed his initial request."[44]

40 *Id.* at 122–23.

41 Interview with Zachary Mider, Reporter, Bloomberg News (Apr. 16, 2019).

42 Telephone Interview with Justin Elliott, Reporter, ProPublica (Apr. 19, 2019).

43 *Id.*

44 Justin Elliott, *The Federal Government No Longer Cares about Disclosing Public Information*, Wash. Post (Mar. 11, 2016), www.washingtonpost.com/opinions/the-federal-government-no-longer-cares-about-disclosing-public-information/2016/03/10/7e0bf1bc-e631-11e5-a6f3-21ccdbc5f74e_story.html.

Charles Seife, a professor of journalism at N.Y.U., cited old information as a significant barrier as well: "By the time you get the documents you need, I mean, we're talking about something that was scandalous in the FDA a decade ago, and it's really hard to get that out there."[45] As independent journalist Seth Freed Wessler summed it up: "[T]he obvious problem with FOIA is that for the vast majority of federal FOIAs that I file and others file, information is either never released or it takes so long for that information to be released that it becomes potentially irrelevant."[46]

Delay is also closely related to the other biggest problem with FOIA cited by journalists: the resources needed to effectively take advantage of the law. Because of unresponsiveness and delay, journalists cannot simply file a FOIA request and expect a response. Will Parrish of the Intercept tied the two problems together in one example: "I filed requests to the Bureau of Indian Affairs, for example, that I haven't been able to get a formal response to in two years. And so, I think that a big problem is there are some agencies that just try to ignore things, and so they're pushed by a legal adjudication or something like that."[47]

Most of the journalists I talked to discussed the need to pester the agencies, the utility of administrative appeals, and, of course, the value of going to court. All of these are time consuming and resource intensive moves. Scott MacFarlane of *NBC News* asserted "[F]ollow up is, more often than not, required."[48] Kevin Bogardus of *E&E News* rarely can dedicate the time required even to administratively appeal: "[F]or appeals, you have to think more creatively and you have to spend more time on it, and they take at least an hour or more."[49]

Mider added to his concern about delay, "[U]nless you are willing to go to court and ask a judge to make them hand it over, then it's almost like a – you almost [are] usually doing FOIA just to kind of make a point . . . ." To state what is perhaps obvious, going to court is expensive and time consuming. Parrish also sees this as a significant barrier: "[T]here are actually untested areas of FOIA . . . where people can't afford the fight or to go to court."[50]

For those reporters I talked to who have mounted lawsuits, they see great power in them. Each, however, cited unique circumstances that afforded them the opportunity to sue, something they see as rare in the industry. Kevin Bogardus previously worked at the Center for Public Integrity and described how he was interested in taking FOIA cases to court, and how as a result of having in house counsel, he was able to challenge some FOIA denials in the judicial process when he was there. But

45 Telephone Interview with Charles Seife, Professor, N.Y.U. (Feb. 15, 2019).

46 Telephone Interview with Seth Freed Wessler, Freelance Investigative Reporter (Apr. 10, 2019).

47 Telephone Interview with Will Parrish, Freelance Investigative Journalist (Feb. 25, 2019).

48 Telephone Interview with Scott MacFarlane, Investigative Reporter, NBC Wash. (Mar. 22, 2019).

49 Telephone Interview with Kevin Bogardus, Reporter, E&E News (Mar. 22, 2019).

50 Telephone Interview with Zachary Mider, *supra* note 41.

it was situational: "I didn't really have that opportunity at *The Hill* newspaper and we haven't pursued that at *E&E News* either."[51]

For his part, Charles Seife explained that he only started finding FOIA really helpful when he started pursuing litigation, which he was only in a position to do once he left his full-time news media job for an academic post: "[I]f I weren't an academic, or if I weren't at a place that had lawyers behind me, yeah, I would never have made that transformation [from a journalist into a FOIA-using journalist]."[52] Seife started by litigating two cases pro se and then did several cases with a lawyer who represented him pro bono and one with a law school clinic also representing him free of charge.

Seth Freed Wessler noted the particular problems faced by independent journalists who, by definition, do not have access to lawyers at their media outlet or nonprofit organization. "When people are working at outlets, sometimes they have access to attorneys that can help them."[53] Since that was not an option for him, he found a lawyer to represent him pro bono and has had great success in the courts. But having to resort to a lawsuit is "not how this should work, and it's not something that everybody can get access to."[54] Wessler saw such a need in this regard that he, along with another freelance journalist, launched an initiative connecting freelance reporters to pro bono legal support for FOIA disputes.[55]

The New York Times provides a perfect case study. Though best estimates put the *Times* squarely in the top ten media requesters government-wide, it is far from the very top of the list. The FOIA Mapper's study pegged the *Times* as the eighth most frequent requester, far behind other legacy outlets such as the *Associated Press* and the *Wall Street Journal*.[56] Yet in terms of litigation, recently the *Times* has been outpacing everyone. According to a recent study by the Transactional Records Access Clearinghouse's FOIA Project, the *Times* has filed nearly twice as many FOIA cases in the last seventeen years as the next highest media plaintiff, Jason Leopold formerly of *Vice* and now of *Buzzfeed News*.[57]

I had the chance to speak with *Times* Vice President and Deputy General Counsel David McCraw and First Amendment Fellow Al-Amyn Sumar who together handle the *Times*' newsroom litigation, more than half of which consists

[51] Telephone Interview with Kevin Bogardus, *supra* note 49.

[52] Telephone Interview with Charles Seife, *supra* note 45.

[53] Telephone Interview with Seth Freed Wessler, *supra* note 46.

[54] *Id.*

[55] GUMSHOE GRP., www.gumshoegroup.org/ (last visited Dec. 2, 2020).

[56] Max Galka, *Who uses FOIA? - An Analysis of 229,000 Requests to 85 Government Agencies*, FOIA MAPPER (Mar. 13, 2017), foiamapper.com/who-uses-foia.

[57] To arrive at this number, I have combined lawsuits filed in the name of *The* New York Times with the lawsuits filed in the name of Charlie Savage, a Times reporter that the Times represents in FOIA matters. *See Media Lawsuits Seeking Government Records Jump under Trump*, THE FOIA PROJECT (Aug. 2, 2018), foiaproject.org/2018/08/02/media-foia-lawsuits-jump-under-trump.

of FOIA cases. One of the first things that came up was that most of the FOIA litigation they bring is over unresponsiveness, not denials. Conceding that this is an unfortunate system, McCraw calls the fee to file a federal lawsuit the "concierge fee," because it is often the only effective way to force an agency to respond to a request.[58]

I asked why they think the *Times* is litigating so many more FOIA cases than other outlets. McCraw pointed to two important factors: the organization's commitment to fighting government secrecy; and the paper's reluctance to hire outside counsel for newsroom litigation, preferring to handle litigation in-house. That means that they have built litigation capacity and do not have to fork over hourly rates to private attorneys every time they want to take a case to court. The barriers to litigation are lower as a result. But it is also clearly an ideological, not just economic, commitment for the *Times*. "[W]e want to be hands-on," he added, "and we think that's a good role for us."[59]

There are good reasons to want all of these reporters and thousands of others like them to have better luck with their requests without having to build the kind of legal capacity that really only the *Times* and possibly a few other large media outlets ever could. Not only do FOIA requests really make a difference in some important arenas, as outlined in Chapter Two, but media requesters are among the most sophisticated FOIA users and thus are able to target their requests effectively and maximize the public benefit reaped for agency resources expended. But many journalists may never get a response in time for it to make a difference, if at all.

E. FOIA INCENTIVIZES THE STATUS QUO

Trying to better align FOIA's workload with its oversight mission may benefit the news media, and in turn, the public's ability to hold government accountable. One very real concern with any move in that direction, however, is what happens to all those interests that are currently being served by FOIA. These interests are very real, and often vitally important. Businesses have a need for information about government initiatives, enforcement, and market data. The benefits of better information for businesses may improve competition, help entrepreneurship, and ultimately accrue to consumers. Perhaps even more salient, individuals have a need for their files when faced with agency enforcement proceedings or when trying to obtain government benefits. Sometimes these administrative determinations are a matter of vital – even life or death – importance.

Accessing government records in these circumstances produces great public benefits. Government records improve the economy, the health and safety of

[58] Telephone Interview with David McCraw, Deputy Gen. Counsel, N.Y. Times, and Al-Amyn Sumar, First Amendment Fellow, N.Y. Times (May 3, 2019).

[59] *Id.*

citizens, the fairness and accuracy of agency proceedings, and other important interests. But, as further detailed below, these interests are not being served particularly well by FOIA. Because FOIA was not designed with these other requesters in mind, often it is not well suited to serving them. Indeed, these requesters mostly resort to FOIA because there is simply no other option. FOIA is a last resort.

Rather than trying to squeeze all of the public's needs for government information into FOIA, reform efforts should focus on requiring or incentivizing agencies to meet other information needs head-on through tailored mechanisms crafted outside of FOIA. No one should be denied the opportunity to avail themselves of FOIA if they want, but if there were better alternatives to access the particular kind of record sought, they would not need to resort to FOIA. As Eggleston, from USCIS told me, "if there were another mechanism, they wouldn't be filing FOIA requests."[60] This approach would reduce (perhaps vastly) the number of FOIA requests that are made, and free up FOIA offices' resources to better serve FOIA's core mission.

As it stands, however, there is little reason for agencies to look to alternatives. Routine requests – the kinds that noncitizens are making by the hundreds of thousands for their immigration files, the kinds that businesses are flooding the Securities and Exchange Commission and the Environmental Protection Agency and the Food and Drug Administration with each year, the kinds that the Social Security Administration sees most often from amateur genealogists – are often the easiest to fulfill. And over time, agencies have specialized in fulfilling the bulk of their requests, not the difficult, one-off requests covering topics of journalistic concern. As a result, agencies fare better in reporting their overall success rates under FOIA when they have lots of routine requests, including faster processing times, higher release rates, and fewer administrative appeals and legal challenges.

Certainly, there is no evidence that agencies consciously avoid non-FOIA alternatives to make their FOIA performance look better, but there is no question the system is set up with a set of FOIA performance metrics that favor jamming nearly everything into FOIA. Agency officials confirm the lack of incentives for finding alternatives to FOIA. For example, Holzer, at DHS, while detailing the department's various proactive disclosure initiatives, still conceded "[t]here really isn't an incentive" for agencies to proactively disclose records.[61]

Indeed, as it stands, FOIA Offices and FOIA Officers often lack power to make meaningful organizational changes about information delivery even within FOIA policy, much less outside it. For one thing, FOIA offices' budgets are not set by Congress, but rather by the agency from its general appropriations. Thus, FOIA budgets compete with programmatic budgets within their agencies, and FOIA is typically not seen as a crucial part of the agency's overall mission. As the US House of Representatives noted in its "FOIA Is Broken" report, "Agencies are responsible

60 Interview with Jill Eggleston, *supra* note 7.

61 Interview with Dr. James V.M.L. Holzer, Jimmy Wolfrey & Amy Bennett, *supra* note 29.

for distributing appropriate resources to the FOIA offices, including a sufficient number of personnel. For this reason, it is primarily the agencies themselves fostering a culture of responsiveness or unresponsiveness."[62] But FOIA offices may not be able to change the calculation, even though they have the expertise to see what is needed.

Helen Foster, formerly of HUD, had also worked within FOIA and Privacy units at the Department of the Treasury and DHS before that. She noted the impact of the agency's culture on FOIA compliance. For example, at Treasury, she said, "FOIA was considered very important," but even there she could not obtain the resources she needed. "Often the staff did have great ideas, but there was no conduit for that and they get no reward for that, and if they make a suggestion and it doesn't work out it could be a real problem for them." But the culture at the Treasury helped because she viewed the Treasury's identity as living up to the gold standard, complying with every legal requirement, and FOIA was part of that. Whereas, at DHS, she summed up the culture as "no 9/11 ever again" and FOIA was viewed as in some tension with that overall goal. At the least, it ate up resources that could be used to find a terrorist, and at the worst, it let loose valuable intelligence information.[63]

But even with the best of cultures, Foster's overriding insight was that FOIA is a "core compliance function[]." The only way it ever matters to the agencies' higher ups or political appointees is when it goes badly, i.e., creates an embarrassment. So do the program staff listen with the FOIA office has ideas for better information delivery practices? "No, oh my god," said Foster, without missing a beat.[64]

The playing field is wide open for intervention. The flood of non-oversight requesters comes at great cost, undermines FOIA's legitimacy, and masks real problems for news media requesters using the law as intended. Worse, those who may be able to see the problem most clearly have little power to do anything about it. What follows is a necessarily incomplete set of strategies agencies could use to "save" FOIA from buckling under the weight of unintended uses and return more of FOIA resources to serving FOIA's core mission.

62 FOIA IS BROKEN, supra note 13, at 7.

63 Telephone interview with Helen Foster, *supra* note 36.

64 *Id.*

10

Affirmative Disclosure

An aggressive affirmative disclosure regime is the first step towards alleviating the burden on FOIA, primarily the vast numbers of requesters not driven by public oversight purposes. This study demonstrates that affirmative disclosure has the potential to preclude the need for requesters – commercial requesters in particular – to file tens of thousands of requests a year. Indeed, some agencies have recognized this potential, experimented with innovative affirmative disclosure initiatives, and succeeded in reducing their volume of FOIA requests without limiting anyone's access to the FOIA process one bit.

There are, however, barriers. Because the types of records for which this strategy might work vary from agency to agency, across the board mandates are difficult to craft. Even those mandates that already exist suffer from abysmal compliance and enforcement. Moreover, agency budget structures, personnel dynamics, and incentives can also pose difficulties. Though now universally celebrated as an aspiration, a comprehensive approach to proactive disclosure has been lacking. This Chapter provides a roadmap from where affirmative disclosure is today to where it could be in the future.

A. FOIA'S EXISTING REQUIREMENTS

Affirmative disclosure, also known as proactive disclosure, is not a new idea. From its inception, FOIA had some limited affirmative disclosure requirements. It always required the publication of agency rules and regulations in the Federal Register, and always required agencies to "make available" without the need for a request, some other limited categories of records, including final agency orders in adjudications.[1] As others have described, these basic requirements essentially made mandatory the

[1] 5 U.S.C. § 552(a)(1)–(2) (2012).

publication of agency "working law" and general government guidance documents.[2]

In 1996, Congress made what seemed like a huge leap forward in amending FOIA with the so-called E-FOIA amendments. Among the many changes designed to "bring[] FOIA into the information and electronic age,"[3] it added an additional affirmative disclosure requirement, mandating agencies make available, "in electronic format," all records that "because of the nature of their subject matter, the agency determines have become or are likely to become the subject of subsequent requests for substantially the same records."[4] In addition, these amendments required agencies to post "a general index of the records" that fall within the agency's affirmative disclosure obligations.[5] And finally, in 2016, Congress further amended this provision to more concretely specify that the requirement applied to records "that have been requested 3 or more times."[6]

The express purpose of these amendments was to reduce the number of FOIA requests filed, not by curtailing FOIA rights, but by preempting the need for a request because the information is already affirmatively available.[7] This is precisely the rationale on which the proposals in this Chapter rely. But for various reasons, the E-FOIA amendments failed to actualize that vision.

First, compliance has always been somewhere between inconsistent and abysmal. Ten years after the amendments, the National Security Archive surveyed agency websites and concluded that only twenty-one percent of federal agencies were posting all four categories of required records in compliance with FOIA's affirmative disclosure provisions, leading the director of the Archive to declare that "Federal agencies are flunking the online test."[8] Another decade later, the Archive returned to the question, finding that only forty percent of agencies systematically posted records to their websites.[9] Importantly, neither of these studies has a method for detecting whether the postings are in any way comprehensive, only that agencies appear to be attempting compliance, and thus these metrics are necessarily overstating compliance significantly. Moreover, even when records are posted, they are

[2] Michael Herz, *Law Lags Behind: FOIA and Affirmative Disclosure of Information*, 7 CARDOZO PUB. L. POL'Y & ETHICS J. 577, 586 n.38 (2009) (this included requiring agencies to publish "descriptions of the agency, statements of its general policies, rules of procedure, and substantive rules and statements of general policy and general applicability.").

[3] *See* Presidential Statement on Signing the Electronic Freedom of Information Act Amendments of 1996, 2 PUB. PAPERS 1743 (Oct. 2, 1996).

[4] 5 U.S.C. § 552(a)(2)(D).

[5] *Id.* at § 552(a)(2)(E).

[6] The FOIA Improvement Act of 2016, Pub. L. No. 114-185, § 2, 130 Stat. 538 (2016).

[7] Delcianna Winders, *Fulfilling the Promise of EFOIA's Affirmative Disclosure Mandate*, 95 DENV. L. REV. 909, 915–16 (2018).

[8] *Agencies Violate Law on Online Information*, NAT'L SEC. ARCHIVE (Mar. 12, 2007), https://nsarchive2.gwu.edu/NSAEBB/NSAEBB216/index.htm.

[9] *Most Agencies Falling Short on Mandate for Online Records*, NAT'L SEC. ARCHIVE (Mar. 13, 2015), https://nsarchive2.gwu.edu/NSAEBB/NSAEBB505.

often posted in a way that makes them relatively difficult to find, thereby defeating the point of preempting the need for FOIA requests.[10]

Second, and perhaps related to noncompliance, is that enforcement has been somewhere between absent and legally uncertain. Lawsuits have only recently been brought to enforce FOIA's affirmative disclosure provisions, rather than to contest the denial of a request filed under FOIA's more well-known access provision. In the first case to reach a circuit court, the D.C. Circuit concluded FOIA did not even provide a cause of action to enforce violations of affirmative disclosure provisions,[11] though a subsequent Ninth Circuit case – in which I represented the plaintiffs – created a direct circuit split on that threshold question.[12] That even this basic question has not been answered definitively – whether FOIA provides a right to sue for affirmative disclosure violations – itself speaks volumes about the lack of enforcement.

That said, the idea of frequently requested records being made affirmatively available has both theoretical and practical appeal. Theoretically, affirmatively disclosing records that are likely to be frequently requested seems like an obvious starting point to reduce would-be duplicative requests to agencies. And practically, it would appear to make sense for agencies to prioritize spending resources posting these records, rather than indiscriminately posting agency records. Indeed, one of the insights from the frequently requested records provision is the interplay between the traditional request-and-response model of FOIA and affirmative disclosure: we can learn what information constituencies want by what they request and respond with targeted affirmative disclosure regimes.

For some agencies, this requirement seems like it may be working or has the potential to work quite well for their requester populations. The Federal Bureau of Investigation (FBI) and the Consumer Product Safety Commission (CPSC) serve as two particularly powerful examples. As previously demonstrated, the FBI gets frequent requests for FBI files of famous people. The FBI had long been proactively disclosing some records on its website, and in Fiscal Year (FY) 2012 unveiled a newly redesigned site called The Vault where it houses a database of records for public access.[13] The website is relatively nimble, allowing users to search by subject matter or individual name, as well as browse through the frequently requested or recently added records.[14]

[10] Laurence Tai, *Fast Fixes for* FOIA, 52 Harv. J. on Legis. 455, 462–64 (2015).

[11] Citizens for Responsibility & Ethics in Wash. v. U.S. Dep't of Justice, 846 F.3d 1235, 1238 (D.C. Cir. 2017).

[12] Animal Legal Def. Fund v. U.S. Dep't of Agric., 935 F.3d 858, 861 (9th Cir. 2019).

[13] U.S. Dep't of Justice, Chief Freedom of Information Act Officer Report for Fiscal Year 2012, at 10 (2012).

[14] FBI Records: The Vault, https://vault.fbi.gov (last visited Nov. 24, 2020).

In addition, the FBI has a relatively refined method for identifying and posting records in The Vault on topics that are the subject of three or more requests.[15] The fact that The Vault has been lauded by the American Library Association and incorporated into various university libraries[16] is indicative of the many information constituents of the FBI who are now able to identify records they seek without having to file a FOIA request. Since particular incidents and people of high public interest will evolve, the FBI's affirmative disclosure regime – driven by FOIA's existing frequently requested records provision – may be a relatively well-tailored approach for this agency.

Another example of an agency where existing affirmative disclosure requirements for frequently requested records could operate as intended is the CPSC. At this agency, there are numerous requests that pertain to particular products or brands. For example, in the study year, there were fifteen requests pertaining to Polaris, a snowmobile company, nine concerning pressure cookers, nine regarding Ikea products, and six concerning hoverboards.[17] These types of frequent requests may be well served by the existing affirmative disclosure requirement. Unlike the FBI, the CPSC does not appear to have an indexed, searchable method of posting frequently requested records. Its website containing these records does not appear to have even been updated in the three years preceding this writing.[18]

The FBI and CPSC demonstrate that for some agencies where a particular person, company, or incident is likely to generate repetitive requests, the existing affirmative disclosure provision – if fully implemented and enforced – may do some important work to alleviate the pressure on the FOIA office to respond to individual requests for records. Nonetheless, for many agencies, this type of affirmative disclosure requirement will barely scratch the surface of affirmative disclosure's potential and, because of its limited applicability, this study did not surface evidence that it substantially reduced the volume of requests at any given agency.

One substantial problem is how limited the requirement is. Though it has not been definitively interpreted by the courts, it appears to require that a particular document be frequently requested to invoke the requirement, rather than a category of documents. At the very least, that is the interpretation the government has espoused.[19] What that means is that even if a certain type of record is often requested, such as agency inspection reports, unless the particular report is likely

[15] U.S. Dep't of Justice, Chief Freedom of Information Act Officer Report for Fiscal Year 2019, at 16 (2019).

[16] U.S. Dep't of Justice, Chief Freedom of Information Act Officer Report for Fiscal Year 2013, at 28 (2013).

[17] FOIA Request Logs, Consumer Product Safety Comm'n, www.cpsc.gov/Newsroom/FOIA/FOIA-Request-Logs (select FY 2018 items).

[18] *Newsroom FOIA*, U.S. Consumer Prod. Safety Comm'n, www.cpsc.gov/Newsroom/FOIA/ReportList (last visited Nov. 6, 2020).

[19] Motion to Dismiss the Complaint, People for the Ethical Treatment of Animals v. USDA, 1:17-cv-00269-CRC, No. 13 (D.D.C. Feb. 13, 2017).

to be requested three or more times, the requirement to publish all inspection reports will not be triggered.

Other problems arise from implementation complexity. For example, the requirement is so specific that it may be difficult, even for the agency, to keep track of which document is requested a certain number of times, much less outside observers, watchdogs, or members of the public seeking to hold the agency accountable for meeting this requirement. Moreover, the requirement does not delineate a format in which the records must be made public, thereby seemingly allowing agencies to post records to a non-searchable, non-indexed website. Sometimes the records are in non-machine readable PDF formats or other inaccessible documents. There is no evidence to suggest agencies intentionally thwart access but rather it seems that a lack of resources and technology within agencies, and particularly the FOIA office, leads to this result.

Despite relatively modest legal requirements, however, affirmative disclosure has gained huge ground in the public discourse about open government. Categorical affirmative disclosure – rather than the individual document disclosure as mandated by FOIA's requirements – has been restyled as an "open data" initiative. Open data, affirmative disclosure, or proactive disclosure, regardless of title, is increasingly centered in policy and lawmaking efforts.

Indeed, the celebrated trio of "Day One" memoranda issued by President Obama on open government focused, in large part, on a style of affirmative disclosure. In one of those documents, President Obama declared federal government information "a national asset" and directed agencies to "harness new technologies to put information about their operations and decisions online and readily available to the public."[20] Later, the Office of Management and Budget (OMB) implemented this policy through a directive ordering agencies to identify "high value" data sets for publication, defining value as increasing agency accountability, adding to public knowledge of agency operations, furthering agency objectives, creating economic opportunity, or responding to information demand.[21] This mandate created Data.gov and was thereafter populated with agency datasets.[22]

The link between open data style affirmative disclosure and FOIA has been clearly stated by others. Beth Noveck identifies one key feature of open data initiatives as "concentrat[ing] on information as a means to solve problems to the end of improving government effectiveness."[23] That is, they are affirmatively tailored toward particular goals, complimenting FOIA's reactive and open-ended access

[20] Memorandum on Transparency and Open Government, 74 Fed. Reg. 4685, 4685 (Jan. 26, 2009).

[21] Memorandum from Peter R. Orszag, Dir., Office of Budget & Mgmt., Exec. Office of the President, to the Heads of Exec. Dept's & Agencies, M-10-06 (Dec. 8, 2009), https://obamawhitehouse.archives.gov/omb/assets/memoranda_2010/m10–06.pdf.

[22] Data.gov, www.data.gov (last visited Nov. 24, 2020).

[23] Beth Simone Noveck, *Is Open Data the Death of FOIA?*, 126 Yale L.J. F. 273 (2016).

scheme.[24] A leading transparency group, the Sunlight Foundation, noted slim evidence to date that proactive disclosure reduces FOIA requests, but the limited resources of government agencies nonetheless means that agencies should prioritize data "demanded by citizens" as evidenced by previous public records requests.[25]

Similarly, the Department of Justice (DOJ), tasked with issuing FOIA guidance for all federal agencies, also embraced affirmative disclosure as a component of FOIA policy. The Attorney General, implementing the Obama memoranda, instructed that "agencies should readily and systematically post information online in advance of any public request. Providing more information online reduces the need for individualized requests and may help reduce existing backlogs."[26] This memorandum further instructed each agency's Chief FOIA Officer to submit annual reports to the Office of Information Policy (OIP) beginning in 2010. Pursuant to OIP's guidance, Chief FOIA Officers, as one of five topics covered in the reports, are required to describe the agency's proactive disclosure measures, including those records released pursuant to the frequently requested records provision as well as additional steps that are useful to the agency's information constituents.[27]

All of which is to say, it is not a new idea to suggest that affirmative disclosure may be used as a pressure valve to release some of the burden on agencies to process individual FOIA requests and better serve the public. That said, it is has been deeply uneven and underprioritized so far. To be sure, some agencies are already creatively using proactive disclosure in ways that are designed to reduce the agency burden of individual FOIA requests while providing better information delivery mechanisms to the public. But many other agencies have opportunities to do the same. From these examples it is possible to imagine better regimes for encouraging or requiring agencies to improve affirmative disclosure, and the promises and limits of affirmative disclosure come into stark relief.

B. EXAMPLES OF SUCCESS

Many agencies have taken up the call to engage in more affirmative disclosure. A few have done so with the apparent or explicit goal to reduce the public's need to rely on FOIA. These agencies have targeted categories of frequently requested records, even if each individual record alone may not meet the technical requirements of FOIA's frequently requested records provision. Their affirmative disclosure

[24] *See id.*

[25] Alena Stern, *Siblings or Silos: How Do Open Data and FOIA Work Together?*, SUNLIGHT FOUND. (Jun. 29, 2018), sunlightfoundation.com/2018/06/29/siblings-silos-open-data-and-foia/.

[26] Memorandum from Eric Holder, Att'y Gen., Office of Att'y Gen., to Heads of Exec. Dep'ts & Agencies (Mar. 19, 2009).

[27] *Content of 2020 Chief FOIA Officer Reports*, U.S. DEP'T OF JUSTICE, (Aug. 2, 2019), www.justice.gov/oip/chief-foia-officer-report-agency-received-more-50-requests-1.

regimes are not document dumps that simply post unorganized, difficult to access, or otherwise badly formatted records on a website. Rather, they created useful platforms tailored to the needs of their information constituents. Several of them noted efficiencies for the agency that have resulted.

Bulk requesting from commercial users is one area that is particularly ripe for this sort of affirmative disclosure initiative. Take, for example, the Environmental Protection Agency (EPA). As described in greater detail in Chapter 6, during the study year, the vast majority of the EPA's requests were for due diligence purposes related to environmental assessments needed to protect against subsequent clean-up liability on commercial property. The EPA itself once estimated that eighty percent of its requests fell in this category.[28] These requests essentially ask the EPA for any records concerning a particular parcel of property to ensure there is no known risk of environmental contamination.[29]

In 2015, the EPA's Chief FOIA Officer cited as a success story the agency's launch of an online tool to make "environmental information about geographic locations available to the public without the need to file a FOIA request."[30] This new search tool, called MyProperty, is listed on the EPA FOIA page under the frequently requested records category, but goes far beyond simply posting records that have been requested three or more times. Rather, it is a "tool for searching facility data that come from multiple EPA data sources," and it is explicit in its purpose:

> This tool allows Real Estate Agents, Mortgage Banks, Engineering and Environmental Consulting Firms and the public to determine if EPA … has records on a specific property without filing a [FOIA] request. The results of this search will be identical to the information you would receive by filing a FOIA request with EPA for these records.[31]

In 2016, the EPA released an "enhanced version" of MyProperty that generated certificates as proof of due diligence, and other improved functions.

While it is difficult to ascertain how many FOIA requests are no longer made because of the MyProperty tool, the agency reported the public had conducted over 12,000 searches using MyProperty in one of the earliest years of its existence.[32] Moreover, the agency, highlighting it as a "success story" declared that

[28] Larry Gottesman, Nat'l FOIA Dir., U.S. Envtl. Prot. Agency, Remarks at the Freedom of Information Act Advisory Committee Meeting (Apr. 19, 2016), www.archives.gov/ogis/foia-advisory-committee/2014-2016-term/documents/04-19-2016-meeting-transcript.

[29] *Id.*; *see also supra* Ch. 6, pt. B.

[30] U.S. Envtl. Prot. Agency, 2015 Chief FOIA Officer Report, www.epa.gov/foia/report-chief-foia-officer-us-department-justice-2015 [hereinafter EPA Chief FOIA Officer Report 2015].

[31] *MyProperty*, U.S. Envtl. Prot. Agency, enviro.epa.gov/facts/myproperty (last visited Nov. 24, 2020).

[32] EPA Chief FOIA Officer Report 2015, supra note 30.

"MyProperty provides the public and EPA staff significant time savings."[33] As recently as 2020, the agency cited this initiative as one of the primary ways it was using technology to facilitate FOIA efficiencies.[34]

Moreover, a very informal scroll through recent requests to the EPA reveals that while some requests are for records pertaining to a particular parcel of land, those requests appear less frequently than in the 2013 logs included in this study. While certainly not reduced by eighty percent, EPA has, in the past five years since MyProperty came online, bucked the trend of ever-increasing numbers of FOIA requests, having fallen from its highwater mark of 11,518 in FY 2017 to 8,869 in FY 2019.[35] Thus, the circumstantial evidence seems to strongly suggest that MyProperty is a model of affirmative disclosure relieving the burden on the individual FOIA requesting process.

Another agency that took a very proactive approach to systematic records disclosure is the Animal and Plant Health Inspection Service (APHIS), a division of the USDA. APHIS, among other things, administers the Animal Welfare Act (AWA), which regulates the treatment of animals in certain commercial animal enterprises.[36] Under this law, APHIS conducts inspections of regulated facilities, issues warning letters for noncompliance, and initiates enforcement proceedings to remedy violations.[37]

In May 2009, APHIS began posting the AWA inspection reports online in a searchable database.[38] In addition, APHIS began publishing annual reports submitted by certain businesses regulated by the AWA as a category of records that were in the public interest.[39] In 2011, APHIS reported comprehensive progress, explaining the recent database postings "have resulted in significant reduction in the number of FOIA requests – 525 fewer requests between FY 2009 and FY 2010, or approximately a 42 reduction in the number of requests received." It also reported reducing its FOIA backlog by almost forty-three percent, what it described as "unprecedented in more than a 10 year backlog and far exceeding our 25% goal for the year."[40]

[33] U.S. Envtl. Prot. Agency, 2016 Chief FOIA Officer Report, www.epa.gov/foia/report-chief-foia-officer-us-department-justice-2016.

[34] U.S. Envtl. Prot. Agency, 2020 Chief FOIA Officer Report 16, www.epa.gov/foia/report-chief-foia-officer-us-department-justice-2020.

[35] U.S. Evtl. Prot. Agency, 2019 Freedom of Information Act Report 10 (2019); U.S. Evtl. Prot. Agency, 2017 Freedom of Information Act Report 5 (2017).

[36] *Animal Welfare Act*, Animal & Plant Health Inspection Serv. (Jul. 23, 2020), www.aphis.usda.gov/aphis/ourfocus/animalwelfare/awa/ct_awa_program_information.

[37] *Id.*

[38] Complaint at paras. 17–18, Humane Soc'y v. U.S. Dep't. of Agric., No. 1:05-CV-00197, 2005 WL 1173393, at *3 (D.D.C. Jan. 27, 2005); *see* Winders, *supra* note 7, at 923–26 (providing a detailed account of this agency's affirmative disclosure history).

[39] U.S. Dep't of Agric., Chief FOIA Officer Report (Mar. 2010), www.epa.gov/foia/report-chief-foia-officer-us-department-justice-2015.

[40] *Id.* at 21.

Yet, APHIS's natural experiment with affirmative disclosure was not over. In February 2017, the agency abruptly blocked public access to its AWA databases on the website.[41] Immediately, requests for these records skyrocketed; one study documented more than double the number of requests submitted to APHIS following the database blackout, resulting in a FOIA backlog 2.5 times as large as it was immediately preceding the blackout.[42] Affirmative disclosure policy thus has a clear connection to the volume of FOIA requests at this agency.

Some agency FOIA officials have offered anecdotes that are difficult to quantify, but nonetheless serve as powerful examples of the positive effects of affirmative disclosure on the volume of requests. For example, at the US Securities and Exchange Commission (SEC), top FOIA officials noted that in the early 2000s the agency was experiencing serious challenges with thousands of backlogged FOIA requests. They explained that, to address demand, the SEC began posting comment letters issued by the SEC in conjunction with companies' required filings and the companies' responses to those comment letters. FOIA officials credited that proactive disclosure policy with substantially reducing the number of requests.[43] Consistent with that account, the SEC's 2006 Annual FOIA Report notes that the SEC's "program of electronic dissemination of filing-related correspondence increased the volume of publicly available information. The effect of this proactive disclosure is measured in the increased number of FOIA requests citing a disposition that indicates the requester was referred to the SEC Public EDGAR website to obtain the requested records. . . . Additionally, requests for this type of records in FY 2007 have decreased by approximately 15%."[44]

Affirmative disclosure in these examples has been used to publish databases of mostly commercial and business information. Many of the other areas discussed below where additional affirmative disclosure is most promising likewise concern commercial records and often commercial information constituents. However, some agencies have experimented with what is essentially affirmative disclosure to specific individuals – making records accessible without a predicate request – without making them *publicly* available. These, too, have the potential to relieve the pressure on the FOIA office to respond to one-at-a-time requests.

One striking example concerns personal financial data at the Pension Benefit Guarantee Corporation (PBGC). In a 2010 Chief FOIA Officer Report, the agency

[41] The reason behind and legality of this decision was the subject of litigation, including one case in which the author was lead counsel. *See* Animal Legal Def. Fund v. U.S. Dep't of Agric., 935 F.3d 858, 861 (9th Cir. 2019); People for the Ethical Treatment of Animals v. USDA, 1:17-cv-00269-CRC (D.D.C. Feb. 13, 2017).

[42] Winders, *supra* note 7, at 926.

[43] Video Conference Call Interview with Barry Walters, Chief FOIA Officer, Olivier Girod, Deputy Chief FOIA Officer, Mark Siford, Counsel to the Dir./Chief FOIA Officer, & John Livornese, FOIA/PA Officer, U.S. Sec. & Exch. Comm'n (July 21, 2016).

[44] U.S. Sec. and Exch. Comm'n., FOIA Annual Report for the Fiscal Year Ending Sept. 20, 2006 (Feb. 8, 2007), www.sec.gov/foia/arfoia06.htm.

explained that "[T]he majority of PBGC's requests come from pension plan participants seeking to access records pertaining to themselves and their pension plan."[45] In the 2011 report, the agency explained it "launched a newly designed web site ... [which] allows participants in our trusted plans greater access to information pertaining to their specific pension plan" and that the effort had reduced the number of FOIA requests received.[46] Even as recently as 2017, the agency again reiterated that numerous FOIA requests were preempted by their affirmative disclosure initiatives:

> [T]he website's greatest influence is to inform potential FOIA requesters as to the records available to and about them via the site, thus eliminating the need to file at all. For example, when potential requesters quickly determine whether or not they are due a pension and/or identify participation terms online, they are less likely to seek records from the Disclosure Division.[47]

In another example, US Customs and Border Protection (CBP) launched a website in 2014 to provide US arrival and departure records, otherwise known as I-94 information after the form that is completed when seeking entry or exit from the United States.[48] The agency explicitly stated that it hoped to preempt the need for FOIA requests for these documents: "This electronic travel-history function means that travelers may no longer need to file [FOIA] requests to receive their arrival/departure history, greatly speeding their process." To avoid mass disclosure of personal data, CBP required an individual to enter certain biographical data, including name, date of birth, and passport information, before access was provided.[49]

To be sure, there is little evidence this initiative succeeded in substantially reducing FOIA requests. It may be because legal disclaimers about reliance on the information provided in this manner litter the website,[50] and many people need these records for submission to a court or an application to an agency. It may be because it does not include the arrival or departure information for lawful permanent residents (green card holders), only those who travel to the US on a nonimmigrant visa.[51] Or, finally, it may just be that most noncitizens need more

[45] Pension Benefit Guar. Corp., 2010 Chief FOIA Officer Report 2 (2010).

[46] Pension Benefit Guar. Corp., 2011 Chief FOIA Officer Report, at Part III (2011).

[47] Pension Benefit Guar. Corp., 2017 Chief FOIA Officer Report 16 (2017).

[48] *Arrival/Departure History Now Available on I-94 Webpage*, U.S. Customs & Border Prot. (Apr. 30, 2014), www.cbp.gov/newsroom/spotlights/arrivaldeparture-history-now-available-i-94-webpage.

[49] *View Travel History*, U.S. Customs & Border Prot., i94.cbp.dhs.gov/I94/#/history-search (last visited Nov. 24, 2020). While privacy might be a concern for some personal records, these records are not of the utmost sensitivity by their nature and thus basic biographical verification is likely sufficient to protect individuals' interests.

[50] *Official Site for Travelers Visiting the United States: Apply for or Retrieve Form I-94, Request Travel History and Check Compliance*, U.S. Customs & Border Prot., i94.cbp.dhs.gov/I94/#/home (last visited Nov. 24, 2020).

[51] *Id.*

comprehensive records pertaining to their immigration status, not the limited arrival and departure data provided on the website. Regardless, the website provides evidence that it is possible to design an affirmative disclosure system for personal information, despite the fact that this particular one apparently did not succeed in reducing reliance on FOIA.

Another example of proactive disclosure of personal information is evident at Centers for Medicare and Medicaid Services (CMS). There, the FOIA page lists as the first bullet point under "Frequently Requested Information" a link to "Download Your Personal Health Information."[52] The link connects the would-be requester with MyMedicare.gov, a website that allows an insured to log into their account and get a report of all personal data with the click of a single button (labeled the "Blue Button data").[53]

These sorts of personal disclosure websites still act as proactive disclosure. The records are already available for the individual, who can access them simply upon some sort of identity verification. The relationship to FOIA is the same as well. These sorts of tools may be able to preempt hundreds or thousands of FOIA requests a year that otherwise would be made by individuals seeking access to their own files. Some agencies are experimenting with affirmative disclosure in just the way that would seem to improve services to information constituents, produce efficiencies for the agency, and, most relevant here, save FOIA for the oversight requesters for whom it was designed.

C. THE UNTAPPED POTENTIAL

Despite some successful examples, there remains huge potential for additional affirmative disclosure initiatives to reduce reliance on individual FOIA requesting. Studying the FOIA logs is precisely the way to identify these opportunities, because the logs reveal what records the public seeks. Indeed, one of the most robust findings of this study is that at any given agency there usually are two or three kinds of records that are routinely requested. That is, categories of records ripe for an alternative to FOIA are often readily identifiable in the agency's FOIA logs. This is particularly true at high-volume FOIA agencies, rather than the smaller FOIA offices.

Nowhere is the potential more evident than at agencies with high-volume commercial requesting. As Chapters 6 and 7 demonstrated, commercial requesting is largely formulaic; that is, businesses are requesting the same types of records over and over again, sometimes by the thousands. Instead of essentially producing an

[52] *Freedom of Information Act (FOIA) Service Center*, CTRS. FOR MEDICARE & MEDICAID SERVS., (Apr. 10, 2015), www.cms.gov/center/freedom-of-information-act-center.html.

[53] *Medicare's Blue Button & Blue Button 2.0*, MEDICARE.GOV, www.medicare.gov/manage-your-health/medicares-blue-button-blue-button-20 (last visited Nov. 24, 2020).

entire category of agency records one by one in response to requests, often, the agency could simply publish the database for all to see. That is, rather than producing inspection reports, contract bids, or warning letters one at a time, agencies could endeavor to proactively make all such records available without waiting for the hundreds or thousands of requests to pour in.

Illustrative examples can be found in many areas of government. Take, for example, the Food and Drug Administration (FDA). There, facilities inspection reports, or Form 483s, are requested en masse by various information resellers who warehouse these records in databases and resell them at a profit. In the study year, 93 percent of these records were released in full, indicating that the overwhelming majority of the information in these records is public. In the most recently posted logs, Form 483 inspection reports were still the subject of 2,879 requests.[54] Publishing these systematically could, therefore, preempt the need for these requesters to obtain them one by one and better serve the agency's information constituents.

Other areas ripe for affirmative disclosure are apparent at the SEC. One of the two big categories of records requested consists of exhibits to required SEC filings that had been withheld from the public under a temporary confidential treatment rule, which expires after a set period of time.[55] These are also largely requested by information resellers, and many requests come in as soon as the temporary confidentiality provision expires.[56] But the SEC already maintains a comprehensive public database of regulated company filings called EDGAR, which could be harnessed to immediately release records upon expiration of the confidential treatment period. Indeed, SEC FOIA officials confirm that such a system would be possible, and indeed has been suggested, but that resource constraints prevented its realization.[57]

That said, the SEC recently adopted a new rule that appears to provide that the agency will not retain copies of records submitted under the confidential treatment rule, but rather destroy or return them to the submitting company.[58] This may well be a serious impediment to access under FOIA or any other regime of records submitted under this provision going forward. Nonetheless, there are decades worth

[54] *See* FOIA Logs FY 2019, U.S. Food & Drug Admin., www.fda.gov/media/131507/download (counting all requests that have a subject matter that contains either "483" or "inspection" or both).

[55] *See* U.S. Sec. & Exch. Comm'n, Freedom of Information Act Response to Sept. 5, 2014 Request by Margaret B. Kwoka (on file with author); FOIA Logs, U.S. Sec. & Exch. Comm'n, www.sec.gov/foia/docs/foia-logs.htm (select "2013" and "2014"). The dataset compiled includes the months between January 2013 and December 2013, representing CY 2013.

[56] *See supra* Ch.7, pt. C; *see also* Video Conference Call Interview with Barry Walters, Olivier Girod, Mark Siford & John Livornese, *supra* note 43.

[57] *See* Margaret B. Kwoka, *Inside FOIA, Inc.*, 125 Yale L.J. F. 265 (2016).

[58] U.S. Sec. and Exch. Comm'n., *New Rules and Procedures for Exhibits Containing Immaterial, Competitively Harmful Information*, U.S. Sec. & Exch. Comm'n (Apr. 1, 2019), www.sec.gov/corpfin/announcement/new-rules-and-procedures-exhibits-containing-immaterial#_ftn1.

of material submitted under the old regime to which an affirmative disclosure policy might fruitfully apply.

Moreover, these exhibits are not the only affirmative disclosure opportunity for the SEC. The other large volume category of requested records are SEC investigative files for particular companies, requested for due diligence purposes. Certainly, investigative files are more complicated because they are carefully reviewed and redacted before release. But due diligence requesters are just as happy (if not more) with a "no records" response; that is, a response that the SEC does not have an investigative file about the company because there has not been an investigation. The SEC could consider a search page that indicates merely whether there are investigative records about a particular company or not. If there are, the inquiring party could file a FOIA request. But if not, it would avoid the need for the request altogether.[59]

An analogous affirmative disclosure solution may be available at the Federal Aviation Administration (FAA), which now receives over 10,000 requests a year.[60] In the study year, as explained in Chapter 5, around half of all requests concerned particular individuals' airman certificate histories, mostly for employment background checks. The FAA maintains a public database that allows anyone to lookup a particular airman certificate and provides basic data, but does not provide the complete airman record.[61] While the logs do not indicate whether records related to a particular request were released in full, released in part, or denied, in the study year the FAA released in full an overall 7,410 of the 8,850 requests for records (or for which responsive records were found), thereby strongly suggesting these records could be proactively disclosed without the need for extensive review or redactions. Indeed, they could be incorporated into the existing database.

Moreover, another 1,691 requests produced "no records" responses, indicating the agency did not have responsive records. This is largely attributed to the fact that many times the request targets enforcement or accident histories, and a "no records response" simply means there is no such negative history.[62] This is precisely the type of information that would be easy to incorporate into a database lookup system.

Finally, there are two categories of records that span various agencies for which affirmative disclosure is a promising alternative to voluminous FOIA requests. Government contracts is one such area. To begin, nowhere would the benefit of

[59] Kwoka, *supra*, note 57.

[60] U.S. Dep't of Transp., FOIA FY 2019 Annual Report (2020).

[61] *See Airmen Inquiry*, Fed. Aviation Admin., https://amsrvs.registry.faa.gov/airmeninquiry/Main.aspx (last visited Nov. 24, 2020).

[62] *See, e.g.*, U.S. Dep't of Transp., 2020 Chief FOIA Officer's Report 5, www.transportation.gov/individuals/foia/chief-foia-officers-reports; U.S. Dep't of Transp., 2019 Chief FOIA Officer's Report 5, www.transportation.gov/individuals/foia/chief-foia-officers-reports; U.S. Dep't of Transp., 2018 Chief FOIA Officer's Report 6, www.transportation.gov/individuals/foia/chief-foia-officers-reports.

an affirmative disclosure policy relating to contracts be more evident than at the Defense Logistics Agency (DLA), where nearly all of the requests submitted are for a particular contract, bids for contracts, or bid abstracts – a full 3,725 requests in the study year.[63] Three-quarters of those records were released in full,[64] suggesting the vast majority of the information requested is releasable. If these were affirmatively posted, the agency's FOIA office would have more resources to meet the needs of the comparatively rare but much more varied requests from news media and other oversight requesters.

But DLA is not the only one. Across the federal government, contracts are requested at various agencies, particularly at military, property management, and scientific agencies, as discussed in Chapter 6. Government contracts are often requested by competitors, but their release may also play important oversight purposes since, after all, they detail the government's spending of taxpayer dollars. Indeed, many newer freedom of information laws in other countries specifically mandate the categorical proactive release of all government contracts.[65] Agencies that affirmatively post their contracts would naturally see a reduction in the number of FOIA requests for those records.

Another category that spans agencies, but which does not pertain to commercial requesters, is health records. Like CMS does for Medicare recipients, electronic health records can be made available to individuals who receive government health services, thereby obviating the need for mostly first-person FOIA requests for medical files. Electronic health records have been promoted by various governmental policies,[66] and the Veterans Health Administration (VHA) has made moves in that direction with its new EHRM system.[67] When I asked a former VHA FOIA official how much electronic health records would help with FOIA request volume, the answer was simple: "A lot."[68]

The truth is, affirmative disclosure has the potential – if done well – to greatly reduce the number of FOIA requests the public has to make. The opportunities are greatest with respect to routine records that the public predictably needs and are easily met through alternative avenues.

63 U.S. Dep't of Def., Def. Logistics Agency, Freedom of Information Act Responses to Oct. 6, 2014 and Feb. 12, 2015 Requests by Margaret B. Kwoka (on file with author).

64 *Id.*

65 *See e.g.*, Adriana García García, Transparency in Mexico: An Overview of Acess to Information Regulations and Their Effectiveness at the Federal and State Level 18 (2016).

66 For example, Congress has incentivized use of electronic health records in the private sector. American Recovery and Reinvestment Act of 2009 § 4101, Pub. L. No. 111-5, 123 Stat. 115, 467 (codified at 42 U.S.C. § 1395w-4 (2012)).

67 VA EHR Modernization, www.ehrm.va.gov (last visited Nov. 24, 2020).

68 Interview with Michael Sarich, FOIA Dir., Veterans Health Admin., U.S. Dep't of Veterans Affairs., in Arlington, Va. (July 23, 2019).

D. FEASIBILITY

It would be disingenuous to suggest that affirmative disclosure is straightforward, without logistical challenges, and universally applicable as a strategy to reduce individual FOIA requests. Typically, the barriers cited to implementing categorical affirmative disclosure programs include agency capacity and resources, the need for individualized review of documents for necessary redactions, and the special requirements of accessibility for any government website imposed by Section 508 of the Rehabilitation Act. In addition, some agency officials rightly point out that not all affirmative disclosure bears meaningfully on reducing FOIA requesting. I do not dispute that these are challenges for affirmative disclosure. But I do seek to lay out options available to overcome each possible barrier, and acknowledge the need to assess feasibility for each potential affirmative disclosure program individually.

Agency resource constraints are probably the most cited reason for not pursuing categorical affirmative disclosure. As Barry Walters at the SEC stated, resource constraints prevented some suggested affirmative disclosure measures from coming to fruition.[69] Ginger McCall joined the Department of Labor's (DOL) FOIA team after a career at an oversight nonprofit working on the requester side of FOIA. She described that what surprised her the "most" was the lack of technology inside government agencies and put funding first on her "wish list" for agency FOIA offices.[70]

Building out a new database feature or function, combing through old records systems to digitize or otherwise index or make searchable stored records, and maintaining a new online service are absolutely costly, both in terms of possible infrastructure needed and in terms of personnel time. And right now, agency FOIA offices are starved for both. Moreover, it is unclear where the resources should come from. If an affirmative disclosure program is not strictly mandated by FOIA, then does funding come from the FOIA office's budget or the program budget for the relevant agency program? Hardly any agency program will prioritize information disclosure when most such offices are already overwhelmed with their primary mission.

Thus, resource constraint objections truly come down to priorities and funding. There is no extant mechanism for agency officials to prioritize these initiatives, especially where the FOIA office is unable to execute such a plan entirely on its own. Even the FOIA offices, as described in Chapter 9, are not really incentivized to find these solutions. Thus, there exists a clear opportunity for structural changes that would facilitate these sorts of measures. Not all of them will necessarily be overall

69 Kwoka, *supra*, note 57.

70 Telephone Interview with Ginger McCall, Former Att'y Advisor, Office of the Solicitor, U.S. Dep't of Labor (May 10, 2019).

cost saving, but they may well be both transparency-promoting and in the public interest, nonetheless. Further, the successful examples above suggest that overall cost saving is a realistic and achievable goal in many instances.

A distinct, but related, possible barrier to affirmative disclosure arises when the category of records in question requires substantive, individualized review because of necessary redactions before the records can be released, whether they be to protect personal privacy, trade secrets, or other protected interests under FOIA's exemptions. Indeed, this concern likely exists in many categories of records, where some small percentage of the requested records contain confidential information and thus review of each record individually is required.

For example, at the FDA, FOIA director Sarah Kotler explained that facilities inspection reports, or Form 483s, require individualized review to identify records that contain confidential information that should be redacted before the records are released. Although 93 percent of the requested 483s in the study year were released in full, identifying the last bit still takes work. Moreover, only between a quarter and a third of all 483s are ever requested each year, causing her to observe that the agency may save time by not having to review and process the unrequested records.[71]

The most promising answer to this challenge is what is being discussed as "transparency by design," as Ginger McCall said, or, as Helen Foster said, "baking transparency in on the front end."[72] Designing documents so they are releasable at the outset, perhaps by putting confidential information in one section that is always blacked out, or by not ever including confidential information on the main form, is one way of ensuring records can be released in database format or in response to a request without the need for individualized review.

Ginger McCall, formerly at DOL, said she thought that if agencies made these sorts of FOIA-ready documents and posted them proactively, it would "cut down on a significant number of requests." She went on to note that any such system would have to be targeted so that agencies did not waste resources on processing records if no one is interested, but nonetheless thought the idea had promise.[73]

Helen Foster cited an example from her time at the Department of Housing and Urban Development (HUD) in which transparency by design was attempted with grant applications. There, the agency started asking companies to submit a redacted and an unredacted version of the application so that the redacted one would be FOIA-ready. When these were posted online, Foster believed this cut down on the

[71] Address by Sarah Kotler, Dir. of the Freedom of Info. Act Program, Food & Drug Admin., at the FOIA Advisory Committee Meeting (Apr. 19, 2016), www.archives.gov/ogis/foia-advisory-committee/2014-2016-term/documents/04-19-2016-meeting-transcript.

[72] Telephone Interview with Ginger McCall, *supra* note 70; Telephone Interview with Helen Foster, Former Chief Privacy and FOIA Officer & Chief Administrative Officer, U.S. Dep't of Housing and Urban Development (May 14, 2019).

[73] Telephone Interview with Ginger McCall, *supra* note 70.

number of requests that had to be processed because people could be referred to the website.[74]

Transparency by design may hold promise even for sensitive records. Jill Eggleston at CIS cited examples where immigration records were designed to make redactions easier. She said the new ELIS electronic records system is introducing form types one at a time and they are making a "FOIA button" that, with a click, creates a copy with the redactions in place. Similarly, she said that refugee officers' interview notes used to be on one unsegregated form, most of which was not released to the person in question, but that after a judicial decision requiring release of factual information contained therein, the FOIA office worked with the refugee office to redesign the form to have all releasable factual information located in one place for easier processing. Many government documents could be redesigned to make affirmative disclosure far more efficient and attainable.[75]

Another logistical hurdle often discussed in the context of affirmative disclosure is the accessibility requirement for all government websites mandated by Section 508 of the Rehabilitation Act. This statute requires that "individuals with disabilities who are members of the public seeking information or services from a Federal department or agency to have access to and use of information and data that is comparable to access to and use of the information and by such members of the public who are not individuals with disabilities."[76] Though there is an "undue burden" exception, in practice this means that agencies must publish information on their websites in a machine-readable format so that those with visual impairments can use dictation software to access the information.[77]

The fundamental hurdle this poses for agencies is that the redaction process they use often strips documents of their metadata, thus turning them into "flat" rather than enriched PDF formats. Moreover, graphics, visuals, charts, and images need metadata tags to be added for the content to be accessible. This process is no doubt time-consuming. This volume offers no comprehensive solution to any tension between the compelling need to make information accessible to all members of the public and affirmative disclosure initiatives that seek to vastly and quickly expand the scope of records available online.

Nonetheless, some ideas have surfaced for alleviating the tension. To begin, the federal government could push for standardization of FOIA processing software to preserve metadata without compromising the confidentiality of redacted portions of records. Beyond that, resources should be allocated so that agencies have sufficient

74 Telephone Interview with Helen Foster, *supra* note 72.

75 Interview with Jill Eggleston, Assistant Ctr. Dir., Freedom of Info. & Privacy Act Unit, Nat'l Records Ctr., U.S. Citizenship & Immigration Servs., U.S. Dep't of Homeland Sec., in Lee's Summit, Mo. (June 12, 2019).

76 29 U.S.C. § 794d(a)(1)(A)(ii) (2019).

77 *See* Information & Communication Technology (ICT) Standards and Guidelines, 82 Fed. Reg. 5790 (Jan. 18, 2017).

funds to meet both their FOIA obligations and their accessibility mandates. In addition, agencies may have circumstances that meet the "undue burden" exception requirements.[78] Some agencies seem to have gone that route by posting records that do not comply with Section 508, but do specify that anyone who wants an accessible version of a record can request it and the office will provide it to them.[79]

Finally, some question the very premise that affirmative disclosure will in fact reduce the number of individual FOIA requests that are made. Indeed, Jill Eggleston at US Citizenship and Immigration Services opined that "[t]he more information we release the more information is requested." She also noted that USCIS records are not typically conducive to proactive disclosure.[80] There is no doubt that at some agencies an affirmative disclosure strategy may not be effective at achieving a reduced reliance on individual requesting. Feasibility has to be assessed on a case-by-case basis. Moreover, the idea that affirmative disclosure might in some cases produce more requests is certainly plausible, as posted records on a hot topic may lead the public to ask for more. But that concern is most present for timely and topical matters of general public interest, not affirmative disclosure programs for categories of routinely produced agency records.

E. DESIGNING A MANDATE

There remains the question of how to mandate affirmative disclosure requirements when the nature of the opportunities for affirmative disclosure, the best method for making records proactively available, and the feasibility of implementation vary so widely from agency to agency. Yet, structural changes could impose requirements and create incentives that achieve this tailored result.

For example, Congress could require agencies to report, as part of their annual FOIA reports to Congress and the DOJ's OIP, an analysis of their own FOIA logs identifying categories of frequently requested records with an accompanying discussion of whether and how it would be feasible to make that category of records proactively available. The analysis could be required to include consideration of a number of factors demonstrated to be relevant by this study: the percent of such records that are eventually requested under FOIA; the percent of that category of

[78] These basic points were made in a FOIA Advisory Committee Recommendation to the National Archies and Records Administration. *See* Freedom of Info. Act Fed. Advisory Comm., Final Report and Recommendations: 2016–2018 Committee Term 7–8 (2018) [hereinafter 2016-2018 Advisory Comm. Final Report].

[79] *See e.g.*, *FOIA Library*, Health.mil, health.mil/Reference-Center/FOIA-Documents (last visited Nov. 24, 2020); *FOIA Library*, U.S. Dep't of Homeland Sec., (Sept. 17, 2020), www.dhs.gov/foia-library.

[80] Interview with Jill Eggleston, *supra* note 75.

records that are released in full; and whether the records could be redesigned to be "FOIA-ready" so that they are immediately releasable upon creation.[81]

Congress could go further by mandating an outcome: that agencies publish whole categories of records when a relatively large portion of the category is eventually requested under FOIA so long as the records require relatively minimal redactions or can be designed to be FOIA-ready. This mandate could be paired with a private right of action to enforce it, subject to an arbitrary and capricious review for discretionary agency decisions.

Moreover, Congress could dictate additional categories of records in FOIA's existing affirmative disclosure requirements. This could include agency contracts, perhaps above a certain value. It could also include certain types of enforcement records such as inspection reports, warning letters, citations, fines and penalties, or other actions taken pursuant to an agency's statutory mandates whether or not they have immediate legal effect. Indeed, the FOIA Advisory Committee has, in the past, attempted to come up with a list of possible categories for proactive disclosure.[82]

Finally, perhaps the most important threshold step to take would be to mandate a uniform format for the publication of agency FOIA logs on an ongoing basis, designating required fields to be included. As this study demonstrates, the logs are essential to understanding agency FOIA operations. And yet, my own experience demonstrates how difficult it is to obtain agency FOIA logs, to obtain logs that contain the fields of information that are most useful, to convert them to a format that can be analyzed, and to compare them across agencies. A detailed draft of such a requirement was adopted as a recommendation by the FOIA Advisory Committee,[83] a body tasked with making FOIA policy recommendations, but should be made mandatory by Congress.

* * *

Affirmative disclosure has perhaps unparalleled promise in rescuing FOIA from its ever-increasing volume of requests. This is the central claim of this Chapter and is alone justification for vigorously pursuing a much more robust set of affirmative disclosure requirements for agencies. If we sensibly shrink FOIA by obviating the need for routine, en masse requesting that does not go to FOIA's oversight purpose, we would remove pressure from FOIA to fill the needs of these other information constituencies.

81 I worked to propose a scheme like this one as an agency best practice recommendation when I served on the FOIA Advisory Committee. *See* Memorandum from Proactive Disclosure Subcomm., to FOIA Advisory Comm. (Oct. 16, 2017), www.archives.gov/files/proactive-disclosure-subcommittee-criteria-recommendation-final.pdf (proactive disclosure subcommittee recommendation on criteria); 2016-2018 Advisory Comm. Final Report, *supra* note 78, at 18.

82 *Id.* at 18–20.

83 *See id.* at 20–21. For full disclosure, the author worked on the drafting of this recommendation.

Beyond that, though, it is worth noting that affirmative disclosure regimes that publish whole categories of records are likely to produce other important benefits for society. Public records would be truly public, for all to see, not warehoused behind the paywalls of information resellers or hoarded for private benefit. Researchers may find uses for the newly published data and document sets to produce knowledge or insights we cannot anticipate. Journalists and public interest groups that previously did not have the resources to put together databases of government records by requesting them individually may find oversight value to records previously used primarily by business. Even the private market may be better off as whole industries would have access to the same information, promoting fairer competition.

To be sure, after some initial investment, agencies may also see cost savings from these strategies by reducing the one-by-one records processing required to respond to FOIA requests. But we should not reduce the requirement to those that merely pass some sort of hair-splitting cost-benefit analysis. Relieving the pressure on FOIA, making public data and records truly public, and having a more transparent, more user friendly, fairer market in government information should be the driving force. Agencies' information constituents – private and public minded – are better served under such a regime.

11

Redesigning Agency Adjudications

This study demonstrates that FOIA often serves as a stand-in for administrative discovery where no such procedure exists, or a method to obtain records needed to be able to apply for a particular agency benefit. That is, requesters are often seeking records from the agency in conjunction with a pending proceeding the requester has with the agency itself. Sometimes the records are needed in order to better position the requester in defending against an enforcement action brought by the agency, and other times they are needed to bolster the requester's attempt to secure benefits the agency administers. Regardless, FOIA in these instances ends up being a parallel agency process the requester must engage to obtain the records on which the agency is relying in an adversarial position or which the requester must produce to secure their position.

To be sure, formalized administrative discovery is commonplace at some agencies. For example, the Federal Trade Commission has broad, federal court–style discovery rights in administrative proceedings before an Administrative Law Judge.[1] Indeed, the Administrative Conference of the United States has provided model adjudication rules for agency consideration that include detailed discovery procedures.[2] But discovery is far from required; courts have never deemed discovery in civil adjudication to be a constitutional right,[3] and the

[1] *See* 16 C.F.R. § 3.31 (2020).

[2] *See* Selected Reports Of The Administrative Conference of the United States, S. Doc. No. 88–24, at 12 (1963); Admin. Conf. of the U.S., Model Adjudication Rules § 102 (2018).

[3] *See* Kelly v. Envtl. Prot. Agency, 203 F.3d 519, 523 (7th Cir. 2000); Alexander v. Pathfinder, Inc., 189 F.3d 735, 741 (8th Cir. 1999); Nat'l Labor Relations Board v. Interboro Contractors, Inc., 432 F.2d 854, 857–58 (2d Cir. 1970); Chafian v. Ala. Bd. of Chiropractic Exam'rs, 647 So. 2d 759, 762 (Ala. Civ. App. 1994); Pet v. Dep't of Health Servs., 542 A.2d 672, 677 (Conn. 1988); In re Herndon, 596 A.2d 592, 595 (D.C. 1991); In re Tobin, 628 N.E.2d 1268, 1271 (Mass. 1994); State ex rel. Hoover v. Smith, 482 S.E.2d 124, 129 (W. Va. 1997).

Administrative Procedure Act baseline procedures for agencies do not require discovery.[4]

As such, many agencies do not provide for discovery rights, particularly for less formal (though sometimes still gravely consequential) agency adjudications. At many of these agencies, FOIA acts as a discovery stand-in. As described in greater detail below, at this group of agencies, providing administrative discovery is a crucial step toward reducing reliance on FOIA for non-public-oversight purposes. And beyond that, administrative discovery is itself a better process in the context of an agency proceeding; it's better at serving the individual information constituents, and it probably makes the agency process more efficient, too.

Agency benefits application processes could also be reworked to eliminate the need for parallel FOIA requests. For example, some agencies will deny benefits without disclosing to the applicant the negative information on which the agency relied. If the applicant wants to know the reason for the decision, they have to file a FOIA request. Other agencies require applicants for benefits to submit paperwork that the agency already has in its files. If the applicant does not have their own copy to submit, they have to file a FOIA request to get the record before they can apply. The following discussion will explain how these agency benefits application processes could be redesigned to incorporate the retrieval of needed records, rather than requiring a parallel FOIA request and possible dispute to be mounted by the applicant.

The following account provides a nonexhaustive list of examples where administrative discovery or other procedural redesign may hold promise. To be sure, immigration plays an outsized presence in FOIA requests and agency procedural design solutions hold the greatest promise in that context, and thus it correspondingly takes up an outsized amount of space in this discussion. Yet, opportunities at other agencies abound, and trans-substantive administrative changes are also therefore possible as an avenue for reform.

A. DISCOVERY IN ENFORCEMENT PROCEEDINGS

Enforcement proceedings – proceedings where agencies are bringing a civil administrative case against an individual for violating the law and seeking some sort of penalty – are the paradigmatic cases where administrative discovery is easily imagined. They are typically very much akin to criminal proceedings in court insofar as there is a charging document alleging a violation of law, an adjudicator, an attorney prosecuting the government's case, and a party defending against the action (albeit in this context with a right to hire a lawyer only at their own expense).

[4] *See* 5 U.S.C. § 555(d) (2012) (Providing only that "Agency subpoenas authorized by law shall be issued to a party on request and, when required by rules of procedure, on a statement or showing of general relevance and reasonable scope of the evidence sought.").

In fact, because of the similarities to judicial proceedings, many people assume that the government's evidence against the defending party must be disclosed in enforcement proceedings, but that is not always the case. FOIA, instead, serves this role at many agencies.

Nowhere is this dynamic more clear than in the immigration context, where removal proceedings (otherwise known as deportation proceedings) are initiated with a charging document (a Notice to Appear), prosecuted by a "Trial Attorney" who works for Immigrations and Customs Enforcement (ICE), and heard by an Immigration Judge who is an employee of the Executive Office for Immigration Review.[5] The noncitizen defending against removal may hire a lawyer, but, because the proceedings are civil and not criminal, does not have a right to a government-appointed attorney.[6] And so one could be forgiven if, as an outsider, one assumed discovery of the government's files about the noncitizen were available to that individual in defending their case.

Not so. The only available discovery mechanism in immigration court is a procedure by which the noncitizen may apply for a subpoena by motion, but courts so routinely deny them that few individuals even attempt this process.[7] At one point the Ninth Circuit seemed to make inroads in requiring a certain amount of discovery as a matter of due process, holding, in a 2010 decision, that the government was obligated to provide certain records demonstrating that the individual subject to removal proceedings in that case was actually a citizen of the United States.[8] Despite this promising ruling, subsequent narrow interpretations and the requirement that the noncitizen show prejudice rendered the decision largely without consequence.[9]

As a result, immigration attorneys uniformly report that discovery as of right is not available in immigration court practice.[10] They also report that when documents are provided by the government attorney to the noncitizen, it is typically through an

[5] *See generally* Exec. Office for Immigration Review, U.S. Dep't of Justice, Fact Sheet: Executive Office for Immigration Review: An Agency Guide (Dec. 2017).

[6] *Id.*

[7] Office of the Chief Immigration Judge, U.S. Dep't of Justice, Immigration Court Practice Manual 93 (May 15, 2017); Geoffrey Heeren, *Shattering the One-Way Mirror Discovery in Immigration Court,* 79 Brook. L. Rev. 1569, 1583 (2014).

[8] Dent v. Holder, 627 F.3d 365, 374–75 (9th Cir. 2010).

[9] Heeren, *supra* note 7, at 1586. *See* DaSilva v. U.S. Att'y Gen., 2013 U.S. Dist. LEXIS 56507, at *5–6 (E.D. La. Apr. 19, 2013) (requiring a robust showing of prejudice to make out a due process claim based on withheld records).

[10] Telephone Interview with Robert Blackshear, Att'y, Law Firm 2 (Apr. 19, 2017); Telephone Interview with Peggy Brewer, Att'y, Law Firm 3 (May 19, 2017); Telephone Interview with Russell Flores, Att'y, Law Firm 1 (Apr. 14, 2017); Telephone Interview with Gloria Glen, Att'y, Law Firm 1 (May 1, 2017); Telephone Interview with Elizabeth Hilton, Att'y, Law Firm 1 (May 2, 2017), Telephone Interview with John Rivera, Att'y, Law Firm 5 (June 1, 2017), Telephone Interview with William Yates, Att'y, Law Firm 4 (May 24, 2017).

informal practice or relationship with the noncitizen's attorney.[11] But far more often these attorneys find themselves filing multiple FOIA requests to various agencies that might have relevant records, including US Citizen and Immigration Service (USCIS), Customs and Border Patrol (CBP), ICE, the Office of Biometric Identity Management (OBIM), and others.[12] And the long processing time under FOIA is frequently problematic. Sometimes, attorneys are forced to ask the immigration court to continue their client's case while they wait for necessary records (with varying degrees of success).[13] Other times, they are forced to move forward without necessary records, potentially prejudicing their client.[14]

The oddity is that, in a removal case, the government has already gone to the trouble to locate all these records for the simple reason that they are the very records found on the desk of the trial attorney prosecuting the case in immigration court.[15] Instead of consolidating the discovery process so that the trial attorney and the

[11] *See, e.g.*, Telephone Interview with Robert Blackshear, *supra* note 10 ("It varies widely between the field offices .... Sometimes some offices will provide you with the I-213, the NTA, anything you need. Especially ones that you're cool with, that you work with all the time. They'll give you what you want and what you need in order to properly represent the guy. Other field offices are like, 'No file FOIA.'"); Telephone Interview with Peggy Brewer, *supra* note 10 (noting that while sometimes a court will order a document to be produced, most of the time as to the most important documents, the attorney will provide them voluntarily); Telephone Interview with William Yates, *supra* note 10 ("Some [trial attorneys] that I[ ] have some kind of relationship with [], they'll tell me like 'Hey, you know what? We have this,' and they'll give [the documents] to me."). *But see* Telephone Interview with Gloria Glen, *supra* note 10 ("[Y]ou can contact government counsel and ask them for whatever specific document you're looking for, but you're almost never going to get it."); Telephone Interview with John Rivera, *supra* note 10 ("[V]ery rarely have I had anybody be cooperative [about discovery].").

[12] For example, Flores said he "automatically do[es] CBP, and USCIS." Telephone Interview with Russell Flores, *supra* note 10 ; *see* Telephone Interview with Gloria Glen *supra* note 10 (explaining she typically files multiple FOIA requests, usually at CBP and ICE); *see also* Telephone Interview with Elizabeth Hilton, *supra* note 10 (explaining that she files a request with USCIS if the client has ever submitted a previous application for any immigration benefit, a request with ICE if they have ever been removed, and a request with CBP if they have ever had any interaction at a port of entry); Telephone Interview with John Rivera, *supra* note 10 (saying that he typically files a USCIS FOIA request and an OBIM request with fingerprints); Telephone Interview with William Yates, *supra* note 10 (explaining that he typically files FOIA requests at USCIS, ICE, CBP, and the Department of State, because "I'm looking for anything or any hit that I can get on my client"). *But see* Telephone Interview with Robert Blackshear, *supra* note 10 (asserting that now that OBIM processes requests with fingerprints, better results come from that one request and multiple requests are needed less often).

[13] *See, e.g.*, Telephone Interview with Peggy Brewer, *supra* note 10; Telephone Interview with Russell Flores, *supra* note 10 (explaining that now they are "not accepting continuances" unless the attorney can show that there is relief available); Telephone Interview with John Rivera, *supra* note 10 (asserting that immigration judges are requiring the client to show prejudice from not having received the response to their FOIA request before granting a continuance).

[14] *See, e.g.*, Telephone Interview with Russell Flores, *supra* note 10 (describing that in the era of the Trump Administration, continuances would not be granted for FOIA request delays if there is no relief available).

[15] *See* Telephone Interview with John Rivera, *supra* note 10; *see also* Telephone Interview with William Yates, *supra* note 10.

judge – those most familiar with the case itself – can make determinations about required releases, FOIA requests are sent to centralized processing offices at each agency or agency component. For example, at USCIS, those requests are all processed at the National Records Center, which is located in The Cave outside Kansas City, Missouri. Moreover, one experienced USCIS processor told me that, because A-Files (permanent immigration records on noncitizens) often contain records that originated with other agencies, there is a need to refer records for processing to at least one other agency "in nearly every case."[16] This means that the FOIA process essentially has to duplicate the evidence gathering process that the prosecutorial arm of ICE has already completed.

To be sure, at USCIS, the only of the immigration agencies that tracks which FOIA requests are related to pending removal proceedings, only three percent of requests in the study year were designated as such.[17] Yet that three percent, as a fraction of USCIS's current level of requests, represents more than 6,000 requests,[18] each one of which concerns a noncitizen who likely filed analogous requests at ICE, CBP, and other agencies at the same time. Moreover, that figure likely significantly undercounts how many requests relate to removal proceedings because to be placed in that priority track the requester must provide documentation of a pending court date, and many requesters may not meet the documentation requirements.[19]

Deputy Chief Privacy Officer at US Department of Homeland Security (DHS), James Holzer, said that his office had considered recommending discovery in immigration court for this very reason.[20] Yet, in addition to the smaller fraction of overall requests at immigration agencies tied to pending removal proceedings, his chief concern was that trial attorneys in immigration court do not currently have the resources to add discovery obligations to their plate. Holzer had personally visited the Orlando immigration court recently at the time I spoke with him, and he put it bluntly: "Trial Attorneys do not have the capacity."[21] Yet, at worst this concern requires shifting resources already being expended on FOIA toward the immigration courts, an investment in that adjudication system that is likely a worthy goal

[16] Interview with Lynn Rossi, Gov't Info. Specialist, U.S. Citizenship & Immigration Servs., in Lee's Summit, Mo. (June 12, 2019).

[17] Electronic Reading Room, US Citizenship & Immigration Servs., www.uscis.gov/about-us/electronic-reading-room (filter by "FOIA Logs"). The dataset compiled includes the months between October 2014 and September 2015, representing FY 2015.

[18] USCIS received, by its own estimate, 191,000 requests in FY 2018. US Citizenship & Immigration Servs., 2018 USCIS Annual Statistical Report 11 (2018).

[19] US Citizenship & Immigration Servs., FOIA Frequently Asked Questions (Jan. 2010), available at www.uscis.gov/sites/default/files/document/questions-and-answers/FOIA%20FAQs.pdf (noting in an FAQ document that if your "track 3" request is denied, it is usually "because the requester failed to provide the proper documentation").

[20] Interview with Dr. James V.M.L. Holzer, Deputy Chief FOIA Officer, Jimmy Wolfrey, Senior Dir., FOIA Operations and Mgmt. & Amy Bennett, Public Liaison, U.S. Dep't of Homeland Sec., in Wash. D.C. (June 5, 2019).

[21] *Id.*

regardless as it would provide fairer, faster, and more accurate results in immigration adjudications.

Indeed, providing discovery rights has been advocated elsewhere as advancing fundamental fairness and dignity interests in immigration court, and it may well save agency resources too.[22] But beyond that, discovery in immigration court would potentially remove from the FOIA processing queues thousands of requests at each of several different immigration-related agencies.

When I observed FOIA processing at USCIS's facility, it was immediately clear that the FOIA operations were set up to handle primarily immigration requests. One of the top FOIA processors was, in the course of our more than two-hour conversation, as knowledgeable about immigration law as many immigration attorneys and about foreign affairs as many foreign service officers.[23] This person was clearly a very experienced specialist – technically in FOIA but even more so in the legal and social framework governing migration. She had an effortless command of immigration filings, visa statuses, grounds for deportation, conditions of work authorization, family relationships as they pertain to immigration benefits, and all manner of family and employment records that would bear on immigration adjudications. She also knew an immense amount about conditions in countless countries around the world, including the specific kinds of violence, hardships, and persecution migrants may be fleeing. Her knowledge base, however, was nontransferrable to the kinds of requests that might be made by journalists.

Rather, journalist requests are processed by the separate, "Significant Interest Group" (SIG) at USCIS's FOIA office. Of 250 full-time positions in the FOIA processing division, only twelve staff were assigned to this unit, where all non-immigration requests are handled. One of their FOIA processors spoke to me, and his job barely resembled the job of the immigration file specialist. Instead, he coordinates with policy offices in the agency, negotiates with requesters, and encourages proactive disclosures.[24] SIG requests are functionally a separate queue in the FOIA office at USCIS, and they are the ones that look more like we imagine FOIA requests to be. Getting the volume of immigration requests out of the FOIA realm would leave room for more specialization in these oversight requests, waste less resources inefficiently poured into FOIA rather than more appropriately dedicated to fair adjudication, and save FOIA from some of the harshest criticisms about agency resource constraints.

Immigration, however, is not the only enforcement area where the government receives significant numbers of FOIA requests that serve as stand-ins for administrative discovery. Tax disputes are another important example. The three principle

[22] Heeren, *supra* note 7, at 1627 ("The truth-finding capacity of adversarial hearings depends on the parties having relatively equal resources at their disposal.").

[23] Interview with Lynn Rossi, *supra* note 16.

[24] Interview with Jarrod T. Panter, Significant Interest Grp. Processor, U.S. Citizenship & Immigration Servs., in Lee's Summit, Mo. (June 12, 2019).

categories of tax disputes are audits, collections, and penalties, all of which can be finally decided by the Internal Revenue Service (IRS) as an administrative matter, unless the taxpayer chooses to challenge the IRS's determination in Tax Court or in federal court. In each of those categories, FOIA plays a significant role in arming the taxpayer with crucial information to which they otherwise would not have access because there is no administrative discovery.

To begin, after the IRS audits a taxpayer it issues audit findings, which the taxpayer can accept or challenge by filing an audit appeal with the Independent Office of Appeals, a division of the IRS. Prior to 2019, the only formal way for a taxpayer to obtain a copy of their file to make their best case at the appeal stage was to file a FOIA request.[25] In 2019, Congress passed the Taxpayer First Act requiring the IRS to "provide[] access to the nonprivileged portions of the case file on record regarding the disputed issue" to the taxpayer.[26] The new provision only applies to taxpayers below an adjusted gross income of $400,000, and in any event attorneys report that the provision is so new that the IRS's implementation has yet to materialize. That said, given that over thirty percent of all IRS requests in the study year were related to an audit,[27] a disclosure provision such as this one – ideally covering all taxpayers and fully implemented – may go a long way to reducing reliance on FOIA.

Similarly, when the IRS finds a taxpayer to have a tax deficiency and attempts to collect the unpaid balance, or when the IRS imposes penalties for noncompliance with the tax code, taxpayers have avenues to challenge those determinations but no opportunity for administrative discovery to uncover any records that may help their case. Attorneys I spoke to cited various specific examples, but one is illustrative. When an employer that is required to withhold taxes for the IRS fails to remit the funds to the agency, the IRS then issues what is called a trust fund recovery penalty assessment to those individuals within the organization who it deems responsible for the failure to pay.[28] Attorneys representing these individuals and challenging those assessments routinely use FOIA to obtain the investigative file, which will show how many other people in the organization were assessed and whether collections were made. Without these records, for which no other discovery mechanism is available, attorneys cannot effectively challenge the determination that their client was

[25] Telephone Interview with Tate Rowe, Att'y, Law Firm 16 (Jan. 12, 2021).

[26] Taxpayer First Act, 26 U.S.C. § 7803(e)(7) (2020).

[27] U.S. Dep't of Treasury, Internal Revenue Serv., Freedom of Information Act Response to order in *Kwoka v. Internal Revenue Serv.*, 1:17-cv-1157-DLF, 2018 U.S. Dist. LEXIS 167547 (D.D.C. Sept. 28, 2018); IRS FOIA Logs, Internal Revenue Serv., www.irs.gov/privacy-disclosure/irs-foia-logs [hereinafter IRS Data]. Out of the 7,228 requests in the study for which a subject matter of the request was ascertained, 2,276 had a subject matter containing either the word "exam" or "audit".

[28] Employment Taxes and the Trust Fund Recovery Penalty (TFRP), Internal Revenue Serv. (Aug. 10. 2020), www.irs.gov/businesses/small-businesses-self-employed/employment-taxes-and-the-trust-fund-recovery-penalty-tfrp.

responsible for the trust funds.[29] The IRS FOIA logs reveal more than 300 such requests in the study year.[30] Administrative discovery in such cases seems plainly in the interests of the fairness of the proceeding and the protection of the taxpayer. Moreover, it would remove these requests from the FOIA queue.

To take another example, the Food and Nutrition Service (FNS), a division of the US Department of Agriculture (USDA), takes administrative actions against businesses enrolled as authorized participants in the Supplemental Nutrition Assistance Program (SNAP, or food stamps) when they are found in noncompliance with the rules.[31] These actions begin with a "charge letter" to which the business may respond and then the agency issues a final determination of any action or sanctions imposed.[32] Once disqualified from the program, the business can request administrative review and, if unsuccessful, judicial review.[33] However, throughout the prejudicial process, no opportunity for administrative discovery is provided.[34]

Enter FOIA. While FNS data was not able to be obtained for this study, USDA annual reports indicate that, in the baseline year of this study, FNS received just shy of 1,000 requests under FOIA. It is likely that many of these requests were in lieu of administrative discovery. At the time, FNS had the practice of holding "in abeyance administrative action against the firm while the FOIA request and appeal is being processed."[35] In 2018, FNS appears to have concluded that using FOIA in this way and the attendant delay in imposing sanctions or other consequences was undesirable. Instead of creating an administrative discovery mechanism, though, the agency proposed a rule curtailing the rights of businesses subject to these enforcement proceedings. It proposed the following language: "A FOIA request for records or FOIA appeal shall not delay or prohibit FNS from taking administrative action against a firm under this part, or delay the effective date of the FNS administrative action."[36]

Issues of fairness are evident with respect to SNAP retailers. An industry group comment on the notice of proposed rulemaking stated that "[t]he ability of SNAP retailers to use [FOIA] to request information is one of the only tools that SNAP retailers possess ... when responding to FNS's administrative charges related to their SNAP licenses."[37] And beyond the fairness concerns, this is a clear opportunity for

[29] Telephone Interview with Chandler Soto, Att'y, Law Firm 17 (Feb. 4, 2021).

[30] IRS Data, *supra* note 27.

[31] 7 C.F.R. § 278.6 (2020).

[32] *Id.*

[33] *Id.*

[34] *See id.*; Jerusalem Halal Meats, Inc. v. United States, No. CV H-17-1423, 2019 WL 1026302, at *6 (S.D. Tex. Feb. 7, 2019).

[35] Taking Administrative Actions Pending Freedom of Information Act (FOIA) Processing, 84 Fed. Reg. 4739 (Feb. 19, 2019) (to be codified at 7 C.F.R. pts. 278, 279).

[36] *Id.* at 4741.

[37] American Food Store Association, Comment Letter on Proposed Rule Taking Administrative Actions Pending Freedom of Information Act (FOIA) Processing (Apr. 22, 2019) (on file with author).

the agency to adopt administrative discovery, thereby eliminating the side-show of a FOIA fight that has little to do with public oversight and everything to do with an individual defending against enforcement.

The Bureau of Prisons (BOP) has a similar dynamic. Of the roughly fifty percent of requests that come from current inmates, one frequent topic is records about disciplinary matters in the prison, either regarding a requester's own complaint against someone else that was investigated, or disciplinary action that was taken against the requester themself.[38] Although there is a Disciplinary Hearing Officer in the prison who issues a final determination and that final decision is provided to the inmate, there is no administrative process for the complainant or the accused to get access to any evidence relied upon.[39] Thus, FOIA requests function in this capacity to target investigatory records, such as statements that were taken, evidence considered, and reports or complaints filed.[40]

Under its current procedures, the BOP tries to refer inmates to their own prison to obtain "local access" to records that might be available there, but this procedure clearly does not eliminate reliance on FOIA.[41] Instead, the regional FOIA office – of which there are six throughout the country – ends up processing volumes of these investigatory records to redact out any confidential personal or law enforcement material before releasing the records.[42] One could imagine disciplinary proceedings that had, at the very least, informal discovery rights for the affected inmates so that the Disciplinary Hearing Officer could be the one to process the records more efficiently and with greater understanding of the competing interests at stake. Likely, this would benefit the inmates in defending their case, and certainly it would remove this burden from the FOIA offices around the country.

Finally, the Equal Employment Opportunity Commission (EEOC) FOIA practices demonstrate another opportunity for administrative discovery to ease the FOIA burden. There, the overwhelming majority of requests are made by individuals who have filed a charge of discrimination, typically against their employer, and are seeking the "charge file," or investigative record, the EEOC compiled.[43] To be sure, this type of dispute is somewhat different from enforcement proceedings that

[38] Telephone Interview with Gene Baime, Supervisory Att'y, FOIA/PA Section, Office of Gen. Counsel, Fed. Bureau of Prisons, U.S. Dep't of Justice (Mar. 30, 2020).

[39] The Discipline Hearing Officer's report to the inmate only requires disclosure of evidence relied upon for the determination; not the full written report of the incident. *See* 28 C.F.R. § 541.8(h) (2011).

[40] Telephone Interview with Gene Baime, *supra* note 38.

[41] *See generally* Fed. Bureau of Prisons, U.S. Dep't of Justice, Change Notice to Program Statement 1351.05, Release of Information (Apr. 2, 2015).

[42] Telephone Interview with Gene Baime, *supra* note 38.

[43] In the 2015 logs, 16,264 out of 17,025 requests for were for a charge file, amounting to more than ninety-five percent of the EEOC's total requests that year. U.S. Equal Emp't Opportunity Comm'n, Freedom of Information Act Response to Apr. 15, 2016 Request and Nov. 15, 2016 Administrative Appeal by Margaret B. Kwoka (on file with author).

the government independently prosecutes against private parties. Rather, this is more like an agency adjudicating third party disputes.

The result of the EEOC process is a "determination on the merits of the charge," which can either be a finding of "cause" to believe discrimination occurred or a finding of "no cause" for such a belief.[44] While not a definitive ruling on the merits, these determinations matter greatly to the parties because they can seriously impact the parties' willingness to engage in settlement negotiations (inside or outside of an EEOC conciliation process), and may pave the way for the EEOC itself to bring a lawsuit to enforce the charging party's rights in federal court.[45]

Yet, there is no meaningful discovery process at the EEOC. The charging party often does not have a way to obtain the position statement filed by the charged party (usually the employer), or the exhibits that the charged party may have relied upon.[46] EEOC attempted to create a uniform disclosure policy,[47] but it appears that the policy simply is not being followed.[48] One plaintiff-side employment discrimination attorney explained that "the EEOC's failure to provide [charging parties] with exhibits ... [leads attorneys to] continue to use FOIA to work around it."[49] Moreover, as detailed in Chapter 5, lawyers who represent charging parties uniformly describe the various ways their clients are prejudiced by having to wait for and go through the FOIA process to obtain these records, including by giving up meritorious claims or failing to make their best arguments before the agency.[50]

44 *What You Should Know: The EEOC, Conciliation, and Litigation*, EEOC-NVTA-0000-21, Equal Emp. Opportunity Comm'n (Jan. 21, 2015), www.eeoc.gov/eeoc/newsroom/wysk/conciliation_litigation.cfm.

45 *Id.*; *see* Telephone Interview with Stephanie Romo, Att'y, Law Firm 10 (Aug. 3, 2017) ("[I]f you happen to be in the class of the very limited number of people who actually get cause findings, then you certainly want to let the EEOC go through that process because it can sometimes have some sway with an employer.").

46 Telephone Interview with Tony Schaver, Att'y, Law Firm 11 (Sept. 27, 2017); Telephone Interview with Stephanie Romo, *supra* note 45.

47 *EEOC Implements Nationwide Procedures for Releasing Respondent Position Statements and Obtaining Responses from Charging Parties*, Equal Emp. Opportunity Comm'n, www.eeoc.gov/eeoc/newsroom/release/position_statement_procedures.cfm (last visited Nov. 24, 2020).

48 Telephone Interview with Stephanie Romo, *supra* note 45; *see* Telephone Interview with Tony Schaver, *supra* note 46 (noting that "generally speaking, every EEOC office operates differently" with respect to providing the position statement); Telephone Interview with Carl Sapp, Att'y, Law Firm 13 (Nov. 15, 2017) (describing how it is "hit or miss" whether the agency provides any attachments or exhibits to the position statement); Telephone Interview with Gerald Prada, Att'y, Law Firm 12 (Nov. 15, 2017) ("We get very little during the investigative process.").

49 Telephone Interview with Stephanie Romo, *supra* note 45.

50 *See, e.g.*, Telephone Interview with Carl Sapp, *supra* note 48 (describing how FOIA requests are sometimes returned only a week before he needs to file a lawsuit, which means that "if there's no case with the client and we say we're not going to represent you, the client doesn't have much time to find a new lawyer."); Telephone Interview with Gerald Prada, *supra* note 48 (explaining that, in one case, his FOIA request for a piece evidence crucial to his ability to plead a claim was returned only one day before the statute of limitations ran out on the claim, forcing him to file the lawsuit without all the relevant information).

As is true for removal proceedings at DHS, for EEOC charges there is an EEOC employee who is tasked with the particular file who is also most familiar with the dispute and the records. This investigator is also often in contact with the charging party and the charged party directly.[51] One could imagine a system in which the EEOC investigator handles routine disclosure of nonconfidential documents related to the file.

This type of procedure would not be unprecedented. The IRS, for example, appears to have such a process, declaring on its FOIA site: "If you are working directly with an IRS employee on an open tax case, you can request information from the file directly from them."[52] A process like this would potentially improve the timeliness and accuracy of disclosures to the parties, improve efficiency for the agency in consolidating the procedures, and, most importantly for this study's purpose, reduce EEOC FOIA requests by as much as ninety-five percent.

B. DISCLOSURE IN BENEFITS APPLICATIONS

The immigration context also reveals voluminous FOIA requesting in another arena: benefits applications. These benefits applications include requesting a new or different kind of visa, adjusting status from a nonimmigrant visa to permanent residency, or going through the naturalization process to become a citizen. Indeed, the rate of FOIA requests associated with noncitizens seeking these affirmative immigration benefits appears to *vastly* outpace requesting associated with removal proceedings.

The process for noncitizens applying for these types of immigration benefits typically requires an in-person interview with a USCIS official after a facially adequate application is submitted. That official usually gathers all the agency documents necessary for the determination. Immigration attorneys describe, however, how those interviews can involve surprises in which a USCIS official makes a claim that the agency has evidence the applicant is ineligible – evidence that may or may not be accurate. As a protective measure, immigration attorneys have to file FOIA requests far in advance of even submitting the application so that they know of whatever documentation might arise. Additionally, if a surprise still arises in the interview, then the immigration attorneys are forced to go file FOIA requests after the interview, further delaying the process.[53]

One could instead imagine a system by which USCIS officials are required to disclose to the applicant any documentation on which they plan to rely in making a determination. This would put the noncitizen on notice, allow them to come to the

[51] *What You Can Expect after a Charge Is Filed*, EQUAL EMP. OPPORTUNITY COMM'N, www.eeoc.gov/employers/process.cfm (last visited Nov. 24, 2020).

[52] *IRS Freedom of Information*, INTERNAL REVENUE SERV. (Sept. 23, 2020), www.irs.gov/privacy-disclosure/irs-freedom-of-information.

[53] Telephone Interview with Elizabeth Hilton, *supra* note 10.

interview prepared with any explanation or rebuttal, and allow some individuals to simply abandon their case and save everyone the time. But regardless, it would prevent the need for possibly thousands – even tens of thousands – of FOIA requests a year.

While immigration is the area where FOIA stands the most to gain from reforming benefits processes, other agencies may have processes that belie similar opportunities for preempting the need for FOIA reliance. For example, the Federal Emergency Management Agency's process for appealing a denial of benefits eligibility lends itself to applicants using FOIA to get a copy of their file to arm themselves for appeal.[54] Automatic provision of the underlying records necessary to file an appeal alongside the determination itself could preempt this class of FOIA requests. Other agencies may well have similar opportunities to provide the records on which benefits eligibility determinations rely so that dissatisfied applicants do not need to resort to FOIA to contest a denial.

C. ELIMINATING REQUEST-AND-RETURN

Some agency benefits applications processes suffer from a different kind of information flow deficiency: they require the applicant to produce documentation that the agency itself already has in its possession but that the applicant very well may not. Those applicants first must go through a FOIA request process to obtain the records – holding up their underlying application for benefits – and then they turn around and return those very same records to the agency with their application. I call this phenomenon "request-and-return" and suggest that agencies should endeavor to eliminate it wherever possible. Oftentimes this could be done with simply an option on the application to rely on documents known to exist within the agency itself.

Once again, immigration processes reveal ample opportunities for this sort of reform. For example, noncitizens who are applying for a green card from within the United States must submit proof they lawfully entered the country, a record of which they may no longer have a copy. An immigration attorney opines:

> [O]ne example is if someone enters lawfully but they have no proof of it, right, you're required to get—they request an I-94 [a form documenting arrivals to the United States]. Oftentimes USCIS has that record, so why do we have to do a FOIA to produce that record? . . . Can you provide us with this proof of entry if we know it exists?[55]

Another example arises when a noncitizen is attempting to adjust their status to permanent residency based on a previously filed family-based petition. There, the

[54] *Request Records through the Freedom of Information or Pivacy Act*, Fed. Emergency Mgmt. Agency (June 22, 2020), www.fema.gov/about/offices/administrative/foia.

[55] Telephone Interview with Peggy Brewer, *supra* note 10.

original petition is needed, but may have been filed years or decades before and the applicant's own copy may be lost in the meantime.[56] FOIA is the only answer for these applicants.[57]

If agencies permitted these applicants to submit their file and simply designate what records they believe the agency holds that supports their application, rather than first going through FOIA to obtain those records only to send them back, that would speed up the process for the applicants, too. In fact, it may allow some applicants to avoid falling out of status or suffer other immigration consequences while they wait for the documentation they need to prove their eligibility for a visa. Beyond that, it would take out of the FOIA queue a whole set of records-processing that does nothing but send documents out of the agency and then receive those same documents back. Agencies should endeavor to eliminate this redundancy. Other than path dependency and the relative lack of power that FOIA offices have to influence administrative reform, this redundancy has no obvious rationale.

Other agencies may have some similar opportunities. For example, at the Veterans Health Administration (VHA), families of recently deceased veterans and the funeral homes handling their arrangements use FOIA routinely to request military discharge forms.[58] Proof of military discharge is necessary to access a military funeral benefit, because only those veterans with other-than-dishonorable discharges are entitled to this funerary support.[59] Yet, one could imagine a process that would allow applicants for the funeral benefit to simply check a box requesting the agency verify the discharge status of the veteran. It may not be much more efficient for the agency, but it could hardly be less efficient than having a separate FOIA process to handle the request. And it would remove what is essentially a verification process from the FOIA office: an office that was instead envisioned to facilitate public oversight requests.

* * *

One might ask whether investing in redesigning agency procedures to include discovery, disclosure, or verification mechanisms, rather than simply leaving those resources in FOIA offices, makes any difference. The clear answer from this study is "yes." The evidence of FOIA's use in this regard reveals inherent weaknesses in

[56] *Petition for Alien Relative, I-130*, U.S. Citizenship & Immigration Servs., www.uscis.gov/i-130 (last visited Nov. 24, 2020).

[57] Telephone Interview with Peggy Brewer, *supra* note 10; Telephone Interview with John Rivera, *supra* note 10 (explaining that "a lot of people lose paperwork over the course of the twenty years that they're waiting for their petition to become current").

[58] In the study year, 367 requests were for this particular kind of form and most of these requests were made by funeral homes. Veterans Health Admin., Dep't of Veterans Affairs, Freedom of Information Act Responses to Apr. 14, 2016 Request by Margaret B. Kwoka (on file with author).

[59] *DD214 and Taps, a Veteran's Final Funeral Benefit, a Tribute from a Grateful Nation*, DD214 (2007), www.dd214.us/funeral.html.

agency procedures that are worthy of addressing in their own right both to promote efficiency and to better serve information constituents. After all, agencies are charged with administering benefits and enforcing the law. They are bettering those goals when their constituents can access benefits more quickly and with less work, and when enforcement efforts promote fairness and accuracy in proceedings.

But again, not having these types of requests in the ambit of FOIA is useful for government transparency, openness, accountability, and public oversight, too. FOIA is doing double and triple duty, and FOIA offices are arranging themselves to serve as stand-ins for enforcement officials, benefits administrators, and other program functions. Let's save FOIA for what it was meant for.

This is one area where Congress could make huge strides by revising the default procedures in the Administrative Procedure Act. Where no default discovery mechanism exists, it could create one. Where notice requirements for agency decisions are minimal, it could add requirements for disclosure of underlying justifications and evidence. Or, Congress could pick off immigration as the right starting point, and overhaul immigration processes to create a fairer, more transparent, more accurate adjudication system that does not require a FOIA-office intermediary. We can learn, in some instances, where the administrative state's relationship with its constituencies has broken down by looking at FOIA. A fix to the underlying problem is also a fix for FOIA.

12

Customizing Information Delivery

Not all systems for providing information upon request have to be consolidated into FOIA. Agencies can and should look at their information constituencies and consider tailored mechanisms for releasing records to those groups of would-be requesters without forcing their requests into the FOIA queue. To be sure, Chapters 10 and 11 document forms of this strategy; affirmative disclosure and reforming administrative procedures are both alternatives to FOIA. But sometimes the strategy can be as simple as making a special process for requesting a certain type of record with uniform attributes and sensible shortcuts.

Some agencies have done this, and their programs evidence the success. Indeed, most people, when provided a choice between a simple and straightforward option and crafting their own FOIA request letter that meets various statutory requirements, will invariably choose simple and straightforward.[1] If there is a process designed just for the kind of records they seek, they will use it. Agencies also benefit from the uniformity and the predictability attendant to tailored request systems for high-volume systems of records.

A. EXAMPLES OF SUCCESS

Many agencies have attempted to remove certain sets of routine requests from their FOIA queues by creating a tailored process for obtaining the records. Importantly, these processes do not appear to curtail anyone's right to file a FOIA request. Rather, the tailored process works because most information constituents are happy to follow a reasonable process specifically designed for them.

Take, for example, the Internal Revenue Service (IRS). The IRS has a separate, non-FOIA process for requesting a copy of one's own tax return. There is a form to fill out solely for this purpose, a flat fee of fifty dollars per copy, and a hotline to call

[1] *See supra* Ch. 1, pt. D (describing the FOIA request process).

if you need help. In addition, if a full copy of the return is unnecessary, the IRS offers a free "transcript" of your tax return, which contains a summary of the information.[2] These "routine access requests" are not considered FOIA requests, not logged as FOIA requests, and not processed as FOIA requests. Indeed, they could not, by definition, be FOIA requests because FOIA does not have a provision allowing for a flat fee per record; rather FOIA requires a computation of costs based on agency personnel time and adherence to various fee categories.[3]

The IRS refers to this program as the "Respond Directly" initiative, which is mentioned in various Chief FOIA Officer reports over the years as one of the agency's initiatives to increase transparency and customer service while "in many cases eliminat[ing] the need for individuals to submit FOIA requests."[4] After the IRS implemented this program, the agency saw a marked decrease in FOIA requests: in 2004, the agency received 51,423 requests, but by 2009, that number had fallen to 14,405, a seventy-two percent reduction in just five years.[5] In its most recent reports, IRS FOIA requests total less than 10,000 per year,[6] bucking the trend of an ever-growing number of FOIA requests government-wide.

An IRS official explained that if someone sends the standard form for their copy of their tax return, that query is not counted as a FOIA request, but, at the same time, no one is precluded from sending in a FOIA request instead of, or in addition to, that form. If someone does send in a written FOIA request, even for the same records, it would also be processed under FOIA; but the vast majority of information-seekers simply use the standard form.[7] Thus, the IRS has efficiently created a separate process that users appear more than willing to comply with, without curtailing anyone's FOIA rights.

National Archives and Records Administration (NARA) is another dramatic example of an agency providing alternative, non-FOIA records delivery systems that operate seemingly to the great satisfaction of their information constituents. In Fiscal Year (FY) 2019, NARA reported 67,466 FOIA requests received. Clearly, this is an extremely high-volume of requests. Indeed, NARA generally trails only the three main immigration components of the Department of Homeland Security in the

2 *Routine Access to IRS Records*, Internal Revenue Serv. (Oct. 1, 2020), www.irs.gov/privacy-disclosure/routine-access-to-irs-records.

3 5 U.S.C. § 552(a)(4) (2016).

4 U.S. Dep't of the Treasury, 2019 Chief Freedom of Information Act Officer Report 10, home.treasury.gov/system/files/236/Chief-FOIA-Officer-Report-2019.pdf.

5 U.S. Dep't of the Treasury, Fiscal Year 2004 Freedom of Information Act Annual Report 11 (Feb. 1, 2015); U.S. Dep't of the Treasury, Fiscal Year 2009 Freedom of Information Act Annual Report 15 (Jan. 5, 2010).

6 U.S. Dep't of the Treasury, 2017 Freedom of Information Act Annual Report 14 (8,255 requests); U.S. Dep't of the Treasury, FY 2018 Freedom of Information Act Annual Report 14 (7,909 requests); U.S. Dep't of the Treasury, FY 2019 Freedom of Information Act Annual Report 13 (8,006 requests).

7 Telephone Interview by Leah Perczak with Karina Smith, FOIA Agent, Internal Revenue Serv. (July 27, 2017).

volume of requests received.[8] Of course, since NARA's mission is to preserve archival records of historical importance, it makes sense that it would be among the high-volume request agencies.

But the shocking thing is that the number of FOIA requests at NARA is absolutely dwarfed by the number of military personnel records requests that NARA processes separately from FOIA. Kevin Pratt, Assistant Director for Military Records at NARA's National Personnel Records Center, outside of St. Louis, Missouri said that his unit receives 1.2 million personnel records requests a year – that's more than the federal government's total annual number of FOIA requests – but nearly all are requests made outside of FOIA. Instead, these requests are made by filling out a relatively simple "Standard Form 180" to request military personnel files.[9] Form 180s are not counted as FOIA requests, nor are they charged as such; rather, this service is run as a fee-for-service operation, with a small flat fee to each requester.[10]

And given the volume of users that avail themselves of this option, it seems like information constituents are happy with this separate, tailored system. It's estimated that more than half of the Form 180 requesters need a DD214 separation document for the service member or the family of a service member to claim veterans' or other benefits; most of the other half of requests are also from service members or their families, but seek more complete personnel records. For most of these Form 180 requests, the agency can turn around the information back to the constituent in an astonishing six days.[11]

Importantly, no one's right to file a FOIA request is ever curtailed. Requesting records under FOIA (even these very same records), is always an option: it's explicitly cited on the agency's website.[12] Pratt explains the agency's position: if a person cites FOIA in the body of the letter, it is counted and processed as a FOIA request; but, he explains, most people fill in the standard Form 180 and are happy with the agency's response. Moreover, if someone is asking for third-party records and isn't happy with what the agency can provide under its routinized service, the agency moves that request into the FOIA queue to be processed under the

[8] *Compare* Nat'l Archives & Records Admin., Fiscal Year 2016 Annual Freedom of Information (FOIA) Report 14 (49,966 requests), *with* U.S. Dep't of Homeland Sec., Privacy Office, 2016 Freedom of Information Act Report, 5 (Feb. 2017) (63,385 requests at Immigration and Customs Enforcement, 66,690 requests at Customs and Border Patrol, 166,732 requests at USCIS).

[9] *Request Military Personnel Records Using Standard Form 180*, Nat'l Personnel Records Ctr., Nat'l Archives (Oct. 13, 2020), www.archives.gov/veterans/military-service-records/standard-form-180.html.

[10] Telephone Interview with Kevin Pratt, Assistant Dir. of Military Records, Nat'l Personnel Records Ctr., Nat'l Archives & Records Admin. (June 17, 2019).

[11] *Id.*

[12] *Access to Official Military Personnel Files (OMPF): Veterans and Next-of-Kin*, Nat'l Personnel Records Ctr. (Sept. 17, 2020), www.archives.gov/personnel-records-center/ompf-access.

statute. As a result, the agency still receives and processes upwards of two-thirds of NARA's total FOIA requests – estimated around 40,000 for FY 2019.[13]

Yet another high-volume FOIA agency, US Citizenship and Immigration Service (USCIS), has pioneered a custom routinized service for certain information requests. USCIS, which otherwise processes upwards of 200,000 FOIA requests mostly pertaining to noncitizens' current immigration situations, also holds historical records that are of interest to people conducting genealogy research. Around 2010, the agency set up a separate program for processing these genealogy requests. It went through a notice-and-comment rulemaking process to create a governing regulatory framework for the program.[14] Under this framework, it charges a flat sixty-five dollar fee for an index search about whether the agency holds records on a particular ancestor, and another sixty-five dollar fee for copies of whatever records there are.[15]

Top agency officials cite the program as helping to reduce the agency's backlog, because otherwise these requests would fall in the FOIA queue. Instead, these records are processed separately, not counted in the FOIA numbers, and funded through the fees charged to the requesters.[16] There is no real reason, as a genealogy requester, to prefer being put in the much larger much longer FOIA queue, other than avoiding a $65 fee. But those who are seeking records out of interest in family history are much more likely to be able and willing to pay this still relatively reasonable fee, as opposed to noncitizens facing removal proceedings or attempting to secure immigration benefits who are not charged fees by this agency under FOIA. Funding a separate program is likely good for everyone, and between 2,000 and 3,000 genealogy requests are received every year and thus diverted from the FOIA queue.[17]

A final fee-for-service example is illustrative of the types of measures agencies are taking to ensure that individuals do not have to resort to FOIA. The Federal Bureau

[13] Telephone Interview with Kevin Pratt, *supra* note 10. Interestingly, Pratt says that the largest increase in FOIA requests has come from employers seeking to claim the Opportunity Tax Credit, a credit for employing veterans that requires documentation of the veterans' status. Since these are third party requests, they are processed under FOIA.

[14] Establishment of a Genealogy Program, 71 Fed. Reg. 20357 (proposed Apr. 20, 2006); Establishment of a Genealogy Program, 73 Fed. Reg. 28026 (notice of final rule May 15, 2008) (to be codified 8 C.F.R. pts. 103, 299).

[15] *See* U.S. Citizenship and Immigration Services Fee Schedule and Changes to Certain Other Immigration Benefit Request Requirements, 85 Fed. Reg. 46788 (Aug. 3, 2020) (confirming that genealogy request fees are currently $65), *and* Immigrant Legal Res. Ctr. v. Wolf, No. 20-CV-05883-JSW, 2020 WL 5798269, at *20 (N.D. Cal. Sept. 29, 2020) (court order restricting, for the time being, the raising of the genealogy request fee).

[16] Interview with Jill Eggleston, Assistant Ctr. Dir., Freedom of Info. & Privacy Act Unit, Nat'l Records Ctr., U.S. Citizenship & Immigration Servs., U.S. Dep't of Homeland Sec., in Lee's Summit, Mo. (June 12, 2019).

[17] *Id.*

of Investigation (FBI), as far back as 1973,[18] set up a separate, non-FOIA system for requesting FBI Identification Records, often referred to as "rap sheets" listing certain criminal history information.[19] The information in this database is submitted in conjunction with fingerprints, and, accordingly, individuals must submit fingerprints to request their own record. Fingerprint submission is nowhere required to make a FOIA request, and nowhere does the FBI seem to count or consider these to be FOIA requests. Moreover, the FBI charges a flat eighteen dollar fee per request.[20] People who need their criminal histories are typically applying for a job or benefit and will willingly engage a non-FOIA process, including fingerprinting, to obtain accurate records they need.

Aside from simply setting up fee-for-service request processes for routine records systems, some agencies have come up with other creative options that preclude the need for information constituents to resort to FOIA. Again at USCIS, a new electronic system called "FIRST" has been introduced to release records to requesters through an online portal instead of mailing out a CD.[21] One of the benefits of this system cited by top FOIA officials is that it acts like a "private reading room" such that the requester, oftentimes the immigration attorney, can retrieve the records again at a later date if the initial set becomes misplaced. This prevents the need for another request to be submitted for the same records that were previously released.[22]

Similarly, at some point in the past, the Bureau of Prisons (BOP) started offering the option to all inmates to receive a copy of their medical records on a CD at the time of their release from custody as part of their out-processing.[23] The idea was that these records were so often needed by formerly incarcerated individuals that providing an electronic copy would better serve the individuals and preempt the need for them to later file FOIA requests for the same records. Of course, it does not prevent those records from being lost and additional copies being requested, but it nonetheless seems to be a step in the direction of avoiding flooding the FOIA office with these information constituents.

Without doubt, many other agencies have these sorts of opportunities for routinized requests. Specially designed fee-for-service records retrieval services are of

[18] Fed. Bureau of Investigation, U.S. Dep't of Justice, Order 556-73, Production of FBI Identification Records in Response to Written Requests by Subjects Thereof (1973) [hereinafter FBI Order 556-73].

[19] *Identity History Summary Checks*, Fed. Bureau of Investigation, www.fbi.gov/services/cjis/identity-history-summary-checks (last visited Nov. 24, 2020).

[20] FBI Order 556-73, *supra* note 18.

[21] *USCIS Expands FIRST: A Fully Digital FOIA System*, U.S. Citizenship & Immigration Servs. (June 25, 2019), www.uscis.gov/news/news-releases/uscis-expands-first-a-fully-digital-foia-system.

[22] Interview with Jill Eggleston, *supra* note 16.

[23] Telephone Interview with Gene Baime, Supervisory Att'y, FOIA/PA Section, Office of Gen. Counsel, Fed. Bureau of Prisons, U.S. Dep't of Justice (Mar. 30, 2020).

particular utility where routine records are requested for predictable reasons, where the processing of those requests takes a predictable amount of agency resources, and where the requester base is formed of information constituents with largely non-public-oversight purposes. Certainly, these conditions are met in the above examples with respect to genealogy records, criminal histories, military personnel records, and previously filed tax returns.

These private information needs are important, but they are largely not seeking government records for public oversight purposes. Agencies should be able to provide services to these other information constituents without cramming them all into FOIA. Agencies can and should look for these opportunities, without denying anyone the right to file a FOIA request if they prefer. These examples show that when presented with a reasonable tailored alternative to FOIA for obtaining a particular type of record, information constituents will gladly comply.

B. SOME THINGS JUST AREN'T FOIA

Sometimes agencies have defaulted to FOIA where FOIA does not apply. That is to say, agencies are calling certain requests FOIA requests even when they are not, and using procedures to process them that clearly are not FOIA procedures. Sometimes the records produced could never be produced under FOIA as the law currently stands, and yet they are logged and counted as FOIA requests. This study revealed this striking pattern found in various corners of the government. It is worth understanding that some things just aren't FOIA.

To begin, FOIA can never be used to force a government agency to create a record that does not already exist. It can only be used to request extant records.[24] Yet, some agencies appear to be using FOIA for requests that are precisely that – requests to create a new record. For example, two separate financial regulatory agencies produce certificates in response to requests made under FOIA that make certifications about companies as of the day that they are issued.

At the Comptroller of Currency, fully half of its 1,606 requests were for a "certificate of corporate existence,"[25] which, as the name suggests, certifies that "a bank was authorized to transact the business of banking on the date the certificate

[24] 5 U.S.C. § 552(a)(3) (2016); *see also* Lipton v. Envtl. Prot. Agency, 316 F. Supp. 3d 245, 250 (D.D.C. 2018) ("The statutory text [of FOIA] clearly contemplates that only extant information, and not information that an agency may create in the future, needs to be published."); Serv. Women's Action Network v. Dep't of Def., 888 F. Supp. 2d 231, 246 (D. Conn. 2012) ("[Agencies] are correct that they are not obligated to create a new record in response to a request for one.) (internal citation omitted); Scaff-Martinez v. Drug Enf't Admin., 770 F. Supp. 2d 17, 22–23 (D.D.C. 2011) ("The FOIA neither requires an agency to answer questions disguised as a FOIA request, nor to create documents or opinions in response to an individual's request for information.") (internal quotations and citation omitted).

[25] Department of Treasury, Office of the Comptroller of the Currency, Freedom of Information Act Response to Mar. 13, 2018 Request by Margaret B. Kwoka (on file with author).

was issued."[26] Except that the date the certificate was issued is the date of responding to the FOIA request, which is to say it is a new record being created, not an extant record that is requested. Moreover, at this agency, there is a separate requesting process for these certificates, and a flat $10 fee: neither procedure is authorized in the statute.[27] Yet, these are counted as FOIA requests and responses.

Similarly, at the Federal Reserve, at least 109 of the agency's 678 requests were for some sort of "certificate" typically for a "certificate of good standing" for a particular entity.[28] These are certificates that again must be created upon the receipt of a request, not extant agency records. While the Federal Reserve does not appear to have created a separate process of requesting these records,[29] it arguably should, and should stop counting them as FOIA requests because they are not.

A similar phenomenon is apparent at the Pension Benefit Guaranty Corporation (PBGC), where "income verification" was the subject of nearly a quarter of the agency's 1,640 requests.[30] Income verification letters are often needed by a pension recipient for the purposes of receiving housing assistance, underwriting a loan, or other matters.[31] By its very nature, an income verification letter is a proof of current pension income, as of the date the letter is issued, rather than a record the agency already has and keeps in its regular course of business. These should never be counted as FOIA requests.

Other agencies have created processes for producing extant records that are clearly outside the normal FOIA process (as in the examples of agencies creating fee-for-service options described above) but still, inexplicably, call them FOIA. Typically, these processes are not in compliance with FOIA in at least two key aspects. First, the request is required to be on a special form or submitted in a special format, not simply a letter that "reasonably describes" the requested records as FOIA requires.[32] And second, the agency typically charges a flat fee, something that may be reasonable for the alternative procedure, but absolutely does not comport with FOIA. FOIA authorizes collection of fees only for "direct costs" of search, duplication, or review.[33] Moreover, FOIA prohibits agencies from collecting fees when the

[26] *Request Certified Documents*, Office of the Comptroller of Currency, www.occ.treas.gov/about/connect-with-us/foia/request-certified-documents.html (last visited Nov. 24, 2020).

[27] *Id.*

[28] Federal Reserve, Freedom of Information Act Response to Mar. 6, 2018 Request by Margaret B. Kwoka (on file with author).

[29] The Federal Reserve's navigation for "Requesting Information" takes a user straight to the "FOIA Request" page. *See Guide to Requesting Records or Information*, Bd. of Governors of the Fed. Reserve Sys. (Dec. 5, 2016), www.federalreserve.gov/foia/about_foia.htm.

[30] Pension Benefit Guaranty Corp., Freedom of Information Act Response to Mar. 26, 2018 Request by Margaret B. Kwoka (on file with author).

[31] *Income Verification Request Procedures*, Pension Benefit Guar. Corp., www.pbgc.gov/about/pg/footer/foia/income-verification-request-procedures.

[32] 5 U.S.C. § 552(a)(3) (2016).

[33] *Id.* at § 552(a)(4)(A)(iv).

cost of responding to the request is minimal, which nearly all these routinized productions would be.[34]

Take, for example, the Social Security Administration (SSA). There, requests for SS-5 and Numident records – the records reflecting original data submitted with social security number applications requested mostly for genealogy research – are processed through a distinct method. A special form, the SSA-711 form, is required, unless an online request is processed through the FOIA Online portal. Even this electronic version, however, invokes a distinct form for these types of requests. Moreover, the agency charges a flat fee of twenty-one dollars for an SS-5, or twenty dollars for Numident records, with an additional ten dollar fee for either one if you want it to be certified.[35]

These just aren't FOIA requests. To be clear, they could be, because these are extant records. But the agency has created a separate, non-FOIA process for the public to gain access. The alternative procedure is eminently reasonable and appears to be an effective means of releasing records that the government possesses. It is precisely the kind of initiative that agencies should take. But SSA still calls it FOIA, counts these as FOIA requests, and logs them into their FOIA logs. And in the study year, these categories of records were requested 11,080 times, representing nearly half of all requests to the SSA.[36]

C. THE BENEFITS OF SAVING FOIA FOR FOIA REQUESTS

We should stop making FOIA do so much work. It cannot be expected to solve everyone's information problems, resolve every need for government records, or satisfy every information constituent. It no doubt seems semantic to suggest that we simply create non-FOIA request processes with tailored forms, mechanisms, and fees for categories of records frequently requested at a given agency that do not have substantial public oversight purposes. But there are actually several very valuable results from segregating out these voluminous requests.

First, they may generate more sustainable funding models. Second, they are potentially much more efficient when designed for the particular record at issue – after all, a specially made request form or procedure will give the agency precisely the data it needs to retrieve the particular record or information requested. And

[34] *Id.* at § 552(a)(4)(A)(iv)(I), (II) (prohibiting collection of fees if the cost of collection of the fee is equal to or exceeds the value of the fee or, for all noncommercial requesters, for the first two hours of search time or 100 pages of duplication).

[35] *FOIA Request Methods and Fees*, Soc. Sec. Admin., www.ssa.gov/foia/request.html (last visited Nov. 24, 2020).

[36] Freedom of Information Act Responses from Soc. Sec. Admin., to Apr. 15, 2016 Request and Mar. 17, 2017 Administrative Appeal by Margaret B. Kwoka (on file with author).

finally, and most importantly for this study, removing these routine records needs from the ambit of FOIA will help alleviate the pressure on FOIA and bring more clarity to the debates concerning FOIA resources and FOIA's benefits. It would, in my view, allow for meaningful improvement in how FOIA serves public oversight requesters.

To take each in turn, stabilizing funding for agencies' information services is hugely important. For most agencies, Congress does not separately appropriate money for FOIA administration; rather, an agency must allocate money for this function from its overall administrative budgets.[37] And charging fees does not allow agencies to recoup any significant percentage of their costs. As described above in Chapter 9, most agencies are recouping tiny percentages of their FOIA costs by charging fees.

Moreover, they are even less likely to be able to charge fees under FOIA for requests for discrete, routine records that are needed for non-oversight purposes. Most of the time, because these types of requests concern a particular record or document, they seek only a few pages of material that are relatively easy to locate within agencies' files. But because agencies cannot charge any noncommercial requester for the first 100 pages of duplication or the first two hours of search time, routine requests for files needed for private reasons are unlikely to reach the threshold for agencies to charge any fee at all.

Finally, if they do charge a fee, it requires the agency to record the amount of time spent by various personnel, their hourly rate, and any materials required (such as CDs) to duplicate the records. Review time – that is the time spent reviewing records for necessary redactions – can never be recouped except from commercial requesters.[38]

A reasonable flat fee for standard information requests is not only more administrable but more likely to reflect agency costs in providing an information service. Genealogy requesters or those needing their criminal histories for an employment requirement or due diligence requesters seeking various compliance certificates are all likely to be perfectly willing to comply with a reasonable fee to access a

[37] U.S. Dep't of Justice, Office of Info. Policy, *FOIA Affected by Budget Constraints*, 11 FOIA Update 1 (Jan. 1, 1990), available at www.justice.gov/oip/blog/foia-update-foia-affected-budget-constraints ("FOIA administration, as a component of agency activities, is not a separate "line item" category in the legislative appropriations for most federal agencies.").

[38] *See* 5 USC. § 552(a)(4)(A)(ii)(II) (2016) ("[F]ees shall be limited to reasonable standard charges for document duplication when records are not sought for commercial use"); *id.* at § 552(a)(4)(iv) ("Fee schedules shall provide for the recovery of only the direct costs of search, duplication, or review. Review costs shall include only the direct costs incurred during the initial examination of a document for the purposes of determining whether the documents must be disclosed under this section and for the purposes of withholding any portions exempt from disclosure under this section. Review costs may not include any costs incurred in resolving issues of law or policy that may be raised in the course of processing a request under this section.").

well-tailored information service the agency offers. Fee-for-service programs may have more success funding themselves from reasonable charges to these non-oversight information constituents.

To be clear, we should continue to provide records for free in conjunction with benefits and enforcement proceedings. No one should be denied their own files when trying to make their best case before an agency, whether immigration proceedings, or employment discrimination claims, or applications for government benefits. Moreover, these types of routine requests that might be better addressed through a fee-for-service model are, as the examples demonstrate, typically not for public-oversight purposes, either. News media, citizens groups, concerned individuals seeking information about government activities simply are not falling in these categories of requesters.

Indeed agencies should allow anyone who is not satisfied with the alternative process the option of filing a FOIA request. If someone invokes FOIA, cites FOIA, or sends something as a FOIA request, it should be processed as such. It is just unlikely that many people will choose FOIA when there is a reasonable tailored alternative specifically designed to get them the records they need as expeditiously as possible.

But the biggest reason to advance this approach is not recouping costs. It is to try to disentangle information services that agencies provide and prevent them all from being lumped under the FOIA umbrella. The behemoth that FOIA has become has strayed far from its goals. It was not designed to do the kind of work described in this chapter and it is not doing it very well. Specialized processes and clearly delineating what is and isn't FOIA are first steps to understanding what FOIA's core value is and whether we can improve its operation as to that core function. If we force FOIA to serve every information need, of course we will eventually conclude that FOIA is not serving oversight requesters well. Indeed, it mostly is not serving oversight requesters at all. Information constituents, the agency, and FOIA, would all be better off by disaggregating information services.

Again, Congress and the various FOIA oversight bodies at DOJ and NARA have roles to play in this regard. For example, the reporting obligations as they currently stand may incentivize counting as FOIA requests as many requests for information as possible. Agencies must provide annual reports that describe the number of requests received, average processing times, and whether records were provided in full, in part, or denied.[39] Given the metrics used to measure agency FOIA performance, reporting requirements may consciously or unconsciously push agencies to count more requests as FOIA requests, especially those that are easy to fulfill quickly and fully such as the routine requests described in this chapter.

[39] *See id.* at § 552(e).

Congress could, however, require reporting on other types of information request processes and thereby give "credit" to non-FOIA options the agency creates. Or Congress could even reward and specifically ask about agency opportunities to create non-FOIA information programs. Incentives would go a long way to helping agencies overcome structural barriers to imagining alternative disclosure regimes. Removing what is not or should not be FOIA from the conversation would likely benefit all involved and would clarify the confounding nature of FOIA reform.

Conclusion

The government is a great repository of information useful to all manner and sector of private and public interests. Indeed, some government agencies view as part of their core mission the delivery of information useful to sectors of the economy, the public, researchers, and more. For example, the Census, the Bureau of Labor Statistics, and the Centers for Disease Control are all agencies dedicated at least in part to amassing information and distributing it sensibly to those who can benefit from it.

But the truth is that all agencies hold information some segments of the public need and want, and right now it is far too often the case that FOIA is the only way for people to get that information. Our rights under FOIA are precious and invaluable. The press, civil society, researchers, and ordinary people in communities throughout the United States are using FOIA to hold our government accountable. It is working, to a degree, and we have every reason to want to vigorously guard our rights to access government records. We should not relinquish them or curtail them. We should protect them and enhance them. But we cannot enhance FOIA's usefulness as an oversight tool when FOIA is forced to be everything to everybody.

Each agency needs to begin to see information delivery as part of its core mission, to identify its principal information constituents, and to be given the authority and incentives to design systems somewhat bespoke to the agency to deliver information in sensible ways. This volume by no means is exhaustive in suggesting what those ways may be. But it is a start. It is the first time we can see the whole – who these one million FOIA requesters are and why they are requesting records under FOIA. Without reimagining the relationship between the public and information held by government agencies, we will never imagine a better future for FOIA.

Appendices

For the full underlying datasets on which this study relies, visit http://hdl.handle.net/1811/92818.

Appendix A

Agency	Requests Received in baseline FY 2016	Request Result	Data Obtained Actual Time Period
Department of Homeland Security, US Citizenship and Immigration Services	166,732	Public Log	FY 2015
Department of Homeland Security, Customs and Border Protection	66,690	Public Log	FY 2015
Department of Homeland Security, Immigration and Customs Enforcement	63,385	Public Log	FY 2015
National Archives and Records Administration	49,966	Incomplete Response	
Department of Justice, Executive Office for Immigration Review	35,500	Incomplete Response	
Social Security Administration	29,631	Data Released	CY 2015
Department of Veterans Affairs, Veterans Health Administration	28,091	Data Released	FY 2015
Department of State	27,856	Public Log	CY 2014
Department of Defense, U.S. Army	25,755	Data Released	CY 2013
Department of Homeland Security, National Protection and Programs Directorate	19,557	Inaccessible Response	
Department of Agricultrue, Farm Service Agency	18,463	Incomplete Response	
Department of Health and Human Services, Centers for Medicare and Medicaid Services	17,917	Incomplete Response	

Equal Employment Opportunity Commission (combined regions)	17,680	Data Released	FY 2015
Department of Justice, Federal Bureau of Investigations	15,202	Data Released	FY 2015
Securities and Exchange Commission	14,458	Data Released Combined with Public Log	CY 2013
Environmental Protection Agency (combined regions)	10,403	Data Released Combined with Public Log	CY 2013
Department of Health and Human Services, Food and Drug Administration	10,374	Data Released	CY 2013
Department of Defense, US Navy	9,605	Data Released	FY 2015
Department of Transportation, Federal Aviation Administration	9,582	Public Log	FY 2018
Department of Labor, Occupational Safety and Health Administration	9,126	Data Released	FY 2015
Department of Treasury, Internal Revenue Service	8,825	Data Released Combined with Public Log	FY 2015
Department of Justice, Bureau of Prisons	7,664	Data Released	CY 2017
Department of Defense, US Air Force	4,918	No Response	
Department of Veterans Affairs, Veterans Benefits Administration	4,784	No Response	
Department of Justice, Executive Office for United States Attorneys	3,982	No Response	
Department of Defense, Defense Logistics Agency	3920	Data Released	CY 2013
Pension Benefit Guaranty Corporation	3,713	Data Released	FY 2017

(*continued*)

(*continued*)

Agency	Requests Received in baseline FY 2016	Request Result	Data Obtained Actual Time Period
Department of Homeland Security, US Coast Guard	3,010	Data Released	FY 2017
National Labor Relations Board	2,679	Data Released	FY 2015
Department of Homeland Security, Federal Emergency Management Agency	2,659	Data Released	FY 2017
Department of Labor, Wage and Hour Division	2,589	Data Released	FY 2015
Central Intelligence Agency	2,547	No Response	
Department of Transportation, Federal Motor Carrier Safety Administration	2,307	Data Released	FY 2016 & 2017
Department of Agriculture, Forest Service	1,977	Data Released	FY 2017
Department of Interior, Bureau of Indian Affairs	1,892	Data Released	FY 2017
Department of Defense, National Security Agency	1,881	No Response	
Department of Defense, Office of the Secretary of Defense and Joint Chiefs	1,794	Data Released	FY 2017
US Postal Service	1,771	Data Released	FY 2017
Department of Justice, US Marshals	1,748	Data Released	FY 2015
Department of Justice, Drug Enforcement Administration	1,724	No Response	
Department of Homeland Security, US Secret service	1,700	Public Log	FY 2018
Department of Treasury, Office of the Comptroller of the Currency	1,432	Data Released	FY 2017
Department of Labor, Employment and Training Administration	1,360	No Response	

Department of Health and Human Services, National Institutes of Health	1,324	Data Released	CY 2013
Federal Trade Commission	1,260	Data Released	CY 2013
Department of Agriculture, Animal and Plant Health Inspection Service	1,143	Data Released	FY 2017
Department of Justice, Bureau of Alcohol, Tobacco, Firearms, and Explosives	1,138	Data Released	FY 2017
Department of Interior, US Fish and Wildilife Service	1,132	Data Released	11/17 to 5/18
Department of Health and Human Services, Centers for Disease Control	1,120	Data Released	FY 2017
Department of Justice, Office of Information Policy	1,071	Data Released	FY 2017
Department of Housing and Urban Development, Headquarters	1,060	Data Released	CY 2013
Department of Labor, Mine Safety and Health Adiministration	1,037	Data Released	FY 2015
Department of Health and Human Services, Office of the Inspector General	1,015	Incomplete Response	
Department of Health and Human Services, Office of the Secretary	985	No Response	
Small Business Administration, Headquarters	979	Data Released	FY 2017
Department of Energy, Headquarters	921	Inaccessible Response	
Department of the Interior, National Park Service	918	Data Released	FY 2017
Department of Defnese, Defense Intelligence Agency	902	Inaccessible Response	
Department of Treasury, Departmental Offices	894	Public Log	FY 2018

(continued)

(continued)

Agency	Requests Received in baseline FY 2016	Request Result	Data Obtained Actual Time Period
General Services Administration	887	Data Released	FY 2017
Department of Interior, Bureau of Land Management	852	Data Released	
Federal Communications Commission	836	Data Released	FY 2017
Department of Justice, Criminal Division	789	Data Released	FY 2017
Nuclear Regulatory Commission	785	Data Released	FY 2017
Department of Defense, Inspector General	772	Data Released	FY 2017
Department of Homeland Security, Transportation Security Administration	769	Data Released Combined with Public Log	FY 2017
Federal Reserve	728	Data Released	FY 2017
US Consumer Product Safety Commission	702	Public Log	FY 2018
Department of Labor, Employee Benefits Security Administration	674	Data Released	CY 2017
Department of Homeland Security, Privacy Office	599	No Response	
Department of Defense, Defense Information Systems Agency	590	Public Log	FY 2018
Department of Defense, Defense Health Agency	572	No Response	
US Department of Agriculture, Food and Nutrition Services	515	No Response	
Department of the Interior, Office of the Secretary	512	Inaccessible Response	
Department of Justice, US Parole Commission	511	Incomplete Response	
Department of Commerce, National Oceanic and Atmospheric Administration	485	No Response	

National Transportation Safety Board	471	No Response	
Federal Deposit Insurance Corporation	465	Data Released	FY 2017
Department of Health and Human Services, Administration for Children and Families	464	Data Released	FY 2015
Department of Commerce, Bureau of the Census	431	Public Log	FY 2013
US Agency for International Development	377	Data Released	FY 2017
National Aeronautics and Space Administration	253	Data Released	FY 2017
Department of Education, Federal Student Aid	233	Inaccessible Response	
Department of Education, Office for Civil Rights Headquarters	192	Data Released	FY 2017
Office of Personnel Management	not reported	Incomplete Response	
Total Requests Made to All Requested Agencies	748,212		
Total Requests Made to Agencies where Data was Obtained	577,892		

Appendix B

Agency	Number of Requests in Baseline FY 2016	Percent News Media Requests in Data Year	News Media Requests Weighted for 2016 Request Total	Count Method
Department of Homeland Security, US Citizenship and Immigration Services	166,732			no count
Department of Homeland Security, Customs and Border Protection	66,690	0.02	13.34	hand count
Department of Homeland Security, Immigration and Customs Enforcement	63,385	0.1	63.39	hand count
Social Security Administration	29,631			no count
Department of Veterans Affairs, Veterans Health Administration	28,091	1.2	337.09	agency count
Department of State	27,856			no count
Department of Defense, U.S. Army	25,755			no count
Equal Employment Opportunity Commission (combined regions)	17,680	0.2	35.36	hand count
Department of Justice, Federal Bureau of Investigations	15,202			no count
Securities and Exchange Commission	14,458	2.6	375.91	agency count
Environmental Protection Agency (combined regions)	10,403	3.5	364.11	agency count

Department of Health and Human Services, Food and Drug Administration	10,374	12	1,244.88	agency count
Department of Defense, US Navy	9,605	3.8	364.99	hand count
Department of Transportation, Federal Aviation Administration	9,582	2.5	239.55	hand count
Department of Labor, Occupational Safety and Health Administration	9,126	4.6	419.80	agency count
Department of Treasury, Internal Revenue Service	8,825	0.4	35.30	hand count
Department of Justice, Bureau of Prisons	7664	1.9	145.62	agency count
Department of Defense, Defense Logistics Agency	3920	0.9	35.28	agency count
Pension Benefit Guaranty Corporation	3,713	0.5	18.57	agency count
Department of Homeland Security, US Coast Guard	3,010	4.2	126.42	agency count
National Labor Relations Board	2,679			no count
Department of Homeland Security, Federal Emergency Management Agency	2,659	4.6	122.31	agency count
Department of Labor, Wage and Hour Division	2,589	6.3	163.11	agency count
Department of Transportation, Federal Motor Carrier Safety Administration	2,307	1	23.07	hand count
Department of Agriculture, Forest Service	1,977	6.5	128.51	agency count
Department of Interior, Bureau of Indian Affairs	1,892			no count

(*continued*)

(*continued*)

Agency	Number of Requests in Baseline FY 2016	Percent News Media Requests in Data Year	News Media Requests Weighted for 2016 Request Total	Count Method
Department of Defense, Office of the Secretary of Defense and Joint Chiefs	1,794	29.4	527.44	agency count
US Postal Service	1,771	4.2	74.38	agency count
Department of Justice, US Marshals	1,748			no count
Department of Homeland Security, US Secret service	1,700	20.7	351.90	hand count
Department of Treasury, Office of the Comptroller of the Currency	1,432	1.4	20.05	hand count
Department of Health and Human Services, National Institutes of Health	1,324	5.2	68.85	agency count
Federal Trade Commission	1,260	14.2	178.92	agency count
Department of Agriculture, Animal and Plant Health Inspection Service	1,143	7.3	83.44	hand count
Department of Justice, Bureau of Alcohol, Tobacco, Firearms, and Explosives	1,138	5	56.90	hand count
Department of Interior, US Fish and Wildilife Service	1,132	19.3	218.48	agency count
Department of Health and Human Services, Centers for Disease Control	1,120	12	134.40	agency count
Department of Justice, Office of Information Policy	1,071	21.4	229.19	hand count
Department of Housing and Urban Development, Headquarters	1,060	13.9	147.34	agency count

Department of Labor, Mine Safety and Health Adiministration	1,037	2	20.74	agency count
Small Business Administration, Headquarters	979	8.8	86.15	hand count
Department of the Interior, National Park Service	918	19.9	182.68	agency count
Department of Treasury, Departmental Offices	894	22.2	198.47	hand count
General Services Administration	887	15.5	137.49	hand count
Department of Interior, Bureau of Land Management	852	11.4	97.13	agency count
Federal Communications Commission	836	29	242.44	hand count
Department of Justice, Criminal Division	789	7.7	60.75	hand count
Nuclear Regulatory Commission	785	12.2	95.77	agency count
Department of Defense, Inspector General	772	11.5	88.78	hand count
Department of Homeland Security, Transportation Security Administration	769	12.9	99.20	hand count
Federal Reserve	728	5	36.40	hand count
US Consumer Product Safety Commission	702	3	21.06	agency count
Department of Labor, Employee Benefits Security Administration	674	11.8	79.53	agency count
Department of Defense, Defense Information Systems Agency	590	5.4	31.86	hand count
Federal Deposit Insurance Corporation	465	8.1	37.67	hand count
Department of Health and Human Services, Administration for Children and Families	464	4.2	19.49	agency count

(*continued*)

(*continued*)

Agency	Number of Requests in Baseline FY 2016	Percent News Media Requests in Data Year	News Media Requests Weighted for 2016 Request Total	Count Method
Department of Commerce, Bureau of the Census	431	5.1	21.98	hand count
US Agency for International Development	377	25.5	96.14	agency count
National Aeronautics and Space Administration	253	3.6	9.11	agency count
Department of Education, Office for Civil Rights Headquarters	192	36.9	70.85	agency count
Total For All Agencies with News Media Counts	**306,397**		**8,081.54**	

Appendix C

Agency	Number of Requests in Baseline FY 2016	Percent First Person Requests in Data Year	First Person Requests Weighted for 2016 Request Total	Count Method	Additional Examples Identified
Department of Homeland Security, US Citizenship and Immigration Services	166,732	98.7	164,564.48	Subject Matter (b)(6)	
Department of Homeland Security, Customs and Border Protection	66,690	97.1	64,755.99	Subject Matter Under Agency Review	
Department of Homeland Security, Immigration and Customs Enforcement	63,385	98.2	62,244.07	Subject Matter (b)(6)	
Social Security Administration	29,631	70.4	20,860.22	Subject Matter SS5 & Numident Requests	
Department of Veterans Affairs, Veterans Health Administration	28,091	77	21,630.07	Request Number Designated As FOIA/PA	
Department of State	27,856	64.3	17,911.41	Requester Name (b)(6)	
Department of Defense, U.S. Army	25,755				Military Police Reports

(continued)

(continued)

Agency	Number of Requests in Baseline FY 2016	Percent First Person Requests in Data Year	First Person Requests Weighted for 2016 Request Total	Count Method	Additional Examples Identified
Equal Employment Opportunity Commission (combined regions)	17,680	95.5	16,884.40	Subject Matter Charge File	
Department of Justice, Federal Bureau of Investigations	15,202	1.9	288.84	Requester Name and Subject Matter Match	
Securities and Exchange Commission	14,458				
Environmental Protection Agency (combined regions)	10,403				
Department of Health and Human Services, Food and Drug Administration	10,374				
Department of Defense, US Navy	9,605	30.9	2,967.95	Requester Name (b)(6)	
Department of Transportation, Federal Aviation Administration	9,582	57.9	5,547.98	Subject Matter (b)(6)	
Department of Labor, Occupational Safety and Health Administration	9,126				Attorneys and Insurance Companies
Department of Treasury, Internal Revenue Service	8,825	36.8	3,247.60	Agency Designation First Party	
Department of Justice, Bureau of Prisons	7,664				Medical Records, Disciplinary Records

Department of Defense, Defense Logistics Agency	3920				
Pension Benefit Guaranty Corporation	3,713	16.7	620.07	Requester Name (b)(6)	
Department of Homeland Security, US Coast Guard	3,010				
National Labor Relations Board	2,679				
Department of Homeland Security, Federal Emergency Management Agency	2,659	68	1,808.12	Subject Matter Claim	
Department of Labor, Wage and Hour Division	2,589				Attorneys
Department of Transportation, Federal Motor Carrier Safety Administration	2,307				Attorneys
Department of Agriculture, Forest Service	1,977	4.6	90.94	Request Number Designated As FOIA/PA	
Department of Interior, Bureau of Indian Affairs	1,892	63.5	1,201.42	Requester Name and Subject Matter Exempt	
Department of Defense, Office of the Secretary of Defense and Joint Chiefs	1,794				
US Postal Service	1,771				
Department of Justice, US Marshals	1,748				Mug Shots

(continued)

(continued)

Agency	Number of Requests in Baseline FY 2016	Percent First Person Requests in Data Year	First Person Requests Weighted for 2016 Request Total	Count Method	Additional Examples Identified
Department of Homeland Security, US Secret service	1,700	33.3	566.10	Requester Name (b)(6)	
Department of Treasury, Office of the Comptroller of the Currency	1,432				
Department of Health and Human Services, National Institutes of Health	1,324				
Federal Trade Commission	1,260	26.4	332.64	Requester Name (b)(6)	
Department of Agriculture, Animal and Plant Health Inspection Service	1,143				
Department of Justice, Bureau of Alcohol, Tobacco, Firearms, and Explosives	1,138	21.9	249.22	Subject Matter Self	
Department of Interior, US Fish and Wildilife Service	1,132				
Department of Health and Human Services, Centers for Disease Control	1,120	18.8	210.56	Subject Matter (b)(6)	
Department of Justice, Office of Information Policy	1,071				

Department of Housing and Urban Development, Headquarters	1,060				
Department of Labor, Mine Safety and Health Administration	1,037				Attorneys
Small Business Administration, Headquarters	979				Small Business Debtors
Department of the Interior, National Park Service	918	7.8	71.60	Request Number Designated As FOIA/ PA	
Department of Treasury, Departmental Offices	894				
General Services Administration	887				
Department of Interior, Bureau of Land Management	852				
Federal Communications Commission	836				
Department of Justice, Criminal Division	789	29	228.81	Agency Designation First Party	
Nuclear Regulatory Commission	785				
Department of Defense, Inspector General	772	56.6	436.95	Requester Name (b)(6)	
Department of Homeland Security, Transportation Security Administration	769	25.3	194.56	Requester Name (b)(6)	

(continued)

(*continued*)

Agency	Number of Requests in Baseline FY 2016	Percent First Person Requests in Data Year	First Person Requests Weighted for 2016 Request Total	Count Method	Additional Examples Identified
Federal Reserve	728	8.6	62.61	Requester Name (b)(6)	
US Consumer Product Safety Commission	702				Attorneys
Department of Labor, Employee Benefits Security Administration	674	4.9	33.03	Subject Matter TAIS	
Department of Defense, Defense Information Systems Agency	590	41.2	243.08	Requester Name (b)(6) and Subject Matter SF61 Form	
Federal Deposit Insurance Corporation	465				
Department of Health and Human Services, Administration for Children and Families	464	64.7	300.21	Subject Matter Immigration	
Department of Commerce, Bureau of the Census	431	16.8	72.41	Requester Name (b)(6)	
US Agency for International Development	377		0.00		
National Aeronautics and Space Administration	253		0.00		
Department of Education, Office for Civil Rights Headquarters	192		0.00		
Total Requests	577,892		387,625.34		

Appendix D

Agency	Number of Requests in Baseline FY 2016	Percent Commercial Requests in Data Year	Commercial Requests Weighted for 2016 Request Total	Additional Examples Identified
Department of Homeland Security, US Citizenship and Immigration Services	166,732			
Department of Homeland Security, Customs and Border Protection	66,690			
Department of Homeland Security, Immigration and Customs Enforcement	63,385			
Social Security Administration	29,631			
Department of Veterans Affairs, Veterans Health Administration	28,091	4.9	1,376.46	
Department of State	27,856			
Department of Defense, U.S. Army	25,755			Resellers and Requests for Contracts
Equal Employment Opportunity Commission (combined regions)	17,680			
Department of Justice, Federal Bureau of Investigations	15,202			

(continued)

(*continued*)

Agency	Number of Requests in Baseline FY 2016	Percent Commercial Requests in Data Year	Commercial Requests Weighted for 2016 Request Total	Additional Examples Identified
Securities and Exchange Commission	14,458	68.6	9,918.19	
Environmental Protection Agency (combined regions)	10,403	79.4	8,259.98	
Department of Health and Human Services, Food and Drug Administration	10,374	74.9	7,770.13	
Department of Defense, US Navy	9,605			Resellers
Department of Transportation, Federal Aviation Administration	9,582			Background Check Companies
Department of Labor, Occupational Safety and Health Administration	9,126	70	6,388.20	
Department of Treasury, Internal Revenue Service	8,825			Corporate Attorneys
Department of Justice, Bureau of Prisons	7,664	0.8	61.31	
Department of Defense, Defense Logistics Agency	3920	95.6	3,747.52	
Pension Benefit Guaranty Corporation	3,713	4.6	170.80	
Department of Homeland Security, US Coast Guard	3,010	44.6	1,342.46	
National Labor Relations Board	2,679			Corporate Attorneys
Department of Homeland Security, Federal Emergency Management Agency	2,659	6.4	170.18	

Department of Labor, Wage and Hour Division	2,589	56.9	1,473.14	
Department of Transportation, Federal Motor Carrier Safety Administration	2,307			Compliance Companies
Department of Agriculture, Forest Service	1,977	12.4	245.15	
Department of Interior, Bureau of Indian Affairs	1,892			
Department of Defense, Office of the Secretary of Defense and Joint Chiefs	1,794	11.8	211.69	
US Postal Service	1,771	35.7	632.25	
Department of Justice, US Marshals	1,748			
Department of Homeland Security, US Secret service	1,700			
Department of Treasury, Office of the Comptroller of the Currency	1,432			Compliance Companies and Corporate Attorneys
Department of Health and Human Services, National Institutes of Health	1,324	36.4	481.94	
Federal Trade Commission	1,260	34.3	432.18	
Department of Agriculture, Animal and Plant Health Inspection Service	1,143			
Department of Justice, Bureau of Alcohol, Tobacco, Firearms, and Explosives	1,138			
Department of Interior, US Fish and Wildlife Service	1,132	7.6	86.03	
Department of Health and Human Services, Centers for Disease Control	1,120	47.8	535.36	

(continued)

(*continued*)

Agency	Number of Requests in Baseline FY 2016	Percent Commercial Requests in Data Year	Commercial Requests Weighted for 2016 Request Total	Additional Examples Identified
Department of Justice, Office of Information Policy	1,071			
Department of Housing and Urban Development, Headquarters	1,060	23.2	245.92	
Department of Labor, Mine Safety and Health Adiministration	1,037	84.7	878.34	
Small Business Administration, Headquarters	979			
Department of the Interior, National Park Service	918	14.6	134.03	
Department of Treasury, Departmental Offices	894			
General Services Administration	887	41.7	369.88	
Department of Interior, Bureau of Land Management	852	14.7	125.24	
Federal Communications Commission	836			
Department of Justice, Criminal Division	789			
Nuclear Regulatory Commission	785	12.6	98.91	
Department of Defense, Inspector General	772			
Department of Homeland Security, Transportation Security Administration	769			
Federal Reserve	728			Business services, corporate registered agents

US Consumer Product Safety Commission	702	74.9	525.80	
Department of Labor, Employee Benefits Security Administration	674	37.4	252.08	
Department of Defense, Defense Information Systems Agency	590			
Federal Deposit Insurance Corporation	465			Resellers and Bank Requesters
Department of Health and Human Services, Administration for Children and Families	464	30.7	142.45	
Department of Commerce, Census Bureau	431			
US Agency for International Development	377	11.3	42.60	
National Aeronautics and Space Administration	253	36.3	91.84	
Department of Education, Office for Civil Rights Headquarters	192	11.4	21.89	
Total Requests	577,892		46,231.93	

Index